Lecture Notes in Computer Science 9923

Commenced Publication in 1973
Founding and Former Series Editors:
Gerhard Goos, Juris Hartmanis, and Jan van Leeuwen

More information about this series at http://www.springer.com/series/7408

Amund Skavhaug · Jérémie Guiochet
Erwin Schoitsch · Friedemann Bitsch (Eds.)

Computer Safety, Reliability, and Security

SAFECOMP 2016 Workshops
ASSURE, DECSoS, SASSUR, and TIPS
Trondheim, Norway, September 20, 2016
Proceedings

 Springer

Editors
Amund Skavhaug
Norwegian University of Science
  and Technology
Trondheim
Norway

Jérémie Guiochet
University of Toulouse
Toulouse
France

Erwin Schoitsch
Austrian Institute of Technology GmbH
Wien
Austria

Friedemann Bitsch
Thales Transportation Systems GmbH
Ditzingen
Germany

ISSN 0302-9743   ISSN 1611-3349   (electronic)
Lecture Notes in Computer Science
ISBN 978-3-319-45479-5   ISBN 978-3-319-45480-1   (eBook)
DOI 10.1007/978-3-319-45480-1

Library of Congress Control Number: 2016948787

LNCS Sublibrary: SL2 – Programming and Software Engineering

Printed on acid-free paper

This Springer imprint is published by Springer Nature
The registered company is Springer International Publishing AG Switzerland

Preface

For many years, the annual SAFECOMP conferences have been complemented by a series of workshops. This year, we accepted proposals for 7 domain-specific high-quality workshops from which four were successful in the end in collecting a sufficient number of high-quality papers or in organizing enough additional invited talks. This volume presents the proceedings of these four workshops held on September 20, 2016, preceding the SAFECOMP 2016 conference from 21 to 23 September, and organized by the Norwegian University of Science and Technology in Trondheim. The SAFE-COMP 2016 proceedings can be found in LNCS volume 9922.

Most workshops were sequels to earlier workshops, which show that the workshop topics are relevant to the scientific and industrial community that deals with safety, reliability, and security in programmable industrial systems. The workshops were organized by well-known chairs and respected Program Committees. This year's workshops (all full-day) were the following:

- ASSURE 2016 - 4th International Workshop on Assurance Cases for Software-Intensive Systems, chaired by Ewen Denney, Ibrahim Habli, and Ganesh Pai;
- DECSoS 2016 - ERCIM/EWICS/ARTEMIS Workshop on Dependable Embedded and Cyber-physical Systems and Systems-of-Systems, chaired by Erwin Schoitsch and Amund Skavhaug;
- SASSUR 2016 - 5th International Workshop on Next Generation of System Assurance Approaches for Safety-Critical Systems, chaired by Alejandra Ruiz, Tim Kelly, and Jose Luis de la Vara;
- TIPS 2016 - 1st International Workshop on the Timing Performance in Safety Engineering, chaired by Laurent Rioux and Marc Geilen.

Another workshop, CPSELabs 2016 - Cyber-Physical Systems Engineering, chaired by Christel Seguin, Holger Pfeifer, and Jérémie Guiochet, was based on invited speakers only, without proceedings. The first four workshops had Calls-for-Papers and a thorough review process. Criteria were different from the main conference since authors were encouraged to submit workshop papers, i.e., on work in progress and topics which may lead to controversial discussions. In total, 30 full papers were accepted, plus 5 invited papers (talks with abstracts in TIPS 2016) and 4 short papers as introductions to the respective workshop. Similar to the SAFECOMP conference, the workshops provided a truly international platform for academia and industry.

It has been a pleasure to work with the publication chair Friedemann Bitsch, the SAFECOMP 2016 program and workshop chairs, the workshop Program and Steering Committees, and the authors. Thank you all for good cooperation and excellent work!

September 2016   Erwin Schoitsch

Organization

EWICS TC7 Chair

Francesca Saglietti   University of Erlangen-Nuremberg, Germany

General Chair

Amund Skavhaug   The Norwegian University of Science and Technology, Norway

Program Co-chairs

Jérémie Guiochet   LAAS-CNRS, University of Toulouse, France
Amund Skavhaug   The Norwegian University of Science and Technology, Norway

Workshop Chair

Erwin Schoitsch   AIT Austrian Institute of Technology, Austria

Publication Chair

Friedemann Bitsch   Thales Transportation Systems GmbH, Germany

Publicity Chair

Elena Troubitsyna   Åbo Akademi University, Finland

Local Organizing Committee

Sverre Hendseth   The Norwegian University of Science and Technology, Norway
Knut Reklev   The Norwegian University of Science and Technology, Norway
Adam L. Kleppe   The Norwegian University of Science and Technology, Norway

Workshop Chairs

DECSoS 2016

Erwin Schoitsch	AIT Austrian Institute of Technology, Austria
Amund Skavhaug	NTNU, Norway

ASSURE 2016

Ibrahim Habli	University of York, UK
Ganesh Pai	NASA Ames Research Center, USA
Ewen Denney	NASA Ames Research Center, USA

SASSUR 2016

Alejandra Ruiz Lopez	Tecnalia, Spain
Jose Luis de La Vara	Carlos III University of Madrid, Spain
Tim Kelly	University of York, UK

TIPS 2016

Laurent Rioux	Thales R&T, France
Chokri Mraidha	CEA List, France
Marc Geilen	Eindhoven University of Technology, The Netherlands
Julio Medina	Universidad de Cantabria, Spain

Sponsoring Institutions

European Workshop on Industrial Computer
Systems Reliability, Safety and Security

Norwegian University of Science and Technology

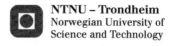

NTNU – Trondheim
Norwegian University of
Science and Technology

Laboratory for Analysis and Architecture
of Systems, Carnot Institute

Lecture Notes in Computer Science (LNCS),
Springer Science + Business Media

International Federation for Information Processing

Austrian Institute of Technology

Thales Transportation Systems GmbH

Austrian Association for Research in IT

Electronic Components and Systems
for European Leadership - Austria

ARTEMIS Industry Association

European Research Consortium for Informatics
and Mathematics

Informationstechnische Gesellschaft

German Computer Society

Austrian Computer Society

European Network of Clubs for Reliability
and Safety of Software-Intensive Systems

Verband österreichischer Software Industrie

Contents

4th International Workshop on Assurance Cases for Software-Intensive Systems (ASSURE 2016)

ASSURE 2016: The 4th International Workshop on Assurance Cases for Software-Intensive Systems 2
  Ewen Denney, Ibrahim Habli, and Ganesh Pai

The Agile Safety Case 5
  Tor Stålhane and Thor Myklebust

Systematic Maintenance of Safety Cases to Reduce Risk 17
  Omar Jaradat and Iain Bate

On Using Results of Code-Level Bounded Model Checking in Assurance Cases 30
  Carmen Cârlan, Daniel Ratiu, and Bernhard Schätz

Configuration-Aware Contracts 43
  Irfan Sljivo, Barbara Gallina, Jan Carlson, and Hans Hansson

Developing SNS Tool for Consensus Building on Environmental Safety Using Assurance Cases 55
  Yutaka Matsuno, Yang Ishigaki, Koichi Bando, Hiroyuki Kido, and Kenji Tanaka

The 6W1H Model as a Basis for Systems Assurance Argument 63
  Shuji Kinoshita and Yoshiki Kinoshita

The Assurance Timeline: Building Assurance Cases for Synthetic Biology ... 75
  Myra B. Cohen, Justin Firestone, and Massimiliano Pierobon

Towards Safety Case Integration with Hazard Analysis for Medical Devices ... 87
  Andrzej Wardziński and Aleksander Jarzębowicz

11th International ERCIM/EWICS/ARTEMIS Workshop on Cyber-Physical Systems and Systems-of-Systems (DECSoS)

DECSoS 2016: The 11th ERCIM/EWICS/ARTEMIS Workshop on Dependable Embedded and Cyber-Physical Systems and Systems-of-Systems: European Research and Innovation Initiatives in the Area of Cyber-Physical Systems and Systems-of-Systems 100
  Erwin Schoitsch and Amund Skavhaug

Testing Safety Properties of Cyber-Physical Systems with Non-Intrusive
Fault Injection – An Industrial Case Study........................... 105
  Joachim Fröhlich, Jelena Frtunikj, Stefan Rothbauer,
  and Christoph Stückjürgen

Quantitative Reliability Assessment for Mobile Cooperative Systems....... 118
  Francesca Saglietti, Ralf Spengler, and Matthias Meitner

An Approach for Systematic In-the-Loop Simulations for Development and
Test of a Complex Mechatronic Embedded System................... 130
  Amir Soltani Nezhad, Johan J. Lukkien, Rudolf H. Mak,
  Richard Verhoeven, and Martijn M.H.P. van den Heuvel

Gate-Level-Accurate Fault-Effect Analysis at Virtual-Prototype Speed...... 144
  Bogdan-Andrei Tabacaru, Moomen Chaari, Wolfgang Ecker,
  Thomas Kruse, and Cristiano Novello

Using SAE J3061 for Automotive Security Requirement Engineering 157
  Christoph Schmittner, Zhendong Ma, Carolina Reyes, Oliver Dillinger,
  and Peter Puschner

Dynamic Safety Contracts for Functional Cooperation of Automotive
Systems... 171
  Sebastian Müller and Peter Liggesmeyer

Time-of-Flight Based Optical Communication for Safety-Critical
Applications in Autonomous Driving.......................... 183
  Hannes Plank, Gerald Holweg, Christian Steger, and Norbert Druml

Limitation and Improvement of STPA-Sec for Safety and Security
Co-analysis 195
  Christoph Schmittner, Zhendong Ma, and Peter Puschner

Security Services for Mixed-Criticality Systems Based on Networked
Multi-core Chips.. 210
  Thomas Koller and Donatus Weber

Analysis of Informed Attacks and Appropriate Countermeasures for
Cyber-Physical Systems................................... 222
  Francesca Saglietti, Matthias Meitner, Lars von Wardenburg,
  and Valentina Richthammer

Advanced Security Considerations in the Arrowhead Framework 234
  Sándor Plósz, Csaba Hegedűs, and Pál Varga

The Role of the Supply Chain in Cybersecurity Incident Handling for
Drilling Rigs 246
  Aitor Couce-Vieira and Siv Hilde Houmb

Control of Cyber-Physical Systems Using Bluetooth Low Energy
and Distributed Slave Microcontrollers.   256
    Øyvind Netland and Amund Skavhaug

**5th International Workshop on Next Generation of System
Assurance Approaches for Safety-Critical Systems (SASSUR)**

SASSUR 2016: The 5th International Workshop on Next Generation of
System Assurance Approaches for Safety-Critical Systems   270
    Alejandra Ruiz, Jose Luis de la Vara, and Tim Kelly

Automotive Safety Concept Definition for Mixed-Criticality Integration on
a COTS Multicore.   273
    Irune Agirre, Mikel Azkarate-askasua, Asier Larrucea, Jon Perez,
    Tullio Vardanega, and Francisco J. Cazorla

Defining Autonomous Functions Using Iterative Hazard Analysis and
Requirements Refinement.   286
    Fredrik Warg, Martin Gassilewski, Jörgen Tryggvesson,
    Viacheslav Izosimov, Anders Werneman, and Rolf Johansson

ASIL Tailoring on Functional Safety Requirements   298
    Markus Fockel

Architecture-driven, Multi-concern and Seamless Assurance
and Certification of Cyber-Physical Systems.   311
    Alejandra Ruiz, Barbara Gallina, Jose Luis de la Vara, Silvia Mazzini,
    and Huáscar Espinoza

Towards the Adoption of Model-Based Engineering for the Development
of Safety-Critical Systems in Industrial Practice   322
    Marc Zeller, Daniel Ratiu, and Kai Höfig

Goal-Oriented Co-Engineering of Security and Safety Requirements in
Cyber-Physical Systems   334
    Christophe Ponsard, Gautier Dallons, and Philippe Massonet

Practitioners' Perspectives on Change Impact Analysis for Safety-Critical
Software – A Preliminary Analysis   346
    Markus Borg, Jose Luis de la Vara, and Krzysztof Wnuk

Seamless Integrated Simulation in Design and Verification Flow for
Safety-Critical Systems   359
    Ralph Weissnegger, Markus Schuß, Christian Kreiner, Markus Pistauer,
    Kay Römer, and Christian Steger

1st International Workshop on Timing Performance in Safety Engineering (TIPS)

TIPS 2016: The 1st International Workshop on Timing Performance in
Safety Engineering   372
    Chokri Mraidha, Laurent Rioux, Julio L. Medina Pasaje,
    and Marc Geilen

Model-Based Real-Time Evaluation of Security Patterns: A SCADA
System Case Study   375
    Anas Motii, Agnès Lanusse, Brahim Hamid, and Jean-Michel Bruel

Invited Papers

ASIL-Conformant Deployment and Schedule Synthesis Using
Multi-objective Design Space Exploration   393
    Sebastian Voss and Bernhard Schätz

Model-Based Contract and Service for Self-managed Components in
Cyber-Physical Systems   394
    DeJiu Chen

Automotive Ethernet: Towards TSN and Beyond   395
    Zhonghai Lu

Dataflow-Based Verification of Temporal Properties for Virtualized
Multiprocessor Systems   396
    Mladen Skelin and Marc Geilen

WARUNA: Modeling and Timing Verification Framework   397
    Rafik Henia

Author Index   399

4th International Workshop on Assurance Cases for Software-Intensive Systems (ASSURE 2016)

ASSURE 2016: The 4th International Workshop on Assurance Cases for Software-Intensive Systems

Ewen Denney[1], Ibrahim Habli[2], and Ganesh Pai[1]

[1] SGT/NASA Ames Research Center, Moffett Field, CA 94035, USA
{ewen.denney, ganesh.pai}@nasa.gov
[2] Department of Computer Science, University of York, York YO10 5DD, UK
ibrahim.habli@york.ac.uk

1 Introduction

This volume contains the papers presented at the 4th International Workshop on Assurance Cases for Software-intensive Systems (ASSURE 2016), collocated this year with the 35th International Conference on Computer Safety, Reliability, and Security (SAFECOMP 2016), in Trondheim, Norway. As with the previous three editions of ASSURE, this year's workshop aims to provide an international forum for presenting emerging research, novel contributions, tool development efforts, and position papers on the foundations and applications of assurance case principles and techniques. The workshop goals are to: (*i*) explore techniques to create and assess assurance cases for software-intensive systems; (*ii*) examine the role of assurance cases in the engineering lifecycle of critical systems; (*iii*) identify the dimensions of effective practice in the development/evaluation of assurance cases; (*iv*) investigate the relationship between dependability techniques and assurance cases; and, (*v*) identify critical research challenges towards defining a roadmap for future development.

2 Program

ASSURE 2016 began with an invited keynote talk by Clive Tomsett, Clinical Strategist at the Cerner Corporation, on healthcare and clinical safety. Eight papers were accepted this year, covering three themes: *lifecycles, formal evidence and tool support*, and applications.

Papers under the lifecycles theme considered topics such as the use of agile development processes in safety case creation, and processes to improve safety case maintenance time. The theme of formal evidence and tool support included papers that dealt with the use of model-checking of code, and the integration of those results into safety cases; safety case contracts that are aware of configuration issues, and tool support for achieving consensus in domains such as environmental safety. Finally, the applications theme comprised papers concerned with models for systems assurance; newer domains for the application of assurance cases such as synthetic biology; and the integration of medical device hazard analysis with safety case development.

Similar to the previous year's workshop, ASSURE 2016 concluded with a panel discussion, comprising researcher and practitioner panelists discussing the role and application of safety cases to a contemporary and emerging problem: the increasing use of autonomy in safety-critical applications.

3 Acknowledgments

We thank all those who submitted papers to ASSURE 2016 and congratulate those authors whose papers were selected for inclusion into the workshop program and proceedings. For reviewing the submissions and providing useful feedback to the authors, we especially thank our distinguished Program Committee members

- Ersin Ancel, NASA Langley Research Center, USA
- Robin Bloomfield, City University, UK
- Reece Clothier, RMIT University, Australia
- Martin Feather, NASA Jet Propulsion Laboratory, USA
- Jérémie Guiochet, LAAS-CNRS, France
- Richard Hawkins, University of York, UK
- Tim Kelly, University of York, UK
- Yoshiki Kinoshita, Kanagawa University, Japan
- John Knight, University of Virginia, USA
- Helen Monkhouse, Protean Electric Ltd., UK
- Andrew Rae, Griffith University, Australia
- Roger Rivett, Jaguar Land Rover, UK
- John Rushby, SRI International, USA
- Mark-Alexander Sujan, University of Warwick, UK
- Kenji Taguchi, AIST, Japan
- Alan Wassyng, McMaster University, Canada
- Sean White, Health and Social Care Information Centre, UK

as well as the additional reviewers:

- Nick Chozos, Adelard, UK
- Shuji Kinoshita, Kanagawa University, Japan
- Makoto Takeyama, Kanagawa University, Japan
- Rui Wang, LAAS-CNRS, France
- Hiroshi Watanabe, AIST, Japan

Their efforts have resulted in an exciting workshop program and, in turn, a successful third edition of the ASSURE workshop series. Finally, we thank the organizers of SAFECOMP 2016 for their support of ASSURE 2016.

The Agile Safety Case

Tor Stålhane[1](✉) and Thor Myklebust[2]

[1] NTNU, 7491 Trondheim, Norway
stalhane@idi.ntnu.no
[2] SINTEF ICT, Strindveien 4, 7034 Trondheim, Norway
thor.myklebust@sintef.no

Abstract. During the last years, there has been an increasing use of agile development methods when developing safety-critical software in order to shorten the time to market, to reduce costs and to improve quality. The Agile Safety Case forces the applicant to be specific about the quality and safety process together with technical safety aspects, enabling the certification process to be done in parallel with development and enabling the certification body to evaluate the current information at any time in the project. Moving from a waterfall/V-model to an agile model affect several parts of the safety case. Only a few international safety standards, like e.g. EN 5129 (Railway) and ISO 26262 (Automotive), require a safety case to be developed. In the future, we expect that more safety standards will include a safety case approach. The railway safety standard EN 50129 does include a list of topics that can be included in safety cases even for other domains.

Keywords: Safety case · Agile · SafeScrum

1   Introduction

Safety cases – also called assurance case or safety demonstration – have for a long time been required for safety critical systems in important industrial areas such as nuclear, automotive and railways. The earliest reference we have found is Def. 00-55:97 from 1997. Safety case is an efficient method for helping the developing company to focus on the simple but important question "How do you know that your system is safe enough?" The idea of a safety case is not to provide a mathematical or statistical proof, but to argue as one would in a court of law – thus the name safety case.

All too often, developing companies have left the important task of creating a safety case to the end of the project. The reason for this has often been that "we need to have complete knowledge of the system before we write the safety case". This has turned out to be a costly solution. It is much more efficient to build the safety case by inserting information when it becomes available during project development – an agile approach also resulting in increased safety awareness and understanding.

Safety cases are used in more and more domain specific standards – e.g., ISO 26262:2011 for automotive – and we expect that the next edition of IEC 61508, which is a generic standard, will require safety cases or have safety case as one option. We have thus started the work to include safety case construction into SafeScrum (http://safescrum.no/). This is part of our general work towards including all or most of the

© Springer International Publishing Switzerland 2016
A. Skavhaug et al. (Eds.): SAFECOMP 2016 Workshops, LNCS 9923, pp. 5–16, 2016.
DOI: 10.1007/978-3-319-45480-1_1

IEC 61508 requirements into SafeScrum. In order to achieve this, we need to include all safety analysis into the agile process. A common approach is to start with evaluating the hazard logs from earlier projects. The next step is often to base the analysis on information such as architecture, operating environment and intended functionality. This might be in conflict with agile development's fear of a "big design up-front". This paper presents out initial thoughts and attempts for a solution to these problems.

2   Related Work

There is a large amount of papers published on safety cases and their use in software assurance. A considerable part of these comes from the University of York, which is an important player in this area. We will here just mention a few of the published papers, covering experiences, methods, some discussions and some of the critique that has been raised against the use of safety cases. For an extensive literature review on safety cases and evidence, the reader should consult Nair et al. [1].

Feather and Marcosian [2] report on their experiences with using safety cases in a NASA project. Their experience is mostly positive but they suffered under lack of experience. Safety case is definitively a method where you need training and experience. Denney et al. [3] also summed up their experience as largely positive. They used safety case on software for an unmanned aircraft and augmented the process with Bayesian belief networks for quantification. They suggest further research on the modularization of the arguments via abstractions to aid argument comprehension. Agacdiken et al. [4] (Euro Control) has reported positive effects of using safety cases as part of the certification activities, while Weinstock [5] has reported positive experience on using assurance cases for software in medical equipment.

A work by Kelly et al. [6] has some bearing on agile development since they start with a preliminary safety case, which is amended throughout the development process. Part of their conclusion is well worth quoting: "By evolving this structure in parallel with development of the architecture, certification concerns were addressed as an integral part of the design process and safety features were built into, rather than 'bolted on' to the design. In our experience, such an approach can help to reduce the risk of having to perform large amounts of rework in order to obtain system certification."

Another important work to amend the safety case method is reported by Greenwell and Knight [7]. They have observed that faults that lead to failures – and the development errors that introduced those faults – manifest themselves as fallacies in the safety argument. They have thus built a tool called Pandora to identify fallacies. Examples of fallacies are circular definitions and that correlation implies causality.

Kaur et al. [8] based their work on the IEC 61508 standard, which they used to build the chain of safety evidence that underlies safety arguments. They have developed a conceptual model which they claim will improve safety cases and prevent many of the problems that often rise during certification. Braun et al. [9] have done research on safety cases and have raised some important issues, such as "when is the safety case complete" and "how can we be sure that the models used are suitable for safety cases". Their conclusion is that "The current state-of-practice, FTA and FMEA, are not sufficient for the complex and interconnected modern systems".

Sun et al. [10] discuss the role of safety case arguments in aircraft certification. As also mentioned by other authors, they observe that that "there is insufficient emphasis (i.e. limited guidance and informal practice only) in existing guidance and practice concerning the explicit reasoning that connects claims of overall safety to the available evidence, and the adequacy of the safety analyses performed in existing guidance and practice".

Safety cases, with their focus on structured arguments and evidences for safety will benefit from a set of patterns. Weaver [11] has published a large set of useful patterns and so has the company AugustaWestland – an Italian company developing helicopters [12]. In addition, Denney and Pai [13] have presented a formal basis for safety cases in a paper where they look into the possibilities of simplifying the safety case process by including domain and safety case ontologies.

Most of the work referenced above has used diagrams – mostly the GSN (Goal Structuring Notation). A lot of the industry, however, has used just unstructured text. A good alternative to this is to use structured text, e.g., as suggested by Holloway [14].

N. Leveson has for a long time presented herself as a strong opponent to safety cases [15]. Although she has written several papers on the subject we will quote only one, which gives a clear view of what she thinks is the main problem with safety cases: To avoid confirmation bias and compliance-only exercises, certification should focus not on showing that the system is safe but in attempting to show that it is unsafe. It is the emphasis and focus on identifying hazards and flaws in the system that provides the "value-added" of system safety engineering. The system engineers have already created arguments for why their design is safe. The effectiveness in finding safety flaws by system safety engineers has usually resulted from the application of an opposite mind set from that of the developers.

To sum up: there are several reports on positive experiences with the use of safety cases. The main problem seems to be lack of training material. Most of the experiences reported have used GSN but there are also some examples of using textual safety cases. There is a lot of research on ontologies, patters and evidence /fallacies related to safety cases. There is, however, little research on the use of safety cases in agile projects and no empirical research at all. The only example we have found is work by Kelly on preliminary safety cases that are elaborated throughout the development project.

3   Some Current Safety Case Standards

Only a few safety standards mention safety case (or assurance case) as an approach to demonstrate compliance with the specified safety requirements. The standard Def. Std. 00-55:97 (military), EN 50129:2003 (railway), DO-178C:2012 (avionics) and ISO 26262:2011 (automotive) requires the use of safety case for demonstration of compliance with safety requirements, while important standards like IEC 61508:2010 (generic) and IEC 62304:2006 (medical) does not. AAMI, however, has issued a safety-assurance case guide AAMI TIR38:2014 that present guidance and examples for how to develop a safety assurance case for medical device with emphasis on the requirements presented in ANSI/ AAMI/ISO 14971:2007/(R) 2010 Application of risk management to medical devices. One of the requirements in Def. Std. 00–55:97 is fully in line with our SafeScrum approach *"The Software Safety Case shall be continually updated to provide a record of the progress of the implementation and evaluation of the safety requirements for the SRS"*. The railway standard has detailed requirements for the contents of the safety case. The requirements and information are distributed through the standard and its annexes.

Three categories of safety case are identified:

- GPSC: Generic product Safety Case (independent of application). A generic product can be re-used for different independent applications
- GASC: Generic application Safety Case (for a class of application). A generic application can be re-used for a class/type of application with common functions.
- SASC: Specific application Safety Case (for a specific application) A specific application is used for only one particular installation. The SASC is divided into:

EN 50129 requires that a safety case shall be developed by the manufacturer and assessed by an independent third party (safety assessor), before the safety authorities approve commissioning of the system.

The requirements for safety case in the ISO 26262 series are presented in part 2 of the standard series: Management of functional safety. The only requirement is "A safety case shall be developed in accordance with the safety plan". The safety case should progressively compile the work products that are generated during the safety lifecycle.

4   Reuse Opportunities and Templates

4.1   Reuse Opportunities

Much of the work invested in generating a safety case can be reused in later safety cases. The descriptions of what was intended for quality and safety management will not change substantially, so only the corresponding evidence of what was actually done needs to be updated. Reuse of documents and the use of templates have several benefits.

- Increased productivity of information and documents
- Reuse of documents and information available as part of the tools
- Reduce duplication effort
- Move information and documents more easily among projects
- Quick and effective process when developing new documents

In the subchapters below, we have first looked at reuse of information and documents and the last chapter look at the use of templates.

If a safety product, for which a safety case already exists, is modified, the new safety case can be based on the existing one. We mainly need to argue for the changes and their effects. This is considerably less work than producing a whole new safety case every time.

Reusable documents have low extra costs. This is documents where parts are reused as is, while remaining parts need to be adapted for each project and even for each sprint for some documents. If reuse is the goal right from the start, the changes between projects or iterations will be small.

As part of a study of relevant proof of compliance documentation when certifying products [16] according to IEC 61508, we found that more than 50 % of the documents can be reused. It is important that the manufacturer make these documents as generic as possible. For documents that has to be updated over several sprints, reuse solutions is important. These documents could e.g. include tables or point lists that are easily updated. Reusability of tests and analysis should also be included in these evaluations – see IEEE 1517:2010 for reuse processes for software. This is also an important part to perform regression tests in an automatic and effective manner.

4.2 The Use of Templates

When doing modification of an already certified product, only a few documents are new [16] e.g. documents required for new tools. These new documents can be based on templates or reuse of similar documents or be automatically generated to further reduce documentation costs.

New documents have high costs. These documents have to be written more or less from scratch for each new project. It is therefore beneficial to make use of already available templates that has been published as industry papers, e.g. [17], or published by different organizations developing guidelines like e.g. Misra (www.misra.org.uk) and AAMI (www.aami.org). Some standards, such as ISO/IEC/IEEE 29119-3:2013 includes procedures and templates for reports such as Test status report, Test completion report, Test data readiness report, Test environment readiness report, Test incident report, Test status report and Test completion report.

As part of the SafeScrum mind set it is important to reduce the amount of documentation and the assessor should be involved early in the project to discuss relevant level of information to be delivered to the assessor. What could be the minimum of documentation delivered to the assessor should therefore be discussed before starting to develop any new document. Some of the information could be reviewed by the assessor, as part of audits and technical meetings.

5 Building a Safety Case with SafeScrum

5.1 The Extended SafeScrum

The present version of SafeScrum includes mainly phase 10 of the IEC 61508 process model – see Fig. 1. For the new, extended version of SafeScrum, we want to include safety cases. We thus also need to include phases 3–5, 7, 9, 13 and 15 of the IEC 61508 process model. These phases are needed in order to have full control over the safety analysis and the evidences produced in each of these phases. The new, extended SafeScrum model is shown in Fig. 2. Even though modifications after release – system maintenance – are handled in an agile way, it is kept outside the development part of SafeScrum.

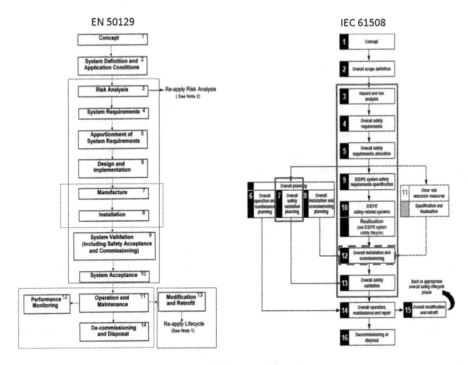

Fig. 1. The EN 50129 and IEC 61508 process models

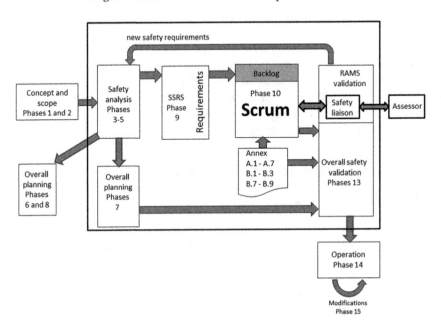

Fig. 2. IEC 61508 and SafeScrum

The standard's requirements for phases 3–5 will not require any changes when applied in an agile setting. Parts of the process will have to be repeated when requirements change or new requirements are added but that will also happen during non-agile development even though it is not part of the planned process. We must keep in mind that there also will be a need for feedback loops from phase 9 to the phases 3–5.

The plan made early in the process – phase 7 – is just the high-level plan. This plan needs to be refined during the SafeScrum process before it is used in phase 13. The refinement will take place when the activities contained in the plan are inserted into the sprint backlog.

5.2   IEC 61508 – Building SSRS and Hazard Log

Before doing a hazard analysis, we need at least the high-level concepts – an extension of the overall concept definition – and the system architecture. As pointed out by Ge et al. [18]: "...for safety-critical projects, the up-front design/plan needs to be incrementally detailed to serve as input to hazard analysis, which in turn informs the safety analysis and certification processes later. Domain-specific checklists or systematic techniques such as Functional Failure Analysis (FFA) are carried out at the start of the development. As part of the design progresses, more detailed analyses are carried out using techniques such as Fault tree analysis (FTA), Hazards and operability analysis (HAZOP), or Failure modes and effects analysis (FMEA)". See also Myklebust et al. [19].

For using FFA or a domain-specific hazard checklist, the important thing is the relationship between the system's functionality – how it interacts with its planned environment – and not how the functionality is realized inside the system. For ways to perform an early hazard analysis, see also Stålhane and Myklebust [20].

In our opinion, safety experts, customer representatives (domain experts) and developers should participate in the sprints concerning phase 3–5 and 9. Making phases 3–5 and 9 part of an agile approach will improve communication between the safety experts and the developers and thus improve the quality of the hazard analysis and increase the safety awareness of the developers. This will improve the company's safety culture.

The initial safety analysis from phases 3–5 will give us the first set of hazards and the necessary input to write the safety requirements – e.g., barrier requirements. The hazards are entered into the hazard log. In addition, we will get safety requirements from the standard. Together with the system's functional requirements, this will be the first product backlog for the SafeScrum development process.

Allocation of a requirement – phase 5 – assigns the requirement to a specific system context. E.g., the derived temperature boundary requirements might be assigned to the temperature measurement hardware, and to the diagnostic software module, respectively. The software safety requirements are derived from the safety requirements and allocated to the software implementation. The intention is to identify all of the requirements, which are related to the software, and to specify the behavior and attributes of the software in testable terms, in order to fulfill the product safety requirements.

The final activity in each sprint should be to prepare the backlog for the next sprint – commonly known as "backlog grooming or refinement". Important activities here are e.g., to improve user stories that are poorly written, estimate resources need for each backlog item, add acceptance criteria and to look deeper into the backlog to do longer-range technical planning. To these activities, we should add work needed to prepare for handling safety requirements in the next sprint, e.g. clarify safety-related requirements and decide whether we need to include customer representatives, domain experts or safety experts (depending on the backlog items) in the next sprint.

When we take work items out of the product backlog and insert them into the sprint backlog, we need to discuss each requirement in details. Two issues are of special importance (1) how shall we realize the safety requirements? A reference to the chosen solution should be entered into the safety case document and (2) are there any new risk related to the functional requirements. This question might lead to a new safety analysis, which is done in the sprint or by sending the requirement back to phase 3–5.

The safety case will need to refer to relevant documents such as code, test results, review results and solution rationales – see Myklebust et al. [20]. This will in some cases put an extra burden on the developers and run counter to the agile concept. However, if it is not done when the code is written it will have to be done later and then requirement much more resources.

5.3   The Safety Case Document

5.3.1   On Safety Cases

Since IEC 61508 does not mention safety cases, we will use the safety case structure suggest by EN 50129, 2003 as our starting point. This standard suggests that the documented safety evidence for the system/sub-system/equipment shall be structured as follows:

- Part 1 Definition of System (or sub-system/equipment). This shall precisely define or reference the system/sub-system/equipment to which the Safety Case refers, including version numbers and modification status of all requirements, design and application documentation.
- Part 2 Quality Management Report. This shall contain the evidence of quality management. This is similar to ISO 9001 requirements.
- Part 3 Safety Management Report. This shall contain the evidence of safety management.
- Part 4 Technical Safety Report. This shall contain the evidence of functional and technical Safety.
- Part 5 Related Safety Cases. This shall contain references to the Safety Cases of any sub-systems or equipment on which the main Safety Case depends. It shall also demonstrate that all the safety-related application conditions specified in each of the related sub-system/equipment Safety Cases are either fulfilled in the main Safety Case, or carried forward into the safety-related application conditions of the main Safety Case.

- Part 6 Conclusion. This shall summarize the evidence presented in the previous parts of the Safety Case, and argue that the relevant system/sub-system/equipment is adequately safe, subject to compliance with the specified application conditions.

Large volumes of detailed evidence and supporting documentation need not be included in the Safety Case and in its parts, provided precise references are given to such documents and provided the base concepts used and the approaches taken are clearly specified. We will focus on part 4 – Technical safety Report – which again consists of six parts. The most important parts are (2) Assurance of correct operation, (3) Effect of faults, (4) Operations with external influences and (5) safety-related application conditions. These issues are contained in the safety case.

5.3.2   Constructing Safety Cases

There are several methods that can be used to present a safety case – e.g. the GSN method and the structured prose method. The GSN-method has several strengths, e.g., a large amount of published patterns, which will simplify the work of developing a safety case. However, a large segment of the relevant industries has used just text. In our opinion, structured text will be an important improvement over plain prose and we will thus start there. GSN should come later. We will take Holloway's work as our starting point. His idea is simple and effective – use the text structure to show the relationships between goals, contexts, strategies, claims, evidences and justifications. The following example is taken from Holloway's paper [14] Chap. 3.3 "Argument outline" – key words in bold. Note the difference between strategy and argument. The strategy describes which type of argument that is best suited for the issue at hand – e.g., hazards or design (inspection) or code (testing). The argument is about what we consider as evidence, e.g., argue that a certain item in the hazard log has been treated in a satisfactory way.

Claim 1: System is acceptably safe
Context 1: Definition of "acceptably safe"
 Claim 1.1: All identified hazards have been eliminated or sufficiently mitigated.
 Context 1.1-a: Tolerability targets for hazards
 Context 1.1-b: Reference to current version of the hazard log

 Strategy 1.1: Arguments over all items in the hazard log
 Claim 1.1.1: Hazard H1 has been eliminated
 Evidence: Document reference, e.g., to the relevant part of the hazard log.
 Claim 1.1.n: Hazard Hn has been satisfactory mitigated
 Evidence: Reference to code analysis and test results
 Claim 1.2: …

This notation is simple to read and provides the necessary structure without being overburdened with too much text. It is also simple to update, which is important in an agile setting. It is important to keep just the structure information in the safety case and use references for all information – e.g., evidences. In this way, we will have a safety case structure that is easy to read and understand.

Both the hazard log and the safety case will change over time, especially in an agile setting. We will start with the hazards found in the hazard log when phase 4 is finished.

After this, necessary updates to the hazard log and to the safety case should be part of the agenda for each sprint retrospective. The structure suggested above makes it simple to add, change and remove items in the safety case. While new hazards can be added to the hazard log as soon as they are identified, the claims, context and evidences must be added later. The need for new evidences will in most cases require new activities, which must be inserted into the sprint backlog. Thus, it is important that we keep a list or library of acceptable evidences related to type of hazard. This must be agreed with the assessor and can then later be reused. We need information on (1) necessary contexts – what do we need as context for a specific type or category of claim and (2) strategies – which strategies are acceptable to the assessor, depending on the type of issue.

By creating and maintaining such a list or library, constructing a safety case will be greatly simplified, and help the author in developing the safety case incrementally. It is, however, important that this approach does not make the safety case construction an automatic process. The list is not intended to be a replacement for thinking, it is just a support intended to remove the more mundane parts of the process of building a safety case.

6 Discussions

Building a safety case will require a certain amount of resources. As mentioned above, several standards require a safety case while some others are on the threshold of requiring it – e.g. IEC 61508. For the rest of us, the important question is whether it is worth it. For people using an agile approach, another important question is how difficult it is to include building a safety case into an agile process such as SafeScrum. In our opinion, all projects that develop safety-critical software should build a safety case, if not for the certification then in order to convince oneself that the system really is safe.

The first important activity is to build a safety validation plan based on the safety requirements. Already here several important questions will surface, such as how do we validate each safety requirement? The safety validation plan is just the high-level plan. We will refine it and add details when we take the high-level activities out of the product backlog and move then into the sprint backlog. In this way, the safety case will be an integrated part of the project and the safety case document will grow incrementally just like the code.

Already during sprint planning, we will get a fruitful discussion in the team, which will increase safety awareness and improve the team's safety culture. In addition we will get an early focus on the certification process and make all participants understand that it is important and needs to be done.

The down side to all this is that a lot of the work will not directly contribute to the development of running software and only indirectly contribute to the test and verification activities. A lot of the documentation necessary will have to be written anyway due to standard requirements but it will still require some extra paper work and extra activities that do not benefit the customer and thus run counter to the agile manifesto's idea of customer focus.

Reuse of documents and use of document templates, however, will reduce the extra effort needed for building a safety case. Working with the safety case will increase system understanding and will thus lead to a more efficient process.

7 Conclusions

Based on the discussions above we can make the following important conclusions, namely: (1) there are no problems building a safety case when using SafeScrum, (2) working with safety cases will increase the team's safety awareness, (3) IEC 50129 provides a good template for writing safety cases, also for other domains than railway, (4) safety cases can be developed incrementally (or continuous as mentioned in DO-55:1997) and (5) structured text works well for writing and presenting safety cases.

References

1. Nair, S., de la Vara, J.L., Sabetzadeh, M., Briand, L.: An extended systematic literature review on provision of evidence for safety certification. Inf. Softw. Technol. **56**, 689–717 (2014)
2. Feather, M.S., Markosian, L.Z.: Building a safety case for a safety-critical NASA space vehicle software system. In: 2011 Fourth IEEE International Conference on Space Mission Challenges for Information Technology (2011)
3. Denney, E., Pai, G., Habli, I.: Perspectives on software safety case development for unmanned aircraft. In: 42nd Annual IEEE/IFIP International Conference on Dependable Systems and Networks (DSN 2012), Boston, Massachusetts, USA
4. Agacdiken, N. et al.: EAD Safety Case, EuroControl, September 2009
5. Weinstock, C.B., Goodenough, J.B.: Towards an Assurance Case Practice for Medical Devices. Carnegie Mellon Software Engineering Institute, October 2009
6. Kelly, T., Bate, I., McDermid, J., Burns, A.: Building a preliminary safety case: an example from aerospace. In: Proceedings of the 1997 Australian Workshop on Industrial Experience with Safety Critical Systems and Software. Australian Computer Society, Sydney, October 1997
7. Greenwell, W.S., Knight, J.C.: Framing analysis of software failure with safety cases. IEEE Trans. Softw. Eng. **33**(5), 347–365 (2010)
8. Kaur, R., Sabetzadeh, M., Briand, L., Coq, T.: Characterizing the chain of evidence for software safety cases: a conceptual model based on the IEC 61508 standard. In: Third IEEE International Conference on Software Testing, Verification and Validation (ICST) (2010)
9. Braun, P., Philipps, J. Schatz, B., Wagner, S.: Model-based safety-cases for software-intensive systems. In: SafeCert (2008)
10. Sun, L., Zhang, W., Kelly, T.: Do safety cases have a role in aircraft certification? In: The 2nd International Symposium on Aircraft Airworthiness (ISAA 2011) (2011)
11. Weaver, R.A.: The Safety of Software – Constructing and Assuring Arguments University of York. Department of Computer Science, September 2003
12. Agusta Westland Limited, BAE SYSTEMS, GE Aviation, General Dynamics United Kingdom Limited, and SELEX Galileo Ltd.: Modular Software Safety Case Process. Description Date: 19 November 2012
13. Denney, E., Pai, G.: Towards an Ontological Basis for Aviation Safety Cases. SGT/NASA Ames Research Center

14. Holloway, C.M.: Safety case notations: alternatives for the non-graphically inclined? In: Johnson, C.W., Casely, P. (eds.) Proceedings of the IET 3rd International Conference on System Safety. IET Press, London (2008)
15. Leveson, N.: The use of safety cases in certification and regulation. J. Syst. Saf. **47**(6) (2011)
16. Myklebust, T., Stålhane, T., Hanssen, G.K., Wien, T., Haugset, B.: Scrum, documentation and the IEC 61508-3:2010 software standard. In: PSAM 12, Hawaii (2014)
17. Myklebust, T., Stålhane, T., Hanssen, G.K., Haugset, B.: Change Impact Analysis as required by safety standards, what to do? In: PSAM 12, Hawaii (2014)
18. Ge, X., Paige, R.F., McDermid, J.A.: An iterative approach for development of safety-critical software and safety arguments. In: AGILE 2010 (2010)
19. Myklebust, T., Stålhane, T., Hanssen, G.K.: Important considerations when applying other models than the Waterfall/V-model when developing software according to IEC 61508 or EN 50128. ISSC 2015, San Diego, USA
20. Stålhane, T., Myklebust, T.: Early Safety Analysis, XP 2016, Edinburgh, UK

Systematic Maintenance of Safety Cases to Reduce Risk

Omar Jaradat[1]([✉]) and Iain Bate[1,2]

[1] School of Innovation, Design, and Engineering,
Mälardalen University, Västerås, Sweden
omar.jaradat@mdh.se
[2] Department of Computer Science, University of York, York, UK
iain.bate@york.ac.uk

Abstract. The development of safety cases has become common practice in many safety critical system domains. Safety cases are costly since they need a significant amount of time and efforts to be produced. Moreover, safety critical systems are expected to operate for a long period of time and constantly subject to changes during both development and operational phases. Hence, safety cases are built as living documents that should always be maintained to justify the safety status of the associated system and evolve as these system evolve. However, safety cases document highly interdependent elements (e.g., safety goals, evidence, assumptions, etc.) and even seemingly minor changes may have a major impact on them, and thus dramatically increase their cost. In this paper, we identify and discuss some challenges in the maintenance of safety cases. We also present two techniques that utilise safety contracts to facilitate the maintenance of safety cases, we discuss the roles of these techniques in coping with some of the identified maintenance challenges, and we finally discuss potential limitations and suggest some solutions.

Keywords: Safety case · Safety argument · Maintenance · FTA · Sensitivity analysis · Safety contracts · Impact analysis

1 Introduction

The size and complexity of safety critical systems are considerable. Without a clear demonstration for the safety performance of a system, it is difficult for inspector organisations or system engineers themselves to build a confidence in the safety performance of the system. System engineers of some safety critical systems are required to demonstrate the safety performance of their systems through a reasoned argument that justifies why the system in question is acceptably safe (or will be so) [10]. This argument is communicated via an artefact that is known as a *safety case*. The safety case is the whole safety justification that comprises every appropriate piece of evidence to make a convincing argument to support the safety performance claims [13].

© Springer International Publishing Switzerland 2016
A. Skavhaug et al. (Eds.): SAFECOMP 2016 Workshops, LNCS 9923, pp. 17–29, 2016.
DOI: 10.1007/978-3-319-45480-1_2

Moreover, safety critical systems can be evolutionary as they are subject to perfective, corrective or adaptive maintenance or through technology obsolescence [24]. Changes to the system during or after development might invalidate safety evidence or argument. Evidence might no longer support the developers' claims because it reflects old development artefacts or old assumptions about operation or the operating environment. After a change, original safety claims might be nonsense, no longer reflect operational intent, or be contradicted by new data [17]. Eventually, the real system will have diverged so far from that represented by the safety case argument and the latter is no longer valid or useful [13]. Hence, it is almost inevitable that the safety case will require updating throughout the operational lifetime of the system. In addition, any change that might compromise system safety involves repeating the certification process (i.e., re-certification) and repeating the certification process necessitates an updated and valid safety case that considers the changes. For example, the UK Ministry of Defence Ship Safety Management System Handbook JSP 430 requires that *"the safety case will be updated ... to reflect changes in the design and/or operational usage which impact on safety, or to address newly identified hazards. The safety case will be a management tool for controlling safety through life including design and operation role changes"* [12,25]. Similarly, the UK Health and Safety Executive (HSE) — Railway safety case regulations 1994 — states in regulation 6(1) that *"a safety case to be revised whenever, appropriate that is whenever any of its contents would otherwise become inaccurate or incomplete"* [6,12].

However, a single change to a safety case may necessitate many other consequential changes — creating a ripple effect [24]. Any improper maintenance in a safety argument might cause unforeseen violations of the acceptable safety limits, which will negatively impact the system safety performance conveyed by the safety case. Hence, a step to assess the impact of this change on the safety argument is crucial and highly needed prior to updating a safety argument after a system change. Despite clear recommendations to adequately maintain and review safety cases by safety standards existing standards offer little advice on how such operations can be carried out [24].

The concept of contract has been around for a few decades in the system development domain. There have been significant works that discuss how to represent and to use contracts (e.g., [3,26]). Also, researchers have used assume-guarantee contracts to propose techniques to lower the cost of developing software for safety critical systems. Moreover, contracts have been exploited as a means for helping to manage system changes in the system domain or in its corresponding safety case [5,9,18]. However, using contracts as a way of managing change was discussed in some works [2,9], but deriving the contracts and their contents have received little support yet [16].

In this paper, we present and discuss techniques that utilises the concept of contracts to facilitate the accommodation of system changes in safety cases to ultimately support the maintainability of safety cases. Our work focuses on: 1. How and where to derive safety contracts and their contents, 2. using the derived contracts to support the decision as to whether or not apply changes, and 3. using the derived contracts to guide developers to the parts in the safety case that might be affected after applying a change. This paper is composed of three further sections. In Sect. 2, we present background information and we also present some safety cases' challenges. In Sect. 3, we describe two techniques to facilitate the maintenance of safety cases. In Sect. 4 we discuss some limitations, draw a conclusion and propose potential future work.

2   Background and Motivation

2.1   Safety Contracts

In 1969, Hoare introduced the pre- and postcondition technique to describe the connection (dependency) between the execution results (R) of a program (Q) and the values taken by the variables (P) before that program is initiated [7]. Hoare introduced a new notation to describe this connection, such as: **P {Q} R**. This notation can be interpreted as: *"If the assertion P is true before initiation of a program Q, then the assertion R will be true on its completion"* [7].

Contracts are widely used in software development. For instance, Design by Contract (DbC) was introduced by Meyer [14,15] to constrain the interactions that occur between objects. Moreover, contract-based design is an approach where the design process is seen as a successive assembly of components where a component behaviour is represented in terms of assumptions about its environment and guarantees about its behaviour [4].

The following is an example that depicts the most common used form of contracts [11]:

Guarantee: The WCET of task X is $\leq 10\,\mathrm{ms}$
Assumptions:
X is:
1. compiled using compiler $[C]$,
2. executed on microcontroller $[M]$ at 1000 MHz with caches disabled, and
3. not interrupted

A contract is said to be a *safety contract* if it guarantees a property that is traceable to a hazard. There have been significant works that discuss how to represent and to use contracts [3,26]. In the safety critical systems domain, researchers have used, for example, assume-guarantee contracts to propose techniques to lower the cost of developing software for safety critical systems. Moreover, contracts have been exploited as a means for helping to manage system changes in a system domain or in its corresponding safety case [5,9,18].

2.2   The Goal Structuring Notation (GSN)

A safety argument organizes and communicates a safety case, showing how the items of safety evidence are related and collectively demonstrate that a system is acceptably safe to operate in a particular context. GSN [1] provides a graphical means of communicating (1) safety argument elements, claims (goals), argument logic (strategies), assumptions, context, evidence (solutions), and (2) the relationships between these elements. The principal symbols of the notation are shown in Fig. 1 (with example instances of each concept).

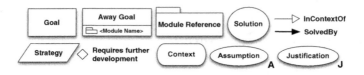

Fig. 1. Notation keys of the Goal Structuring Notation (GSN)

A goal structure shows how goals are successively broken down into ('solved by') sub-goals until eventually supported by direct reference to evidence. Using the GSN, it is also possible to clarify the argument strategies adopted (i.e., how the premises imply the conclusion), the rationale for the approach (assumptions, justifications) and the context in which goals are stated.

2.3 Safety Cases Maintainability: What Does it Mean?

The goal of the work which is being discussed in this paper is to **facilitate the accommodation of system changes in safety cases to ultimately enhance safety case maintainability.** Hence, it is vital to explicitly define what do we mean by safety case maintainability. We refer to *"Safety Case Maintainability"* as the ability to repair or replace the impacted elements of a safety case argument, without having to replace still valid elements, to preserve the validity of the argument. The maintainability degree is said to be high whenever the following three activities are done efficiently:

1. Identifying the impacted elements and those that are not impacted.
2. Minimising the number of impacted elements.
3. Reducing the work needed to make the impacted elements valid again.

However, the work presented by this paper does not focus on how to measure the efficiency of achieving these three activities, but rather it strives to enable them and improve on them. In order to achieve this goal, we should resolve the problems that affect the accommodation of system changes in safety cases.

2.4 Safety Cases Maintainability: Why Is it Painstaking?

Safety assurance and certification are amongst the most expensive and time-consuming tasks in the development of safety-critical embedded systems [10]. A key reason behind this is because the increasing complexity and size of these systems combined with their growing market demands. The cost of system changes including the cost of the activities that will follow them (e.g., regression testing), are another key reason that exacerbates the problems of cost and time in safety certification. Coherent strategies are required to reduce the cost and time of safety certification.

One of the biggest challenges that affects safety case revision and maintenance is that a safety case documents a complex reality that comprises a complex web of interdependent elements. That is, safety goals, evidence, argument, and assumptions about operating context are highly interdependent. Hence, seemingly minor changes may have a major impact on the contents and structure of the safety argument. Basically, operational or environmental changes may invalidate a safety case argument for two main reasons as follows:

1. Evidence is valid only in the operational and environmental context in which it is obtained, or to which it applies. During or after a system change, evidence might no longer support the developers' claims because it could reflect old development artefacts or old assumptions about operation or the operating environment.
2. Safety claims, after introducing a change, might be nonsense, no longer reflect operational intent, or be contradicted by new data. Changing safety claims might change the argument structure.

In order to deal with problems that impede safety cases maintenance, we start by identifying and describing these problems.

Main Problem: *Maintaining safety cases after implementing a system change is a painstaking process.* This main problem is caused by three sub-problems.

Sub-problem (1): *The lack of documentation of dependencies among the safety cases contents.*

Developers of safety cases are experiencing difficulties in identifying the direct and indirect impact of change due to high level of dependency among safety case elements. If developers do not understand the impact of change then they have to be conservative and do wider verification (i.e., check more elements than strictly necessary) and this increases the maintenance cost. The use of GSN might help to produce well-structured arguments that clearly demonstrate the relationships between the argument claims and evidence. However, GSN has not solved the problem of documenting dependencies among the safety cases contents [22]. In other words, a well-structured GSN argument helps the developers to mechanically propagate the change through the goal structure. However, it does not evaluate whether the suspect elements of the argument are still valid or not (or it does not show why the element is impacted), but rather it can bring these elements to the developers' attention [22].

Safety is a system level property; assuring safety requires safety evidence to be consistent and traceable to system safety goals [24]. Moreover, current standards and analysis techniques assume a top-down development approach to system design. One might suppose that a safety argument structure aligned with the system design structure would make traceability clearer. It might, but safety argument structures are influenced by four factors: (1) modularity of evidence, (2) modularity of the system, (3) process demarcation (e.g., the scope of ISO 26262 items [8]), and (4) organisational structure (e.g., who is working on what) [2]. These factors often make argument structures aligned with the system design structure impractical. However, the need to track changes across the whole safety argument is still significant for maintaining the argument regardless of its structure.

As explained in Sect. 2.1, a contract is conceived as an extension to the specification of software component interfaces that specifies preconditions and postconditions to describe what properties a component can offer once the surrounded environment satisfies one or more related assumption(s). Based on this description, safety contracts can be used as a means to record the dependencies among system components. If we assume a one-to-one mapping between a system component and all the claims that are articulated about it, dependencies among safety argument elements can be conceived through the dependencies between components of the corresponding system that are recorded in contracts. In practice, this notion is far from straightforward because it is infeasible to be achieved and impossible to prove the completeness of the generated contracts, and the expected number of contracts will be too large to easily manage.

Sub-problem (2): *The lack of traceability between a system and its safety case.*

We refer to the ability to relate safety argument fragments to system design components as component traceability (through a safety argument). We refer to evidence across a system's artefacts as evidence traceability.

System developers need both top-down and bottom-up impact analysis approaches to maintain safety cases. A top-down approach is dedicated for analysing the impacted artefacts from the system domain down to the safety argument. In contrast, a bottom-up approach is dedicated for analysing impacted elements from the argument to the corresponding artefacts such as a safety analysis report, test results or requirements specification, etc. The lack of systematic and methodical approaches to analysing impact of change is a key reason behind the maintenance difficulties. However, conducting any style of impact analysis requires a traceability mechanism between the system and safety arguments.

There has been significant work on how to use safety contracts as a means to establish the required traceability [2]. The guaranteed properties in the contracts can be mapped to safety argument goals. If the derived safety contracts are associated with the corresponding argument elements, any broken contracts will reveal (i.e., highlight) the associated argument elements and thus enabling easier identification for the impacted parts in the argument due to a system change. However, this is not as simple as it first appears because we still do not know which contracts were affected by the change. In other words, how does a change lead to broken contracts?

Predicting system changes before building a safety argument can be useful because it allows the safety argument to be structured to contain the impact of these changes. Hence, anticipated changes may have predictable and traceable consequences that will eventually reduce maintenance effort. Nevertheless, planning the maintenance of a safety case still faces a key problem.

Sub-problem (3): *System changes and their details cannot be fully predicted and made available up front.*

Modularity has been proposed as the key element of the 'way forward' in developing systems [19,21]. Although the most influential approach for using modularity effectively in software design is information hiding, modularity can also be beneficial for systems maintenance. For modular systems, it is claimed that the required maintenance efforts to accommodate predicted changes can be less than the required efforts to accommodate arbitrary changes. This is because having a list of predicted changes during the system design phase allows system engineers to contain the impact of each of those changes in a minimal number of system's modules. Predicting system changes before building a safety argument can be useful because it allows the safety argument to be structured to contain the impact of these changes. Hence, predicted changes may also have predictable and traceable consequences that will eventually reduce the maintenance efforts. Nevertheless, planning the maintenance of a safety case still faces two key issues: (1) system changes cannot be fully predicted and made available up front, especially, the software aspects of the safety case as software is highly changeable and harder to manage as they are hard to contain and (2) those changes can be implemented years after the development of a safety case [16].

3   Sensitivity Analysis for Enabling Safety Argument Maintenance (SANESAM)

Sensitivity analysis can be defined as: *"The study of how uncertainty in the output of a model (numerical or otherwise) can be apportioned to different sources of uncertainty in the model input"* [23]. The analysis helps to establish reasonably acceptable confidence in the model by studying the uncertainties that are often associated with variables in models.

In our previous work [16], we introduced a Sensitivity ANalysis for Enabling Safety Argument Maintenance (SANESAM) technique, in which we apply sensitivity analysis on FTAs to measure the sensitivity of outcome A (e.g., a safety requirement being true) to a change in a parameter B (e.g., the failure probability in a component). The sensitivity is defined as $\Delta B/B$, where ΔB is the smallest change in B that changes A (e.g., the smallest increase in failure probability that makes safety requirement A false). The failure probability values that are attached to FTA's events are considered input parameters to the sensitivity analysis. A sensitive part of a FTA is defined as one or multiple FTA events whose minimum changes (i.e., the smallest increase in its failure probability due to a system change) have the maximal effect on the FTA, where effect means exceeding failure probabilities (reliability targets) to inadmissible levels. SANESAM was extended by SANESAM+ [11] to consider the change's impact on: (1) intermediate events of FTAs, (2) multiple events, and (3) duplicated events.

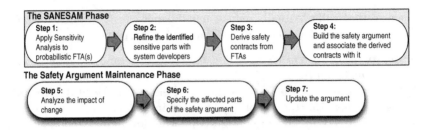

Fig. 2. Process diagram of SANESAM and SANESAM+ [16]

The key principle of both techniques is to determine, for each system component, the allowed range for a certain parameter within which a component may
change before it compromises a certain system property (e.g., safety, reliability,
etc.). Sensitivity analysis is used in the techniques as a method to determine
the range of failure probability parameter for each component. The techniques
assume the existence of a probabilistic FTA where each event in the tree is spec-
ified by a current estimate of failure probability $FP_{Current|event(x)}$. In addition,
they assume the existence of the required failure probability for the top event
$FP_{Required(Topevent)}$, where the FTA is considered unreliable if:

$$FP_{Currentl(Topevent)} > FP_{Required(Topevent)} \ [16].$$

The steps of SANESAM are shown in Fig. 2 and described as follows [16]:

Step 1. Apply the sensitivity analysis to a probabilistic FTA: In this
step the sensitivity analysis is applied to a FTA to identify the sensitive
events whose minimum changes have the maximal effect on the $FP_{Topevent}$.
Identifying those sensitive events requires the following steps to be performed:

1. Find the Minimal Cut Set (MC) in the FTA. The minimal cut set definition is: *"A cut set in a fault tree is a set of basic events whose (simultaneous) occurrence ensures that the top event occurs. A cut set is said to
   be minimal if the set cannot be reduced without losing its status as a cut
   set"* [20].
2. Calculate the maximum possible increment to the failure probability parameter of event x before the top event $FP_{Required(Topevent)}$ is no longer
   met, where $x \in MC$, and

$$(FP_{Increased|event(x)} - FP_{Current|event(x)}) \nRightarrow$$
$$FP_{Increased(Topevent)} > FP_{Required(Topevent)}.$$

3. Rank the sensitive events from the most sensitive to the less sensitive.
   The most sensitive event is the event for which the following formula is
   the minimum:

$$\frac{FP_{Increased|event(x)} - FP_{Current|event(x)}}{FP_{Current|event(x)}.}$$

Step 2. Refine the identified sensitive parts with system developers: In this step, the generated list of sensitive events from Step 1 should be discussed by system developers (e.g., safety engineers) as they should choose the sensitive events that are most likely to change. The list can be extended to add any additional events by the developers. Moreover, it is envisaged that some events might be removed from the list or the rank of some of them might change.

Step 3. Derive safety contracts from FTAs: In this step, a safety contract or contracts should be derived for each event in the list from Step 2. The main objectives of the contracts are to: (1) highlight the sensitive events to make them visible up front for developers attention, and (2) to record the dependencies between the sensitive events and the other events in the FTA. Hence, if the system is later changed in a way that increases the failure probability of a contracted event where the increased failure probability is still within the defined threshold in the contract, then it can be said that the contract(s) in question still hold (intact) and the change is containable with no further maintenance. The contract(s), however, should be updated to the latest failure probability value. On the other hand, if the change causes a bigger increment to the failure probability value than the contract can hold, then the contract is said to be broken and the guaranteed event will no longer meet its reliability target. It is worth noting that the role of safety contracts in SANESAM is to highlight sensitive events, and not to enter new event failure probabilities. Figure 3 an example of a derived safety contract from FTA.

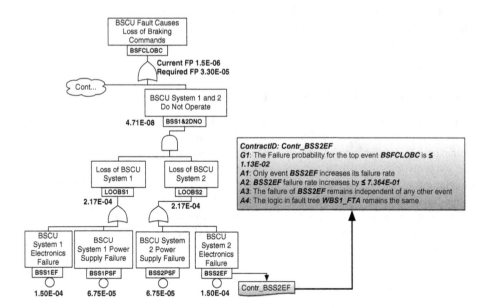

Fig. 3. Example of a derived safety contract

*Step 4. Build the safety argument and associate the derived contracts
with it*: In this step, a safety argument should be built and the derived
safety contracts should be associated with the argument elements. Essentially, SANESAM calculates the maximum possible increment to the failure probability parameter of only one event at a time before the top event
$FP_{Required(Topevent)}$ is no longer met. It considers the events within the MC
only. SANESAM+ was introduced to provide more freedom by considering
multiple events at a time and not only the events in the MC. The key principle of SANESAM+ is to distribute $\Delta FP_{(Topevent)}$ over all of the events in
FTA, or over the events that are relevant to a particular change. Hence, the
difference between SANESAM and SANESAM+ is observed only in Step 1,
all other steps are identical.

3.1   The Roles of Safety Contracts in SANESAM and SANESAM+

SANESAM and SANESAM+ derive safety contracts for the identified sensitive parts. The main objectives of the contracts is to (1) highlight the sensitive
events to make them visible up front for developers attention and (2) to record
the dependencies between the sensitive events and the other events in the FTA.
Hence, if any contracted event has received a change that necessitates increasing
its failure probability where the increment is still within the defined threshold
in the contract, then it can be said that the contract(s) in question still holds
(intact) and the change is containable with no further maintenance. The contract(s), however, should be updated to the latest failure probability value. On
the contrary, if the change causes a bigger increment in the failure probability
value than the contract can hold, then the contract is said to be broken and the
guaranteed event will no longer meet its reliability target. Hence, SANESAM
and SANESAM+ may address the first and the second identified sub-problems
in Sect. 2.4.

3.2   Support the Prediction of Potential System Changes

Expectedly, if we ask system engineers to anticipate the potential future changes
for a system they might brainstorm and come up with a list of changes. However, the list can be incomplete or contain unlikely changes that might influence
the system design to little or no avail. Instead, we propose providing system
developers a list of system parts that may be more problematic to change than
other parts and ask them to choose the parts that are most likely to change. Of
course our list can be augmented by additional changeable parts that may be
provided by the system developers. Hence, SAMESAM and SANESAM+ may
address the third identified sub-problem in Sect. 2.4.

4   Conclusion and Future Work

System developers should understand the change and the potential risks that it
might carry before they identify the impacted parts. For example, a change might

turn some implicit assumptions about the context in which a system should operate to be wrong. Misunderstanding the change might lead to skip those parts of the system which are dependent on that assumptions. Also, the developers need to understand the dependencies between the system parts to identify the affected parts correctly. Hence, there is a pressing need for acceptable methods and techniques to enable easier change accommodation in safety critical systems without incurring disproportionate cost compared to the size of the change.

In this paper, SANESAM and SANESAM+ were discussed as techniques to facilitate the maintenance of safety cases. The techniques were introduced and illustrated in our previous work. More specifically, we proposed SANESAM [16] through which we: (1) measure the sensitivity of FTA events to system changes using the events' failure probabilities, (2) derive safety contracts based on the results of the analysis, and (3) map the derived safety contracts to a safety argument to improve the change impact analysis on the safety argument. We used an aircraft Wheel Braking System (WBS) to illustrate the application of SANESAM. We also developed SANESAM+ [11] as another version of SANESAM to cover wider variety of change scenarios, where we also used the WBS to illustrate it. This paper also identifies some challenges in the maintenance of safety cases, and shows how the techniques might help to address them.

A foreseen limitation in the techniques is that they can be less useful while dealing with software changes as it is recognised as being difficult to quantify the failure probabilities of the system software components.

To further develop the approach, SANESAM+ is being migrated to timing. More specifically, the problem of the Worst Case Execution Time (WCET) is considered as the property where sensitivity is judged in terms of its impact on the ability to meet the system's timing requirements. We also plan to create several case studies to validate both the feasibility and efficacy of the techniques.

Acknowledgment. This work has been partially supported by the Swedish Foundation for Strategic Research (SSF) through SYNOPSIS and FiC Projects. The work is also partially supported by SafeCOP project.

References

1. GSN community standard version 1. Technical report, Origin Consulting (York) Limited, November 2011
2. Modular Software Safety Case (MSSC) – Process Description, November 2012. https://www.amsderisc.com/related-programmes
3. Benveniste, A., Caillaud, B., Ferrari, A., Mangeruca, L., Passerone, R., Sofronis, C.: Multiple viewpoint contract-based specification and design. In: de Boer, F.S., Bonsangue, M.M., Graf, S., de Roever, W.-P. (eds.) FMCO 2007. LNCS, vol. 5382, pp. 200–225. Springer, Heidelberg (2008)
4. Benvenuti, L., Ferrari, A., Mazzi, E., Vincentelli, A.L.S.: Contract-based design for computation and verification of a closed-loop hybrid system. In: Egerstedt, M., Mishra, B. (eds.) HSCC 2008. LNCS, vol. 4981, pp. 58–71. Springer, Heidelberg (2008)

5. Graydon, P., Bate, I.: The nature, content of safety contracts: challenges and suggestions for a way forward. In: Proceedings of the 20th IEEE Pacific Rim International Symposium on Dependable Computing (PRDC), November 2014
6. Health and Safety Executive (HSE). Railway Safety Cases - Railway (Safety Case) Regulations - Guidance on Regulations (1994)
7. Hoare, C.A.R.: An axiomatic basis for computer programming. Commun. ACM **12**(10), 576–580 (1969)
8. ISO 26262:2011. Road Vehicles – Functional Safety, Part 1–9. International Organization for Standardization, November 2011
9. Fenn, J.L., Hawkins, R., Williams, P.J., Kelly, T., Banner, M.G., Oakshott, Y.: The who, where, how, why and when of modular and incremental certification. In: Proceedings of the 2nd IET International Conference on System Safety, pp. 135–140. IET (2007)
10. Jaradat, O.: Enhancing the maintainability of safety cases using safety contracts, Mälardalen University, Västerås, Sweden, November 2015. http://www.es.mdh.se/publications/4082-
11. Jaradat, O., Bate, I.: Deriving hierarchical safety contracts. In: The 21st IEEE Pacific Rim International Symposium on Dependable Computing, November 2015
12. Kelly, T.: Arguing Safety - A Systematic Approach to Managing Safety Cases. Ph.D. thesis, Department of Computer Science, University of York (1998)
13. Maguire, R.: Safety Cases and Safety Reports: Meaning, Motivation and Management. Ashgate Publishing Ltd., Aldershot (2012)
14. Meyer, B.: Design by contract. Technical report TR-EI-12/CO, Interactive Software Engineering Inc. (1986)
15. Meyer, B.: Object-Oriented Software Construction, 1st edn. Prentice-Hall Inc., Upper Saddle River (1988)
16. Jaradat, O., Bate, I., Punnekkat, S.: Using sensitivity analysis to facilitate the maintenance of safety cases. In: Proceedings of the 20th International Conference on Reliable Software Technologies (Ada-Europe), pp. 162–176, June 2015
17. Jaradat, O., Graydon, P., Bate, I.: An approach to maintaining safety case evidence after a system change. In: Proceedings of the 10th European Dependable Computing Conference (EDCC), Newcastle, UK, August 2014
18. Conmy, P., Carlson, J., Land, R., Björnander, S., Bridal, O., Bate, I.: Extension of techniques for modular safety arguments. Deliverable d2.3.1, Technical report, Safety certification of software-intensive systems with reusable components (SafeCer) (2012)
19. Parnas, D.L.: On the criteria to be used in decomposing systems into modules. Commun. ACM **15**(12), 1053–1058 (1972)
20. Rausand, M., Høyland, A.: System Reliability Theory: Models Statistical Methods and Applications. Wiley-Interscience, Hoboken (2004)
21. Bates, S., Bate, I., Hawkins, R., Kelly, T., McDermid, J., Fletcher, R.: Safety case architectures to complement a contract-based approach to designing safe systems. In: Proceedings of the 21st International System Safety Conference (ISSC) (2003)
22. Wilson, S., Kelly, T., McDermid, J.: Safety case development: current practice, future prospects. In: Shaw, R. (ed.) Safety and Reliability of Software Based Systems, pp. 135–156. Springer, London (1997)
23. Saltelli, A.: Global Sensitivity Analysis: The Primer. Wiley, New York (2008)

24. Kelly, T.P., McDermid, J.A.: A systematic approach to safety case maintenance. In: Felici, M., Kanoun, K., Pasquini, A. (eds.) SAFECOMP 1999. LNCS, vol. 1698, pp. 13–26. Springer, Heidelberg (1999)
25. U.K. Ministry of Defence, "JSP 430 - Ship Safety Management System Handbook", Ministry of Defence, January 1996
26. Damm, W., Hungar, H., Bernhard, J., Peikenkamp, T., Stierand, I.: Using contract-based component specifications for virtual integration testing and architecture design. In: Proceedings of the Design, Automation & Test in Europe Conference & Exhibition, pp. 1–6 (2011)

On Using Results of Code-Level Bounded Model Checking in Assurance Cases

Carmen Cârlan[1]([⊠]), Daniel Ratiu[2], and Bernhard Schätz[1]

[1] Fortiss GmbH, Munich, Germany
{carlan,schaetz}@fortiss.org
[2] Siemens CT, Munich, Germany
daniel.ratiu@siemens.com

Abstract. Software bounded model checkers (BMC) are today powerful tools to perform verification at unit level, but are not used at their potential in the safety critical context. One reason for this is that model checkers often provide only incomplete results when used on real code due to restrictions placed on the environment of the system in order to facilitate the verification. In order to use these results as evidence in an assurance case, one needs to characterize the incompleteness and mitigate the assurance deficits. In this paper we present an assurance case pattern which addresses the disciplined use of successful but possibly incomplete verification results obtained through C-level bounded model checking as evidence in certification. We propose a strategy to express the confidence in incomplete verification results by complementing them with classical testing, and to mitigate the assurance deficits with additional tests. We present our preliminary experience with using the CBMC model checker and the mbeddr environment to verify three safety-critical software components.

Keywords: Assurance cases · Bounded model checking · Confidence arguments

1 Introduction

Modern software model checkers are powerful enough to verify complex properties of programs at unit level. In the field of safety critical systems development, formal verification is used only for highest critical functions and when it is highly recommended by safety standards like IEC 61508 [2]. Instead, current functional verification of software is mostly based on testing.

Figure 1 presents three fragments of an assurance case (in a Goal Structuring Notation-like notation [3]) for the correct implementation of a safety requirement by a software component. In test-based verification (Fig. 1-left-up), the assurance of the correctness of the developed software is split into two parts: the *conformance of the implemented behavior* with the test-suite demonstrating the *validity* of the correctness claim with respect to the selected test case, and the *analysis*

© Springer International Publishing Switzerland 2016
A. Skavhaug et al. (Eds.): SAFECOMP 2016 Workshops, LNCS 9923, pp. 30–42, 2016.
DOI: 10.1007/978-3-319-45480-1_3

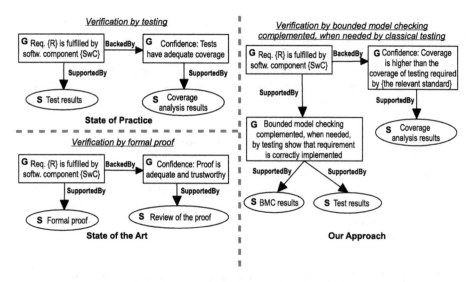

Fig. 1. Existing approaches for providing evidence in assurance cases: testing or formal proofs (left); Our approach proposes to combine model checking with testing (right).

of the coverage of the implemented behavior by the selected test-cases demonstrating the confidence in the correctness claim. The required coverage grows with the assurance level, in case of the IEC 61508 from statement via branch to MC/DC. In the case of verification by formal proofs (Fig. 1-left-down), one argues the confidence in the results by claiming adequacy and trustworthiness of the proof as a demonstration that SwC fulfills R.

The idea of splitting the argumentation in a part focusing on the conformance of the implemented behavior with the requirements, and a part focusing on the confidence [14] can also be applied in the verification which uses bounded model checking (Fig. 1-right). In this case, we split the argumentation into the proof of the correctness of the implemented behavior with respect to a specification under restricting assumptions, and the demonstration of sufficient confidence in the respective restricting assumptions. If the confidence argument is not strong enough, we propose to use classical testing for compensating the identified assurance deficits.

In this paper, we present an assurance case pattern which can be used at the interface between developers, verification engineers, safety managers and third party assessors to tackle the following questions: **(Q1)** *How can we use successful verification results of software bounded model checkers as evidence for the correctness of the implementation of software components?* **(Q2)** *How can we cover the assurance deficits due to incomplete verification using classical testing?* This work is part of our efforts at fortiss GmbH and Siemens to enable practicing engineers to use successful results of code level bounded model checking as evidence for certification.

Contributions. We present a pattern to use successful, but possibly incomplete bounded model checking verification results as evidence in assurance cases. In case these verification results are incomplete, we develop a confidence argument by comparing the input and the state coverage of incomplete model-checking with coverage requirements for classical testing. We present our experience with using bounded model checking on three real-world safety-critical software components.

Structure of this Paper. In Sect. 2, we present an assurance case pattern to incorporate results of the bounded model checker-based verification as evidence for assurance (Q1). In Sect. 3, we characterize the confidence in incomplete verification results and the additional testing in an argument structure pattern (Q2). In Sect. 4, we present our experience with verifying three software components. In Sect. 5, we discuss variability points of our approach. The last two sections contain the related work and conclusions.

2   Using BMC Results as Formal Verification Evidence

Testing is the state-of-the-practice verification method. However, safety standards recommend the usage of formal verification results as evidence for certification, because formal verification allows exploration of all possible behaviors while assessing the satisfaction of a certain safety property. When complete verification is not possible, standards require that the limits of the coverage of the performed verification are explicitly expressed. If bounded model checking is used (as alternative verification method), DO-178C recommends the construction of an assurance case in order to argue the adequacy and trustworthiness of the verification results for demonstrating that safety goals have been met. In the following, we develop an assurance case pattern for arguing that the objective related to the functional correctness of a software module has been met by bounded model checking accompanied by testing, when needed.

System Under Verification. Our focus is on code-level functional verification of reactive software components. A software component (SwC) possesses an internal state, a set of input variables with different types $I = \{i_1 : T_1, ..., i_n : T_m\}$ and a set of output variables. Each type T_l defines a set of possible values which can be taken by an input variable. Being a reactive system, the component is called in a (possibly infinite) main loop. For each of the steps of the loop, each of these input variables can take a different value – let i_l^t denote the value of an input variable i_l at time step t. The value i_l^t conforms to the type of i_l, namely $i_l^t \in T_l$.

Main Pattern. Figure 2 presents a pattern that captures the structure of an assurance argument, which uses as evidence bounded model checking results together with classical testing, if the verification is incomplete. Our top-level goal $G1$ is that a software component SwC implements a safety requirement formalized as a property P, given the environmental constraints Env^{SwC} $(C0)$. Env^{SwC} assigns to each input variable its step-dependent range: $Env^{SwC}(i_l)(t) \subseteq T_l$.

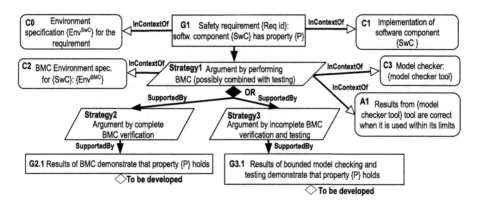

Fig. 2. Main pattern for arguing that a software component implements a safety requirement. The argument's strategy is to use results from bounded model checking verification complemented, when necessary, by testing.

Strategy 1: Argument by Combining BMC with Testing. Our strategy to decompose the top-level goal is to use bounded model checking on the source code of the component ($C1$), possibly combined, when needed, with testing. The bounded model checker uses the environment definition Env^{BMC} ($C2$), and the checking is performed with a given model checker tool ($C3$). The environment definition determines whether the verification is performed completely or just partially. As an answer to our research question $Q1$, there are two main possible outcomes of the verification: either the verification is complete (in which case the pattern is instantiated with the choice of *Strategy* 2); or, in the case when the system under verification is too complex, compromises are made (i.e. environment restrictions and limited loop unwindings) and thereby the verification is incomplete (in which case *Strategy* 3 is applied).

Strategy 2: Argument by Complete Verification Using BMC. There are many cases in which verification results obtained with bounded model checking are complete. In these cases the functional correctness of the implementation of property P by SwC is guaranteed by the model checker itself. The bounded model checking verification is complete when the environment constraining the inputs of the model checker Env^{BMC} (verification harness) is relaxed enough to cover all inputs of the environment Env^{SwC} specified by the requirement $ReqId$: $Env^{SwC} \subseteq Env^{BMC}$. In this case, the verification results can be used with the highest confidence as evidence, under the assumption ($A1$).

Strategy 3: Argument by Incomplete BMC Verification and Testing. Due to the complexity of the system under verification, often exhaustive verification is not possible, and the verification is performed under several restrictions of Env^{SwC}, namely Env_i^{BMC}, where $\bigcup Env_i^{BMC} = Env^{BMC}$. There are two orthogonal dimensions in which the environment is restricted: (1) Env^{BMC} restricts the set of possible values taken by the inputs of the software component, or, (2) Env^{BMC} restricts the number of steps which are used to verify the component.

In both cases, only a part of the space of behaviors is covered by the model checker. Consequently, there are behaviors possible in the environment of the component which are specified by the requirement (Env^{SwC}), but not captured in the verification environment (Env^{BMC}). Thus, the assurance deficits caused by incomplete verification must be accompanied by additional evidence in a confidence argument. In the following section, we elaborate on the assurance deficits of incomplete bounded model checking verification and how to compensate for this deficits.

3   Confidence in Incomplete Results

Testing is the most common evidence for functional verification required by safety certification standards. Thereby, in order to be accepted as evidence, the results of a formal verification technique must be shown to be more trustworthy than the results of testing required by the standards [13].

In Fig. 3, we describe an argument structure pattern for combining incomplete bounded model checking verification with manually written tests. *Intuitively, the main confidence argument is that the simplifying assumptions under which the bounded model checking is performed are permissive enough to cover test vector sets which satisfy the requirements of the certification standard. If this is not the case, additional test-cases are added to cover the deficits of the bounded model checking verification results (Q2).*

Strategy 3 deals with incomplete bounded model checking verification ($G3.1$) and additional manually written test cases ($G3.2$). The amount of additional

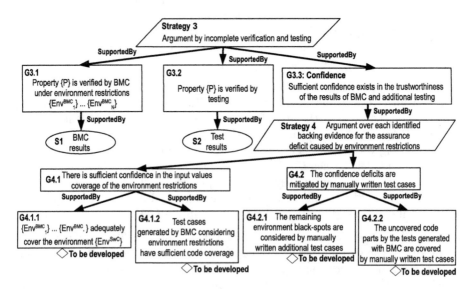

Fig. 3. Pattern for combining the incomplete bounded model checking results with testing. We argue the confidence in bounded model checking results by comparison to testing.

testing should be enough to reach the required confidence ($G3.3$). The strategy for arguing confidence (*Strategy* 4) is to explicitly mitigate the assurance deficits caused by incomplete bounded model checking due to environment restrictions ($G4.1$, $G4.2$).

Adequacy of Environment Partitioning. We argue that the sum of environment restrictions ($Env_1^{BMC}, ..., Env_i^{BMC}$) adequately covers the environment Env^{SwC} ($G4.1.1$) – e.g., adequacy can be defined by IEC 61508, which recommends the partitioning of the valid input domain in equivalence classes and the consideration of boundary values. Environment black-spots ($Env^{SwC} \setminus Env^{BMC}$) are parts of the environment which were not covered by the environment definition for the model-checker. These black-spots must be identified, made explicit in an assurance case, and a mitigation method for the risk that they could lead to bugs must be developed. The black-spots are considered by manually writing additional test cases ($G4.2.1$).

Sufficiency of the Code Covered by Bounded Model Checking. Similarly to measuring the code coverage of tests, we can measure the code covered by the bounded model checker when it is run under the verification assumptions. To do this, we use test case generation from the same environment as the verification. Test vectors which satisfy required coverage criteria (e.g. statement, condition, MC/DC) can be generated by the model checker starting from the environment definition ($G4.1.2$). When the required coverage cannot be achieved, it is an indication that the environment restrictions are too narrow. In this case, either the environment must be relaxed such that the required coverage can be reached, or additional test cases must be manually written ($G4.2.2$).

4   Preliminary Experience

In order to operationalize our approach we use the *CBMC* model checker [9] integrated in the *mbeddr* development environment [18]. Besides checking assertions, CBMC also possesses the needed capabilities to generate test cases with a specified coverage. We use the same environment restrictions and CBMC settings to perform the functional verification and to generate test cases. We use mbeddr because it features a user friendly integration of CBMC.

In the following, we present our experience with the verification of three software components, which implement critical functionality. The purpose of our experiments is to investigate the extent to which bounded model checking verification can achieve better coverage than classical testing on software components. These experiments mirror the verification strategies proposed in the patterns.

4.1   Traffic Collision Avoidance System

In our first experiment we verified a software component which implements part of the Traffic Alert and Collision Avoidance System (TCAS) available from the benchmark algorithms for testing [12]. The TCAS component implements a highly critical functionality because its malfunctioning could lead to collision of planes. The component uses as inputs the positions and speeds of the planes and does not have internal state.

We have checked two properties of the system, namely *P1: Safe advisory selection* and *P2: Best advisory selection*, as in [12]. We have chosen to restrict the values of the variables representing the tracked altitudes of the two planes, based on the constraints on the valid inputs given by the TCAS standard [1]. CBMC managed to fully verify the specified properties under no additional input restrictions in a few seconds and hence obtain 100 percent input coverage. This experiment confirmed us the fact that, with bounded model checking, one can provide, for certain cases, results of exhaustive verification much easier than with any testing method.

4.2   Hamming Error Detection and Correction Algorithm

For our second experiment we chose to verify a commonly used algorithm for detecting and correcting errors based on Hamming codes. We took an algorithm which uses Hamming codes which is based on [16]. This algorithm is representative for a class of error detection and correction algorithms which are often used as parts of the critical functions. Standards like IEC 61508 or ISO 26262 explicitly recommend the use of these algorithms for detecting data failures.

```
harness {
    // Generate random message
    for (uint16 i = 1;i <= size_of_info; i++ ) {
        nondet assign info[i]; constraints {
            info[i] in [0..1]
        }
    } // for
    encode_message();
    // inject error
    nondet assign error_pos; constraints {
        error_pos in [1..size_of_transmitted_data]
    }
    transmitted_data[error_pos] ^= 1;
}
correct_transmitted_message();
// check
for (uint16 i = 1;i <= size_of_info; i++ ) {
    assert(info[i] == received_info[i]);
} // for
```

```
// Correct error if needed
if (syn != 0) {
    transmitted_data[syn] ^= 1;
} // if
```

```
harness {
    // Generate random message
    for (uint16 i = 1;i <= size_of_info; i++ ) {
        nondet assign info[i]; constraints {
            info[i] in [0..1]
        }
    } // for
    encode_message();
    // choose whether to inject the error or not
    nondeterministic_choice: {
        choice: {
            // inject error
            nondet assign error_pos; constraints {
                error_pos in [1..size_of_transmitted_data]
            }
            transmitted_data[error_pos] ^= 1;
        }
        choice: {
            // no error
        }
    }
}
correct_transmitted_message();
// check
for (uint16 i = 1;i <= size_of_info; i++ ) {
    assert(info[i] == received_info[i]);
} // for
```

Fig. 4. Environment definition, error injection and verification condition for the Hamming coding algorithm. On the left-hand an initial definition which prevented us to reach branch coverage (left-bottom). On the right-hand side is the corrected environment definition which considers also messages without error.

Figure 4 shows an example of a harness definition for the Hamming coding algorithm using mbeddr. On the upper-left-hand side there is an initial definition of the environment – at first we initialize the message to be sent (stored in binary form in the vector info), then we encode this message using the Hamming algorithm, we choose an arbitrary position where the error is injected (error_pos) and correct the message. The verification condition checks that the initial message is the same as the message decoded upon receival. This harness covers exhaustively all possible vectors of size_of_info and all possible one bit errors which can occur within the transmitted vector (transmitted_data contains the information together with the corresponding parity bits).

When trying to generate test-cases with branch coverage based on this environment, CBMC could not cover all branches – e.g. the branch from Fig. 4-left-bottom was always taken. Manual investigation revealed the fact that our harness did not consider the case when no error happens during transmission. At this point we could have either relaxed the verification environment or we could have manually written some test cases to also verify the uncovered branch. We chose to enhance the harness (Fig. 4-right) with a non-deterministic choice to inject/not-inject the error and thereby we could obtain a higher branch coverage. In Fig. 5, we present the running time required by CBMC for different lengths of the message. We could exhaustively verify the correct functioning of the algorithm for messages with a length up to 64 bits. Exhaustive testing of these messages would require 2^{58} test-cases and thereby is completely unfeasible. Our conclusion is that bounded model checking can be used to exhaustively check the correctness of the algorithm for relatively small input messages. Correct encoding of messages with a higher length could not be verified by the model checker because the time step bound k was less than the diameter of the transition system that abstractly models the program. In order to cover this assurance deficit, the embedded engineers must manually write additional test-cases, which comply with standards. This experiment shows that the bounded model checker can exhaustively verify cases when the length of the input message is small enough.

number_of_parity_bits	4	6	7
size_of_info	11 bits	58 bits	121 bits
analysis time	2s	60s	> 600s (timeout)

Fig. 5. Time required by CBMC when choosing different lengths of the message to be encoded. CBMC is fast up to messages with total length 64 bits (58 info + 6 parity).

4.3   Case Study 3: Patients Trolley

Our third experiment is the verification of a controller for a smart trolley which assists healthcare professionals in drug administration and other bedside procedures. The smart trolley has several drawers and can serve multiple patients.

The trolley responds with different actions to the inputs given by a doctor. We chose this system because (1) it is built as a state machine and can be run infinitely (2) it is a safety-critical system because, if it does not function properly, the patient might get the wrong medicine, a fact which might endanger his life.

We chose two properties of the system to verify, namely: *P1: There are never two drawers open at the same time* and *P2: Only the drawers corresponding to the selected patient can be opened*. Both properties come directly from the requirements specification document of the system. Figure 6-left shows the harness definition for the property *P1* – in the main loop we send an arbitrary event to the state machine and we check that in between two events for opening drawers (EVENT_OPEN_DRAWER) there is always an event for closing the drawer (EVENT_DISPLAY_CLOSED). This only works under the assumption that there is no transition that opens two different drawers at once. This assumption could be checked by code reviewing. In Fig. 6-right we present the harness definition for *P2*. We check that the system opens only the valid drawers for a patient.

The state-machine can run infinitely, but we chose to restrict the number of steps in the main loop and thereby the number of events that we send to the state-machine. Thus we performed complete verification up to MAX_EVENT_NUMBER. Even with a small value of MAX_EVENT_NUMBER we were able to cover all statements of the state-machine. However, the trolley can run for much longer time, and thereby our verification is incomplete. The assurance deficit occurs for long runs of the trolley system. For these cases the developers must use additional manual tests, which comply with standards. The patients trolley example shows the usefulness of bounded model checker based verification on a reactive system which runs infinitely.

```
harness {
  boolean drawer_already_opened = false;
  for (i ++ in [0..MAX_EVENT_NUMBER[) {
    nondet assign crt_event_id; constraints {
      valid_enum(crt_event_id)
    }
    // call the system
    executeEvent(crt_event_id);
    // property: only one drawer can be open
    assert(!(drawer_already_opened &&
        lastEvent == EVENT_OPEN_DRAWER));

    if (state == STATE_DRAWER_SELECTED) {
      if (lastEvent == EVENT_OPEN_DRAWER) {
        drawer_already_opened = true;
      } else if (lastEvent == EVENT_DISPLAY_CLOSED) {
        drawer_already_opened = false;
      }
    }
  }
}
```

```
harness {
  for (i ++ in [0..MAX_EVENT_NUMBER[) {
    nondet assign crt_event_id; constraints {
      valid_enum(crt_event_id)
    }
    if (crt_event_id == EVENT_PATIENT_SELECTED) {
      nondet assign patient_in; constraints {
        patient_in in [1..3]
      }
    }
    if (crt_event_id == EVENT_DRAWER_SELECTED) {
      nondet assign drawer_in; constraints {
        drawer_in in [1..9]
      }
    }
    // call the system
    executeEvent(crt_event_id);
    // property: only the drawers corresponding to
    // the current patient can be open
    if (state == STATE_DRAWER_SELECTED) {
      assert(patient == 1 -> (drawer in [1..3]));
      assert(patient == 2 -> (drawer in [4..6]));
      assert(patient == 3 -> (drawer in [7..9]));
    }
  }
}
```

Fig. 6. Environment definition and verification condition for the smart trolley system: on the left we check property *P1* and on the right we check property *P2*.

5   Discussion

On Simplifying Assumptions. In practice, there are a multitude of factors that must be considered when analyses tools replace the execution of the tests on the target hardware. For example, the C compiler used to produce the binary from the sources might have itself bugs or have a different interpretation of corner cases of the C language than the verification tool. Furthermore, hardware particularities like the endianess, word length or memory model must be treated soundly by the verification tool. These aspects are not in the scope of this paper, but should be thoroughly considered during the development of a real-world assurance case.

On Automating the Complementary Testing. When the bounded model checking is incomplete, we propose to cover the assurance deficits using manually written test-cases. However, recent developments in verification based on conditional model checking [7] are able to characterize the state space of the program covered by the verification tool and use this information to generate test-cases for the uncovered parts [10]. The information about the uncovered code parts can be used in the confidence argument and part of the test vectors can be obtained in an automatic manner.

On Using Tests Vectors Generation to Measure Confidence. One of the means we proposed to measure the completeness degree of incomplete verification is to generate test vectors starting from the same enviromental assumptions. However, empirical studies on the effectiveness of coverage-directed tests generation to uncover bugs show disappointing results [17]. Thereby, structural coverage criteria can indicate weaknesses in our assumptions (when these criteria are NOT fulfilled) and offer only a weak confidence in the verification when the criteria are fulfilled.

On Practicality and Costs. Our approach builds a bridge between two extreme cases. The first case is when the model checker can explore the space of behaviors exhaustively; the second case is when the model checker cannot produce any meaningful result, even when a narrow environment is used. In the first case, the verification is complete; in the second case, we rely completely on the results of traditional testing. In this paper, we argue for a middle way to complement the verification results with testing. Finding a sweet-spot, in which the cost-benefits of applying formal verification is the highest, is of a paramount importance for the adoption of the approach, especially for functions at lower criticality levels.

On Using the CBMC Bounded Model Checker. CMBC is still in need of verification and validation in order to be used as assurance evidence generator. However, the reason for using CBMC in our work is that it provides out-of-the-box features which are key enablers for our approach. Firstly, the CBMC analyses are bit-precise and thereby accurate. Secondly, CBMC offers the possibility to instrument loops (and recursion) to detect insufficient unwindings and to warn about incomplete results. Thirdly, CBMC offers the function to generate tests with a given code coverage and we use these tests as backing evidence for the coverage degree of the bounded model checking verification. Last but not least, CBMC allow the specification of verification environment. There are, however, other bounded model checking tools which could be used instead of CBMC.

6   Related Work

Formal Verification for Assurance. Habli [13] and Denney [11] present a generic safety argument for the use of formal methods results for certification. Basir [5] proposes a method to derive safety cases from formally verified code using Hoare-style inferences. Bennion [6] develops an assurance case for arguing the compliance of the Simulink Design Verifier model checker to DO-178C. We propose an argument structure pattern for using successful, but possibly incomplete bounded model checking results as certification evidence. For the cases when the verification is incomplete, our pattern uses results of additional testing as evidence and comprises a confidence argument.

Confidence of Evidence. Habli [13] emphasizes the need of including all the known limitations of the used formal verification technique in order to achieve trust in the results. Hawkins [14] defines assurance deficits as a prohibiting factor of perfect confidence in a claim about an assurance evidence. Ayoub [4] proposes the usage of separate argumentation legs for arguing that certain confidence exists in a certain assurance evidence. This is done by explicitly listing identified assurance deficits and the measures taken against them. They call these argumentation legs confidence arguments. The usage of complementary diverse evidence is encouraged by Littlewood [15], who demonstrates an increase of confidence in the argument about the system safety when having both a verification and a testing argument leg. We propose a confidence argumentation structure for explicitly describing the assurance deficits of this verification method and for providing corresponding backing arguments.

Complementing Verification with Testing. Conditional model checking [7] is a technique to characterize the state space of the program which was covered by the model checker and use this information for subsequent analyses or to generate test cases for the uncovered parts Czech [10]. Christakis [8] uses a similar technique in order to explicitly specify all assumptions which the verification engine performed and thereby, to enable collaborative verification. The focus of these works is on making the deficits of model checking explicit and cover these deficits by other verification methods. The above mentioned works are complementary to our work and they can be used to better characterize the confidence in incomplete results, to increase the automation of the tests generation, or to use other complementary verification methods to minimize the deficits.

7   Conclusions

In this paper, we presented an approach to use successful results of software bounded model checking in an assurance case. We propose to use additional testing to mitigate the possible assurance deficits of incomplete bounded model checking. Our longer term goal is to enable practitioners who develop safety critical systems to benefit from the bounded model checking technology. As future work, we plan to investigate in detail heterogeneous backing evidence from other verification methods (e.g., code review) to reinforce incomplete model checking results.

Acknowledgments. The research leading to these results has received funding from the European Union's Seventh Framework Programme FP7/2007–2013 under grant agreement n°610640.

References

1. Introduction to TCAS II version 7.1, November 2000
2. International standard IEC 61508 (2008)
3. GSN community standard version 1. Technical report, November 2011
4. Ayoub, A., Kim, B.G., Lee, I., Sokolsky, O.: A systematic approach to justifying sufficient confidence in software safety arguments. In: Ortmeier, F., Lipaczewski, M. (eds.) SAFECOMP 2012. LNCS, vol. 7612, pp. 305–316. Springer, Heidelberg (2012)
5. Basir, N., Denney, E., Fischer, B.: Constructing a safety case for automatically generated code from formal program verification information. In: NFM (2010)
6. Bennion, M., Habli, I.: A candid industrial evaluation of formal software verification using model checking. In: ICSE (2014)
7. Beyer, D., Henzinger, T.A., Keremoglu, M.E., Wendler, P.: Conditional model checking: a technique to pass information between verifiers. In: FASE (2012)
8. Christakis, M., Müller, P., Wüstholz, V.: Collaborative verification and testing with explicit assumptions. In: Giannakopoulou, D., Méry, D. (eds.) FM 2012. LNCS, vol. 7436, pp. 132–146. Springer, Heidelberg (2012)
9. Clarke, E., Kroning, D., Lerda, F.: A tool for checking ANSI-C programs. In: Jensen, K., Podelski, A. (eds.) TACAS 2004. LNCS, vol. 2988, pp. 168–176. Springer, Heidelberg (2004)
10. Czech, M., Jakobs, M.-C., Wehrheim, H.: Just test what you cannot verify!. In: Egyed, A., Schaefer, I. (eds.) FASE 2015. LNCS, vol. 9033, pp. 100–114. Springer, Heidelberg (2015)
11. Denney, E., Pai, G.: Evidence arguments for using formal methods in software certification. In: WoSoCer (2013)
12. Gotlieb, A.: TCAS software verification using constraint programming. Knowl. Eng. Rev. **27**, 343 (2012)
13. Habli, I., Kelly, T.: A generic goal-based certification argument for the justification of formal analysis. Electron. Notes Theor. Comput. Sci **238**, 27–39 (2009)
14. Hawkins, R., Kelly, T., Knight, J., Graydon, P.: A new approach to creating clear safety arguments. In: Dale, C., Anderson, T. (eds.) Advances in Systems Safety, pp. 3–23. Springer, London (2011)
15. Littlewood, B., Wright, D.: The use of multilegged arguments to increase confidence in safety claims for software-based systems: a study based on a BBN analysis of an idealized example. IEEE Trans. Softw. Eng. **33**, 347–365 (2007)

16. Morelos-Zaragoza, R.H.: The Art of Error Correcting Coding. Wiley, New York (2006)

17. Staats, M., Gay, G., Whalen, M., Heimdahl, M.: On the danger of coverage directed test case generation. In: de Lara, J., Zisman, A. (eds.) Fundamental Approaches to Software Engineering. LNCS, vol. 7212, pp. 409–424. Springer, Heidelberg (2012)

18. Voelter, M., Ratiu, D., Kolb, B., Schätz, B.: mbeddr: instantiating a language workbench in the embedded software domain. Autom. Softw. Eng. **20**, 339–390 (2013)

Configuration-Aware Contracts

Irfan Sljivo$^{(\boxtimes)}$, Barbara Gallina, Jan Carlson, and Hans Hansson

Mälardalen Real-Time Research Centre, Mälardalen University, Västerås, Sweden
{irfan.sljivo,barbara.gallina,jan.carlson,hans.hansson}@mdh.se

Abstract. Assumption/guarantee contracts represent the basis for independent development of reusable components and their safety assurance within contract-based design. In the context of safety-critical systems, their use for reuse of safety assurance efforts has encountered some challenges: the need for evidence supporting the confidence in the contracts; and the challenge of context, where contracts need to impose different requirements on different systems.

In this paper we propose the notion of configuration-aware contracts to address the challenge contract-based design faces with multiple contexts. Since reusable components are often developed with a set of configuration parameters that need to be configured in each context, we extend the notion of contract to distinguish between the configuration parameters and the other variables. Moreover, we define a multi-context reusable component based on the configuration-aware contracts. Finally, we demonstrate the usefulness of the multi-context components on a motivating case.

1 Introduction

Software intensive safety-critical systems are nowadays rarely developed from scratch or by a single company. Instead, parts of the system are usually either reused or developed independently of the system [11]. To move towards components with pedigree and thus to fully benefit from reuse within safety-critical systems, the integrator companies need to reuse not only the components themselves, but also the accompanying safety artefacts [7]. The difficulty with reusing safety artefacts is that they are often context-specific. To enable out-of-context development, the notion of Safety Element out-of-Context (SEooC) was introduced within ISO26262 [5] as well as a corresponding life-cycle. This SEooC-related life-cycle requires that a set of context assumptions is identified for the reusable component and validated when the component is reused in the context of a particular system. These assumptions represent a way for the supplier of the reusable component to impose certain requirements on the usage of the provided component, in order to guarantee the specified behaviour of the component.

The term context is usually described as *any information that can be used to characterise the situation of an entity* [4]. In terms of SEooC, in-context is defined as all the information about the particular system, while out-of-context means that very little or no information is known about the environment in which

© Springer International Publishing Switzerland 2016
A. Skavhaug et al. (Eds.): SAFECOMP 2016 Workshops, LNCS 9923, pp. 43–54, 2016.
DOI: 10.1007/978-3-319-45480-1_4

the component will execute. Moving a SEooC to a particular context means that we are gradually increasing the knowledge about the environment in which the component will execute until we gain the full knowledge about the environment.

Component contracts in software engineering represent a way to support independent development of reusable components by specifying behaviours of the components in assumption/guarantee pairs [1]. The guarantees state the behaviours of the component, provided that the environment behaves according to the assumptions. By supporting such contracts with evidence and relating them to the safety requirements allocated to the component, they can be used to semi-automatically generate assurance case argument-fragments [10]. A characteristic of the assumptions and guarantees is that they represent properties of entire traces, unlike assertions in program analysis that constrain the state space of a program at a particular point. In the traditional assumption/guarantee contracts [1] this means that the assumptions cannot include detailed information about different contexts, which are often contradictory. The distinction on strong and weak contracts allows for capturing those context-specific properties within the weak contracts [9], while the strong contracts capture properties of behaviours in all the different contexts. The weak contract assumptions are not required to be satisfied, while the strong contract assumptions, just as the traditional ones, are required to be satisfied.

Contract assumptions allow the developer of the component to impose requirements on the environment in which the component is used. But currently this imposing of requirements can be done only for all contexts, and since not all requirements are safety relevant in every context, an approach is needed to facilitate imposing requirements on only some contexts where they are actually safety-relevant. For example, an integrator company asks one of its suppliers for a reusable component and provides the specification on how this component should behave. These specifications should be addressed by the guarantees of the contracts of the reusable component. The supplier develops the component and in that process identifies assumptions under which the component exhibits the guaranteed behaviours. For such a component to be used in a particular system, all of the assumptions stated in the component contracts need to be satisfied by the system. The contract assumptions thus represent a way in which the supplier can constrain the set of environments in which the component can be used. Such reusable components are often developed with a set of usage profiles in mind that are characterised by different configuration parameters of the component. The different configuration parameters imply different behaviour of the component, and may require different constraints on different environments to guarantee the same safety requirement. Since the assumptions need to be consistent, otherwise no environment could fulfil them, the suppliers of reusable components are forced to weaken the assumptions of the contracts for the sake of specifying behaviour of the component under different configuration parameters. One way of achieving this weakening is by specifying the context-specific information in the weak contracts. But weak contracts do not impose any constraints on the component environment, since its assumptions are not required to be satisfied.

In this work, we extend the notion of contract to handle the multi-context setting of reusable components by explicitly distinguishing between assumptions on configuration parameters and operational variables. We introduce the configuration-aware contracts and demonstrate how they can be used to achieve similar flexibility as the strong and weak contracts, while providing the possibility to the supplier to explicitly impose requirements on only some contexts. Finally, we demonstrate the usefulness and the applicability of the configuration-aware contracts on a motivating case where a safety-relevant component is developed for reuse within a family of wheel-loaders.

The rest of the paper is structured as follows: In Sect. 2 we recall essential background information. We present the configuration-aware contracts and the related reasoning in Sect. 3. In Sect. 4 we present the application of the proposed extensions on a motivating case. We present related work in Sect. 5. Finally, we bring conclusions and future work in Sect. 6.

2   Background

In this section we recall the essential information on contracts. Moreover, we introduce the motivating case we use for illustrative purposes as well as demonstration of usefulness of the configuration-aware contracts.

2.1   The Assumption/Guarantee Contracts

The component model of the assumption/guarantee contract theory is based on a set V of variables, where each **variable** represents some relevant information about a component (e.g., input and output ports) [1]. A **contract** C is defined over the set of variables V as a pair $C = (A, G)$ of assertions, called the assumptions (A), and the guarantees (G).

We denote the **strong contracts** with (A, G) and the **weak contracts** with (B, H) [9]. The strong assumptions (A) need to be met by the environment of the component, and in return the component provides the guarantees (G). In contrast, the weak guarantees (B) are not necessarily offered in every environment. Only when both the strong and the weak assumptions are met, the corresponding weak guarantees(H) are offered. Such strong and weak contracts can be represented as traditional contracts by transforming the weak contracts into implications stated in the guarantees. The resulting contract is in conjuncted form where only the strong assumptions remain as the contract assumptions, while the guarantees represent the conjuncted strong guarantees and the implications from weak contracts, i.e., (A, G) and (B, H) can be represented as a single traditional contract $(A, G \wedge (B \Rightarrow H))$.

Just as the contracts, the environment E and implementation I are also defined in terms of the assertions over the set of variables V. When dealing with distinct sets of variables an **environment** is defined as a tuple $E=(V_E, P_E)$ and **implementation** is defined as $I=(V_I, P_I)$, where V_E and V_I are the sets of variables of the environment and implementation respectively, and P_E and

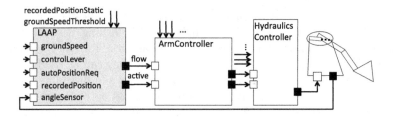

Fig. 1. The assumed structure of the lifting arm unit context

P_I are the sets of behaviours over the corresponding set of variables for the environments and implementations respectively. An implementation I is said to implement a contract $C = (A, G)$ if it provides the contract guarantees G, subject to the assumptions A, i.e., $P_I \cap A \subseteq G$. An environment E satisfies the contract C if it fulfils its assumptions, i.e., $P_E \subseteq A$. A **component** S is defined as a tuple $S = (V, C_S, I)$ where C_S is a set of contracts over the set of variables V, while I is a possibly empty set of implementations of the contracts [1].

2.2   Motivating Case

In this section we present the motivating case based on a real-world scenario where a single component Loading Arm Automatic Positioning (LAAP) is developed for reuse in different wheel-loaders.

Wheel-loaders are usually equipped with a loading arm, which can perform up and down movements. The software controller Loading Arm Controller Unit (LACU) handles both manual and automated arm movement. LACU calculates the arm movement commands based on the sensory data and user input, and then issues them to a hydraulic controller that moves the arm physically. The assumed structure of a representative LACU is shown in Fig. 1.

LACU is composed of two main subcomponents: the LAAP component that handles automatic arm positioning; and the Arm Controller component that issues the final command for both automatic and manual arm positioning. LAAP monitors the control lever that is used to lift/lower the arm manually and an automatic position request button that positions the arm in a predefined position. LAAP is activated by pressing the automatic positioning button, and it can be stopped by moving the control lever, as LAAP gets deactivated on detection of any movement of the control lever. When active, LAAP uses an arm angle sensor to determine the current arm position, while the target position is indicated by the recorded position port. The recorded position port is related to the *recordedPositionStatic* configuration parameter, which indicates whether the recorded position is predefined and constant, or if it can be set to a custom value. The ground speed port indicates the current ground speed of the vehicle and is used together with the *groundSpeedThreshold* configuration parameter such that the component deactivates if the current speed is greater than the specified threshold. Moreover, LAAP uses *maxGroundSpeed* that indicates the maximum ground speed of the vehicle to determine whether a faulty ground speed sensor can influence LAAP to move the arm when not supposed to.

3 The Configuration-Aware Contracts

In this section we define the context and the configuration-aware contracts. Moreover, we define the reusable component for the multi-context based on the notion of the configuration-aware contracts. Finally, we discuss the differences between the configuration-aware contracts and the corresponding traditional contracts.

3.1 A Component Configuration Context

As mentioned in Sect. 1, the context represents all information about a particular system. The fact that a component is developed out-of-context does not mean that no information about the system is known. Reusable components are usually developed with a set of usages in mind that are characterised by different configuration parameters of the component. We refer to the set of such parameters as the configuration context of the component. To define the configuration context, we first partition the set V of variables of the reusable component S: $V = V_{Sop} \uplus V_{Sconf}$, such that we distinguish between the operational (V_{Sop}) and the configuration (V_{Sconf}) variables. The distinction between the two types of variables is that the configuration variables, also referred to as parameters, can have only one value in a particular environment. The parameters allow component implementations to be prepared for use in different environments.

For each environment where the component may be used, there is a corresponding set of parameter values, which is why they can be viewed as constants when the component is used in a specific configuration context. We define a *configuration context* of a component as an assignment of a value to each variable from the set of configuration parameters V_{Sconf}. For example, *ground-SpeedThreshold* and *recordedPositionStatic* in our motivating example are configuration variables that are constant in the context of a particular vehicle. Based on the values of these two parameters we can distinguish between different configuration contexts of the LAAP component. The recorded position can be fixed and the ground speed threshold set to zero, which represents the environment where likelihood of propagation of failures through LAAP is minimal. Another configuration context could be when the recorded position is dynamic and the ground speed threshold is at a higher vehicle speed e.g., 20 kmph. To reduce the likelihood of failures propagating through LAAP in environments that fit this context, requirements on the failure behaviours of the components providing recorded position and ground speed need to be imposed.

3.2 Configuration-Aware Contracts

As discussed in Sect. 1, using traditional contract assumptions to capture both the configuration and operational variables can lead to unwanted weakening of the assumptions. To overcome this problem we define the notion of *configuration-aware contract* to clearly distinguish between the assumptions on the configuration parameters and those over the operational variables. A *configuration-aware contract* is defined as a tuple $C = (A_c, A_o, G)$ where:

- A_c represent assumptions over the configuration variables, and is defined as an assertion over the set of configuration variables V_{Sconf};
- A_o represent assumptions over the operational variables, and is defined as an assertion over the set of operational variables V_{Sop};
- G represent the contract guarantees defined as an assertion over V.

The contract C states that the assertion A_o needs to be satisfied in all contexts satisfying A_c, and under these conditions G is guaranteed. While we model assertions over operational variables as sets of traces, assertions over the set of configuration variables can be simply modelled as sets of configuration contexts.

A correct implementation of a configuration-aware contract behaves according to the specified guarantees, provided that the corresponding assumptions on both types of variables are met. We define a configuration-aware *implementation* over the set of variables V as $I = (V, P_{Ic}, P_{Io})$ where:

- P_{Ic} represent a set of configuration contexts over the set of configuration variables V_{Sconf};
- P_{Io} represent an assertion over the set of operational variables V_{Sop}.

While an implementation considers the different values of the configuration parameters, an environment establishes a single configuration context, i.e., it considers only a single value for each configuration parameter. We define an environment over the set of variables V as $E = (V, p_{Ec}, P_{Eo})$ where:

- p_{Ec} represent the configuration context of the environment E over the set of configuration variables V_{Sconf};
- P_{Eo} represent an assertion over the set of operational variables V_{Sop}.

3.3   A Multi-context Component

As mentioned earlier, a reusable component can exhibit different behaviours in different configuration contexts. This makes the configuration context interesting for contract-based development because once a configuration context of a component is determined by a particular environment, then only behaviours of the component exhibited in that particular configuration need to be analysed. Hence, the configuration context information of an environment allow us to filter out the contracts relevant for the particular environment.

We define a multi-context component by considering its configuration contexts and the corresponding configuration-aware contracts. Formally, we define *multi-context component* as $S = (V, P_{Sc}, C_S, I_S)$ such that

- V is the set of variables composed of the sets of operational and configuration variables $V = V_{Sop} \uplus V_{Sconf}$;

- P_{Sc} is the set of configuration contexts over V_{Sconf};
- C_S is the set of configuration-aware contracts over V such that the set of configuration contexts of each of the contracts is a subset of P_{Sc};
- I_S is a possibly empty set of implementations over V.

As a multi-context component S is moved to the context of a particular system, it needs to be instantiated to an in-context component. We define an *in-context component* as a special case of a multi-context component where the set of configuration contexts P_{Sc} contains only one configuration context. Consequently, the set of contracts is reduced to only those matching the particular context. Given an environment $E_1 = (V, p_{E1c}, P_{E1})$ such that $p_{E1c} \in P_{Sc}$, we define an *instantiation* of an in-context component from the component S as $S_1 = (V, p_{S1c}, C_{S1}, I)$, where:

- $p_{S1c} = p_{E1c}$
- $C_{S1} = \{c \in C_S \mid c = (A_c, A_o, G) \wedge p_{S1c} \in A_c\}$

3.4   From Configuration-Aware Contracts to Traditional Contracts

To transform a set of configuration-aware contracts to a traditional contract, we conjunct them such that the assumptions that need to hold for all configuration contexts are preserved, while other operational assumptions together with the assumptions on configuration variables are transferred to the traditional contract guarantees. The latter is done by implications in guarantees, expressing that if the transferred assumptions are satisfied they imply the corresponding configuration-aware contract guarantees. This is similar to how the strong and weak contracts are conjuncted into traditional contracts. This way the assumptions and guarantees transferred as implications behave as the weak contracts, while the assumptions and guarantees that hold in all configuration contexts behave as assumptions and guarantees of strong contracts.

The traditional conjuncted form does not distinguish between the different configuration contexts. While the two types of contracts are the same in terms of implementations, i.e., implementations of the conjuncted contract are the same as the implementations of the configuration-aware contracts, they differ in terms of environments. A correct environment of a contract in conjuncted form is every environment that satisfies only the overall contract assumptions, while the configuration-aware contracts of an in-context component offer the possibility for a more fine-grained constraining of the different environments without weakening the assumptions to only the assumptions that hold in all configuration contexts.

For example, if we consider *groundSpeedThreshold* configuration parameter in our motivating case from Sect. 2.2. LAAP is disabled when the ground speed value is greater than the threshold parameter. For contexts where the threshold value is lower than the maximum speed of the vehicle, the groundSpeed port failure can contribute to LAAP running when not supposed to, e.g., when groundSpeed is faulty and shows that the vehicle is moving slower than it actually is. For such contexts it is important to impose a requirement on the groundSpeed port value to be highly reliable. But when the threshold value is equal or greater than the maximum speed of the vehicle, then even if the groundSpeed port reports faulty value it cannot lead to LAAP running when not supposed to. Hence for the first set of contexts, it is important to impose the requirement on reliability of the groundSpeed port, while for the second case such requirement is not necessary and in fact is too strong. For traditional contracts, this can be expressed only in the conjuncted form where no requirements on the environment would be made regarding the reliability of groundSpeed, or if such requirement would be made for all contexts, it would be too strong for certain cases.

The concept of configuration-aware contracts can be used to facilitate capturing optional behaviours in terms of weak contracts by defining a boolean parameter and using it only for the particular configuration-aware contract that is intended to be optional. This concept facilitates similar flexibility of the weak contracts, although it may result in a large number of configuration parameters for the different weak contracts.

4   Ilustrative Case

In this section we demonstrate, using the motivating case introduced in Sect. 2.2, how capturing of the contracts as configuration-aware can influence the constraints imposed by the contract assumptions in a specific environment. Since the component is intended for a family of wheel-loaders, the requirement that needs to be satisfied in all the systems of the family is that the LAAP does not move the loading arm when not supposed to. Hence, the property that the LAAP outputs are not faulty needs to be satisfied in all the different systems. We model LAAP as a multi-context component and demonstrate how configuration-aware contracts can provide the mechanism for ensuring that the LAAP is not faulty in the different configuration contexts without making the assumptions too strong.

To compare the configuration-aware and traditional way of capturing the contracts, we consider how would capturing the same information using the two contract approaches influence the strength of the assumptions that a particular environment needs to fulfil. We first capture the configuration-aware contracts, shown in Table 1. The example shows five configuration-aware contracts where the first LAAP1 contract is valid for all the configuration contexts, since it checks whether the received values on the input ports are in the specified range. If not, then it disables the component outputs. The LAAP2-LAAP5 contracts are specific to the four different configuration contexts described in Sect. 2.2. The LAAP2 contract specifies the LAAP component behaviour when the maximum ground speed is greater than the ground speed threshold and the predefined arm position does not change. In this configuration context, for the component not to propagate any failures, the assumptions need to be made so that the ground speed value will not be faulty, while any faults of the recorded position do not influence the LAAP output. In contrast to this configuration context, when ground speed threshold is greater or equal to the maximum ground speed, as specified in the LAAP4 contract, the environment does not need to fulfil the requirement that the ground speed value is not faulty.

Table 1. A set of LAAP configuration-aware contracts

$\mathbf{A}_{c-LAAP1}$:	-;
$\mathbf{A}_{o-LAAP1}$:	*groundSpeed* within [0, 200] km/h AND *angleSensor* within [0,3] rad AND *controlLever* within ± 1 rad AND *recordedPosition* within [0,3] rad;
$\mathbf{G}_{LAAP1}$:	(*groundSpeed* not within [0, 200] km/h OR *angleSensor* not within [0,3] rad OR *controlLever* not 0 rad OR *recordedPosition* not within [0,3] rad;) **implies** (*Active* = false and *Flow* = 0);
$\mathbf{A}_{c-LAAP2}$:	*groundSpeedThreshold* < *maxGroundSpeed* AND *recordedPositionStatic*;
$\mathbf{A}_{o-LAAP2}$:	**not** *faultAngleSensor* AND **not** *faultAutoPositionReq* AND **not** *faultControlLever* AND **not** *faultGroundSpeed*;
$\mathbf{G}_{LAAP2}$:	**not** *faultFlow* AND **not** *faultActive*;
$\mathbf{A}_{c-LAAP3}$:	*groundSpeedThreshold* < *maxGroundSpeed* AND **not** *recordedPositionStatic*;
$\mathbf{A}_{o-LAAP3}$:	**not** *faultAngleSensor* AND **not** *faultRecordedPosition* AND **not** *faultAutoPositionReq* AND **not** *faultControlLever* AND **not** *faultGroundSpeed*;
$\mathbf{G}_{LAAP3}$:	**not** *faultFlow* AND **not** *faultActive*;
$\mathbf{A}_{c-LAAP4}$:	*groundSpeedThreshold* ⩾ *maxGroundSpeed* AND *recordedPositionStatic*;
$\mathbf{A}_{o-LAAP4}$:	**not** *faultAngleSensor* AND **not** *faultAutoPositionReq* AND **not** *faultControlLever*;
$\mathbf{G}_{LAAP4}$:	**not** *faultFlow* AND **not** *faultActive*;
$\mathbf{A}_{c-LAAP5}$:	*groundSpeedThreshold* ⩾ *maxGroundSpeed* AND **not** *recordedPositionStatic*;
$\mathbf{A}_{o-LAAP5}$:	**not** *faultAngleSensor* AND **not** *faultRecordedPosition* AND **not** *faultAutoPositionReq* AND **not** *faultControlLever* AND **not** *faultGroundSpeed*;
$\mathbf{G}_{LAAP5}$:	**not** *faultFlow* AND **not** *faultActive*;

Table 2. The corresponding LAAP traditional contract

$\mathbf{A}_{cf-LAAP}$:	$\mathbf{A}_{o-LAAP1}$ AND **not** *faultAngleSensor* AND **not** *faultAutoPositionReq* AND **not** *faultControlLever* ;
$\mathbf{G}_{cf-LAAP}$:	$\mathbf{G}_{LAAP1}$ AND ((($\mathbf{A}_{c-LAAP1}$ AND **not** *faultGroundSpeed*) OR ($\mathbf{A}_{c-LAAP2}$ AND **not** *faultRecordedPosition* AND **not** *faultGroundSpeed*) OR ($\mathbf{A}_{c-LAAP3}$) OR ($\mathbf{A}_{c-LAAP4}$ AND **not** *faultRecordedPosition*)) **implies** (**not** *faultFlow* AND **not** *faultActive*));

Since the traditional way of specifying contracts cannot capture the configuration variables in the contract assumptions, the assumptions need to be weakened to exclude the configuration variables. As described in Sect. 3.4, we transform the set of configuration-aware contracts to a traditional contract (Table 2) and also to the resulting in-context component overall contracts (Table 3). By comparing the assumptions of the traditional contract and the specific in-context overall contracts derived from the multi-context LAAP component, we notice that the assumptions for the different configuration contexts are in-general stronger than the assumptions of the traditional contract. This can for instance be seen on the in-context overall contract LAAP-C1 (Table 3), which besides the assumptions included in the traditional contract and the context-specific

Table 3. The in-context LAAP overall contracts of the LAAP configuration contexts

$\mathbf{A}_{cf-LAAP-C1}$:	$\mathbf{A}_{o-LAAP1}$ AND **not** *faultAngleSensor* AND **not** *faultAutoPositionReq* AND **not** *faultControlLever* AND **not** *faultGroundSpeed* AND $\mathbf{A}_{c-LAAP2}$;
$\mathbf{G}_{cf-LAAP-C1}$:	$\mathbf{G}_{LAAP1}$ AND **not** *faultFlow* AND **not** *faultActive*;
$\mathbf{A}_{cf-LAAP-C2}$:	$\mathbf{A}_{o-LAAP1}$ AND **not** *faultAngleSensor* AND **not** *faultAutoPositionReq* AND **not** *faultControlLever* AND **not** *faultGroundSpeed* AND **not** *faultRecordedPosition* AND $\mathbf{A}_{c-LAAP3}$;
$\mathbf{G}_{cf-LAAP-C2}$:	$\mathbf{G}_{LAAP1}$ AND **not** *faultFlow* AND **not** *faultActive*;
$\mathbf{A}_{cf-LAAP-C3}$:	$\mathbf{A}_{o-LAAP1}$ AND **not** *faultAngleSensor* AND **not** *faultAutoPositionReq* AND **not** *faultControlLever* AND $\mathbf{A}_{c-LAAP4}$;
$\mathbf{G}_{cf-LAAP-C3}$:	$\mathbf{G}_{LAAP1}$ AND **not** *faultFlow* AND **not** *faultActive*;
$\mathbf{A}_{cf-LAAP-C4}$:	$\mathbf{A}_{o-LAAP1}$ AND **not** *faultAngleSensor* AND **not** *faultAutoPositionReq* AND **not** *faultControlLever* AND **not** *faultRecordedPosition* AND $\mathbf{A}_{c-LAAP5}$;
$\mathbf{G}_{cf-LAAP-C4}$:	$\mathbf{G}_{LAAP1}$ AND **not** *faultFlow* AND **not** *faultActive*;

configuration parameters, also assumes that the ground speed value is not faulty. The strengthening of the in-context overall contract assumptions is done not only in terms of configuration parameters, but also in terms of assumptions over operational parameters. This way of deriving an in-context overall contract based on the configuration-aware contracts allows us to impose additional requirements in terms of assumptions that the corresponding environment of the particular in-context component needs to fulfil.

5   Related Work

Contract-based design has emerged as an interesting approach that facilitates a range of activities such as independent development, requirements structuring, compositional verification, and safety assurance argument generation, all useful for the development of safety-critical systems. Westman et al. [12] generalises the established contract theory [1] to environment-centric contracts to provide support for practical engineering and expressing of safety requirements using contracts. The environment-centric contracts relax the constrains on the scope of the assumptions and guarantees beyond the interface of the corresponding component. While environment-centric contracts theory does not distinguish explicitly between the rigid variables such as configuration parameters and other operational variables, Cimatti et al. [2] present a tool-supported contracts-refinement proof system that distinguishes between the two types of variables. Although they can be separately specified, they are treated equally within the contract assumptions, and hence the explicit distinction does not alleviate the challenge contracts have with the different context.

Schneider et al. [8] introduce the Digital Dependability Identities (DDIs) as a way to assure dependability of cyber-physical systems. DDIs represent modular, composable and possibly executable specification. One of the main goals of

DDIs is to provide the basis for run-time certification for the dynamically reconfigurable systems. Conditional Safety Certification (ConSert) represent an initial implementation of DDIs. The conditions in ConSerts are captured between the potentially guaranteed safety requirements (guarantees), and the corresponding demanded safety requirements (demands). In contrast, in our work we use contracts to capture the safety-relevant behaviours needed for satisfaction of safety requirements. Similarly to the conditions in ConSert, we extend the notion of contracts to act as conditions based on the configuration parameters and identify which component behaviours are relevant for a particular system. Since contracts can be used for generation of argument-fragments [10], the configuration-aware contracts can be viewed as means to achieve conditional safety arguments offline. Although configuration-aware contracts have potential for run-time certification for reconfigurable systems, that work is out of the scope of this paper.

Oliveira et al. [3] present a method for automatic allocation of safety requirements to components of a Software Product-line (SPL) by building upon HiP-HOPS (Hierarchically Performed Hazard Origin & Propagation Studies) [6]. The proposed method enumerates the SPL products enriched with hazard and failure information, and then uses HiP-HOPS for automatic allocation of ASILs (Automotive Safety Integrity Levels). Based on the ASIL allocations for each of the products, the proposed method identifies the most stringent allocation for each of the SPL components across the entire product family. In contrast, the configuration-aware contracts of a component can be used to verify that the SPL products in which the component is reused meet the minimum needed requirements to ensure that the requirements allocated to the reusable component are met. By using configuration-aware contracts, we alleviate the need for all the neighbouring components of the reusable component to be allocated with the most stringent ASIL in all configuration contexts.

6   Conclusions and Future Work

Contract-based design is a promising approach to facilitate independent development of components and their safety assurance within safety-critical systems. One of the challenges it faces is the troublesome issue of context when dealing with safety requirements. While one requirement can be safety-relevant in the context of a particular system, it may not be relevant in the context of some other system. In this paper we have argued that there is a need for more fine-grained handling of the context within the contracts. We have proposed to clearly distinguish between assumptions on configuration parameters and other operational variables. Unlike the operational variables, the configuration parameters have constant values within a particular system, and this makes them a useful source of information when developing a reusable component for a set of different contexts. We have proposed extended configuration-aware contracts that use the configuration parameters to filter out the assumptions over the operational parameters for the different configuration contexts. We have demonstrated on a real-world example how the multi-context components enriched with configuration-aware contracts provide a mechanism for imposing requirements on only those environments where actually needed.

As our future work, we intend to align this work with product-line engineering for safety-critical systems. While product-line feature modelling is done at a higher level, the configuration-aware contracts allow for tailoring the safety behaviour and the corresponding safety assurance case. We plan to investigate the usefulness of configuration-aware contracts for systems where cloud-computing is used to provide service to safety functions. We also plan to explore how configuration-aware contracts can be used to assist reuse of safety assurance artefacts across different system concerns such as safety and security.

Acknowledgements. This work is supported by the Swedish Foundation for Strategic Research (SSF) via project SYNOPSIS and FiC, as well as EU and VINNOVA via the ECSEL Joint Undertaking projects AMASS (No 692474) and SAFECOP (No 692529).

References

1. Benveniste, A., Caillaud, B., Nickovic, D., Passerone, R., Raclet, J.-B., Reinkemeier, P., Sangiovanni-Vincentelli, A., Damm, W., Henzinger, T., Larsen, K.G.: Contracts for system design. Research report RR-8147, Inria, November 2012
2. Cimatti, A., Tonetta, S.: Contracts-refinement proof system for component-based embedded systems. Sci. Comput. Programm. **97**(3), 333–348 (2014)
3. Oliveira, A.L., Papadopoulos, Y., Azevedo, L., Parker, D., Braga, R., Masiero, P.C., Habli, I., Kelly, T.: Automatic allocation of safety requirements to components of a software product line. IFAC-Pap. OnLine **48**(21), 1309–1314 (2015)
4. Dey, A.K.: Understanding and using context. Pers. Ubiquitous Comput. **5**(1), 4–7 (2001)
5. Road vehicles — Functional safety — Part 10: Guideline on ISO 26262. International Organization for Standardization, Geneva (2011)
6. Papadopoulos, Y., Walker, M., Parker, D., Rüde, E., Hamann, R., Uhlig, A., Grätz, U., Lien, R.: Engineering failure analysis and design optimisation with HiP-HOPS. Eng. Fail. Anal. **18**(2), 590–608 (2011)
7. Redmill, F.: The COTS debate in perspective. In: Voges, U. (ed.) SAFECOMP 2001. LNCS, vol. 2187, p. 119. Springer, Heidelberg (2001)
8. Schneider, D., Trapp, M., Papadopoulos, Y., Armengaud, E., Zeller, M., Höfig, K.: WAP: digital dependability identities. In: 26th International Symposium on Software Reliability Engineering, pp. 324–329. IEEE (2015)
9. Sljivo, I., Gallina, B., Carlson, J., Hansson, H.: Strong and weak contract formalism for third-party component reuse. In: 3rd International Workshop on Software Certification, International Symposium on Software Reliability Engineering Workshops (ISSREW), pp. 359–364. IEEE, November 2013
10. Sljivo, I., Gallina, B., Carlson, J., Hansson, H.: Generation of safety case argument-fragments from safety contracts. In: Bondavalli, A., Di Giandomenico, F. (eds.) SAFECOMP 2014. LNCS, vol. 8666, pp. 170–185. Springer, Heidelberg (2014)
11. Varnell-Sarjeant, J., Andrews, A.A., Stefik, A., Strategies, C.R.: An empirical evaluation of developer views. In: 8th International Workshop on Quality Oriented Reuse of Software, pp. 498–503. IEEE (2014)
12. Westman, J., Nyberg, M.: Environment-centric contracts for design of cyber-physical systems. In: Dingel, J., Schulte, W., Ramos, I., Abrahão, S., Insfran, E. (eds.) MODELS 2014. LNCS, vol. 8767, pp. 218–234. Springer, Heidelberg (2014)

Developing SNS Tool for Consensus Building on Environmental Safety Using Assurance Cases

Yutaka Matsuno[1(✉)], Yang Ishigaki[2], Koichi Bando[2],
Hiroyuki Kido[3], and Kenji Tanaka[2]

[1] Nihon University, Tokyo, Japan
matsuno.yutaka@nihon-u.ac.jp
[2] The University of Electro-Communications, Chofu, Japan
[3] The University of Tokyo, Tokyo, Japan

Abstract. Systems have been connected and interacted with each other around our daily lives. The boundaries of the systems are no more exist, and the safety of the systems involves various stakeholders including professionals, governments, and ordinary citizens. Therefore, for the safety of systems and the environments, consensus building among various stakeholders (e.g., professionals, developers, government, citizens) is crucial. However, ordinary citizens usually does not have sufficient knowledge about the safety and risk of systems around them. To solve this problem, we aim to develop methods and tools for consensus building specially with citizens using assurance cases written in GSN. This paper specifies the initial study for the goal. We take radiation information as an example. We implement prototype tools for visualizing structured argument by GSN about radiation information for citizens, and conduct an experiment for the effectiveness of the tool. The preliminary result indicates that the tool based on GSN is statistically significantly effective for sharing correct radiation information with citizens.

1 Introduction

Systems have been connected and interacted with each other around our daily lives. The boundaries of the systems are no more exist, and the safety of the systems involves various stakeholders including professionals, governments, and ordinary citizens. In particular, ordinary citizens usually does not have sufficient knowledge about the safety and risks of systems around them.

In the Fukushima nuclear plant disaster in 2011, a very serious problem was that scientifically correct information about radiation did not necessarily distributed to ordinary citizens. SNS (Social Networking Service) such as Twitter and Facebook were widely used by ordinary citizens for getting fast information about the radiation disaster. However, unfortunately, incorrect information was also distributed through the internet. Figure 1 shows a typical incorrect discussion in SNS (modified from actual discussion in Facebook). This discussion is wrong: radiation doze measurement changes according to the weather. In this paper, we aim to develop methods and tools to correct such scientifically incorrect discussion, and facilitate more discussion.

© Springer International Publishing Switzerland 2016
A. Skavhaug et al. (Eds.): SAFECOMP 2016 Workshops, LNCS 9923, pp. 55–62, 2016.
DOI: 10.1007/978-3-319-45480-1_5

– User A: When I used dosimeter when raining, radiation dose becomes twice!! Yesterday it was 0.1 μSv/h, but now it becomes 0.2 μSv/h! This must be by Radioactive iodine from the collapsed Fukushima nuclear plants!
– User B: Radiation dose is not increased by raining. Water absorbs radiation dose, so radiation dose must be decreased. Then why...
– User C: I have never heard that radiation dose measurement significantly changes by the weather. It might be due to measurement error.
– User D: Oh, my god! I heard that re-criticality of the nuclear plant is in the process. The Fukushima disaster seems not ending... I will take care of radiation when raining.

Fig. 1. An example of Facebook discussion about radiation doze measure

To avoid such incorrect discussion on SNS, our main idea is to use assurance cases [1] written in GSN (Goal Structuring Notation) [6] as reference for ordinary citizens discussing about radiation on SNS to lead scientifically correct discussion. Figure 2 shows the architecture of tool chain. The tool chain consists of two tools: *Smart Structure* and *Crowd Talks*.

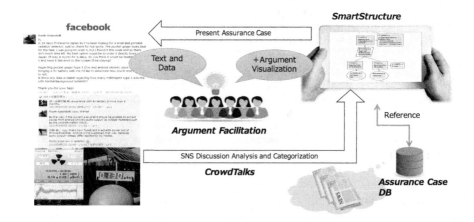

Fig. 2. Architecture of tool chain

– Smart Structure. When SNS user wants to share related information of the SNS discussion, Smart Structure presents the related information in GSN. GSN is generated semiautomatically by a database of the newspaper information and the government office, public, including the Web information. "Smart" is meant to expect that the tool to be used easily like smartphones.
– Crowd Talks. It analyses argument contents on SNS and passes the analyzed results to Smart Structure. Based on the information, Smart Structure presents appropriate GSN to the users. "Crowd" is meant to expect that the tool to be used by crowds (ordinary citizens), not only by experts.

Currently prototypes of Smart Structure and Crowd Talks have been implemented, and tested the feasibility by a preliminary experiment with 20 subjects. The functions of semi-automatically generating GSN (Smart Structure) and SNS argument content analyzing (Crowd Talks) are in initial phases. Assurance cases in GSN used in the preliminary experiments are made manually with radiation experts. Figure 3 shows a screenshot of Smart Structure. In the screenshot, a GSN diagram for the SNS discussion in Fig. 1 is shown (in Japanese), which is translated into English in the righthand side. The top goal of the GSN is "Weather affects measurement of radiation dose." For the top goal, we use the strategy node "Argument over weather." The sub goals are "Measured radiation dose is decreased by snowing" and "Measured radiation dose is increased by raining." For these sub goals, evidence "Measured radiation dose data when snowing" and "Measured radiation dose data when raining" are attached. In Smart Structure, for each node in GSN, more detailed documents can be presented by clicking the node. For the evidence, the actual measured radiation dose data are attached. The case for snowing is not directly necessary, but with multiple cases including raining, ordinal citizens could understand that radiation doze is affected by the weather.

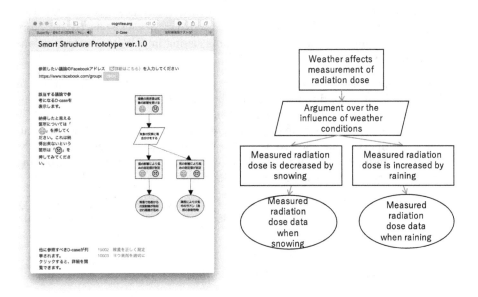

Fig. 3. A Screenshot of smart structure and GSN

Screenshots of Crowd Talks is shown in Fig. 4. Crowd Talks analyses Facebook discussions using LDA analysis [5], and elicits discussion topics in the Facebook discussions. It also visualises the topics.

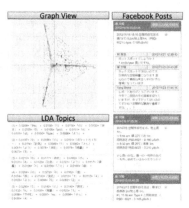

Fig. 4. Screenshots of crowd talks

As a mean for risk communication, assurance cases have been introduced mainly in safety-critical area for showing that the system is safe under a given environment in a goal oriented manner, based on evidence. Assurance cases are based on a general scientific research field called *argumentation theory* [3], in particular on Toulmin's model [11]. We observe that if assurance cases are effective for system assurance in safety-critical area, then they are also effective in more general risk communications with citizens, discussing in SNS. Our contributions are as follows.

– We develop prototype tools to present scientifically correct information in GSN, when users are discussing about the safety of systems and environment in SNS (e.g., radiation in the environment).
– We conduct a preliminary experiment with 20 subjects (undergraduate students), comparing the effectiveness of newspapers, web browsing, and GSN. The result indicates GSN is more effective than newspapers and web browsing for leading the users to scientifically collect discussion.

The structure of the paper is as follows. In Sect. 2, we explain preliminary experiment and the results. Section 3 discusses related work. In Sect. 4 we state concluding remarks.

2   Preliminary Experiment

To show the effectiveness of assurance cases (GSN) for leading SNS discussion scientifically correct discussion, we conduct a preliminary experiment with 20 subjects (undergraduate students). A snapshot of the experiment is shown in Fig. 5.

We assume that the 20 subjects have similar knowledge on radiation as ordinary citizens. 20 subjects are asked to see Facebook discussion as in Fig. 1. Then they are asked to use either newspapers, web browsing, or GSN for complementing the SNS discussion:

Fig. 5. A snapshot of experiment

- Newspapers: a set of articles related to the radiation topic.
- Web browsing: the subjects are allowed to use the internet freely.
- GSN: the subjects can use prototyped Smart Structure and see related GSN of the Facebook discussion. Currently, GSN is manually written with experts of radiation.

They are asked to do three tasks of different topics on radiation information. For each task, they can refer to either newspapers, web, or GSN. 20 subjects are divided into 6 groups (each of group consists of 3 or 4 subjects), and takes three tasks as in Table 1, in order to reduce order effect. The three topics are as follows.

- Weather affects radiation dose measurement (GSN for this topic is shown in Fig. 1).
- Iodine preparation is not necessary for ordinary citizens.
- Measuring equipment for radiation doze should be correctly chosen according to the purpose.

Sometimes incorrect information on radiation has been distributed in the internet. For example, some web pages propagates that Iodine preparation is a must thing for citizens living near Fukushima. We aim to provide scientifically correct information in GSN, and reduce adverse effect of such web pages.

Table 1. Structure of preliminary experiment

Group	Task 1	Task 2	Task 3
Group 1	Web	Newspaper	GSN
Group 2	Newspaper	Web	GSN
Group 3	GSN	Web	Newspaper
Group 4	GSN	Newspaper	Web
Group 5	Web	GSN	Newspaper
Group 6	Newspaper	GSN	Web

2.1 Experimental Result

After each task, we asked the 20 subjects how do they think that the Facebook discussions are correct or not (by questionnaire). Actually, all the Facebook discussions used in our experiments were scientifically wrong. This implies

Our hypothesis is that by the content of GSN with its argument structure and evidence, the subjects can reach to scientifically correct conclusion with the group members, and not so well by newspapers and web browsing.

Currently we are analyzing the experiment result. The preliminary analysis is shown in Fig. 6. We conduct analysis of variance for two criteria: satisfaction of tool usage and correctness. These criteria are measured by results of several questionnaire. For example, satisfaction score is calculated using five questionnaire (1 to 5 points scored by the subjects): usefulness of the information, understandability, degree of agreeing, degree of interest, and degree of facilitation using GSN, newspaper, or web browsing.

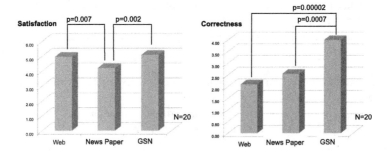

Fig. 6. Preliminary result of the experiment

For satisfaction criteria, our GSN presenting tool is not statistically advance on web browsing, but on newspapers. This indicates that reading articles of newspapers is not convenient for the subjects (undergraduate students). They tend to like web browsing, and our GSN tool is liked by them in similar level. For the correctness criteria, GSN leads the subjects to more correct conclusion than newspaper (the p value is 0.0007) and web browsing (the p value is 0.00002). This indicates that the structure of GSN is a better media for presenting information, comparing with newspaper (un-structured document) and web browsing (easy to use, but contains incorrect and huge information).

There are several considerations. One interest topic is that is there really a different between presenting just a top goal or a whole GSN tree structure. A comment of the subjects indicates that a whole GSN tree is valuable for understanding why the top goal is supported, by following the argument steps (strategy nodes in GSN) and evidence. It is interesting to conduct an experiment for difference between the two cases.

There are also several threats to validity. One is that the subjects are undergraduate students, so they might not be representatives of general public. Also, the results of the experiment are biased because the GSN diagram is a "distilled" and correct argument, whereas the other sources were not refined, and were not correct. Our main aim of this experiment is to show the effects of the tools (Smart Structure and Crowd Talks) when they are fully developed. Therefore we compare the current usage of SNS with newspapers and web browsing and our proposed usage of GSN. It is worth experimenting on such basic comparisons, including comparing natural language text and its corresponding GSN, where both have the same information.

3   Related Work

Assurance cases and GSN have been introduced for risk communication including safety regulations. There are, however, some criticisms of assurance cases. In [8], Leveson wrote, "Most papers about safety cases express personal opinions or deal with how to prepare a safety case, but not whether it is effective." This paper has conducted a preliminary experiment for evaluating the effectiveness of GSN with statistical argument. We believe our tool and experiment is a first step for evaluating the effectiveness of GSN in a statistical setting with subjects.

In [2], Cheikes et.al. conducted an empirical analysis of Toulmin's argument structure. The results were mixed, with the formalism having a positive impact for only one of the two articles. The paper focused on the impact of generating Toulmin's argument structure by the participants, and not directly comparing the understandability of natural text and argument structure of the same information. We also plan to do experiment of generating GSN by participants, because such active behavior would make more positive effect to participants.

4   Concluding Remarks

This paper has described our prototype tool for sharing scientifically correct information among citizens using GSN. The preliminary experiment suggests that the structure of assurance cases in GSN is effective, comparing with other methods such as newspapers and web browsing. Currently we are extending the tool and planning more general experiment not limited to on radiation information, but also on such as whether automatic driving cars are good or not. The tool will be freely used by the public on our web page[1]. We would like to report our progress in near future.

Acknowledgement. This work has been partially conducted as a part of "Research Initiative on Advanced Software Engineering in 2015" supported by Software Reliability Enhancement Center (SEC), Information Technology Promotion Agency Japan (IPA) and a part of KAKENHI 15K15971.

References

1. Workshop on Assurance Cases: Best Practices, Possible Obstacles, and Future Opportunities, DSN 2004 (2004)
2. Adelman, L., Lehner, P.E., Cheikes, B.A., Taylor, M.F.: An empirical evaluation of structured argumentation using the toulmin argument formalism. IEEE Trans. Syst. Man Cybern. Part A: Syst. Hum. **37**(3), 340–347 (2007)
3. Besnard, P., Hunter, A.: Elements of Argumentation. MIT Press, Cambridge (2008)
4. Bishop, P., Bloomfield, R.: A methodology for safety case development. In: Redmill, F., Anderson, T. (eds.) SSS 1998, pp. 194–203. Springer, London (1998)
5. Ng, A.Y., Blei, D.M., Jordan, M.I.: Latent dirichlet allocation. the. J. Mach. Learn. Res. **3**, 993–1022 (2003)
6. GSN contributors. GSN standard version 1.0 (2011)
7. Tim, K., Rob, W.: The goal structuring notation - a safety argument notation. In: Proceedings of the Dependable Systems and Networks, Workshop on Assurance Cases (2004)
8. Leveson, N.: The use of safety cases in certification and regulation. In: ESDWorking Paper Series, Boston, MIT (2011)
9. Matsuno, Y.: D-Case Editor Homepage. http://www.dcase.jp/editor_en.html
10. Cullen, L.: The public inquiry into the piper alpha disaster, vols. 1 and 2 (Report to Parliament by the Secretary of State for Energy by Command of Her Majesty) (1990)
11. Toulmin, S.E.: The Use of Argument, Updated. Cambridge University Press, Cambridge (2003)

---

[1] www.matsulab.org.

The 6W1H Model as a Basis for Systems Assurance Argument

Shuji Kinoshita[1,2(✉)] and Yoshiki Kinoshita[1,2]

[1] Department of Information Sciences, Kanagawa University, Hiratsuka, Japan
shuji@progsci.info.kanagawa-u.ac.jp
[2] Research Institute for Programming Science, Kanagawa University,
Hiratsuka, Japan

Abstract. The basis of an assurance argument must be built on top of explicit specification of the target system. Nevertheless, identification of a municipal disaster management system out of existing documents is a non-trivial task. We propose an approach applying 6W1H models. A 6W1H model is a tree of actions equipped with "6Ws" (Who, What, Whom, When, Where, Why) that provide necessary explication of the system for assurance argument. The approach is exemplified by identifying a system and building an assurance case out of water supply activities prescribed in the Local Disaster Management Plan of Hiratsuka city.

Keywords: Assurance argument · Systems modelling · Disaster management

1 Introduction

This paper introduces an approach using a 6W1H model to specification of systems for the purpose of assurance argument. A 6W1H model is a tree of actions equipped with "6Ws" (Who, What, Whom, When, Where, Why) that provide necessary explication of the system for assurance argument.

The 6W1H model is a part of our ongoing work on assuring the dependability of the disaster management activities in Hiratsuka city. The procedure for dependability argument contains three phases as follows (Fig. 1):

1. Identify a disaster management system out of the documents which prescribe disaster management activities[1];
2. Specify a system life cycle of the disaster management system;
3. Develop assurance cases that demonstrate that the disaster management system life cycle has a dependability.

Identification of a system out of the documents (Fig. 1, highlighted in yellow) is a non-trivial task. The municipal disaster management activities are prescribed

---

[1] The term "activity" here is used as an everyday word, not as a technical word in system life cycles.

© Springer International Publishing Switzerland 2016
A. Skavhaug et al. (Eds.): SAFECOMP 2016 Workshops, LNCS 9923, pp. 63–74, 2016.
DOI: 10.1007/978-3-319-45480-1_6

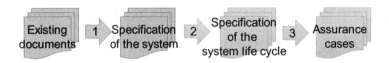

Fig. 1. Three phases for assuring systems dependability (Color figure online)

in Local Disaster Management Plan (LDMP) by each local governments. These LDMPs are neither easy to grasp a complete view of the system, nor easy to comprehend the system in detail.

The "6W1H model" provides an ontological framework or taxonomy that gives uniform structure to the contents of LDMP documents. It supports explicit system specification that works as a basis of assurance argument on LDMP by means of a tree whose nodes correspond to actions specified by six items (6Ws: Who, What, Whom, When, Where and Why). An action may be decomposed by "How" relation into a set of other actions.

The proposed approach is exemplified by identifying a system and building an assurace case out of water supply activities prescribed in the LDMP of Hiratsuka city. The purpose of water supply subsystem is to supply water to disaster-affected people in emergency response. By application of the 6W1H approach, a system of water supply activities is specified explicitly with satisfiable rigour.

The main contributions of this paper are: (i) spotting the research problem for identification of a system out of activities provided in a set of documents, not necessarily assuming the concept of systems; (ii) proposal of "6W1H" taxonomy (modelling approach) for identification of a system out of a set of documents that provide activities. Unlike the case of computer software and hardware, the concept of system is weakly presumed in the description of human intensive systems such as disaster management activities. 6W1H approach is anticipated to be effectively applicable to building the specification of those systems.

The rest of the paper is organised as follows: Sect. 2 gives relevant background information. Section 3 gives a leading example of water supply activities that have the inherent complexities in the specification documents. Section 4 presents the 6W1H models and their usage. Section 5 gives a case study of applying 6W1H model to water supplying activities. Section 6 shows related work and Sect. 7 concludes the paper.

2   Background

The procedure for dependability argument of the municipal disaster management activities is based on the notion of "Open Systems Dependability" [1]. In this section, we give details of them and the definition of "system" in international standards, which is a guideline to identify the system.

2.1 Disaster Management Activities in Hiratsuka City

The disaster management activities of each municipal in Japan are documented by Local Disaster Management Plan (LDMP) [2]. The national government set up the law "Disaster Countermeasures Basic Act" [3] in 1961 that prescribes provision of an LDMP by each local government. This means there are more than thousand LDMPs. The target disasters of LDMPs are both natural disasters (e.g., earthquake, tsunami, storm and flood, volcano, snow) and accident disasters (e.g., maritime, aviation, railroad, nuclear disaster). Each LDMP describes several disaster management issues, such as disaster prevention and preparedness, disaster emergency response, disaster recovery and reconstruction.

Hiratsuka city, where our university is located, has many natural disaster risks. Earthquakes and typhoons must be considered all over Japan. In particular, there is also heavy tsunami risks in this city, facing the Sagami bay. The latest public damage estimation [4] shows that tsunami height is expected to exceed 5 m around the Hiratsuka area when heaviest earthquake occurs. Furthermore, recent volcanic activity in Hakone (only 30 km from Hiratsuka) must be taken into account.

Against these disaster risks, the Hiratsuka LDMP [5] have developed and revised over and over from 1960s. As a result, they become large and complex documents. Table 1 shows the LDMP of Hiratsuka city, which describe its disaster management activities. In this paper, the emergency response activities against Earthquake are in focus.

Table 1. The LDMP of Hiratsuka city

Title of fascicle	Number of pages
LDMP against Earthquake	196
LDMP against Storm & Flood	181
LDMP against Tokai Earthquake	24
LDMP against Extraordinary Disasters	33
Appendices	288

2.2 Open Systems Dependability

Open Systems Dependability is a new dependability concept in the sense that it is for an open system, which boundaries, functions and structure change over time and are recognised differently from different points of views. Various methods are proposed, such as D-Case (an extension of assurance case) [1, Chap. 4], D-Case in Agda (a tool support for formal assurance argument) [1, Chap. 6] [6]. The international standard IEC 62853 [7] is forthcoming.

Municipal disaster management activities are "open systems" in the sense that these activities change by the estimation of disaster risks (e.g., earthquake damage estimation), the national/international regulation (e.g., exposed dose from nuclear plants) or public opinion.

2.3 International Standards for Systems

We employ the definition of "system" in ISO/IEC/IEEE 15288 [8], which defines system life cycle processes. Since Open Systems Dependability can be clarified as requirements for system life cycle in the sense of ISO/IEC/IEEE 15288 [1, Chap. 10]. The standard provides a framework of process descriptions for specifying the life cycle of systems created by humans.

The term "system" is defined as *"combination of interacting elements organized to achieve one or more stated purposes"* [8, 4.1.45]. This imply the hierarchical relationship between the system and its complete set of system elements. Figure 2 show this hierarchical tree structure of a system. Our proposed "6W1H model" employ this structure, because one of our aim is to reformulate the municipal disaster management activities in the form suitable for application of ISO/IEC/IEEE 15288.

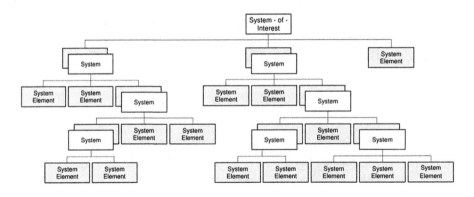

Fig. 2. System-of-interest structure (source: [8, 5.2.2 System structure])

3   Leading Example: Water Supply Activities

Our study of 6W1H model is motivated by our investigation of LDMP to identify a "system" in the sense of [8]. In this section, we describe the following two difficulties inherent in the LDMP. (i) grasp a complete view of the system; (ii) comprehend the system in detail. As an example, consider water supply activities in emergency response.

Water supply activities supply water to disaster-affected people in emergency response. The activities includes possessing water, preparing for water supplying, transferring vehicles, supplying water at evacuation centres and other relevant activities. Note that the daily water and sewage services are not included in these activities.

3.1   Grasp a Complete View of the System

Tables 2 and 3 both show the list of water supplying activities in emergency response against earthquakes. According to the staff at the disaster management department of Hiratsuka city office, the source of Table 2 is a definition of all activities of every division in emergency response. On the other hand, the source of Table 3 is documented in the section of Water supplying activities. Therefore, Table 3 should be the refinement of Table 2. It is appropriate that one activity in Table 2 is decomposed into a set of individual activities in Table 3.

Table 2. Excerpt of the list of activities in Hiratsuka disaster management headquarters (source: [5, Appendices, p. 13], translated by the authors)

Division	Activities
Water supply division	1. Activity related to possession of drinking water
	2. Activity related to water supplying and transferring to the evacuation centres
	3. Activity related to communication and coordination between the Water and Sewage Service Office and other relevant organisations
	4. Activity related to water supplying from other organisations
	5. Activity related to emergency response missions

However, there is not such a good correspondence between two tables. For example, Activity 1 in Table 2 corresponds to Activity (1), (2) and (4) in Table 3. Activity 2 in Table 2 corresponds to Activity (2), (3), (4) and (5) in Table 3. Moreover, these correspondence are neither specified in this document nor common sense for the staff.

3.2   Comprehend the System in Detail

Table 4 indicates the excerpt of the detailed description of water possession in water supplying activities. At a glance, there is no ambiguous statement and it describes one activity precisely. However, the following issues must be addressed:

- "In case of no road damage" assumes that we can know whether there is some road damage or not without any problems. Who investigate the level of road damage and how do we know them?
- There is no subject word in this sentence. Who possess the water, who transfer the truck?

Table 3. List of water supply activities in Water supply division (source: [5, Earthquake Fascicle, p. 131], translated by the authors)List of water supply activities in Water supply division (source: [5, Earthquake Fascicle, p. 131], translated by the authors)

Relevant organisations	Activities
Water supply division	(1) Collecting information regarding damaged area, outlook for recovery and other relevant information related to water supplying, communication and coordination with Hiratsuka Water & Sewage Service Office and organisations with agreement
	(2) Grasping the total demands of water, Coordinating the places and the methods for supplying water
	(3) Possession of tanks for supplying water and request for cooperation with Truck Association and other relevant transportations through the General affairs division
	(4) Possession of water and transferring to the water supplying place and medical institution, supplying water
	(5) Supplying water by employing emergency water storage tanks
	(6) Request for cooperation with the local governments which have the agreement on supporting activities, the Prefectural government, the Self-Defence Forces through the General response division, receiving and coordination of activities

Table 4. Excerpt of the methods of water possession (source: [5, Earthquake Fascicle, p. 133], translated by the authors)

Order	Methods of possession
1st	In case of no road damage, possess drinking water and water for medical inst. from the Hiratsuka Service Reservoir by employing water trucks or water containers

3.3   Discussion

As shown above, the current description in the LDMP is not directly regarded as a specification of the disaster management system and not suitable for application of ISO/IEC/IEEE 15288 to build system life cycle. The complexity of LDMP is an issue not only in Hiratsuka city but in many other municipalities in Japan, according to our investigation.

The law [3] prescribes what to provide rather than how to provide them in disaster management activities. This result in increasing complicatedness and an underlying ontological structure is necessary to make it comprehensive to the stakeholders. The 6W1H modelling is our solution to this problem.

4   6W1H Model

The 6W1H model is a framework for supporting system specification as a basis for systems assurance argument. This is inspired by the "5W1H" or "five Ws" in journalism. This framework specifies a system into a tree of "actions". An action is a task which can be implemented by some person or some organisation. The description of each action is equipped with the hexad called **"6Ws"** (**Who, What, Whom, When, Where, Why**).

In general, an action may be implemented by means of other actions. **"How"** provides a functionality that decomposes an action into several, that gives a hierarchical tree structure to a set of actions. A level of a node corresponds to a level of abstraction. This tree structure of 6W1H model enables us to do stepwise refinement of the specification through arguments between stakeholders.

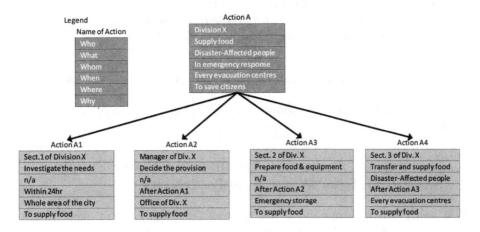

Fig. 3. An example of the specification of food supply system employing 6W1H model

Figure 3 shows a simple example of the specification of food supply system in emergency response employing 6W1H model and supplementary graphical notations. The top of action is "To save citizens, division X supplies food to the disaster-affected people at every evacuation centres in emergency response". This action is decomposed into four actions with detailed specification such as "Investigate the needs", "Decide the provision", "Prepare food and equipments" and "Transfer and supply food". These four action can be recursively decomposed into several actions until stakeholders of the system agree with the execution of "leaf" actions of the tree. For example, Action A1 (To supply food, Sect. 1 of division X investigate the needs over the whole area of the city within 24 h.) can be decomposed into several actions equipped with a specification of the area.

The steps for building the specification of a system by employing 6W1H model are as follows:

1. Specify a "What" of top action out of existing documents.

2. Fill in the other 6Ws of it by searching adjacent or relevant statements. If not possible, discuss with the stakeholders of a system and specify them.
3. If you would like to, decompose the action into several actions. Specify "What" of several actions out of existing documents (recursively cont'd).

These "6Ws" are suitable for identifying a system out of documents with complexity as follows: **"What"** is the basis of 6Ws. Nothing can be done without clear specification of "What". **"Who"** clarifies an owner of the action. This is particularly effective for null-subject languages like Japanese. **"Whom"** suggests other actions which have "Who" field as its "Whom". This prevents lack of actions. **"When"** suggests an order of actions. The order of actions give us an opportunity for discussing necessary condition of the action. **"Where"** clarifies communication channel between actions. Namely, if a product of an action is information, how to inform is an issue. This is essential for disaster management systems, since communication channels are often out of service in case of emergency. **"Why"** emphasises a purpose of the action. An action is to be implemented to achieve its "Why". To specify "Why", the following issues can be discussed:

– Is this action necessary to implement a parent action (Should it be moved to other branches or not)?
– Is this group of actions fully implement a parent action (Should we add more actions or not)?

5   Building an Assurance Argument of Water Supply Subsystem from Water Supply Activities

Now we show how to apply our "6W1H" modelling approach to identifying a system and building an assurance argument. The examples are as same as shown in Sect. 3. A "6W1H" specification of water supply subsystem is developed out of water supply activities in LDMP. An assurance case can be built from the specification.

5.1   Grasp a Complete View of the System

A top of specification of water supply subsystem as a "6W1H" tree of height 2 is developed (Fig. 4). This is based on Tables 2, and 3, other relevant statements in [5] and discussion between the staff. At first, we specified Action W (To save the life of citizens, disaster management headquarters supply water to the disaster-affected people at evacuation centres etc. in emergency response). Then we divided Action W into three basic actions (Action W1, W2, W3) such as "Decide the provision", "Prepare the provision" and "Provide water supplying" (specified with "What").

In comparison with the Table 2 (5 activities) and Table 3 (6 activities), this 6W1H tree has few actions. However, this division can classify several activities naturally. For example, the statement "Collecting information regarding

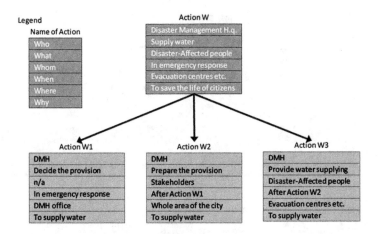

Fig. 4. Top of the specification of Water supply subsystem by 6W1H model

damaged area" of Activity (1) in Table 3 belongs to Action W1 "Decide the provision", since collected information is a basis for decision to supply water. Activity (2) in Table 3 apparently belongs to Action W2 "Prepare the provision". This means that the top of specification is suitable to grasp a complete view of water supply subsystem.

5.2   Comprehend the System in Detail

Seven actions are developed out of the statement in Table 4 (Fig. 5). Action W, W1, W2 and W3 is equivalent to that of Fig. 4. Out of the statement "In case of no road damage", we specified Action W1-03 (Investigate road damage) and W1-04 (Report road damage) as child node of W1 (Decide the provision). Out of the statement "possess drinking water and water for medical inst. from the Hiratsuka Service Reservoir", we specified Action W2-03 (Confirm amount of water) and W2-04 (Report amount of water) as child node of W2 (Prepare the provision). Note that there is no difference between "drinking water" and "water for medical institution" according to the staff. Out of the latter statement and "by employing water trucks or water containers", we specified Action W3-01 (Transfer water truck from the disaster management headquarters office to the reservoir), W3-02 (Transfer water) and W3-03 (Transfer water truck from the reservoir to evacuation centres) as child node of W3 (Provide water supplying). Through the discussion, we specified that the transferring activities are in the provision rather than the preparation.

Some of specification came from other relevant statements in [5] and discussion between the staff. For example, "Facility Reconstruction Division" ("What" of W1-03, W1-04) are from other pages in [5]. We specified "Water & Sewage Service Office" ("What" of W2-03, W2-04) through the discussion with the staff. This means that the 6W1H modelling framework promote explicate system specification to comprehend the system in detail. As a result, 7 actions under the

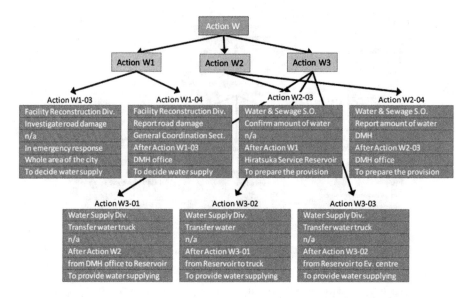

Fig. 5. Excerpt of the detailed specification of Water supply subsystem by 6W1H model

action W1, 23 actions under the action W2, 19 actions under the action W3 are specified. The details of them is beyond the scope of this section.

5.3   Building an Assurance Case Based on the 6W1H Model

An assurance case can be built from the hierarchical tree structure of 6W1H model as follows:

1. Specify each *goals* out of each "6Ws" action nodes of the 6W1H model.
2. Connect each goals and sub-goals by specifying precise *strategies*.
3. Develop a glossary of the 6W1H model and add to the assurance case as a *context*.

Each *evidence* of sub-goals may be a detailed description of actions for operation, or a report of disaster drill, which is out of the 6W1H model. Note that the assurance case is not a result of the phase 3 of Fig. 1. For assuring Open Systems Dependability of the disaster management system, a system life cycle of the system must be specified and assurance cases for its system life cycle must be developed on the basis of the 6W1H model and the assurance case.

An argument pattern can be found in the 6W1H model. Namely, the three basic actions in Fig. 4 (Action W1, W2, W3) such as "Decide the provision", "Prepare the provision" and "Provide water supplying" indicate the argument pattern "Decide, Prepare and Provide" (Fig. 6). This pattern would be applicable for other activities in emergency response such as food supply and human resource management.

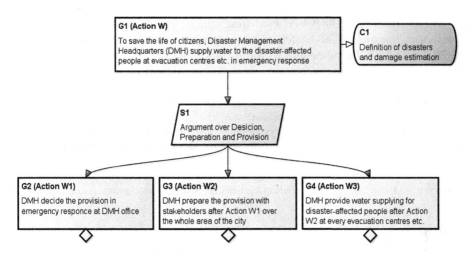

Fig. 6. The argument pattern "Decide, Prepare and Provide"

6   Related Work

There has been some work on systems modelling for disaster management systems. Sommerville et al. [9] employ responsibility modelling [10] for analysis of contingency planning documents in Cumbria County, England. Their purpose is to analyse the complex documents to improve understandings, which is similar to ours. They developed the model with an emphasis on "responsibility", which is expressed as relationships between stakeholders.

The responsibility relation may be formulated by "How", the parent-child relation between the action nodes. For example, Action W1 and W1-03 in Figs. 4, and 5 indicates the following issues in the sense of [9].

– Facility Reconstruction Div. are responsible for investigating road damage.
– Disaster Management Headquarters is the authority for the responsibility.

7   Conclusion and Future Work

This paper introduced "6W1H models" for supporting system specification as a basis for systems assurance argument. The effectiveness of proposed approach was exemplified by a specification of water supply subsystem of the municipal disaster management system.

As shown in Fig. 1, this paper is only a first step towards our goal. To improve the dependability arguments of municipal disaster management activities, the following work remains: (i) to specify a system life cycle of the disaster management system, where the definition of "system" follows ISO/IEC/IEEE 15288; and (ii) to develop and evaluate assurance cases that demonstrate the dependability of the system life cycle.

We anticipate that the 6W1H modelling applies to any system with intensive human aspects, such as food safety management or governmental policy making. Application of 6W1H modelling to improvement of these activities remains as future work.

Acknowledgements. The authors thank the staff of the disaster management department of Hiratsuka city office for clarification of the details of LDMP and fruitful discussions. Dr. Makoto Takeyama gave critical yet insightful and constructive comments on early manuscript of this paper. The authors are also grateful to the support of Mr. KojOkuno.

This work was partially supported by the Research Initiative on Advanced Software Engineering (RISE) by the Information-technology Promotion Agency (IPA), Japan.

References

1. Tokoro, M. (ed.): Open Systems Dependability: Dependability Engineering for Ever-Changing Systems, 2nd edn. CRC Press, Boca Raton (2015)
2. Cabinet Office, Government of Japan.: Disaster management in Japan (2015). URL: http://www.bousai.go.jp/1info/pdf/saigaipamphlet_je.pdf (in English and Japanese)
3. Ministry of Internal Affairs and Communications, Government of Japan.: Disaster countermeasures basic act (2015). URL: http://law.e-gov.go.jp/htmldata/S36/S36HO223.html (in Japanese)
4. Safety and Disaster Management Department of Kanagawa Prefectural Government.: Earthquake Damage Estimation (2015). URL: http://www.pref.kanagawa.jp/cnt/f5151/p15579.html (in Japanese)
5. Disaster Management Department of Hiratsuka City Office (ed.): Hiratsuka local disaster management plan (2015). URL: http://www.city.hiratsuka.kanagawa.jp/bousai/plan.htm (in Japanese)
6. Kinoshita, Y., Takeyama, M.: Assurance case as a proof in a theory: towards formulation of rebuttals. In: Assuring the Safety of Systems - Proceedings of the Twenty-First Safety-critical Systems Symposium, Bristol, UK, pp. 205–230, 5–7 February 2013
7. IEC 62853/Ed1.0: Open Systems Dependability, Work in progress by IEC TC56 PT4.8
8. ISO, IEC, IEEE 15288: 2015 Systems and software engineering - System life cycle processes
9. Sommerville, I., Storer, T., Lock, R.: Responsibility modelling for civil emergency planning. Risk Manage. **11**, 179–207 (2009)
10. Sommerville, I., Lock, R., Storer, T., Dobson, J.: Deriving information requirements from responsibility models. In: van Eck, P., Gordijn, J., Wieringa, R. (eds.) CAiSE 2009. LNCS, vol. 5565, pp. 515–529. Springer, Heidelberg (2009)

The Assurance Timeline: Building Assurance Cases for Synthetic Biology

Myra B. Cohen$^{(\boxtimes)}$, Justin Firestone, and Massimiliano Pierobon

University of Nebraska - Lincoln, Lincoln, NE 68588, USA
{myra,jfiresto,pierobon}@cse.unl.edu

Abstract. Recent research advances in modifying and controlling DNA have created a booming field of biological engineering called synthetic biology. In synthetic biology engineers manipulate and modify living organisms to change (and produce entirely novel) functionality, which has led to new fuel sources or the ability to mitigate pollution. Synthetic biology research is also expected to lead to methods of intelligent drug delivery. In synthetic biology, designs are first built using biological programming languages and then implemented in a laboratory. These synthetic organisms can be considered living programs that will sense, respond and interact with humans while they persist in the natural environment. We argue that we should view these as safety critical devices which can be both regulated and certified. Since the synthetically engineered organisms follow a regular cycle of reproduction and replication that involves mutations, they will eventually adapt and evolve new behavior over time. In this paper we propose the use of an assurance case for synthetically engineered organisms, and present an orthogonal dimension, an assurance timeline, that can be used to reason about the dynamic, evolving aspects of these systems. We present a case study based on a real application to illustrate our ideas.

Keywords: Assurance case · Synthetic biology · Evolution

1 Introduction

The emerging science of synthetic biology is providing novel tools for the design, realization, and control of biological processes through the programming of cells' genetic code [21]. These tools are allowing engineers to study and access the basis of molecular information processing, and to develop software with specific functionality that can be engineered into living organisms [33]. Synthetically engineered biological organisms (SEBOs) are leading to novel applications that include the enhancement of soil quality [6], the creation of novel sources for biofuels [36], the development of engineered biological tissue [26,31], and the synthesis of biocompatible intelligent drug delivery systems [24].

SEBOs are created by manipulating and combining genetic components in the laboratory to modify existing organisms' traits or to generate entirely new functionality, including computational components (both analog and digital [32]).

© Springer International Publishing Switzerland 2016
A. Skavhaug et al. (Eds.): SAFECOMP 2016 Workshops, LNCS 9923, pp. 75–86, 2016.
DOI: 10.1007/978-3-319-45480-1_7

This will open the road to the development of biological computers [5]. From the identification of sequences of DNA genetic code with precise biological functions, to the design of components into more complex programs with information processing and logical control capabilities, software principles are used in every SEBO. As a consequence, SEBOs are truly software-intensive systems [17].

While synthetic biology is opening doors to the programming of living organisms, questions should be posed about the interaction of these programs with human life and the environment. Even if we ignore the possible malicious uses of this technology [22], or the bioethical aspects [2], faults and failures in biological programs can pose serious threats, such as by the inadvertent production of compounds toxic to humans, or by polluting the environment, or colonizing ecological niches. If SEBOs are used for drug delivery or to protect us from harm, then we must also rely on the intended behavior occurring as expected. However, SEBOs are living and therefore their programs are dynamic in nature. They are subject to mutations, and regular evolution, and this has made it difficult to build a framework for their certification, and ultimately for governmental regulation and guidance [1,25].

To date, there has been little research that provides systematic techniques to verify biological systems in general [8]. In this paper we argue that it is possible to build assurance cases (more specifically safety cases) for reasoning about the behavior of SEBOs. We first show how they are similar to software systems, and as such we can build arguments and evidence for their safety. However, we also identify some key challenges due to the their mutation and evolution over time. We propose a new dimension to the assurance case, the *assurance timeline*, which leverages recent work on dynamic assurance cases [10], and at the same time addresses a new problem, random changes in the system to be assured. Since the software code itself mutates as it evolves, it can change functionality over time. The assurance timeline captures this new dimension through the identification of intervals that may require either new evidence or a new set of claims and arguments. We present an example of an SEBO assurance case and discuss its potential evolution, based on a real SEBO project from the literature.
The contributions of this paper are:

- The proposed use of assurance cases for SEBOs;
- A new kind of assurance case - the assurance timeline; and
- An illustrative example demonstrating how these might be applied to a real-world SEBO.

The rest of the paper is organized as follows. In the next section we present some background on synthetic biology and motivation for the use of assurance cases. We follow this with an example of applying the assurance case and an assurance timeline in Sect. 3. We then present related work in Sect. 4 and finally conclude in Sect. 5.

2   Background and Motivation

Consider a strain of high yield soybeans that thrives on a specific type of protein. If that protein is only produced by bacteria that also produce a toxic protein which can seep into the water supply, the cultivation of these soybeans would be an environmental hazard. A synthetic biologist might recognize an opportunity and solve this problem by (i) modifying the soybeans to utilize a different protein while retaining a high yield, or by (ii) designing a *program* with protein inhibitors and repressors that will prevent the production of the toxic protein in the pre-existing bacteria, or by iii) developing a new version of the bacteria that only produces the beneficial protein and does not output the toxin at all. In the rest of this section we describe how this type of programming is achieved in SEBOs and then discuss the need for building assurance cases.

2.1 Synthetic Biology

In synthetic biology, engineers design *plasmids* and insert them into living cells. A plasmid is a DNA sequence that is not part of a cell's chromosome but that can trigger the ribosomes to synthesize new proteins. Ribosomes are responsible for creating proteins, which underlie most cellular functions [4]. Engineers have already implemented various logic gates within SEBOs including AND, NOR, and NOT gates [4]. They have also realized more complicated systems, including feedback loops, intercellular signaling, biological on/off switches, oscillators, and counters, leading also to the idea of cellular memory [4].

A language called the Synthetic Biology Open Language (SBOL) [14] has been developed to represent programs for SEBOs (or SEBO parts). Figure 1(a) shows a small (abstract) program in SBOL. At the top left is a promoter. A promoter is a short DNA sequence that causes transcription to occur (transcription is how DNA copies itself). It is followed by a ribosome binding site that allows ribosomes to bind to the transcribed mRNA to start its translation into a protein. This is followed by a coding sequence which contains the information to synthesize a protein. Finally, it ends with a transcription terminator which indicates where to stop the transcription of DNA into mRNA. The circular line back to the promoter indicates a repetition operator in this process. A concrete version of this program would indicate specific instances of promoters, terminators, ribosome binding sites, etc. If we consider SBOL as a programming language, we can view the DNA sequences as our byte code and the transcription and translation of the DNA into proteins as compilation, after which point we have proteins which perform as binary code, yet are not humanly readable.

The International Genetically Engineered Machine (iGEM) Competition, hosted by MIT since 2004, is an exemplar of the widespread use of SEBO programming. It is a competition for students ranging from high school through to graduate school. Teams are given a kit of biological parts and develop novel functionality. The parts are added to *biological chassis* such as *E. coli* or other common bacteria. iGEM encourages modularity, reusability, and interoperability of parts. As such there are over 20,000 parts, or BioBricks, with known functionality in the iGEM parts registry [19]. An example of a *Reporter* part from the registry, which causes an organism to fluoresce under certain conditions, is shown in Fig. 1(b). This part can be obtained from iGEM and added to a team's own program in combination with a multitude of other parts.

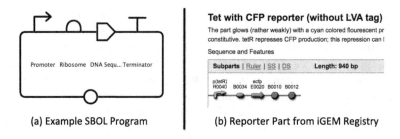

(a) Example SBOL Program

(b) Reporter Part from iGEM Registry

Fig. 1. An example of (a) an SBOL program and (b) concrete instance of a reporter part that creates fluorescence from [18]

2.2   An Argument for SEBO Assurance Cases

Given the ability to mix and match thousands of promoters, ribosome binding sites, sequences, terminators, etc. and to define concrete logic for their combination, we can view this in a similar fashion to designing a program. We have an abstract model and should be able to predict behavior under a variety of conditions (inputs). While the programs and parts developed by iGEM are by default restricted to the laboratory environment, students are required to present informal safety arguments about their systems (if they were to be released) and the long term goal of synthetic biology is to make variants of organisms that can actually co-exist in the environment. Given that these new programs will interact with humans and their environment, we need confidence that the devices work safely as expected. In this direction, it is possible that synthetic biological systems can be designed with *kill switches*, which force the bacteria to die under specific conditions, but these too must be reliable. Assurance safety cases seem to be the natural way to provide the necessary evidence for these systems.

While we believe that safety cases are a good starting point for SEBOs, we also argue that they have novel characteristics which may add challenges to their formal definition. Given that they are living systems, once the code is compiled, we cannot assume (as in most software systems) that the software will remain unchanged. In fact, we expect that random mutations will occur during each generation of the organisms lifecycle and that new (previously unknown) functionality may appear over time. While a single mutation is unlikely to dramatically change an SEBO's function, the cumulative effect over many generations can lead to strains that do not adhere to the original safety case. At the same time, SEBOs are subject to evolution, where natural selection will tend to promote mutated strains that best fit the environmental conditions, by growing and reproducing at a faster rate than others. Hence, while SEBOs share characteristics with other dynamic systems and may benefit from a dynamic safety case, the peculiarity of their mutation and evolution processes differentiates them from other systems studied in previous literature, such as unmanned aircraft systems (UASs)[10]. However, we also believe that the seemingly overwhelming complex nature of SEBO mutations and evolution can be successfully captured at regular time intervals, which can allow identifying when new evidence (or new safety cases) are needed. This will lead to what we call the *assurance timeline*, presented in the next section.

3   Assuring SEBOs: An Illustrative Example

To illustrate our ideas we have studied a project from the 2012 iGEM competition and used their safety documents as the basis for our example. This project, called *the Food Warden*, was created by the Groningen team [16]. The goal of Food Warden is to engineer *Bacillus subtilis* to change color when it detects spoiled meat in a refrigerator. Spoiled meat releases ammonia, and ammonia contains nitrogen. The team uses the PsboA promoter that causes a color change in the bacteria *Bacillus subtilis* (or *B. subtilis* for short) to alert in the presence of nitrogen. The design includes a semi-permeable "sticker" with an outer membrane made from an FDA-approved material, Polymethylpentene, which has nanopores large enough to allow passage of gases, but small enough to prevent the bacteria from escaping. The sticker relies on sensing nitrogen molecules from the rotten meat through a process known as quorum sensing. When a threshold number of signaling molecules is detected by a sufficient number of bacteria, it will trigger a response. The bacteria will produce yellow fluorescent proteins to visually indicate meat spoilage. The sticker also features a breakable inner packet of Luria broth as a growing medium, which is activated when ready to use. If the bacteria escape the packet, the team claims that the bacteria cannot live without the food source in the sticker, and that the original bacteria are known to be non-harmful to humans or to the environment.

The team identified five separate threads of safety requirements. The first two, general safety of synthetically engineered organisms, and safety in the lab, are out of the scope of our assurance example presented here. The other three, we discuss briefly. First, the team identifies the safety of their sticker design which contains the engineered organisms. They consider this a public safety issue, since *B. subtilis* needs to remain isolated from the consumer and the meat. Second, they highlight food safety, which includes protecting the consumer from the effects of eating spoiled meat, i.e. the color must be visible and reliable. Last they highlight environmental safety, in the case the bacteria should accidentally be released into the environment (all iGEM projects are laboratory based, however if this project was to move out of the laboratory, it would become an issue).

3.1   Initial Assurance Case

We have built an initial (partial) safety assurance case using the goal structuring notation (GSN), to demonstrate its feasibility for SEBOs. We show this in Fig. 2. The top level Goal (G0) is that Food Warden is safe for humans. Using arguments over identified hazards as the strategy (S0) there are four subgoals for this case (G1-G4). G4 has an open diamond showing that it is not complete. G1 is the goal that the sticker will keep the bacteria isolated under normal conditions.

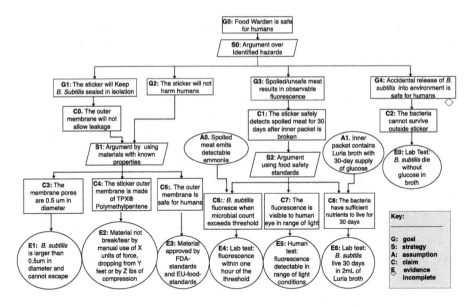

Fig. 2. Food Warden (partial) SEBO assurance case using GSN

This goal has a claim that the sticker membrane will not allow leakage of the bacteria. G2 says that the sticker is not harmful to humans. Both use a strategy (S1) that identifies known material properties, which connects to three subclaims (C3-C5), namely, the membrane material is smaller than 0.5 μm in diameter, it is made of a known material with strong properties, and, finally, it is safe (C4) for humans. Evidence for these claims includes testing the diameter of *B. subtilis*, confirming the strength of the material, and the existence of FDA approval of human safety of the material.

Subgoal G3 reasons about the safety of the system's logic – it will correctly identify meat that is unsafe for humans. It states that spoiled meat will result in observable fluorescence of the bacteria. This has a subclaim that the sticker works for 30 days once the inner packet is broken. For these goals the strategy used is that of existing food standards. Two assumptions are included. A0 states that spoiled meat will emit ammonia consistent with the total aerobic microbial count (TAMC) which is used to measure the degree of spoilage as determined by FDA acceptable levels. Since the bacteria *sense* the ammonia which then cause them to fluoresce, this assumption must hold. The second assumption (A1) states that the inner packet contains Luria broth with a 30-day supply of glucose (required for growth). Claims 6, 7 and 8 argue that the bacteria fluoresce once the TAMC threshold is reached, that this is visible under a range of light conditions and that there is sufficient nutrients for 30 days.

Finally, Goal 4 requires that release into the environment will not be harmful to humans. We have only partially expanded this goal (the team identified several other subgoals). Claim 2 says that the bacteria cannot live outside of the sticker, with evidence (E0) that shows via laboratory tests that *B. subtilis* will die without the glucose in the broth.

3.2   Evolution in SEBOs

While we show that a safety case can be built for a system such as Food Warden, this case is static. It does not account for evolution. Denney et al. [10] describe the need for dynamic assurance cases for systems such as unmanned aircraft systems. We argue that SEBOs are also dynamic. Not only do their environmental conditions change, so too does their "software" which is subject to random changes at regular intervals via evolution and natural selection. Since *B. subtilis* are living, there will be mutations to the organism's DNA. However, we have models of the organisms and know their evolution frequency and magnitude, therefore we should be able to reason about the likelihood of a behavior change at a point in time. Assuming that we have this information, we can allow the safety case to hold for a specified regular time interval before re-assurance.

We show how the safety case can evolve in two ways (see Fig. 3). First it may require a change in evidence. Second, it is possible that the entire structure of a branch of the assurance case will change. We discuss each of these next. Assume the bacteria are engineered to only digest glucose in the Luria broth and that there is only enough glucose to keep the bacteria alive for 30 days. If the bacteria evolve or mutate to digest an alternate sugar such as lactose as well, then we would need new evidence for assumption 1 (A1) and claim 8 (C8), because the system has changed [20]. We can either provide evidence that there is no lactose in the Luria broth or the meat, or that there is an insufficient combination of lactose in the Luria broth to keep the bacteria alive for more than 30 days. We depict this evolution in Fig. 3A where E0 has been updated to E0' at time interval 1 and A1 has been updated to A1'. This type of evolution does not change the assurance case - it simply requires that new evidence and assumptions are provided.

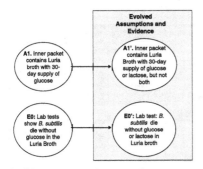
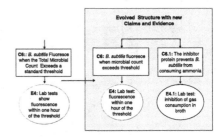

A. Change in evidence and arguments   B. Change to the assurance case structure

Fig. 3. Two types of SEBO assurance case evolution. A. shows a change required in the evidence and arguments, while B. shows a change in the assurance case structure.

A second possibility for evolution, is that the bacteria develop the ability to digest the gases from the spoiled meat, and they no longer fluoresce to warn consumers since the gas has been consumed. It is possible, that an inhibitor protein may need to be added to the bacteria to prevent this behavior from happening. This would require a change in the structure of the safety case itself. We would need a new claim that provides evidence for the functionality of the inhibitor. We show this in Fig. 3B.

3.3   The Assurance Timeline

We now present the *assurance timeline*, an orthogonal assurance case that reasons about our confidence in the stability of the current assurance case. It argues that within specific times slices, evolution is unlikely to impact the existing case.

While biological mutations are random, if we use known models of organisms, we can infer the possible trajectories of evolution at a given point in time and group the potential changes into an *evolution envelope*. The envelope then contains a set of possible behavior changes which are reflected as changes to our current assurance case. We illustrate this idea in Fig. 4. Based on the set of possibilities within an envelope, we can analyze the evolved system to select the new assurance case. In Fig. 4 we see that at time T_2, a change in evidence occurs, while at T_3 a change in structure occurs. Within each time slice, there is a decay in our confidence of the current assurance case.

The assurance timeline itself can be viewed as an assurance case. Figure 5 shows this view (note that this is generic and may not be accurate for a specific organism such as *B. subtilis*). The top goal states that the system behavior is stable for 10 days (our time interval for this assurance case). The subgoals and claims are based on the known evolution of the organism. The evidence comes from empirical data or *in silico* computational models. The timeline can be

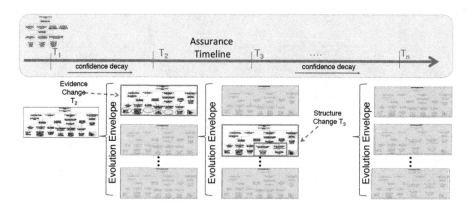

Fig. 4. Assurance timeline informs times intervals for re-assurance. Confidence decay occurs between timeslices. Evolution envelope contains set of possible changes at that interval. Selected changes are shown.

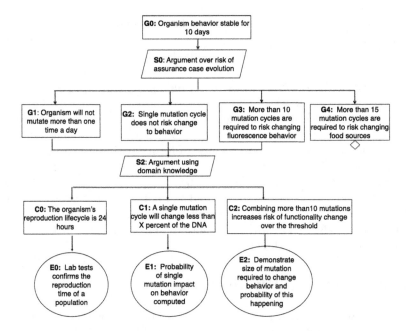

Fig. 5. Assurance timeline as an assurance case.

combined with other elements of a dynamic assurance case such as increased traceability for a through-life assurance as proposed by Denney et al. [10].

4 Related Work

Safety assurance cases have been applied to a wide variety of domains. The list includes offshore drilling operations, railroads, nuclear power plants, avionics, national defense, automobiles, and medical devices [11,23]. There has been research on how to build safety cases, such as showing evidence traceability [30], automating the collection of evidence [28], creating a controlled and structured textual language [3], arguing the need for a hierarchical structure [12], and automating safety case generation from tabular requirements specifications [9]. Although the trend has been to build more structure, formalism, and consistency, there have been arguments against formalism because safety cases require natural language which is open to multiple interpretations [15]. This work differs in that we are applying an assurance case to a biological domain.

The most closely related area to synthetic biology is the medical and medical devices domain. Within the medical domain there has been a push towards using assurance cases [7,27,35], however there have also been arguments against this idea [34]. Sujan et al. argue that since the healthcare industry is one where the "level of maturity of safety management systems is arguably still lower than in traditional safety-critical industries" it might be best to use safety cases only for internal purposes, rather than to have regulators mandate them. SEBOs may suffer similar issues.

There has been research on formal methods for biological organisms. David et al. [8] proposed use model checking and Petri nets for runtime verification of a biological oscillator, while Ellis et al. and Lutz et al. applied automated software requirement analysis and probabilistic model checking to DNA self-assembly [13,29]. Both of these threads focus on a single biological function rather than the entire system within their environment, including mutations and evolution, and neither propose the use of formal assurance cases.

Finally, Denney et al. [10] propose dynamic safety cases which consider *through-life* assurance. In this type of safety case, environmental conditions change and emergent behaviors appear and the notion of continuous assurance over the life of the system is needed. We view our assurance timeline as a variation a dynamic safety case, where not only the environment, but the software itself is subject to random changes.

5   Conclusions and Future Work

In this paper we have shown that the emerging field of synthetic biology is a novel direction for building safety assurance cases. We have illustrated how we can build a safety case for an existing project from the iGEM competition. However, we also differentiate an SEBO assurance case in that there is an expected evolution over time given the living nature of these systems. We show how the assurance case can evolve in two ways. One simply requires new evidence, however the other may change the structure. We argue that the evolution itself can be reasoned about and propose the use of an assurance timeline, an assurance case for the evolution itself. This will provide arguments and evidence for the necessary time intervals at which the assurance case will change. As future work we will build larger, more complete assurance cases for other projects and work with biological engineers to develop evidence. We will also explore the use of regression testing techniques to reason about impactful change.

Acknowledgments. This work was supported in part by NSF grants CCF-1161767 and MCB-1449014.

References

1. Adam, L., Kozar, M., Letort, G., Mirat, O., Srivastava, A., Stewart, T., Wilson, M.L., Peccoud, J.: Strengths and limitations of the Federal guidance on synthetic DNA. Nat. Biotechol. **29**(3), 208–210 (2011)
2. Anderson, J., Strelkowa, N., Stan, G.-B., Douglas, T., Savulescu, J., Barahona, M., Papachristodoulou, A.: Engineering and ethical perspectives in synthetic biology. EMBO Rep. **13**(7), 584–590 (2012)
3. Attwood, K., Kelly, T.: Controlled expression for assurance case development. In: Proceedings of the 23rd Safety-Critical Systems Symposium on Engineering Systems for Safety, pp. 143–165 (2015)

4. Baldwin, G.: Synthetic Biology: A Primer. World Scientific, London (2016)
5. Benenson, Y.: Biomolecular computing systems: principles, progress and potential. Nat. Rev. Genet. **13**, 455–468 (2012)
6. Bereza-Malcolm, L.T., Mann, G., Franks, A.E.: Environmental sensing of heavy metals through whole cell microbial biosensors: a synthetic biology approach. ACS Synth. Biol. **4**(5), 535–546 (2015)
7. Chapman, R.: Assurance cases for external infusion pumps. U.S. Food and Drug Administration (2010). www.fda.gov/downloads/medicaldevices/newsevents/workshopsconferences/ucm219685.pdf
8. David, A., Larsen, K.G., Legay, A., Mikučionis, M., Poulsen, D.B., Sedwards, S.: Runtime verification of biological systems. In: Margaria, T., Steffen, B. (eds.) ISoLA 2012, Part I. LNCS, vol. 7609, pp. 388–404. Springer, Heidelberg (2012)
9. Denney, E., Pai, G.: A lightweight methodology for safety case assembly. In: Ortmeier, F., Lipaczewski, M. (eds.) SAFECOMP 2012. LNCS, vol. 7612, pp. 1–12. Springer, Heidelberg (2012)
10. Denney, E., Pai, G., Habli, I.: Dynamic safety cases for through-life safety assurance. Int. Conf. Softw. Eng. **2**, 587–590 (2015)
11. Denney, E., Pai, G., Pohl, J.: AdvoCATE: an assurance case automation toolset. In: Ortmeier, F., Daniel, P. (eds.) SAFECOMP Workshops 2012. LNCS, vol. 7613, pp. 8–21. Springer, Heidelberg (2012)
12. Denney, E., Pai, G., Whiteside, I.: Formal foundations for hierarchical safety cases. In: IEEE 16th International Symposium on High Assurance Systems Engineering (HASE), pp. 52–59. IEEE (2015)
13. Ellis, S.J., Henderson, E.R., Klinge, T.H., Lathrop, J.I., Lutz, J.H., Lutz, R.R., Mathur, D., Miner, A.S.: Automated requirements analysis for a molecular watchdog timer. In: International conference on Automated software engineering (ASE), pp. 767–778 (2014)
14. Galdzicki, M., Clancy, K., Oberortner, E., Pocock, M., Quinn, J., Rodriguez, C., Roehner, N., Wilson, M., Adam, L., Anderson, J., Bartley, B., Beal, J., Chandran, D., Chen, J., Densmore, D., Endy, D., Grünberg, R., Hallinan, J., Hillson, N., Johnson, J., Kuchinsky, A., Lux, M., Misirli, G., Peccoud, J., Plahar, H., Sirin, E., Stan, G., Villalobos, A., Wipat, A., Gennari, J., Myers, C., Sauro, H.: The synthetic biology open language (SBOL) provides a community standard for communicating designs in synthetic biology. Nat. Biotechnol. **32**(6), 545–550 (2014)
15. Graydon, P.J.: Formal assurance arguments: a solution in search of a problem? In: 45th Annual IEEE/IFIP International Conference on Dependable Systems and Networks (DSN), pp. 517–528. IEEE (2015)
16. Hendriks, E., van Lente, T., Raaphorst, R., Purwanto, A., Poljakova, W., Parrish, J., Daszczuk, A., Dessalegne, Y., Jo, E., Oldebesten, A., Drenth, I., Kuipers, O., Veening, J., Herber, M.: iGEM: team groningen: food warden (2012). http://2012.igem.org/Team:Groningen
17. Hölzl, M., Rauschmayer, A., Wirsing, M.: Engineering of software-intensive systems: state of the art and research challenges. In: Wirsing, M., Banâtre, J.-P., Hölzl, M., Rauschmayer, A. (eds.) Soft-Ware Intensive Systems. LNCS, vol. 5380, pp. 1–44. Springer, Heidelberg (2008)
18. iGEM. http://igem.org/Main_Page
19. iGEM Parts Registry. http://parts.igem.org/
20. Jaradat, O., Graydon, P., Bate, I.: An approach to maintaining safety case evidence after a system change. arXiv preprint (2014). arXiv:1404.6846
21. Kahl, L.J., Endy, D.: A survey of enabling technologies in synthetic biology. J. Biol. Eng. **7**(1), 13 (2013)

22. Kelle, A.: Beyond patchwork precaution in the dual-use governance of synthetic biology. Sci. Eng. Ethics **19**(3), 1121–1139 (2013)
23. Kelly, T., Weaver, R.: The goal structuring notation-a safety argument notation. In: Dependable Systems and Networks Workshop on Assurance Cases (2004)
24. Kis, Z., Pereira, H.S., Homma, T., Pedrigi, R.M., Krams, R.: Mammalian synthetic biology: emerging medical applications. J. Roy. Soc. Interface **12**(106), 20141000 (2015)
25. LaVan, D.A., Marmon, L.M.: Safe and effective synthetic biology. Nat. Biotechnol. **28**, 1010–1012 (2010)
26. Lee, E.J., Tabor, J.J., Mikos, A.G.: Leveraging synthetic biology for tissue engineering applications. Inflamm. Regen. **34**(1), 015–022 (2014)
27. Lin, C.-L., Shen, W.: Generation of assurance cases for medical devices. In: Lee, R. (ed.) CIS. SCI, vol. 566, pp. 127–140. Springer, Heidelberg (2015)
28. Lin, H., Wu, J., Yuan, C., Luo, Y., van den Brand, M., Engelen, L.: A systematic approach for safety evidence collection in the safety-critical domain. In: Annual IEEE International on Systems Conference (SysCon), pp. 194–199. IEEE (2015)
29. Lutz, R.R., Lutz, J.H., Lathrop, J.I., Klinge, T.H., Mathur, D., Stull, D.M., Bergquist, T., Henderson, E.R.: Requirements analysis for a product family of DNA nanodevices. In: IEEE International Requirements Engineering Conference (RE), pp. 211–220, September 2012
30. Nair, S., de la Vara, J.L., Melzi, A., Tagliaferri, G., de-la-Beaujardiere, L., Belmonte, F.: Safety evidence traceability: problem analysis and model. In: Salinesi, C., Weerd, I. (eds.) REFSQ 2014. LNCS, vol. 8396, pp. 309–324. Springer, Heidelberg (2014)
31. Rossello, R.A., David, H.: Cell communication and tissue engineering. Commun. Integr. Biol. **3**(1), 53–56 (2010)
32. Sarpeshkar, R.: Analog synthetic biology. Philos. Trans. A Math. Phys. Eng. Sci. **372**, 20130110 (2014)
33. Slusarczyk, A., Lin, A., Weiss, R.: Foundations for the design and implementation of synthetic genetic circuits. Nat. Rev. Genet. **13**(6), 406–420 (2012)
34. Sujan, M.A., Habli, I., Kelly, T.P., Pozzi, S., Johnson, C.W.: Should healthcare providers do safety cases? lessons from a cross-industry review of safety case practices. Saf. Sci. **84**, 181–189 (2016)
35. Weinstock, C.B., Goodenough, J.B.: Cmu/sei-2009-tn-018: towards an assurance case practice for medical devices. Software Engineering Institute, Technical report, Carnegie Mellon (2009)
36. Whitaker, W.B., Sandoval, N.R., Bennett, R.K., Fast, A.G., Papoutsakis, E.T.: Synthetic methylotrophy: engineering the production of biofuels and chemicals based on the biology of aerobic methanol utilization. Curr. Opin. Biotechnol. **33**, 165–175 (2015)

Towards Safety Case Integration with Hazard Analysis for Medical Devices

Andrzej Wardziński[1,2] and Aleksander Jarzębowicz[1,2(✉)]

[1] Department of Software Engineering, Faculty of Electronics,
Telecommunications and Informatics, Gdańsk University of Technology,
Narutowicza 11/12, 80-233 Gdańsk, Poland
{andrzej.wardzinski, olek}@eti.pg.gda.pl
[2] Argevide sp. z o.o., Gdańsk, Poland
{andrzej.wardzinski,
aleksander.jarzebowicz}@argevide.com

Abstract. Safety case is one of system safety lifecycle products and should be consistent with other lifecycle products like hazard analysis results. In this paper we present a method of safety case integration with hazard tables based on the use of parametrized argument patterns. We describe a hazard table metamodel, a safety argument pattern and a mechanism of pattern instantiation using a linking table which represents references to system lifecycle artefacts. We report and comment results of a feasibility study of pattern application for medical device hazard analysis. Finally we discuss the opportunities of applying such solution to safety case development and maintenance and the perspectives of further development of this approach.

Keywords: Safety case · Hazard table · Safety argument pattern · Infusion pump · Medical device

1 Introduction

A safety case is a way of arguing system's safety used in many industry sectors. In recent years a growing interest in application of safety cases in healthcare can be noticed [1–3]. Such interest is also reflected in regulatory requirements, in particular U.S. Food and Drug Administration (FDA) published a guidance document for manufacturers of medical devices (infusion pumps), strongly recommending delivering safety cases as a part of pre-market notification [4]. It is expected that the safety case approach will be extended for other medical devices in the coming years. The mentioned guidance is complemented by other documents which address other safety-related aspects of medical devices like software components [5] and security [6].

Safety cases are usually based on the results of hazard analysis. FDA recommends tabular form of hazard analysis results presentation for medical devices containing software premarket notifications [5]. The recommended standard describing the process of hazard analysis for medical devices is ISO 14971 [7], which does not impose any particular form of hazard analysis results presentation. Tabular presentation is descri-bed by Jones and Taylor [8], who present an idea of transforming hazard tables into

© Springer International Publishing Switzerland 2016
A. Skavhaug et al. (Eds.): SAFECOMP 2016 Workshops, LNCS 9923, pp. 87–98, 2016.
DOI: 10.1007/978-3-319-45480-1_8

instantiations of argument patterns to be included in a safety case. They also provide an example of a generic pattern.

Our goal is to develop a method to establish and maintain relationship between safety case elements and hazard analysis results through the pattern instantiation process. We use NOR-STA tool [9, 10] to develop safety cases and argument patterns. The tool allows to save the safety argument in XML format conformant to OMG SACM standard [11]. The approach we present is based on processing XML data for safety cases and hazard analysis.

In Sect. 2 we present the background and related work including safety cases for medical devices, safety argument patterns and pattern instantiations. In Sect. 3 we describe the metamodel of hazard table and the safety argument pattern mapping to hazard table elements. A case study of the instantiation process is presented in Sect. 4. The achieved results and future work is discussed in Sect. 5. In Sect. 6 we discuss the main conclusions to summarize the presented work.

2 Background

The work presented in this paper concerns safety cases for medical devices, safety case patterns and pattern instantiation.

2.1 Safety Cases for Medical Devices

Safety cases (or assurance cases as referred to in many papers) are a relatively new tool for managing safety of medical devices. One of the first research reports on safety cases for medical devices was published in 2009 by Weinstock and Goodenough [12]. They presented the example of an assurance case for the generic infusion pump and discussed the applicability of assurance case approach for medical devices, especially in the context of FDA's review processes. Ray and Cleaveland [13] introduce an approach to the creation of assurance cases for pre-market submissions of medical devices. It includes argumentation schemes of addressing hazards and providing mitigation mechanisms. Wassyng et al. [14] propose capturing the requirements of a standard (or a guideline) in the form of an assurance case template. As already mentioned, Jones and Taylor [8] designed a safety argument pattern using data from hazard tables documenting risk analysis process for a medical device.

A large repository of safety-related resources for medical devices can be found at the Generic Infusion Pump Research Project website [15]. A number of contributions from University of Pennsylvania was dedicated to several aspects of assurance cases for medical devices e.g. a pacemaker assurance case [16], from_to pattern [17] or a high-level safety argument for the PCA closed-loop system [18]. Also, Larson developed a draft assurance case for Open PCA infusion pump as an example to illustrate how to apply FDA guidelines [19].

2.2   Safety Argument Patterns

The first ideas of safety argument patterns and their role in development of safety cases were described by Kelly and McDermid in [20, 21]. The first catalogue of patterns was included in Kelly's PhD thesis [22]. In the following years the concept and applications of patterns were further elaborated, mostly by the researchers affiliated with the University of York (e.g. [23, 24]).

A number of pattern catalogues was published over the years: [22, 25–28]. Recently, Denney and Pai summarized the existing catalogues and provided a description of six new patterns [29]. An online pattern catalogue including a substantial set of patterns derived from the available sources has been published by Gdańsk University of Technology in NOR-STA tool [30].

The process of pattern application is called instantiation and it requires to define values for pattern parameters, which are specific for a given system [22]. Hauge and Stølen [31] introduce a pattern-based method, called Safe Control Systems (SaCS), which focuses on pattern compositions (integrating sets of patterns) and their instantiations. Khalil et al. [32] describe a reusable pattern library for automotive safety cases and the mechanism for their instantiation.

Denney and Pai [29] provide a formalized definition of safety argument patterns which includes aspects of their instantiation. The mechanism of patterns instantiation consists of an algorithm and data tables, which store traces between template elements and their instantiations. The mechanism was implemented in AdvoCATE tool [33]. The presented instantiation requires interaction from the user of the tool, who is supposed to provide concrete values for pattern parameters. The earlier paper of the same authors [34] focuses on assembling parts of a safety case on the basis of external artefacts in tabular form: hazard tables and two kinds of requirements tables. Two argument patterns for representing contents of hazard tables and requirements tables are proposed. The contents of a hazard table and the structure of corresponding argument pattern are specific to NASA standards and guidelines.

Hawkins et al. [35] present a way of pattern instantiation using a weaving model, which is the main source of information for the instantiation program. The weaving model stores the dependencies between the elements of safety argument patterns and reference information metamodels, as well as additional interdependencies. Reference information models of various notations and tools, based on different metamodels (e.g. system components, errors) can be used to provide values for pattern parameters.

3   Safety Case to Hazard Table Relationship

Safety cases refer to hazards, their causes and control measures. Our work is based on the hazard table format specified in [8] which includes the following table columns:

- Hazardous situation – circumstances in which people, property or environment are exposed to a hazard;
- Causes of the hazardous situation – events and circumstances necessary to the occurrence of hazardous situation;

- Risk estimation before mitigation or severity of harm – risk arising from a hazardous situation, calculated on the basis of probability of occurrence and severity of consequences (or just severity if probability cannot be assessed);
- Control measure(s) – mechanisms applied by the manufacturer to reduce unacceptable risk by addressing causes of the hazardous situation;
- Safety decision rationale – justification why a control measure is chosen and considered to be effective;
- Verification of effectiveness (methods & objective evidence) – verification whether control measure is effective in the context of design specifications and expected behavior;
- Verification of implementation & objective evidence (validation) – validation whether the control measure is fit for purpose in the context of device intended use.

We have specified a hazard table metamodel in the form of an UML class diagram to precisely specify hazard analysis artefacts and their relationship (Fig. 1).

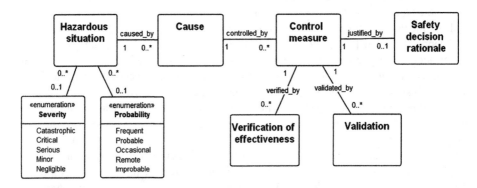

Fig. 1. A metamodel of hazard table elements and their relationships.

The model in Fig. 1 corresponds to top-down approach. We accept optional relationships (0..*) to address situations when hazard analysis is still in progress and is not complete (for example control measures are not yet defined for a given cause). On the other hand we do not accept low level artefacts (e.g. validation evidence) not connected to any control measure. The hierarchy presented in Fig. 1 can be directly mapped to the safety case argument hierarchy. The mapping is described in Table 1.

Safety argument pattern presented in Fig. 2 is based on this hierarchical relationship. The pattern is expressed in textual hierarchical notation used in NOR-STA software tool [36]. The notation is compatible to OMG SACM and includes its main concepts. The types of the elements are denoted by icons and by mnemonics: C – claim, A – argumentation strategy, F – fact, R – rationale, Ctx – context. Argument elements related to hazard table columns are marked with a corresponding column number (ID) specified in Table 1. One should note that NOR-STA notation does not currently implement structural abstraction relations such as multiplicity and choice. Temporary solution presented in Fig. 2 is to describe the relation in UML-like style: "1..*". NOR-STA notation is planned to be extended to cover structural abstraction.

Table 1. Mapping between a hazard table and a safety case.

ID	Hazard table column	Safety case element
1	Hazardous situation	Claim: hazardous situation is mitigated
		Context: hazardous situation definition
2	Risk estimation/severity of harm	Context: severity
3	Causes of the hazardous situation	Claim: cause is addressed by control measures
		Context: cause description
4	Control measure(s)	Claim: control measure is effective
		Context: control measure description
5	Safety decision rationale	Rationale: rationale for the choice of control measures
6	Verification of effectiveness – methods and objective evidence	Fact: control measure's effectiveness verified
		Evidence: verification evidence
7	Verification of implementation and objective evidence (validation)	Fact: control measure validated
		Evidence: validation evidence

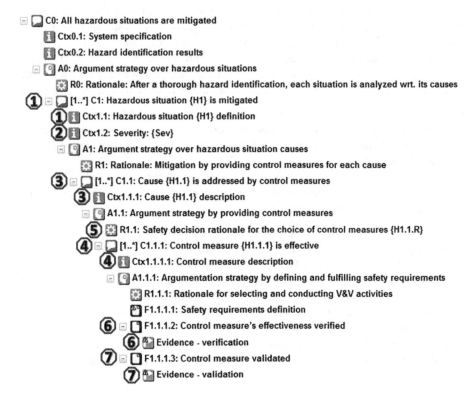

Fig. 2. A structure of a safety argument pattern based on hazard table.

The presented safety argument pattern is simplified and does not cover issues like: hierarchical hazard decomposition, re-evaluation of the residual risk following application of control measures, mitigation strategies other than addressing causes of hazardous situations. The real safety case would also have to be extended by arguments and evidence demonstrating the confidence in safety claims. For example, one could doubt whether hazard identification uncovered all hazardous situations. Such doubts should be addressed by a separate confidence case or by local confidence arguments supporting Rationale elements [37], in this case a confidence argument for R0 in Fig. 2.

4   Hazard Table Integration with Safety Case

Hazard analysis results mapping to safety case elements can be established in the safety case pattern instantiation process. In this section we will present the use of parametrized patterns to integrate safety case and hazard table and to track the relationships. First we will describe safety argument instantiation mechanism and then present how it can be applied to safety case integration with hazard tables.

4.1   Pattern Instantiation Process

The objective of the instantiation process is to produce a safety argument compiled from an argument pattern and references to the artefacts of types specified by pattern parameters. Pattern parameters may refer to any system model or artefact.

Our basic assumption for pattern instantiation process is the use of XML representation for all system models, the safety case and patterns. We introduce a linking table to track relationships between models. The linking table is divided into two parts:

- Abstract part is created for each pattern to specify the type of referenced models and the type of target elements for each pattern parameter. For example we can specify a pattern parameter to be related to a *ControlMeasure* type specified in the hazard object model (Fig. 1).
- Instantiation part defines relationships on detailed system model level. For each pattern parameter a specific model element can be selected by the user or the parameter value is entered manually.

Both parts of the linking table are presented in their context in Fig. 3. During the instantiation process, a user has to select elements of a specified type in the system model. Let's take an example of {H1} parameter in the pattern presented in Fig. 2. The abstract linking table can specify that {H1} parameter is related to objects of *HazardousSituation* type in the hazard table class model (Fig. 1). During the instantiation process, the user will be asked to point to an XML file for hazard table data and then select objects of the *HazardousSituation* type. As a multiplicity operator [1..*] is defined for {H1} parameter in the template, the user will be asked to select any number of objects and an argumentation subtree will be created for each of them.

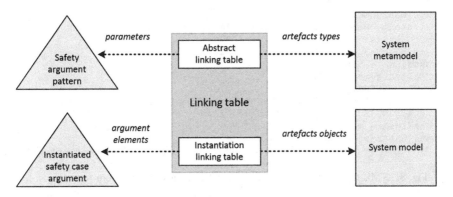

Fig. 3. Linking table and referenced models (arrows show references).

4.2 Integration with Hazard Table Case Study

We will demonstrate the instantiation process for a simple example of a hazard decomposition argument. All the input information used in the process is represented in XML formal, as well as the final output. From a technical point of view it is an XML transformation process. We will present model excerpts in XML format or GSN-like diagrams. NOR-STA tool generates graphical argument diagrams, however some symbols used differ a bit from standard GSN, for example the context elements. We assume the differences will not impede understanding of the diagrams.

The pattern presented in Fig. 4 is a fragment of the pattern from Fig. 2. As XML representation takes much more space than the diagram, we present only a small excerpt containing claim C1 and context Ctx1.2, represented as XML in Fig. 5.

There are three parameters in this pattern fragment: hazardous situation {H1}, severity {Sev} and cause {H1.1}. The abstract linking table (Table 2) allows us to map these parameters to hazard analysis metamodel elements (Fig. 1).

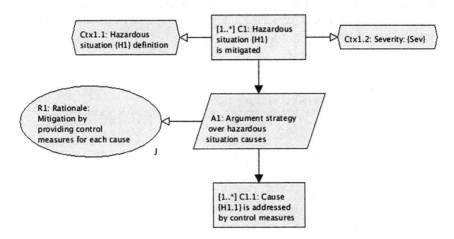

Fig. 4. Safety case pattern excerpt for hazard decomposition by causes.

```
<containsArgumentElement
    content="Hazardous situation {H1} is mitigated"
    identifier="[1..*] C1" xmi:id="7" xsi:type="ARM:Claim">
    <taggedValue key="order" value="1"/>
</containsArgumentElement>
<containsArgumentElement
    content="Severity: {Sev}"
    identifier="Ctx1.2" xmi:id="9" xsi:type="ARM:InformationElement">
    <taggedValue key="order" value="2"/>
</containsArgumentElement>
<containsAssertedRelationship
    source="7" target="9" xmi:id="30" xsi:type="ARM:AssertedContext"/>
```

Fig. 5. XML representation of C1 and Ctx1.1 elements of the pattern from Fig. 4.

Table 2. Abstract linking table.

Pattern parameters		System metamodel	
Pattern name	Parameter name	Model type	Element type
HazardDecomposition	H1	HazardAnalysis	HazardousSituation
HazardDecomposition	Sev	HazardAnalysis	Severity
HazardDecomposition	H1.1	HazardAnalysis	Cause

To instantiate the pattern we will need a hazard model for the system under analysis. Our safety case example refers to PCA infusion pump system [38]. Excerpt of the hazard analysis in XML format is presented in Fig. 6. This fragment describes one cause (sensor failure) for a hazardous situation 'air in line'. The possible consequence is the injection of air into the patient bloodstream which can be dangerous for patient life and health.

During safety argument's instantiation the user has to select value for each pattern parameter. The value can be an element of the hazard model of appropriate type or the value may be entered manually by the user. The result of this step is recorded in the instantiation linking table (Table 3). For each parameter, the table specifies corresponding safety case elements (presented in Fig. 7) and system model elements (XML excerpt of a hazard table in Fig. 6),

```
<hazardElement
    content="Air in line"
    xsi:type="HA:HazardousSituation" xmi:id="H1">
    <attribute xsi:type ="HA:Severity" xmi:id="S1" name="Critical"/>
    <attribute xsi:type ="HA:Probability" xmi:id="P1" name="Occasional"/>
</hazardElement>
<hazardElement
    content="Sensor does not signal error when air is present in IV line"
    xsi:type="HA:Cause" xmi:id="C1">
</hazardElement>
<relationship
    xsi:type="HA:CausedBy"
    xmi:id="H1C1" source="H1" target="C1">
</relationship>
```

Fig. 6. Model excerpt for one hazardous situation and one of its causes.

Table 3. Instantiation linking table.

Parameter name (abstract linking table)	Safety case		System model	
	Pattern root element id	Elements ids	Filename	Element id
H1	C1	C1, Ctx1.1	PCA_hazards.xmi	H1
Sev	C1	Ctx1.2	PCA_hazards.xmi	S1
H1.1	C1	C1.1	PCA_hazards.xmi	C1

C1: Hazard <Air in line> is mitigated

    Ctx1.1: Hazard <Air in line> description

    Ctx1.2: Severity: <Critical>

A1: Argument strategy over hazard causes

    R1: Rationale: Hazard is mitigated by providing control measures for all its causes

    C1.1: Cause <Sensor signals normal state 'Fluid detected' when air is present in IV line> is mitigated by control measures

Fig. 7. Excerpt from the instantiated argument pattern.

The instantiation linking table directly points argument elements to the values of the specified model elements.

The instantiation linking table is not deleted after the instantiation as it allows for tracking the relationship even in case the model changes. In case any hazard table element is modified, the change can be propagated to dedicated safety case elements provided objects identifiers are maintained.

5   Summary of the Case Study and Further Work

The presented case study demonstrates how the linking table can be used to establish the lasting relationship between a safety case and a hazard table. The established relationship should be maintained throughout the system lifecycle. The linking table can be used to track and propagate changes. Let's consider a situation when a hazard cause has been modified in the hazard table. Having the linking table filled in, we can detect the change and react to it. When the change is to be propagated to the safety case, we can re-instantiate safety case elements affected by the change or even restart the whole instantiation process and produce new and up-to-date safety case. If we want this process to be effective, we should forbid manual safety argument modifications or limit them to safety case areas not covered by the automatic instantiation process.

Change propagation in the opposite direction is also possible, however we should be careful in allowing changes to be propagated from a safety case to a hazard table. From a technical point of view it will not be difficult to implement a two way change propagation mechanism. The issue is whether it is necessary and secure to allow changing the safety case without the actual update of the hazard analysis.

Propagation of structural changes is more difficult and will require extending the linking table with additional information. As a structural change we understand adding or removing any model element. For example when a new hazard cause has been identified. Change propagation would require creation of a new argument subtree. And vice versa, when an element is deleted (let's imagine we have to delete one of the hazard causes) from the hazard table, the change propagation mechanism would cause removal of the related argument parts as specified in the linking table.

We plan to extend the linking table to comprehend data necessary for propagation of structural changes in the hazard table. This would enable continuous consistency maintenance between a safety case and a hazard table.

The pattern described in Sect. 3 bears similarities to Extended Hazard Directed Breakdown Pattern [29], however the latter includes hierarchical decomposition of hazards into lower-level ones. This is possible with the use of loop construct which is not available in NOR-STA notation (as NOR-STA data structure is based on directed graph, not hypergraph). We can use dedicated Link elements to represent loops in NOR-STA notation to achieve the same effect.

6   Conclusions

We presented the approach of integrating safety cases and hazard tables based on the use of parametrized safety argument patterns. The essential concept is the use of the linking table which stores references to the elements of safety case and hazard table both on abstract (pattern parameters, hazard table columns) and instantiation (claims, hazardous situations etc.) levels. On the abstract (pattern) level we map pattern parameters to metamodel elements and then on the instantiation level we map each parameter value to a particular model element. The linking table allows to track the relationships and maintain consistency between the safety case and hazard table.

This approach can be generalized from the hazard table presented in this paper to other system models, provided we can specify a metamodel and provide an XML interface, for example for AADL specifications. The approach can also be applied to other safety argument patterns however the user would need to specify appropriate system models for all pattern parameters.

This paper presents work in progress and the linking table may evolve as the approach matures. The presented approach will be developed further to effective management and maintenance of the relationship between safety cases and hazard tables.

References

1. Sujan, M., Koornneef, F., Chozos, N., Pozzi, S., Kelly, T.: Safety cases for medical devices and health IT - involving healthcare organisations in the assurance of safety. Health Inform. J. **19**(3), 165–182 (2013)
2. Chen, Y., Lawford, M., Wang, H., Wassyng, A.: Insulin pump software certification. In: Gibbons, J., MacCaull, W. (eds.) FHIES 2013. LNCS, vol. 8315, pp. 87–106. Springer, Heidelberg (2014)
3. Sujan, M., Habli, I., Kelly, T., Pozzi, S., Johnson, C.: Should healthcare providers do safety cases? Lessons from a cross-industry review of safety case practices. Saf. Sci. **84**, 181–189 (2016)

4. FDA: Infusion Pumps Total Product Life Cycle, Guidance for Industry and FDA Staff (2014)
5. FDA: Guidance for the Content of Premarket Submissions for Software Contained in Medical Devices (2005)
6. FDA: Content of Premarket Submissions for Management of Cybersecurity in Medical Devices. Guidance for Industry and Food and Drug Administration Staff (2014)
7. ISO: ISO 14971:2007. Medical Devices – Application of Risk Management to Medical Devices (2007)
8. Jones, P.L., Taylor, A.: Medical device risk management and safety cases. Bio-med. Instrum. Technol. **49**(1), 45–53 (2015)
9. Górski, J., Jarzębowicz, A., Miler, J., Witkowicz, M., Czyżnikiewicz, J., Jar, P.: Supporting assurance by evidence-based argument services. In: Ortmeier, F., Daniel, P. (eds.) SAFECOMP Workshops 2012. LNCS, vol. 7613, pp. 417–426. Springer, Heidelberg (2012)
10. NOR-STA tool website. https://www.argevide.com/en/products/assurance_case
11. OMG: Structured Assurance Case Metamodel (SACM), Version 1.1 (2015)
12. Weinstock, C., Goodenough, J.: Towards an assurance case practice for medical devices. Software Engineering Institute, Technical Note CMU/SEI-2009-TN-018 (2009)
13. Ray, A., Cleaveland, R.: Constructing safety assurance cases for medical devices. In: Proceedings of the 1st International Workshop on Assurance Cases for Software-Intensive Systems, pp. 40–45. IEEE Press (2013)
14. Wassyng, A., Singh, N.K., Geven, M., Proscia, N., Wang, H., Lawford, M., Maibaum, T.: Can product specific assurance case templates be used as medical device standards? IEEE Des. Test **32**(5), 45–55 (2015)
15. Generic Infusion Pump Research Project website. https://rtg.cis.upenn.edu/gip/
16. Jee, E., Lee, I., Sokolsky, O.: Assurance cases in model-driven development of the pacemaker software. In: Margaria, T., Steffen, B. (eds.) ISoLA 2010, Part II. LNCS, vol. 6416, pp. 343–356. Springer, Heidelberg (2010)
17. Ayoub, A., Kim, B., Lee, I., Sokolsky, O.: A safety case pattern for model-based development approach. In: Goodloe, A.E., Person, S. (eds.) NFM 2012. LNCS, vol. 7226, pp. 141–146. Springer, Heidelberg (2012)
18. Feng, L., King, A., Chen, S., Ayoub, A., Park, J., Bezzo, N., Sokolsky, O., Lee, I.: A safety argument strategy for PC a closed-loop systems: a preliminary proposal. In: 5th Workshop on Medical Cyber-Physical Systems, vol. 36, pp. 94–99 (2014)
19. Larson, B.R.: Open PCA Pump Assurance Case, SAnToS Research Group, Kansas State University (2014). http://openpcapump.santoslab.org/
20. Kelly T., McDermid, J.: Safety case construction and reuse using patterns. In: Proceedings of SAFECOMP 1997, pp. 55–69 (1997)
21. Kelly, T., McDermid, J.: Safety case patterns – reusing successful arguments. In: Proceedings of IEE Colloquium on Understanding Patterns and Their Application to System Engineering, London, UK (1998)
22. Kelly T.: Arguing safety – a systematic approach to safety case management. Ph.D. thesis, Department of Computer Science, University of York (1998)
23. Hawkins, R., Kelly, T.: A systematic approach for developing software safety arguments. In: Proceedings of the 27th System Safety Society (SSS) International System Safety Conference (ISSC), 3–7 August 2009, Huntsville AL, USA (2009)
24. Hawkins, R., Clegg, K., Alexander, R., Kelly, T.: Using a software safety argument pattern catalogue: two case studies. In: Flammini, F., Bologna, S., Vittorini, V. (eds.) SAFECOMP 2011. LNCS, vol. 6894, pp. 185–198. Springer, Heidelberg (2011)
25. Weaver R.: The safety of software – constructing and assuring arguments. Ph.D. thesis, Department of Computer Science, University of York (2003)

26. Ye, F.: Justifying the use of COTS components within safety critical applications, Ph.D. thesis, Department of Computer Science, University of York (2005)
27. Alexander R., Kelly T., Kurd Z., McDermid J.: Safety cases for advanced control software: safety case patterns, Technical report, University of York (2007)
28. Hawkins, R., Kelly, T.: A software safety argument pattern catalogue, Technical report, University of York (2013)
29. Denney, E., Pai, G.: safety case patterns: theory and applications, NASA/TM–2015–218492 Technical report (2015)
30. Assurance Case Patterns Online Catalogue, Gdańsk University of Technology. http://www.nor-sta.eu/en/en/news/assurance_case_pattern_catalogue
31. Hauge, A.A., Stølen, K.: A pattern-based method for safe control systems exemplified within nuclear power production. In: Ortmeier, F., Lipaczewski, M. (eds.) SAFECOMP 2012. LNCS, vol. 7612, pp. 13–24. Springer, Heidelberg (2012)
32. Khalil, M., Schätz, B., Voss, S.: A pattern-based approach towards modular safety analysis and argumentation. In: Embedded Real Time Software and Systems Conference (ERTS 2014), Toulouse, France (2014)
33. Denney, E., Pai, G., Pohl, J.: AdvoCATE: an assurance case automation toolset. In: Ortmeier, F., Daniel, P. (eds.) SAFECOMP Workshops 2012. LNCS, vol. 7613, pp. 8–21. Springer, Heidelberg (2012)
34. Denney, E., Pai, G.: A lightweight methodology for safety case assembly. In: Ortmeier, F., Lipaczewski, M. (eds.) SAFECOMP 2012. LNCS, vol. 7612, pp. 1–12. Springer, Heidelberg (2012)
35. Hawkins R., Habli I., Kolovos D., Paige R., Kelly T.: Weaving an assurance case from design: model-based approach. In: 2015 IEEE 16th International Symposium on High Assurance Systems Engineering (HASE) (2015)
36. Argevide: NOR-STA Argument Notation White paper. https://www.argevide.com/sites/default/files/docs/Argevide%20WP2%20-%20NOR-STA%20argument%20notation.pdf
37. Jarzębowicz, A., Wardziński, A.: Integrating confidence and assurance arguments. In: 10th IET System Safety and Cyber Security Conference, Bristol, UK (2015)
38. Larson, B.R., Hatcliff, J., Chalin, P.: Open source patient-controlled analgesic pump requirements documentation. In: 5th International Workshop on Software Engineering in Health Care (SEHC), pp. 28–34 (2013)

11th International ERCIM/EWICS/ARTEMIS Workshop on Cyber-Physical Systems and Systems-of-Systems (DECSoS)

DECSoS 2016: The 11th ERCIM/EWICS/ARTEMIS Workshop on Dependable Embedded and Cyber-Physical Systems and Systems-of-Systems

European Research and Innovation Initiatives in the Area of Cyber-Physical Systems and Systems-of-Systems

Erwin Schoitsch[1] and Amund Skavhaug[2]

[1] AIT Austrian Institute of Technology GmbH, Vienna, Austria
Erwin.Schoitsch@ait.ac.at

[2] Department of Production and Quality Engineering,
NTNU (The Norwegian University of Science and Technology),
Trondheim, Norway
Amund.Skavhaug@ntnu.no

1 Introduction

The DECSoS workshop at SAFECOMP follows already its own tradition since 2006. In the past, it focussed on the conventional type of "dependable embedded systems", covering all dependability aspects as defined by Avizienis, Lapries, Kopetz, Voges and others in IFIP WG 10.4. To put more emphasis on the relationship to physics, mechatronics and the notion of interaction with an unpredictable environment, the terminology changed to "cyber-physical systems" (CPS) and "Systems-of-Systems" (SoS). Collaboration and co-operation of these systems with each other and humans, and the interplay of safety, security and reliability are leading to new challenges in verification, validation and certification/qualification respectively. Examples are e.g. the smart power grid with power plants and power distribution and control, smart transport systems (rail, traffic management with V2V and V2I facilities, air traffic control systems), advanced manufacturing systems ("Industry 4.0"), mobile co-operating autonomous robotic systems, smart health care, smart buildings up to smart cities and the like.

Society as a whole strongly depends on CPS and SoS - thus it is important to consider dependability (safety, reliability, availability, security, maintainability, etc.), resilience, robustness and sustainability in a holistic manner. CPS and SoS are a targeted research area in Horizon 2020 and public-private partnerships such as the ECSEL JU (Joint Undertaking) (Electronic Components and Systems for European Leadership), which integrates the former ARTEMIS (Advanced Research and Technology for Embedded Intelligence and Systems), ENIAC and EPoSS efforts, where industry and research ("private") are represented by the three industrial associations ARTEMIS-IA, AENEAS (for ENIAC, semiconductor industry) and EPoSS (for "Smart Systems Integration"), the public part are represented by the EC and the national public authorities of the member states which take part in the ECSEL Joint Undertaking. Funding comes from the EC and the national public authorities ("tri-partite funding": EC, member states, project partners).

2 ARTEMIS/ECSEL: The European Cyber-Physical Systems Initiative

This year the workshop is co-hosted by the ARTEMIS and Horizon 2020 projects

- CRYSTAL ("Critical Systems Engineering Factories", http://www.crystal-artemis.eu),
- ARROWHEAD[1] ("Ahead of the Future", http://www.arrowhead.eu/),
- EMC2 ("Embedded Multi-Core systems for Mixed Criticality applications in dynamic and changeable real-time environments", http://www.artemis-emc2.eu/) and
- R5-COP ("Reconfigurable ROS-based Resilient Reasoning Robotic Co-operating Systems", http://www.r5-cop.eu/)
- CP-SETIS ("Towards Cyber-Physical Systems Engineering Tools Interoperability Standards", http://cp-setis.eu/), which is not an ARTEMIS but a Horizon 2020 project, funded only by the EC, but executed by ARTEMIS-IA members.

The recently started co-hosting ECSEL projects are AMASS (Safety & Security Multi-Concern Assurance), ENABLE-S3 (Automated Vehicles), IoSENSE (IoT and Industry 4.0) and SemI40 (Semiconductor - Industry 4.0).

ARTEMIS was one of the European, industry-driven research initiatives and is now part of the ECSEL PPP. The current ARTEMIS projects will, however, be continued according to the ARTEMIS rules, but managed by the ECSEL JU. The five co-hosting ARTEMIS projects are described briefly, the "newcomers" have just started this year so it was too early to present first results before the deadline Spring 2016:

R5-COP focuses on agile manufacturing paradigms and specifically on modular robotic systems. Based on existing and newly developed methods for a formal modelling of hardware and software components, R5-COP will support model-based design, engineering, validation, and fast commissioning. Using existing interface and middleware standards, R5-COP will strongly facilitate integration of components from various suppliers.

CRYSTAL, a large ARTEMIS Innovation Pilot Project (AIPP), aims at fostering Europe's leading edge position in embedded systems engineering by facilitating high quality and cost effectiveness of safety-critical embedded systems and architecture platforms. Its overall goal is to enable sustainable paths to speed up the maturation, integration, and cross-sector reusability of technological and methodological bricks in the areas of transportation (aerospace, automotive, and rail) and healthcare providing a critical mass of European technology providers. CRYSTAL will integrate the contributions of previous ARTEMIS projects (CESAR, MBAT, iFEST, SafeCer etc.) and further develop the ARTEMIS RTP (Reference Technology Platform) and Interoperability Specification.

CP-SETIS ("Towards Cyber-Physical Systems Engineering Tools Interoperability Standards") is a H2020 support-action-like IA which aims to leverage on these various initiatives mentioned in context of CRYSTAL by proposing and implementing sustainable cooperation and governance structures to (a) facilitate long-term and sustainable cooperation between all involved stakeholder organizations – End Users, Tool Vendors, Research Organizations, Standardization bodies, R&D projects, etc. – and (b) support extensions, advancements and formal standardization of the IOS.

ARROWHEAD, a large AIPP addressing the areas production and energy system automation, intelligent-built environment and urban infrastructure, is aiming at enabling collaborative automation by networked embedded devices, from enterprise/worldwide level in the cloud down to device level at the machine in the plant. The goal is to achieve efficiency and flexibility on a global scale for five application verticals: production (manufacturing, process, energy production and distribution), smart buildings and infrastructures, electro-mobility and virtual market of energy.

EMC^2 is up to now the largest ARTEMIS AIPP bundling the power of innovation of 100 partners from embedded industry and research from 19 European countries and Israel with an effort of about 800 person years and a total budget of about 100 million Euro. The objective of the EMC^2 project is to develop an innovative and sustainable service-oriented architecture approach for mixed criticality applications in dynamic and changeable real-time environments based on multi-core architectures.

It provides the paradigm shift to a new and sustainable system architecture which is suitable to handle open dynamic systems:

- Dynamic Adaptability in Open Systems, scalability and utmost flexibility,
- Utilization of expensive system features only as Service-on-Demand in order to reduce the overall system cost,
- Handling of mixed criticality applications under real-time conditions,
- Full scale deployment and management of integrated tool chains, through the entire lifecycle.

The AIPPs ARROWHEAD and EMC^2 are addressing "Systems-of-Systems" aspects in the context of critical systems, whereas CRYSTAL and CP-SETIS are devoting their major efforts towards creating a sustainable eco-system of a CRTP (Collaborative Reference Technology Platform) and the harmonization of efforts towards an IOS (set of standards, specifications and guidelines for tool interoperability).

3   This Year's Workshop

The workshop DECSoS'15 provides some insight into an interesting set of topics to enable fruitful discussions during the meeting and afterwards. The mixture of topics is hopefully well balanced, with a certain focus on cybersecurity & safety co-analysis and on modelling, simulation and verification. Presentations are mainly based on the ARTEMIS/ECSEL projects mentioned above and on nationally funded (basic) research respectively industrial developments of partners' companies and universities.

The session starts with an introduction and overview to the ERCIM/EWICS/ARTEMIS DECSoS Workshop setting the European Research and Innovation scene. The first session on **Analysis, Test and Simulation** comprises four presentations: (1) An industrial case study on fault injection (Siemens and fortiss, Germany), (2) "Reliability assessment of mobile robotics systems" (R5-COP project), (3) "In-the-loop Simulations for Development and Test of a Complex Mechatronic Embedded System" (CRYSTAL project) and (4) "Gate-Level-Accurate Fault-Effect Analysis at Virtual-Prototype Speed" (German project EffektiV, Federal Ministry of Education and Research, BMBF).

The second session covers the **Automotive Domain** by three papers: (1) "The use of Standard SAE J3061 for Automotive Security Requirement Engineering" (EMC^2 project, SCRIPT project (Vienna Business Agency)), (2) "Dynamic Safety Contracts for Functional Cooperation of Automotive Systems" (Germany) and (3) "Time-of-Flight based Optical Communication for Safety-Critical Applications in Autonomous Driving" (EMC^2).

The session after lunch is dedicated to **Safety & Cybersecurity Analysis and Co-Engineering**: (1) The new hazard analysis technique STPA based on system thinking, as proposed by Nancy Leveson not long ago, is extended by STPA-SEC for safety and security co-analysis and evaluated in a practical use case (ECSEL project AMASS), (2) "Security Services for Mixed-Criticality Systems based on Networked Multi-Core Chips" describes the results of the DREAMS project (Framework Program FP7), and (3) "Analysis of Informed Attacks and Appropriate Countermeasures for Cyber-Physical Systems" allows modelling and analysis of cybersecurity attacks on CPS, as achieved through the German project SMARTEST funded by the Federal Ministry of Economic Affairs and Energy (BMWi).

The last session of the day is about large and small **Dependable Industrial Applications**: (1) "Advanced Security Considerations in the Arrowhead Framework" is about results of the ARROWHEAD project on secure collaborative automation, (2) "The Role of the Supply Chain in Cybersecurity Incidents at Drilling Rigs" covers an important safety and security topic in a complex safety and environmental critical industrial automation application, and (3) "Control of Cyber-Physical Systems using Bluetooth Low Energy and Distributed Slave Microcontrollers" covers the small (SME-related, low cost) side of dependable industrial CPS applications in industrial control.

As chairpersons of the workshop, we want to thank all authors and contributors who submitted their work, Friedemann Bitsch, the SAFECOMP Publication Chair, and the members of the International Program Committee who enabled a fair evaluation through reviews and considerable improvements in many cases. We want to express our thanks to the SAFECOMP organizers, who provided us the opportunity to organize the workshop at SAFECOMP 2016 in Delft. Particularly we want to thank the EC and national public funding authorities who made the work in the research projects possible. We do not want to forget the continued support of our companies and organizations, of ERCIM, the European Research Consortium for Informatics and Mathematics with its Working Group on Dependable Embedded Software-intensive Systems, and EWICS, the creator and main sponsor of SAFECOMP, with its working groups, who always helped us to learn from their networks.

We hope that all participants will benefit from the workshop, enjoy the conference and accompanying programs and will join us again in the future!

Erwin Schoitsch

Amund Skavhaug

AIT Austrian Institute of Technology, Digital Safety & Security Department, Vienna, Austria

NTNU, Norwegian University of S&T, Department of Production and Quality Engineering, Trondheim, Norway

Acknowledgements. Part of the work presented in the workshop received funding from the EC (ARTEMIS/ECSEL Joint Undertaking) and the partners National Funding Authorities through the projects R5-COP (grant agreement 621447), CRYSTAL (332820), ARROWHEAD (332987) and EMC2 (621429), and through the EC only in Horizon 2020 (CP-SETIS (645149) or via purely national funding sources (see individual acknowledgements in papers). The ECSEL JU and nationally ("tri-partite") funded projects just started are AMASS (grant agreement 692474), ENABLE-S3 (692455), IoSENSE (692480) and SemI40 (692466).

International Program Committee

Bettina Buth	HAW Hamburg, Department Informatik (DE)
Friedemann Bitsch	Thales Transportation Systems GmbH (DE)
Maya Daneva	m.daneva@utwente.nl (NL)
Peter Daniel	EWICS TC7 (UK)
Wolfgang Ehrenberger	University of Applied Science Fulda (DE)
Francesco Flammini (IT)	Ansaldo, University "Federico II" of Naples (IT)
Virginia Franqueira	v.franqeira@derby.ac.uk (UK)
Janusz Gorski	Gdansk University of Technology (PL)
Denis Hatebur	University of Duisburg-Essen (DE)
Maritta Heisel	University of Duisburg-Essen (DE)
Andrea Herrmann	AndreaHerrmann3@gmx.de (DE)
Floor Koornneef	TU Delft (NL)
Willibald Krenn	AIT Austrian Institute of Technology (AT)
Peter Ladkin	University of Bielefeld (DE)
Dejan Nickovic	AIT Austrian Institute of Technology (AT)
Odd Nordland	SINTEF ICT (NO)
Frank Ortmeier	Otto-von-Guericke-University Magdeburg (DE)
Thomas Pfeiffenberger	Salzburg Research (AT)
Francesca Saglietti	University of Erlangen-Nuremberg (DE)
Christoph Schmitz	Zühlke Engineering AG (CH)
Erwin Schoitsch	AIT Austrian Institute of Technology (AT)
Rolf Schumacher	Schumacher Engineering Office (DE)
Amund Skavhaug	NTNU Trondheim (NO)
Mark-Alexander Sujan	University of Warwick (UK)
Meine van der Meulen	DNV GL (NO)

Testing Safety Properties of Cyber-Physical Systems with Non-Intrusive Fault Injection – An Industrial Case Study

Joachim Fröhlich[1]([⊠]), Jelena Frtunikj[2], Stefan Rothbauer[1], and Christoph Stückjürgen[1]

[1] Siemens AG, Otto-Hahn-Ring 6, 81739 Munich, Germany
froehlich.joachim@siemens.com
[2] Fortiss GmbH, Guerickestrasse 25, 80805 Munich, Germany

Abstract. Non-intrusive, deterministic fault-injection tests provide evidence for making reliable statements about the behavior of safety-critical, real-time systems in the presence of software faults and component failures. These tests are derived from system safety requirements for the detection and handling of value and time errors. That the approach presented here works for distributed, time-triggered systems that process data cyclically and reserve resources exclusively for testing purposes has been demonstrated by an industry study confirming the feasibility of the concepts for a fail-operational electric car.

Keywords: Cyber-physical system · Fault-tolerant system · Safety requirement · Fault injection test

1 Introduction

An open question for fault-tolerant, cyber-physical systems is how to reliably demonstrate their safety properties. Since the root causes of failures are faults, fault injection is an established practice for testing systems. There are promising approaches for injecting hardware and software models with faults without adversely affecting the simulation time during simulation runs [1,9]. However simulation-based fault-injection of executable system models ultimately fails to hold for operation systems, essentially for two reasons: (1) By their very nature, system models abstract implementation details and cannot be fully accurate in every aspect for operational systems in the field that need to execute under tight real-time constraints. (2) System environment models are hard to parametrize accurately with realistic simulation data. Software Implemented Fault Injection (SWIFI) is an established technique for fault injection into operational software systems, but has a significant disadvantage: SWIFI changes the timing behavior due to probe effects. The same disadvantage applies for tests in general and in particular for fault injection tests that stimulate and check the behavior of distributed systems online solely on the network level (see for example [6]). Another

© Springer International Publishing Switzerland 2016
A. Skavhaug et al. (Eds.): SAFECOMP 2016 Workshops, LNCS 9923, pp. 105–117, 2016.
DOI: 10.1007/978-3-319-45480-1_9

issue is the limited observability and controlability of systems under test. The limits of SWIFI tests define the fundamental objective of this work: to accurately test real-time systems with tight schedules while running free of side effects. The scope of the system which these tests observe and control shall be maximized to let concise tests illuminate otherwise obscure locations and behaviors of the system under test.

The contributions of this work are twofold: (1) demonstration of deterministic tests of safety requirements to provide reliable statements on fault-tolerant systems in operation; (2) an explanation of when, where, and why such tests provide reliable statements.

This paper is structured as follows: Sect. 2 introduces a consistent set of terms for characterizing target systems, assigned safety requirements and tests. Section 3 presents safety requirements used as driving examples. Section 4 characterizes target systems that implement fault-tolerance mechanisms and enable the execution of fault-injection tests without inadmissible probe effects. Section 5 specifies tests in ALFHA[1] [5] that verify the fulfillment of the safety requirements. The tests are executed with VITE[2]. Section 6 checks the plausibility of results that the test system produces. We use RACE[3] as our reference target system [2,4,8].

2   Terms

Throughout the paper we use a consistent set of terms for characterizing target systems, assigned safety requirements and tests for these requirements. Some terms are implemented as system predicates and used in test procedures (Sect. 5), such as **Platform Node**, **Dual Platform Node** and **Master Host**. Figure 1 provides an overview of selected terms explained in the following.

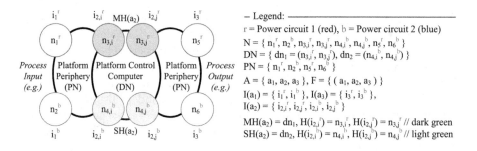

Fig. 1. An example target system with platform network (rings) (Color figure online)

---

[1] Assertion Language for Fault-Hypothesis Arguments.
[2] Verification and Integration Testing Environment, www.aviotech.de.
[3] Reliable Automation and Control Environment, www.projekt-race.de/en.

Platform Mechanism. Code block that implements a fault-tolerance mechanism such as, in general terms, error detection (ed), error recovery (er) and/or error mitigation (em), or a basic operating system mechanism such as input/output data processing and operation scheduling. Let $M = \{ed, er, em, ...\}$ denote the set of all platform mechanisms. Each platform mechanism $m \in M$ can be instantiated to an instance $i \in I(m)$, with $I(m)$ denoting the set of all instances $\{i_1, i_2, ...\}$ of m.

Platform Node. Node for short. Computer n consisting of a CPU, a clock generating cyclic ticks of constant duration, main memory, an access point to the network of all platform nodes $N = \{n_1, n_2, ..., n_n\}$ of the target system, an access point to a test network (not shown in Fig. 1 but in Fig. 3), and deployed instances of platform mechanisms. Each computer n is connected to either the "red" power circuit (n^r) or to the "blue" power circuit (n^b).

Platform. Instantiated and deployed platform mechanisms providing together fault-tolerance (safety) mechanisms to platform applications.

Platform Application. Application for short. Code block that uses platform mechanisms. Let $A = \{a_1, a_2, ...\}$ denote the set of all platform applications. Each platform application $a \in A$ can be instantiated to an instance $i \in I(a)$ that is deployed on a platform node. $I(a)$ denotes the set of all instances $\{i_1, i_2, ...\}$ of a. For clarity, we sometimes write i^r or i^b if the underlying platform node n is connected to the "red" power circuit (n^r) or to the "blue" power circuit (n^b).

Dual Platform Node. Dual node for short. Pair of platform nodes $dn = \{n_i, n_j\}$, with $n_i, n_j \in N$ running in lockstep mode and being connected to the same power circuit. In context of a dual platform node n_i and n_j are also called twin nodes.

Platform Control Computer. All dual platform nodes $DN = \{dn_1, dn_2, ..., dn_n\}$, with $\forall dn_i, dn_j \in DN : dn_i \cap dn_j = \emptyset$; that is, dual platform nodes run in disjoint node pairs.

Platform Periphery. All periphery nodes $PN = \{n : n \in N \wedge \nexists dn \in DN : n \in dn\}$. In other words, a node n belongs either to the platform periphery (sensing process inputs or controlling process outputs) or to the platform control computer.

Node Cycle. Instant of a cyclic process running in linear time [7] on a platform node, also called local instant. The clock of platform node n generates subsequent cycle numbers defined as numerical time series of node cycles $clock(n) = (0, 1, 2, ...)$. Cycle numbers of two different platform nodes n_i, n_j can differ at the same global instant, e.g., when the platform is up and running and when n_i started before n_j or when the clocks of n_i and n_j drift.

Platform Cycle. Instant of a cyclic process running in linear time on the platform, also called global instant. At platform start, the cycles generated by the clock of the first started platform node n determines the numerical time series of platform cycles $clock = (0, 1, 2, ...)$.

Variable. Addressable location $v(n)$ in the data segment of the main memory of platform node n. Platform mechanisms and platform applications exchange values via variables during a cycle and between cycles. We denote the value of a variable $v(n)$ at cycle x as $v(n)_x$, or simply v_x if n is irrelevant. Depending on the context, x denotes a (local) node cycle or a (global) platform cycle. Variables also take on values of input signals (process inputs originating from sensors in the platform periphery) and output signals (process outputs targeting actuators in the platform periphery).

Data Store. Section $V(n)$ in the data segment of the main memory of node n which contains all variables; that is, $V(n) = \{v_1(n), v_2(n), ...\}$. The data store of the platform contains all variables in the data stores of all nodes; that is, $V = \bigcup_{n \in N} V(n)$. Typically only a subset $W = \{v_1, v_2, ...\}$ of all variables V is in the test scope, that is $W \subseteq V$ and v_1, v_2 are different variables of possibly different nodes. The data stores of all nodes contain some common variables with node-specific values, e.g., node cycle and node state.

Trace. Chronologically ordered values of all variables in the test scope denoted as $(W_i)_{i=x..y} = (W_x, W_{x+1}, ..., W_y)$. Depending on the context, x and y denote (local) node cycles or (global) platform cycles.

System Function. All functionally coherent platform applications which together transform input signals from system sensors (related to nodes in the platform periphery) to output signals for system actuators (related to nodes in the platform periphery) defined as $F \subseteq A \times A \times ... \times A$. Instances of one or more platform applications instantiate a concrete system function.

Host. Platform node n that executes an instance i of platform application a at cycle x; that is, $H(i)_x = n \in N$. If x is not relevant then we write $H(i)$.

Master Host. Dual platform node MH whose nodes n_i and n_j both execute instances i_i and i_j of the same platform application a at cycle x; that is, $MH(a)_x = (n_i, n_j) \in DN$ with $i_i, i_j \in I(a)$, so that $H(i_i)_x = n_i$ and $H(i_j)_x = n_j$. $MH(a)$ operates as an open gate in the sense that $MH(a)$ transports signals or data to (input) and from (output) application a.

Slave Host. Dual platform node SH whose nodes n_i and n_j both execute instances i_i and i_j of the same platform application a at cycle x in hot-standby mode to $MH(a)_x$; that is, $SH(a)_x = (n_i, n_j) \in DN$ with $i_i, i_j \in I(a)$, so that $H(i_i)_x = n_i$ and $H(i_j)_x = n_j$. In contrast to $MH(a)$, $SH(a)$ operates as a half-side open gate in the sense that $SH(a)$ only transports signals or data to (input) application a.

3   Safety Requirements

3.1   Application Context

Our example system is an electric car built using software-intensive electronic devices. Safety-critical car functions, such as steering and braking, must be highly available and work reliably. In the following, we consider only car steering. In basic configuration, the steering system takes input from the driver, i.e., steering wheel position, and translates it into control commands for car wheels. An advanced variant of the steering system is controlled by additional parameters such as car speed, weight, weight distribution, yaw angle, and road and weather conditions. Regardless of the variant, the steering function, as well as the communication network and the on-board power supply, must stay operational in the presence of permanent or temporary faults in steering and non-steering car components.

3.2   System Scope

We assume that every fault-tolerant function roughly consists of three parts: input from the platform periphery (Fig. 1, sensors on the left), data processing in the platform control computer (Fig. 1, central nodes) and output to the platform periphery (Fig. 1, actuators on the right). Hence, the steering function consists of three platform applications $F = \{(sws, sc, wc)\}$ with: (1) *steering wheel sensing* (*sws*) having two redundant instances $I(sws) = \{sws^r, sws^b\}$ on two redundant steering wheel sensors $n_1^r, n_2^b \in PN : n_1^r = H(sws^r) \land n_2^b = H(sws^b)$; (2) *central steering control* (*sc*) having four redundant instances $I(sc) = \{sc_i^r, sc_j^r, sc_i^b, sc_j^b\}$ on four pairwise redundant, central nodes $(n_{3,i}^r, n_{3,j}^r), (n_{4,i}^b, n_{4,j}^b) \in DN : n_{3,i}^r = H(sc_i^r) \land n_{3,j}^r = H(sc_j^r) \land n4_i^b = H(sc_i^b) \land n4_j^b = H(sc_j^b)$ and (3) *wheel controlling* (*wc*) having two redundant instances $I(wc) = \{wc^r, wc^b\}$ on two redundant steering boxes $n_5^r, n_6^b \in PN : n_5^r = H(wc^r) \land n_6^b = H(wc^b)$. Redundant communication links and redundant power circuits complete the system. The following requirements concern availability properties of safety-critical system functions and thereby the steering function.

3.3   Requirement R1: Redundant Input Signals

R1.1 Safety property: Continuous data available. Host $n = H(i)_x$ shall provide a signal value to instance i of data processing application a in each node cycle. The signal value shall be free from those errors that platform mechanisms are responsible to detect and process.

For example, for car steering we assume the difference between two succeeding steering angles (v_x, v_{x-1}) of a safe longitudinal movement to lie within variable limits, that is, $|v_x - v_{x-1}| \leq delta$, even when a redundant steering wheel sensor fails. Driving situations, physical values and technical properties determine *delta*.

R1.2 Error detection. Host $n = H(i)_x$ shall check signal value $v(n)_x$ for errors that the platform mechanisms shall detect before providing $v(n)_x$ to i.

R1.3 Error mitigation. Host $n = H(i)_x$ shall provide signal value $v_2(n)_x$ to i when $v_1(n)_x$ is missing (no signal value received in cycle x) and if $v_2(n)$ is redundant to $v_1(n)$ and free of errors. Redundant signals $v_1(n)_x, v_2(n)_x$ from redundant senders $n_1, n_2 \in PN$ reach n in redundant, local variables $v_1(n), v_2(n)$.

R1.4 Sender abstraction. Instance i of application a cannot distinguish redundant signal values $v_1(n)_x$ and $v_2(n)_x$.

3.4   Requirement R2: Fail-Operational Data Processing

R2.1 Safety property: Master host available. Exactly one master host $MH(a)_x$ shall execute application a at platform cycle x.

R2.2 Error detection. Slave host $SH(a)$ shall detect the failed $MH(a)$ within $d > 0$ cycles, that is, in the interval from cycle $x+1$ to cycle $x+d$, when $MH(a)$ fails at platform cycle x.

R2.3 Error recovery. Slave host $SH(a)$ shall become $MH(a)$ within $s > 0$ cycles, that is, in the interval from cycle $x + d' + 1$ to cycle $x + d' + s$, when $SH(a)$ has detected the failed $MH(a)$ after d' cycles, with $d' \leq d$, and if the master-selection strategy selects $SH(a)$.

R2.4 Safety property: Master unavailable. Application a can run without $MH(a)$ for $d + s$ number of cycles, that is, in interval from cycle x to cycle $x + d + s$. Properties of the containing system function F and the situation dependent system environment determine the durations d and s.

R2.5 Host abstraction. Instances of application a cannot distinguish $MH(a)$ from $SH(a)$ at platform cycle x.

4   Target System

4.1   Platform Safety Mechanisms

The car system must stay fail-operational. To operate dependably such systems are realized as distributed, redundant components with replicated communication channels and redundancy control to tolerate all faults. System functions rely on redundancy handling and fault processing mechanisms built into the system platform. These mechanisms factored out into the platform simplify the implementation, integration, and testing of platform applications.

The heart of the example target system is the platform control computer built of several dual nodes (DN in Fig. 1). Single or redundant sensors and actuators in the platform periphery (PN in Fig. 1) connect the system to the system environment. Platform safety mechanisms ($\{ed$ = error detection, eh = error handling, ...$\}$) are instantiated once for each node. They automatically detect and handle value errors and time errors [3] or combinations thereof (Table 1).

Safe steering, for example, relies on the availability, reliability and integrity of the underlying system platform. In case of an inconsistency in the platform control computer, the faulty node immediately backs out so as not to jeopardize steering. For detecting inconsistencies, dual nodes pairwise monitor input data, output data and node states in every cycle (Table 1: f). If the inconsistent dual node is the master host of the central *steering control*, cyclic exchange of platform states and checks within all other dual nodes detect the faulty master host (Table 1: g). Then one of the hot standby slave hosts, still exchanging platform states, takes over the role of the master host (Table 1: j, k). As the steering function must constantly work alongside the redundant steering-wheel sensor,

Table 1. Detecting (ed) and handling (eh) of value (V) and time (T) errors

Platform mechanisms		Examples	V	T
Data plausibility	ed	a. Host checks value range in cycle	+	-
		b. Host checks value delta in subsequent cycles	+	-
Protocol integrity	ed	c. Host checks CRC of frames in cycle	+	+
		d. Host checks frame counters in subsequent cycles	+	+
		e. Host checks frame arrival time	-	+
Node integrity	ed	f. Nodes of dual nodes cyclically compare status	+	+
Platform integrity	ed	g. Dual nodes cyclically compare status	+	+
Vote signals (error mitigation)	eh	h. Host selects one of several redundant signals	+	+
Compensate signal (error mitigation)	eh	i. Host provides safe signal: last valid or default	+	+
Reconfigure platform (error recovery)	eh	j. Dual nodes determine one master host	+	+
		k. Dual nodes isolate faulty nodes	+	+

the platform mechanisms of the platform control computer check steering angles (and signal values in general, Table 1: *a–e*), vote, and select one per cycle to ensure that instances of the central *steering control* application obtain quality signal values in every cycle (Table 1: *h*).

4.2   Non-Intrusive Test Probe Mechanism

For demonstrating system safety in different system configurations of varying degrees of redundancy, the system platform must enable by design the test system to non-intrusively monitor and manipulate signal values, communication packets, system states and data quality indicators. Tests must be able to intervene simultaneously and instantaneously in different nodes. A target system is testable if it permits these interventions without accidentally altering system functionality and timing—neither in lab tests nor in field tests. The following properties of the system platform meet these requirements (Fig. 2):

Time-triggered architecture. Time-triggered systems behave deterministically because systems control events and not vice versa (as in event-triggered systems). Hence schedulers activate instances of platform applications and platform mechanisms in a time-triggered way.

Node data store. Instances of platform applications and platform mechanisms, on each node, communicate via a data store. A node data store captures signal

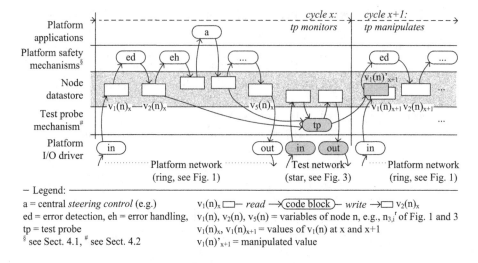

Fig. 2. Data flow in a node with built-in test probe

values, communication packets, node and platform states and quality indicators, for one cycle and for every cycle anew.

Test probe. Each node contains a built-in test probe which is a platform test service. Test probe operations are always scheduled at the very end of every cycle. In this position, a test probe can (1) monitor data accumulated in the data store during the last cycle (in Fig. 2: *cycle x*) and (2) manipulate data for the next cycle (in Fig. 2, *cycle x+1*).

Exclusive test resources. Test probes use exclusive time slots (CPU times), memory areas, and access points to a separate test network. Time, space and bandwidth available to a test probe are set to upper limits, constant across all node cycles. Other mechanisms and applications cannot use resources of a test probe, even when it is deactivated. Otherwise test probes would be intrusive.

5   Safety Tests

Test requirement R1: *Redundant input signals* (Sect. 3.3). The minimalistic system under test consists of three nodes: two sensor nodes determine the position of the steering wheel (in Fig. 1: n_1^r, n_2^b) and provide redundant steering angles to any central node (in Fig. 1: one of $\{n_{3,i}^r, n_{3,j}^r, n_{4,i}^b, n_{4,j}^b\}$) that hosts $(n = H(i))$ any instance (i) of the central *steering control* application $(i \in I(sc)$, enumerated in Sect. 3.2). The test idea is to manipulate the output of a sensor with different values for different time periods so that the central node must assume that the sensor has a temporary or permanent problem. While one sensor fails temporarily or permanently (controlled by different test data vectors), the central *steering control* shall obtain steering angles from the redundant, error-free sensor.

Test 1. Tolerate failing sensor

```
 1: TEST Tolerate failing sensor WHAT 2 redundant sensors WHEN 1 sensor fails WITH
 2:     N1,a, N2,N3, // Control computer node N1, periphery nodes N2,N3 (sensors), application a
 3:     M, vM, vMx, // Node M where value vMx is injected into variable vM
 4:     c, cc, // Injection instant (cycle c) and injection duration (number of cycles cc)
 5:     t // Delta across two succeeding sensor (signal) values
 6: EXPECT Application continuously receives correct signal values
 7: PROVIDED THAT // System predicates checking the applicability of the test to the target
 8:     IsIn(DN, N1) AND IsIn(PN, N2, N3) AND N2 ≠ N3 // Sets DN and PN as def. in Sect. 2
 9:     IsHost(N1, a) // Node N1 executes an instance of application a as def. in Sect. 2
10:     IsIn(V(M), vM) // Set V(M) of the names of all variables of node M as def. in Sect. 2
11:     IsIn({N1, N2, N3}, M) // Via node M faults can be injected into one of N1, N2 or N3
12: CYCLE LENGTH 10 // Specified in milliseconds e.g., 10
13: MAX CYCLES 100 // Obtain definite verdicts within a maximum of 100 cycles
14: SETUP Tolerate failing sensor WITH N1, N2, N3 // Setup of target system (sys. under test)
15: START eNormal == N*State // Start test clock after SETUP when all nodes operate normally
16: INVARIANT // Safety property (R1.1, Sect. 3.3) must hold in each test clock cycle
17:     N1.a.In == N1.a.In@[-1] DELTA t // In each test cycle compare current with former value
18: CYCLE // Test clock cycles
19:     FROM c TO c + cc - 1 DO M.vM = vMx // Inject value vMx into variable vM of node M
20: STOP
```

Test 2. Tolerate failing master host

```
 1: TEST Tolerate failing master WHAT 1 master and 1 slave WHEN Master fails WITH
 2:     N1i, N1j, N2i, N2j, a, // Dual nodes $dn_1$, $dn_2$ executing 4 instances of application a
 3:     vN1, vN1ix, vN1jx, // Inject values v1N1ix and v1N1jx in variables vN1 of N1i and N1j
 4:     c, cc, // Injection instant (cycle c) and injection duration (number of cycles cc)
 5:     d, // Number of cycles for the slave to detect the failed master (SH, MH in Sect. 2)
 6:     s // Number of cycles for switching the master
 7: EXPECT Slave becomes master in time
 8: PROVIDED THAT // System predicates checking the applicability of the test to the target
 9:     IsIn(DN, N1i, N1j, N2i, N2j) // Set DN as def. in Sect. 2
10:     IsDN(N1i, N1j) AND IsDN(N2i, N2j) AND N1i≠N2i // Test for 2 different dual nodes
11:     IsIn(V(N1i),vN1) AND IsIn(V(N1j),vN1) // Sets of variables V(N1i), V(N1j) as in Sect. 2
12:     vN1ix ≠ vN1jx AND d > 0 AND s > 0
13: CYCLE LENGTH 10 // Specified in milliseconds e.g., 10
14: MAX CYCLES 100 // Obtain definite verdicts within a maximum of 100 cycles
15: CONDITIONS // System predicates which can change values during runtime
16:     IsMH(Ni, Nj, A): eMaster == Ni.A.Authority AND eMaster == Nj.A.Authority
17:     IsSH(Ni, Nj, A): eSlave == Ni.A.Authority AND eSlave == Nj.A.Authority
18: SETUP Tolerate failing master WITH // Setup of target system (system under test)
19:     N1i, N1j, Delay1 = 0, // $dn_1$ starts with no delay to become the master
20:     N2i, N2j, Delay2 = 10, // $dn_2$ starts with 10 cycles delay to become the slave
21:     StateExpected = eNormal // Setup finished when all nodes operate normally
22: START IsMH(N1i, N1j) // Start test clock after SETUP, when $dn_1$ is master.
23: INVARIANT // Safety property (R2.1 and R2.4, Sect. 3.4) must hold in each test clock cycle
24:     (IsMH(N1i, N1j, a) XOR IsMH(N2i, N2j, a)) OR IsSH(N1i, N1j, a) OR IsSH(N2i, N2j, a)
25: CYCLE // Test clock cycles
26:     FROM 0 TO c - 1 DO IsMH(N1i, N1j, a) // Master of a is $dn_1$ because of starting earlier
27:     FROM c TO c + cc - 1 DO N1i.vN1 = vN1ix; N1j.vN1 = vN1jx // Break the master
28:     FROM c + d + s DO IsMH(N2i, N2j, a) // Master of a is $dn_2$ after master switch
29: STOP
```

Test 1 checks safety property R1.1 throughout a test run as a test invariant (line 17), also while manipulating a variable of one of the nodes under test for cc cycles (line 19). It is not necessary for the test to simulate the environment because, with RACE, nodes can start and run in a neutral mode processing default values. With the steering wheel in neutral position (default), dependable delivery of steering angles to the central *steering control* can be tested with the following test vector:

N1 = $n^r_{3,i}$, N2 = n^r_1, N3 = n^b_2, M = n^r_1, // Nodes of the target system (Fig. 1)

a = SteeringControl, // Corresponds to a_2 in Fig. 1

vM = Out.SteeringAngle, // Corresponds to $v_5(n)$ in Fig. 2 with n = M = N2

vMx = 0xDEAD, t = 1.0, c = 30, cc = 2 // Irregular steering angles for 2 cycles

To test the reaction on permanent sensor failure, we extend the fault injection period cc from 2 to, say, 1000 cycles. For scoping the fault region differently, e.g., when looking for fault reasons with exploratory tests during system maintenance, the test can intervene in the data flow in the central node by manipulating the signal quality attribute on the side of the signal receiver, with all other test vector arguments unchanged, as follows: M = $n^r_{3,i}$, vM = In.SteeringAngle.Error, vMx = eErrorConfirmed. If these tests pass, then we can say that the central *steering control* application is indifferent to the sender of the steering angle (R1.4), as well as to other tested faults.

Test requirement R2: *Fail-operational data processing* (Sect. 3.4). The minimally realistic system under test is a core platform of two dual nodes: $dn_1 = (n^r_{3,i}, n^r_{3,j})$, $dn_2 = (n^b_{4,i}, n^b_{4,j})$ in Fig. 1. The test idea is to shock the nodes of the master host $(MH(sc))$ of the central *steering control* (sc) application so that $(MH(sc))$ backs out. The slave host $(SH(sc))$ shall become $MH(sc)$ within the required time period, including the time needed for error detection plus the time needed for error recovery (switching from SH to MH).

Test 2 checks safety properties R2.1 and R2.4 (line 24) throughout a test run, also while the test injects (line 27) different values vN1ix and vN1jx in the duplicated variables N1i.vN1 and N1j.vN1 (line 3). The safety mechanisms of both nodes must detect this inconsistency (shock) and switch off the master host. The slave host takes over the master role (line 28) and continues executing the platform application. With the following test vector, Test 2 does not inject a fault into an arbitrary memory cell or I/O buffer. Rather, Test 2 attacks the system under test later in the data flow where the platform's error detection service stores the quality (error) indicator for further processing:

N1i = $n^r_{3,i}$, N1j = $n^r_{3,j}$, N2i = $n^b_{4,i}$, N2j = $n^b_{4,j}$, // Platform control comp. (Fig. 1)

a = SteeringControl, // Corresponds to a_2 in Fig. 1

vN1 = Twin.ErrorIndicator, vN1ix = 7, vN1jx = 0, c = 10, cc = 1, d = 3, s = 2.

6   Plausibility Check and Test Analysis

Safety tests written in ALFHA provide reliable statements on system behavior without probe effects, because: (1) Target systems are designed for testability with lifelong built-in test probes (special modules) and data stores decoupling modules (code blocks), see Sect. 4.2; (2) Accurate and understood tests are written in an appropriate domain-specific language that describes fault-injection tests of testable target systems, see Sect. 5; (3) A test system with a central test controller is decoupled from target systems via test probes and separate test networks, see Sect. 4.2 and sketched in Fig. 3; (4) Traces produced by the test controller enable plausibility checks, e.g., Trace 1 for a *tolerate failing master host* test (Test 2) of the target system RACE in operation, see Fig. 4.

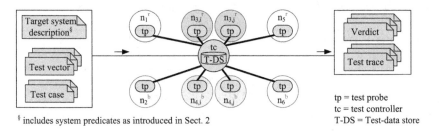

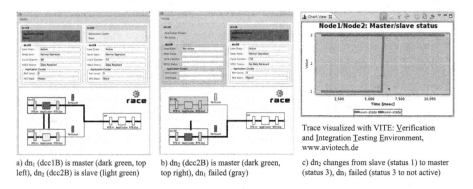

Fig. 3. Test system connected to the target system (Fig. 1) by a separate star network (Color figure online)

a) dn_1 (dcc1B) is master (dark green, top left), dn_2 (dcc2B) is slave (light green)   b) dn_2 (dcc2B) is master (dark green, top right), dn_1 failed (gray)   c) dn_2 changes from slave (status 1) to master (status 3), dn_1 failed (status 3 to not active)

Fig. 4. Demonstration of the *Tolerate failing master host* test (Color figure online)

Once the test system and a testable target system are set up and connected, the focus of plausibility checks moves to analyses of tests and related traces. Test traces document the bindings between test (vector) arguments and parameters of test procedures (Trace 1, lines 1–9) on the basis of structural descriptions of target systems. The test controller uses target system descriptions also for checking whether test cases can be applied to target systems before test runs (e.g., Test 2, lines 9–11). In Trace 1 the test controller documents that in platform cycle 298 test probes of $n_{3,i}^r$ and $n_{3,j}^r$ are instructed to manipulate variables C ($n_{3,i}^r.Twin.ErrorIndicator$) and G ($n_{3,j}^r.Twin.ErrorIndicator$) in platform cycle 308. Trace 1 filtered (1) for values that test probes send to the test controller (gray lines, platform cycles 299, 300, ..., 309, ..., 398) and (2) for values of variables that indicate the role of a dual node (green boxes, variables D and H for dual node dn_1, L and P for dual node dn_2, MH = 3, SH = 1) shows that the target system (platform control computer in Fig. 1) satisfies requirement R2 (Sect. 3.4) for this test run. Snapshots of a RACE-specific trace visualizer (Fig. 4) for another *tolerate failing master host* test of a RACE system can be mapped to Trace 1 as follows: snapshot (a) corresponds to, e.g., platform cycle 308 (test cycle 9) and snapshot (b) corresponds to, e.g., platform cycle 398.

Test Trace 1 Trace of a *Tolerate failing master host* test

```
 1: T-DS 1.1 :A: n^r_{3,i}.Cycle                       # N1i = n^r_{3,i}, Node cycle in scope by default
 2: T-DS 1.8 :B: n^r_{3,i}.State                       # N1i = n^r_{3,i}, Node state in scope by default
 3: T-DS 1.23:C: n^r_{3,i}.Twin.ErrorIndicator         # N1i = n^r_{3,i}, vN1 = Twin.ErrorIndicator
 4: T-DS 1.44:D: n^r_{3,i}.SteeringControl.Authority   # N1i = n^r_{3,i}, a = SteeringControl
 5: ...
 6: T-DS 2.23:G: n^r_{3,j}.Twin.ErrorIndicator         # N1j = n^r_{3,j}, vN1 = Twin.ErrorIndicator
 7: ...
 8: T-DS 3.44:L: n^b_{4,i}.SteeringControl.Authority   # N2i = n^b_{4,i}, a = SteeringControl
 9: ...
10:          #:  A:B:C:D:  E:F:G:H:  I:J:K:L:  M:N:O:P:
11:          #===========================================
12: ...
13: CYCLE:298:  :>:   : :7: :   : :0: :   : : : :   : : : : @9=1 // Controller tc in Fig. 3
14:      instructs n^r_{3,i}, n^r_{3,j} to manipulate C, G in test cycle 9 for 1 cycle (see line 24 below)
15: CYCLE:299: 0:<:299:3:0:3:299:3:0:3:289:3:0:1:289:3:0:1: // Monitor A, B, ..., P
16: CYCLE:299: 0:w:   : : :3:   : : :3:   : : :1:   : : :1: %24 // Invariant holds, line 24
17: CYCLE:299: 0:v:   : : :3:   : : :3:   : : : :   : : : : %26 // IsMH passes, line 26
18: CYCLE:300: 1:<:300:3:0:3:300:3:0:3:290:3:0:1:290:3:0:1: // Monitor A, B, ..., P
19: CYCLE:300: 1:w:   : : :3:   : : :3:   : : :1:   : : :1: %24 // Invariant holds, line 24
20: ...
21: CYCLE:308: 9:<:308:3:0:3:308:3:0:3:298:3:0:1:298:3:0:1: // Monitor A, B, ..., P
22: CYCLE:308: 9:w:   : : :3:   : : :3:   : : :1:   : : :1: %24 // Invariant holds, line 24
23: CYCLE:308: 9:v:   : : :3:   : : :3:   : : : :   : : : : %26 // IsMH passes, line 26
24: CYCLE:308: 9:c:   : :7: :   : :0: :   : : : :   : : : : %27 // tp manipulate C and G
25: CYCLE:309:10:<:   : : : :   : : : :   : : :299:3:0:1:299:3:0:1: // Monitor I, J, ..., P
26: CYCLE:309:10:w:   : : : :   : : : :   : : :1:   : : :1: %24 // Invariant holds, line 24
27: ...
28: CYCLE:398:99:<:   : : : :   : : : :   : : :388:3:0:3:388:3:0:3: // Monitor I, J, ..., P
29: CYCLE:398:99:w:   : : : :   : : : :   : : :3:   : : :3: %24 // Invariant holds, line 24
30: CYCLE:398:99:v:   : : : :   : : : :   : : :3:   : : :3: %28 // IsMH passes, line 28
31: VERD 0       #=========================================== // Test passes (0: no errors)
```

7 Summary

The tests presented in this paper demonstrated a method of proving safety-related statements about a fault-tolerant system, like "a steer-by-wire car remains steerable when one computer of the central platform computer fails." More fault-injection tests for the same target at different points of attack (e.g., nodes and variables) and in different situations (e.g., degradation modes and load levels) are necessary to increase the confidence in and precision of such statements. Test probes permanently built into all nodes of a fault-tolerant, cyber-physical system that executes time-controlled behavior provide the necessary testability.

References

1. Ayestaran, I., et al.: Modeling and simulated fault injection for time-triggered safety-critical embedded systems. In: 2014 IEEE 17th International Symposium on Object/Component/Service-Oriented Real-Time Distributed Computing (ISORC), pp. 180–187, June 2014
2. Becker, K., et al.: RACE RTE: a runtime environment for robust fault-tolerant vehicle functions. In: 11th European Dependable Computing Conference on CARS Workshop - Dependability in Practice. IEEE, September 2015
3. Bondavalli, A., Simoncini, L.: Failure classification with respect to detection. In: Proceedings of 2nd IEEE Workshop on Future Trends of Distributed Computing Systems, 1990, pp. 47–53, September 1990
4. Büchel, M., et al.: An automated electric vehicle prototype showing new trends in automotive architectures. In: International Conference on Intelligent Transportation Systems (ITSC 2015). IEEE, September 2015
5. Frtunikj, J., et al.: Qualitative evaluation of fault hypotheses with non-intrusive fault injection. In: 5th International Workshop on Software Certification (WoSoCer 2015). IEEE, November 2015
6. Kane, A., Fuhrman, T., Koopman, P.: Monitor based oracles for cyber-physical system testing : practical experience report. In: 44th IEEE/IFIP International Conference on Dependable Systems and Networks (DSN), pp. 148–155, June 2014
7. Kopetz, H.: Real-Time Systems: Design Principles for Distributed Embedded Applications. Springer, New York (2011)
8. Sommer, S., et al.: RACE: a centralized platform computer based architecture for automotive applications. In: Vehicular Electronics Conference and the International Electric Vehicle Conference (VEC/IEVC). IEEE, October 2013
9. Svenningsson, R., Vinter, J., Eriksson, H., Törngren, M.: MODIFI: a MODel-implemented fault injection tool. In: Schoitsch, E. (ed.) SAFECOMP 2010. LNCS, vol. 6351, pp. 210–222. Springer, Heidelberg (2010)

Quantitative Reliability Assessment for Mobile Cooperative Systems

Francesca Saglietti[✉], Ralf Spengler, and Matthias Meitner

Software Engineering (Informatik 11), University of Erlangen-Nuremberg,
Martensstr. 3, 91058 Erlangen, Germany
{francesca.saglietti,matthias.meitner}@fau.de,
ra.spengler@web.de

Abstract. This article proposes a systematic approach to statistical testing for cooperative systems consisting of autonomous mobile agents. Based on Coloured Petri Net models of cooperative behaviour, it analyses different sources of randomness and defines an automatic test case generation procedure to derive cooperative scenarios according to a given operational profile. As an example, the approach is applied to a model of trolleys moving within a common environment. The results allow for quantitative reliability estimations of cooperative behaviour on the basis of statistical sampling theory.

Keywords: Reliability · Robots · Autonomous agents · Cooperation · CPN modelling · Statistical testing · Operational profile

1 Introduction

For reasons of flexibility and cost efficiency there is an increasing tendency towards the operation of autonomous systems in a common environment, thus yielding complex systems-of-systems. These differ in an essential way from classical component-based systems, in that components are newly developed or re-used within a development project in order to serve a common purpose, i.e. the service(s) to be provided by the system they compose; on the other hand, the integration of independently developed and autonomously working agents into a new system-of-systems additionally requires sophisticated a posteriori checks about the fulfilment of complex co-existence and cooperation rules.

The benefits offered at this higher level of interaction evidently concern both economy and performance; in fact, this novel development and operation paradigm allows to re-use pre-developed applications, at the same time aiming at enriching their behaviour by additional functionality "emerging" from their interplay.

Intended emergent behaviour usually concerns the provision of complex services requiring the cooperative performance, or at least the safe co-existence of different services in a common operational environment. Typical examples concern robotic applications or car-to-car communication, where mobile agents perform individual tasks as autonomously as possible, but can contribute to increase safe co-existence and performance by easing individual decision-making through provision of diverse feedback information, enabling agents to temporarily delegate decision-making or actions to other agents provided with more appropriate sensing, perception or action capabilities,

© Springer International Publishing Switzerland 2016
A. Skavhaug et al. (Eds.): SAFECOMP 2016 Workshops, LNCS 9923, pp. 118–129, 2016.
DOI: 10.1007/978-3-319-45480-1_10

achieving a complex task by cooperative use of complementary individual capabilities, supporting the safe parallelization of individual, heterogeneous operations within a common environment.

Obviously, all benefits mentioned involve an increase in functional complexity due to the resulting combinatorial behavioural multiplicity; if not appropriately analysed, such complexity may induce unintended emergent behaviour, i.e. unpredicted inacceptable behaviour resulting from the inappropriate interplay of autonomous systems. Therefore, a thorough reliability analysis is of utmost importance; as usual, it must rely on two successive assessment phases: a preliminary *qualitative* verification and validation phase devoted to maximising the chances of fault detection by means of systematic testing techniques, followed by a successive *quantitative* verification and validation phase devoted to the probabilistic assessment of correct performance under expected operational conditions.

While the former issue built the focus of past research effort, e.g. within the ARTEMIS project R3-COP, the latter one still poses a serious challenge to the robotic community and is being currently investigated in the ongoing successor project R5-COP. The present article aims at illustrating some of the preliminary results meanwhile achieved. It is structured as follows: after these introductory remarks, the benefits of Coloured Petri Nets (CPN) in offering the required expressiveness and scalability are shortly recollected and illustrated by an example addressing the cooperative behaviour of linen-carrying trolleys within a hospital environment (Sect. 2). Successively, Sect. 3 addresses in more detail the difference between qualitative and quantitative reliability analysis and summarise the progress already achieved with respect to the first target, while stressing the challenge still posed by the second one. The following Sect. 4 proposes a systematic procedure to analyse the operational variability of a cooperative mobile application for the purpose of generating independent, operationally representative test data on which to base statistical testing. The procedure is subsequently instantiated in terms of the example previously introduced. The results obtained are presented in Sect. 5. They include the derivation of quantitative results as well as some conclusions on benefits and limitations of the technique developed.

2   Modelling Cooperative Behaviour

2.1   Coloured Petri Nets

Especially for applications with ultrahigh reliability requirements as in case of safety demands, the challenge posed by the task of verifying and validating the logic of systems-of-systems is even higher than is already the case for ordinary centralised automatic control software. In fact, an accurate reliability analysis of mobile agents must address, in addition to classical reliability considerations concerning the autonomous behaviour of each individual agent in a stand-alone operational mode, the combination of several further aspects like the usage profile of the whole system-of-systems, the potential modes of interplay between agents (such as communication, physical cooperation or collision avoidance), the potential impact of environmental anomalies on individual and cooperative system performance. The coincidental consideration of so diverse information evidently requires appropriate formal modelling techniques allowing to address the underlying behavioural multiplicity at an adequate abstraction level. CPN reveals as a particularly suitable modelling formalism; after a short recollection of its highlights and benefits, its application to cooperative mobile agents will be demonstrated in the light of an example inspired by a hospital logistic system based on linen-transporting trolleys.

The modelling formalism offered by *Coloured Petri Nets* (CPN, [1]) revealed as particularly suitable to achieve this task. Like for classical Petri Nets, the operational semantic of the model is defined by allowing actions to take place via the "firing" of corresponding CPN transitions. Such a transition firing takes place under given pre-conditions captured by

- *expressions* annotating the ingoing arcs of the CPN transition to be evaluated in the light of the data-specific tokens present in the corresponding input places; a legal assignment of expression variables with available tokens is denoted as an enabling variable binding;
- additional arc-unspecific predicates annotating the transition considered (so-called *transition invariants*) and required to be fulfilled.

After firing a transition, the effect of the corresponding action is captured by a new marking (*CPN state*) resulting from the previous one by

- *removing* from each input place of the CPN transition tokens in type and number as indicated by the input arc expression w.r.t. the enabling variable binding;
- *adding* to each output place of the CPN transition tokens in type and number as indicated by the output arc expression w.r.t. the same variable binding.

For further details concerning CPN syntax and semantics the reader is kindly referred to [1]. A major benefit of CPN is the fact that it easily allows to separate

- *static information* on the net structure (places and transitions as well as directed arcs connecting a place with a transition or vice versa) which can be taken to represent all application-specific, invariant information like actions enabled by robot capabilities within a pre-defined plant topology, and
- *dynamic information* on data-specific tokens (marking the CPN places) which can be taken to represent all relevant, time-dependent information concerning current tasks, agent states and temporary environmental conditions.

This neat separation between static and dynamic information by different graphical entities adds to the scalability of the CPN language, as it allows an arbitrary increase in number of cooperating agents without need to adapt the underlying net structure. Moreover, it supports also the enrichment of regular behaviour by capturing additional reconfiguration techniques via appropriate composition of generic actions.

2.2 Example

The benefits and potential of CPN for the purpose of capturing and verifying complex cooperative behaviour are illustrated by means of the following example inspired by a hospital application based on autonomously moving, linen-carrying trolleys.

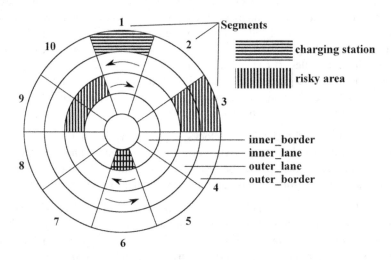

Fig. 1. Plant topology with charging stations and hazardous areas

As sketched in Fig. 1, the working environment traversed by the trolleys is assumed to consist of 4 concentric rings, each partitioned into 10 numbered segments, resulting on the whole in 40 pairwise disjoint areas with the following properties:

- segments consist of *inner borders*, *inner lanes*, *outer lanes* and *outer borders*;
- for safety reasons, each area must be traversed by at most one trolley at any time;
- a subset of inner and outer borders provide working or parking facilities;
- a subset of inner and outer borders provide energy charging facilities;
- ease of moving or working may vary from segment to segment;
- inner lanes are to be traversed in *clockwise*, outer lanes in *anti-clockwise* direction.

The operator-defined missions to be assigned to the trolleys are characterised by

- a segment number to be targeted by the entrusted trolley;
- a subset of capabilities from {*move, lift, tow*}, where *move* is always required;
- the present mission status revealing the progress achieved so far, i.e. *available*, *assigned*, *completed* or *degraded* (i.e. only partially achieved).

Available missions are assigned to idle trolleys fulfilling corresponding functional requirements. As soon as it is assigned a new mission, the entrusted trolley approaches as far as possible its target by moving in the direction requiring to traverse the shortest distance, and proceeding as far as possible on free areas and with its energy resources. When reaching its target, the trolley accesses the adjacent border, if free. In case a passive obstacle or a parking trolley occupy the target border, it moves to the next free border area on its way; finally, if the target border is momentarily occupied by a trolley intending to leave, it switches its position with this trolley.

Before being assigned a new mission, trolleys recharge their battery. The following reconfiguration strategies help increase flexibility and efficiency:

- as soon as it perceives an obstacle (including a defect trolley) on its way, a trolley informs the operator and changes its direction by moving to the alternative lane;
- as soon as its energy level falls below a predefined threshold, the trolley accesses the closest free charging station on its way, recharges its battery and resumes its original mission, unless it can reach its target before the charging station;
- trolleys moving in consecutive areas build a common platoon led by the front trolley in a queue-like way [2]; platoons are split as soon as a member needs to branch off to reach its target border or to recharge.

In order to reduce the risk of deadlocks, it is assumed that the plant operator manually initiates a shutdown if at least 2 obstacles were sensed and reported.

The CPN modelling the application described above allows to store the temporary information concerning trolleys, missions and environment in 4 CPN places:

- 'Mission Pool' stores information on current missions still available or ongoing;
- 'Finished Missions' stores information on missions totally or partially concluded;
- 'Robot Platoons' stores information about trolleys including moving formations;
- 'Areas' stores information about variable environmental properties.

The behavioural model is based on 11 CPN transitions representing corresponding atomic actions, where the following 5 CPN transitions relate to regular behaviour not requiring any conflict resolution:

- 'Assign Mission' represents the entrustment of idle trolleys with new missions;
- 'Move Forward' represents the stepping forward of a single trolley or of a whole trolley formation by one segment length either on the inner or on the outer lane;
- 'Move To Border' represents the movement from lane areas to adjacent border areas;
- 'Finish Mission' represents the successful conclusion of a mission;
- 'Charge' represents a trolley recharging its battery.

On the other hand, the following CPN transitions help avoid occupied areas preventing trolleys from proceeding:

- 'Change Lane' represents the movement of an individual trolley or of a trolley platoon towards the adjacent area on the alternative lane;
- 'Switch Border Lane' represents the switch of position between a trolley on a lane area encountering a trolley on an adjacent border area;
- 'Switch Lane' represents the position switching of facing trolleys on adjacent lanes;
- 'Find Alternative Finish Area' represents the movement to an alternative target border.

Finally, the following 2 transitions model the building and splitting of formations:

- *'Join Platoon'* represents the autonomous partial and temporary release of decisional autonomy of a trolley determining to follow another trolley;
- *'Leave Platoon'* represents the restoring of the full decisional autonomy of a platoon member leaving a platoon formation.

In view of the variety of data types and of the control logic complexity involved, a complete and legible CPN representation illustrating all transitions guards and arc expressions is beyond the spatial scope of this article. For this reason, the representation shown in Fig. 2 is limited to the underlying net structure.

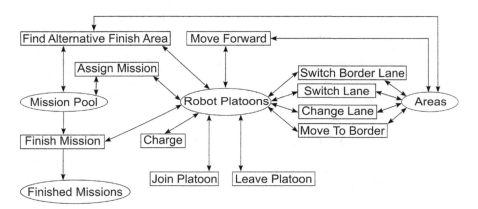

Fig. 2. Net structure of CPN model (rectangles denote CPN transitions, ellipses denote CPN places)

3   Model-Based Reliability Analysis

Qualitative Reliability Analysis. A preliminary approach consists of validating the robot behaviour w.r.t. test scenarios covering as accurately as possible the functionality encoded in the CPN. Based on different CPN entities, several objectively reproducible coverage measures have been considered, e.g. [3, 4]. While [4] focuses on generic actions or system snapshots by use of CPN transitions, transition pairs and states, [3] allows for different levels of behavioural expressiveness by use of CPN transitions, events and state pairs.

Corresponding test case generation tools based on analytical search algorithms or heuristic multi-objective optimization techniques were successively developed [3]. Conclusions on system reliability as perceived during structural testing can be merely of qualitative nature, as test case selection exclusively depends on the CPN net structure and marking and does not refer in any way to the expected, planned or experienced usage. Moreover, most CPN coverage criteria depend on the initial marking; CPN events and state pairs, for example, are defined w.r.t. given initial conditions which are likely to vary throughout plant operation. Therefore, though beneficial as a preliminary, fault detection approach, structural testing is not considered as appropriate for the purpose of determining meaningful reliability estimations at predefined confidence levels.

Quantitative Reliability Analysis. By definition, reliability denotes the probability of survival of an agent in a given time interval under given operational conditions. The latter refer to any variable aspect potentially exerting influence on system performance. In case of centralised applications, the major variability factor typically concerns the user-specific demand profile reflecting both the relative frequency of functional demands and the distribution of data per functional demand. An estimation of the expected operational profile can be used for the purposes of

- *generating* a data-independent sample of operationally representative test cases executing independently (i.e. by memoryless sequencing), or
- *extracting* from operational experience such a data-independent sample of operationally representative runs executing independently [5].

In both cases, the resulting sample can be analysed in the light of statistical sampling theory to derive sound reliability figures [6]. More precisely, in case of an event occurring a number k of times within a sample of size n, its probability p can be bound at a given confidence level α by

$$p_\alpha(0) = 1 - \sqrt[n]{1 - \alpha} \qquad \text{if } k = 0 \qquad (1)$$

$$p_\alpha(k) = \frac{(k+1) \cdot F_{2(k+1),2(n-k)}(\alpha)}{n - k + (k+1) \cdot F_{2(k+1),2(n-k)}(\alpha)} \qquad \text{otherwise} \qquad (2)$$

While the estimation of the operational profile already poses serious problems in case of centralised automatic controllers, this challenge becomes even harder in case of parallel multi-tasking operation where several agents are assigned individual missions in a fully asynchronous way; in addition, agents may influence each other in terms of decision-making and action and must react to anomalous internal or environmental conditions by counteractions. In such cases the nature of randomness governing the operational profiles is not simply restricted to the intended user's demands, but must be rather extended to include unintended random effects like hazardous environmental conditions, premature consumption of resources and conflicting decision-making among agents. An extensive, systematic analysis of random sources is proposed within the scope of the next chapter.

4   Model-Based Instantiation of Operational Profile

4.1   Systematic Analysis and Generation of Random Events

In analogy to the definition of the CPN model it is suggested to structure a preliminary analysis of the operational profile on the basis of the triple (users' demands, agents, environment) [7], distinguishing for each of the 3 elements between permanent information and variable information:

- *users' demands* consist of a time-varying number of individual demands, where some demands already exist upon operation start, while others follow and each demand includes a permanent part (the functionalities to be provided and the location(s) to be accessed) and a variable part (its current progress status);
- the *set of agents* consists of a fixed number of units, each characterised by its identification number and variable information on the availability of its resources;
- the *environment* consists of a fixed number of areas characterised by permanent information (identification number, facilities hosted, risk), as well as of variable information on accessibility.

Therefore, the randomness governing operation must be simulated by two-fold random generation: first, an initial marking is generated according to a preliminary estimation of the users' needs. Successively, intermediate markings are repeatedly manipulated to represent the arising of new missions or the accidental occurrence of functional failures and/or of passive obstacles according to predefined probabilistic distributions. To do so, inherent dependencies between the occurrences of such anomalies must be analysed beforehand. Moreover, in order to be able to apply formulae (1) resp. (2) relying on statistical sampling theory, it must be taken care that test case definition supports the independence of test case executions, preferably without enforcing an external resetting intervention. Both aspects will be considered in the next section.

4.2   Example

Test data generation must rely on predefined data types underlying the token marking.

Areas. At any time, an area is represented as a 5-tuple consisting of: segment number (integer between 1 and 10); area type (inner border/inner lane/outer lane/outer border); occupation status (free/active robot/passive robot/further obstacle); danger (normal/risky); availability of charging station (Boolean).

Robots. At any time, a robot is represented as a 7-tuple consisting of: unique identifier (integer between 1 and 5); segment number (integer between 1 and 10); area type (inner border/inner lane/outer lane/outer border); target segment (integer between 1 and 10); rotation movement (clockwise/anti-clockwise); functional capabilities offered (Boolean triple for moving, lifting and towing capabilities); energy level (integer between 0 and 60).

Missions. At any time, a mission is represented as a quadruple consisting of: target segment (integer between 1 and 10); functional demands (Boolean triple for moving, lifting and towing capabilities); status (available/assigned/completed/degraded); robot entrusted (integer between 1 and 5 or −1 if status available).

In addition to the basic properties introduced in Sect. 2, operation was assumed to rely on the functional capabilities provided by the 5 robots as shown in Table 2 and on risk levels and availability of charging facilities per area as shown in Table 3.

Moreover, forward movement by one segment was assumed to require 3 energy units in case of autonomous stand-alone or formation front trolleys, while trolleys passively following a front robot were assumed to consume only 2 energy units for the same movement thanks to the simpler sensing and recognition tasks involved.

Dependencies. Before starting with the random generation of scenarios, it is important to identify stochastic correlations restricting test data selection as the following ones:

- between mission targets and areas: the probability of a segment being a target is likely to depend a. o. on its being suitable for loading tasks (see Table 4);
- between mission functions and areas: given functionalities (except for moving) are more likely to be required in certain locations than in others (see Table 5);
- between initial robot positions and areas: as long as robots can successfully carry out their missions, they will end on an inner or an outer border, where they will start their next mission (see Table 6);
- between functional failures and areas: the failure probability of robot functions is likely to depend on the risk level of its sojourn area (see Table 7).

Based on these inherent dependencies, test case generation must take into account both intended and unintended random sources. Intended demands are initially simulated by uniform random generation of 3 to 7 missions. During execution, new available missions were randomly added to the mission pool such that after each transition firing at most one new mission was generated and that the number of transitions firing between successive mission generations was assumed to be binomially distributed with parameters n = 30 and p = 0.3.

Unplanned behaviour includes random physical failures of robots (where aging and wear-out effects were outside the scope of the article) as well as the occurrences of external obstacles. Both are simulated by random manipulation of initial and intermediate marking(s). For any robot, random physical failures are independently injected before any transition firing by changing its corresponding functional capability parameter at a probability determined by the risk level associated with its momentary sojourn area (see Table 7). On the other hand, the sudden occurrence of a passive obstacle in a free area can be simulated before any transition firing by changing its occupation parameter at probability 0.005 %.

This random mission generation procedure is interrupted as soon as one of the following stopping criteria is fulfilled:

- every intact robot has successfully achieved at least one mission;
- every intact robot has been assigned a mission but cannot proceed due to deadlock;
- 2 or more obstacles are present in different areas (leads to operation shutdown).

After every test case execution, any functional incapability and any obstacle are assumed to be removed. By further requiring that after mission completion the successful robots fully recharge their batteries, the independent execution of successive test cases can be ensured, thus enabling the application of statistical sampling theory.

5   Results

The test case generation procedure introduced in Sect. 4 was implemented with the help of CPN Tools [8] to derive an independent sample of 4606 test cases. These test cases were subsequently evaluated in terms of model-based reliability and availability estimates by distinguishing between the following cases:

- whether the presence of at least 2 obstacles would have resulted in a human intervention (case denoted as *shutdown*);
- whether 1 or more intact robots could be prevented from moving further by 1 obstacle or any other intact robots (case denoted as *livelock*);
- whether all robots could continue operating in the absence of obstacles and even in the presence of at most 1 obstacle (case denoted as *OK*).

The results are shown in Table 1, where the 54 livelocks identified could be further partitioned into 2 disjoint classes:

Table 1. Results ('n.a.', denoting 'not applicable', refers to impossible combinations of events)

# obstacles		# test cases				
		Shutdown	Livelocks			OK
			Type 1	Type 2	Types 1 and 2	
0		0	n. a.	10	n. a.	3975
1	1 failed robot	0	7	0	0	28
	1 passive object		35	2	0	453
	Partial sum		42	2	0	481
≥ 2		96	n. a.	n. a.	n. a.	n. a.
Sum		96	54			4456

- *type 1-livelocks* denote the case where 1 intact trolley is prevented from leaving a border area by an obstacle on the adjacent lane area;
- *type 2-livelocks* denote the case where 4 robots on 4 adjacent lane areas prevent each other from carrying out a circular manoeuvre.

The application of sampling theory (see Sect. 3) to this independent sample yields the following estimations at a confidence level of 95 %:

$$p_{0.95}(shutdown) = \frac{(96+1) \cdot F_{2(96+1),2(4606-96)}(0.95)}{4606 - 96 + (96+1) \cdot F_{2(96+1),2(4606-96)}(0.95)} \approx 0.0246$$

Similarly, the livelock probability can be bounded by $p_{0.95}(livelock) \approx 0.0147$.

On the other hand, unreliable behaviour due to shutdown or livelock conditions was observed in 150 test cases, its probability being bounded by $p_{0.95}(shutdown\_or\_livelock) \approx 0.0372$.

In particular, this means that – assuming model accuracy and faithful implementation – the probability of reliable operation (in spite of sporadic obstacles) would amount to ca. 0.9628 at the same confidence level. Obviously, accurate reliability estimations can only be achieved by running the test sample in a real environment. When this may require a prohibitive effort, it may be considered to restrict field testing to the most critical scenarios identified as well as to filter operational data in order to obtain operational independent samples of operating experience [5].

6   Conclusion

This article proposed a systematic approach to statistical testing for cooperative systems consisting of autonomous mobile agents. Based on Coloured Petri Net models of cooperative behaviour, it analysed different sources of randomness and defined an automatic test case generation procedure to derive independent cooperative scenarios according to a given operational profile.

As an example, the approach was applied to a model of 5 trolleys moving within a hospital environment. The evaluation of the resulting sample allowed for both qualitative insight in terms of types of anomalous scenarios and quantitative insight in terms of conservative reliability estimations based on statistical sampling theory.

To overcome the main limitations of the approach presented, namely its dependence on model accuracy and its requiring considerable testing effort, it is suggested to make use of operating experience such as to extract significant independent samples by appropriate filtering of operational data.

Acknowledgment. The authors gratefully acknowledge that part of the work presented was carried out within the European Research Programme ARTEMIS (Advanced Research and Technology for Embedded Intelligence and Systems), project R5-COP (Reconfigurable ROS-based Resilient Reasoning Robotic Co-operating Systems), supported by the German Federal Ministry of Education and Research (BMBF).

Appendix

See Tables 2, 3, 4, 5, 6 and 7.

Table 2. Initial function availability of robots (-: function unavailable, X: function available)

Trolley ID	Move	Lift	Tow
1	X	X	-
2	X	X	-
3	X	-	X
4	X	-	X
5	X	X	X

Table 3. Risk level and charging facility per area (-: normal, X: risky, N: no charge, Y: charge)

Segment no./type	1	2	3	4	5	6	7	8	9	10
Inner border	-, N	-, N	-, N	-, N	-, N	X, Y	-, N	-, N	-, N	-, N
Inner lane	-, N	-, N	-, N	-, N	-, N	-, N	-, N	-, N	X, N	X, N
Outer lane	-, N	-, N	X, N	-, N	-, N	-, N	-, N	-, N	-, N	-, N
Outer border	-, Y	-, N	X, N	-, N	-, N	-, N	-, N	-, N	-, N	-, N

Table 4. Probability of areas being mission targets

Segment number	1	2	3	4	5	6	7	8	9	10
Probability	0	1/6	1/6	1/12	1/12	0	1/6	1/6	1/12	1/12

Table 5. Probability of areas being mission targets with given functional demands

Segment no.	1	2	3	4	5	6	7	8	9	10
Only move	-	0.1	0.1	0.1	0.1	-	0.1	0.1	0.1	0.1
Move and lift	-	0.5	0.5	0.3	0.3	-	0.3	0.3	0.1	0.1
Move and tow	-	0.3	0.3	0.2	0.2	-	0.5	0.5	0.6	0.6
Move, lift and tow	-	0.1	0.1	0.4	0.4	-	0.1	0.1	0.2	0.2

Table 6. Probability of segment types being robot starting positions

Inner border	Inner lane	Outer lane	Outer border
0.5	0	0	0.5

Table 7. Failure probability of robot functions in normal and risky areas

Area function	Move	Lift	Tow
Normal	0.01 %	0.1 %	0.1 %
Risky	1.00 %	0.1 %	0.1 %

References

1. Jensen, K., Kristensen, L.M.: Coloured Petri Nets. Springer, Heidelberg (2009)
2. Bergenhem, C., Shladover, S., Coelingh, E.: Overview of Platooning Systems. In: Proceedings of the 19th World Congress on Intelligent Transportation Systems (ITS) (2012)
3. Saglietti, F., Föhrweiser, D., Winzinger, S., Lill, R.: Model-based design and testing of decisional autonomy and cooperation in cyber-physical systems. In: Proceedings of the International Conference on Software Engineering and Advanced Applications. IEEE Xplore Digital Library (2015)
4. Cai, Z., Zhang, J., Liu, Z.: Generating test cases using colored petri net. In: Proceedings of the 2nd International Symposium on Information Engineering and Electronic Commerce. IEEE Xplore Digital Library (2010)
5. Söhnlein, S., Saglietti, F., Bitzer, F., Meitner, M., Baryschew, S.: Software reliability assessment based on the evaluation of operational experience. In: Müller-Clostermann, B., Echtle, K., Rathgeb, E.P. (eds.) MMB & DFT 2010. LNCS, vol. 5987, pp. 24–38. Springer, Heidelberg (2010)
6. Störmer, H.: Mathematische Theorie der Zuverlässigkeit. Oldenbourg, Munich (1983)
7. Nehmzow, U.: Scientific Methods in Mobile Robotics. Springer, Heidelberg (2006)
8. CPNTools and Access/CPN by AIS Group, Eindhoven University of Technology and CPN Group, Aarhus University

An Approach for Systematic In-the-Loop Simulations for Development and Test of a Complex Mechatronic Embedded System

Amir Soltani Nezhad[(✉)], Johan J. Lukkien, Rudolf H. Mak,
Richard Verhoeven, and Martijn M.H.P. van den Heuvel

Mathematics and Computer Science Department,
Eindhoven University of Technology (TU/e), P.O. Box 513,
5600 MB Eindhoven, The Netherlands
{a.soltaninezhad,j.j.lukkien,R.H.Mak,P.H.F.M.Verhoeven,
m.m.h.p.v.d.heuvel}@tue.nl

Abstract. Simulations are widely used in the engineering workflow of complex mechatronic embedded systems in various domains, such as healthcare, railway, automotive and aerospace, for analyzing, testing and validating purposes. This paper focuses on the development and test of the control software of complex mechatronic embedded systems from the perspective of software interfaces (e.g., driver APIs) and presents a systematic approach for testing the control software during the various stages of an engineering process. Since we assume that the physical (hardware) components of an under-control plant could be replaced with simulation models, various kinds of in-the-loop simulations, ranging from MiL to HiL, can be consequently acquired. Additionally, we present a mathematical model of MESes required to formally describe the approach and also a healthcare case study to which our approach was applied.

Keywords: Development of mechatronic embedded systems · In-the-Loop simulations · Software-in-the-Loop (SiL) · Hardware-in-the-Loop (HiL) · Driver APIs

1 Introduction

A Mechatronic Embedded System (MES) typically consists of complex combinations of hardware and software components. Such a system is often software-intensive, and therefore the development and test or evolution of its control software is largely costly (time and money) over the development process. Due to this software complexity, manufactures and OEMs are interested in techniques and tools to shorten the development, verification and validation engineering workflow (typically V model-based), while maintaining or even improving the quality of the control software and in turn the entire product.

For instance, in recent years, simulations have been widely used during the development and test of MESes, especially for the control unit, in different domains, such as healthcare, railway [5], automotive [7], and aerospace.

© Springer International Publishing Switzerland 2016
A. Skavhaug et al. (Eds.): SAFECOMP 2016 Workshops, LNCS 9923, pp. 130–143, 2016.
DOI: 10.1007/978-3-319-45480-1_11

The key reason is to discover faults and inconsistencies with design in advance without postponing tests until the availability of implemented control software or of hardware components of the plant, which might be under parallel development. It can also be used for comparing different alternatives prior to taking a critical design decision. In complex embedded systems, there are well-know simulation techniques in which a control unit can be tested against its under-control plant, while different abstraction levels of the control and the components of the plant could participate in the simulations. Some examples of these techniques include Model-in-the-Loop (MiL), Software-in-the-Loop (SiL), Processor-in-the-Loop (PiL) and Hardware-in-the-Loop (HiL) simulations, which differ from each other based on the level of abstraction.

For instance, MiL is a technique, with the highest abstraction, in which there is no target hardware involved in the system and only simulation models are integrated for testing and validating purposes. On the other hand, HiL, among other definitions, is a simulation technique, with the lowest abstraction, in which a target control unit is tested while connected to an under-control, fully-simulated plant.

Deploying in-the-loop simulations, especially HiL, to accelerate the development and test of embedded systems in various domains and applications has been widely investigated [1–4]. However, these works mostly focus on in-the-loop simulations to validate different control algorithms in various domains, such as power electronic systems and mechanics.

In this paper, however, we are interested in looking at the problem of the development and test of the control software of a MES from the higher-level perspective of driver APIs of the plant. Through these APIs, a MES's control software controls the plant, typically via other sub-control systems. We consider these sub-control systems as part of the MES's plant. The in-the-loop simulation works in the literature mainly focus on validating these sub-control systems unlike this work that concentrates on the higher-level control software of a MES. To clarify more the research question, assuming that the under-development control software is going to be tested against the plant, given the driver APIs of the plant components, such as motors and sensors, we investigate a systematic way for testing such control software and its interaction with the plant through the APIs. It is essential to note that not all the components of the plant must be physically available. This means that we can arbitrarily replace any number of physical components with their simulated counterparts.

By solving this problem, we can consequently provide the engineers of a MES's control software with a mechanism by which various in-the-loop simulations in different abstractions could be realized.

Furthermore, observing the increasingly widespread adoption of the Model Based System Engineering (MBSE) paradigm, our solution could benefit from MBSE for the development of MESes. Because, since MBSE operates based on models throughout an entire engineering process, our approach could enjoy from MBSE by deploying, for example, early executable models of a plant for testing the early model of the control software.

A general idea of this paper was published in [6]. In this paper, we present the following contributions:

1. A mathematical model for a MES and running in-the-loop simulations, which can be found in Sect. 2.
2. A formal explanation of our methodology is addressed, which can be found in Sect. 3.
3. A detailed explanation of an industrial case study from the healthcare domain to which the methodology was applied, which can be found in Sect. 4.

Finally, Sect. 5 concludes this paper and presents the future directions of this work.

2   System Model

In this section, we introduce the key concepts of our system model (see Fig. 1 for an overview). The model considers that a MES is composed of components that interact solely via well-defined interfaces. For the scope of this paper, we assume that all systems are built from a known set of components taken from a fixed repository named $\mathcal{R}$.

Definition 1 (Repository). The repository $\mathcal{R}$ is a pair $(\mathcal{R}.\mathcal{I}, \mathcal{R}.\mathcal{C})$, where $\mathcal{R}.\mathcal{I}$ is a set of interfaces and $\mathcal{R}.\mathcal{C}$ is a set of components.

To enforce correct interaction patterns between components, some detail about their interfaces needs to be available.

Definition 2 (Interface). An interface $i \in \mathcal{R}.\mathcal{I}$ is a pair $(i.n, i.s)$ where $i.n$ is a unique name, and $i.s$ is a set of signatures (prototypes) of methods, i.e., method names with input/output parameters.

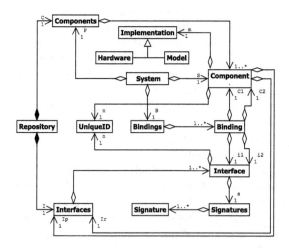

Fig. 1. System model overview

Occasionally, we need to express that sets of interfaces are identical apart from the names that make each interface unique. For this, we introduce the notion of signature equivalence.

Definition 3 (Signature Equivalence). Two sets of interfaces $I_1, I_2 \subseteq R.\mathcal{I}$ are *signature equivalent*, denoted by $I_1 \equiv_{sig} I_2$ when their bags of signatures are equal, i.e., when

$$\biguplus_{(n_1,s_1)\in I_1} \{s_1\} = \biguplus_{(n_2,s_2)\in I_2} \{s_2\}$$

A component uses interfaces both to provide functionality to its environment and to require functionality from other components. Thus, its provided functionality arises as a combination of its own implementation and the functionality obtained via the required interfaces.

Definition 4 (Component). A component $C \in \mathcal{R}.\mathcal{C}$ is a quadruple $(C.n, C.I_p, C.I_r, C.m)$, where $C.n$ is a unique name, $C.I_p, C.I_r \subseteq \mathcal{R}.I$ is the set of its provided and required interfaces, respectively, and $C.m$ is the C's implementation, which is a set of implemented artifacts. Moreover, we denote the set $(C.I_p \cup C.I_r)$ (i.e., all the interfaces) by $C.I$.

Based on the nature of its implementation, we distinguish two types of components.

Definition 5 (Component Type). A component is called a *hardware (physical) component* when its implementation is given by actual piece(s) of hardware, such as sensors or motors. It is, however, called a *simulated component*, if it is made of executable simulation model(s). A component whose implementation is of software but still need to be embedded in the targeted device is also called a simulated component.

The interaction patterns between the components of a system are captured by bindings. Each binding involves a pair of interfaces of opposite roles, such that all methods required by one component are provided by the other. However, within a binding, not all provided methods need to be required.

Definition 6 (Binding). A binding between components from $\mathcal{R}$ is a quadruple (C_1, i_1, C_2, i_2), where $C_1, C_2 \in \mathcal{R}.\mathcal{C}$, $i_1 \in C_1.I_p$, and $i_2 \in C_2.I_r$ such that $C_1.n \neq C_2.n$ and $i_2.s \subseteq i_1.s$.

For the purpose of an in-the-loop simulation, a MES is divided into two parts: control software[1] and a plant. In contrast to the control software component, which is of the simulated component type, the plant may consist of the both component types, simulated and hardware. Furthermore, in order to perform an in-the-loop simulation of a system, the bindings present between the control software and the plant must satisfy certain rules.

---

[1] In this work, our focus is on the software part of a MES's control than on the entire control unit.

Definition 7 (Valid System). A valid system is a triple (S, P, B), where $S \in \mathcal{R}.\mathcal{C}$ is a simulated component called the *control software*, and $P \subseteq \mathcal{R}.\mathcal{C} \setminus \{S\}$ is a set of components called the *plant*. In contrast to S, the components of P may be of either type, i.e., a plant may consist of both simulated and hardware components. Furthermore, B is a set of bindings such that:

1. $\forall_{i_r \in S.I_r} : \left[\exists_{C \in P, i_p \in P.I_p} : (C, i_p, S, i_r) \in B \right]$
2. $\forall_{i_r \in P.I_r} : \left[\exists_{C \in P, i_p \in S.I_p} : (S, i_p, C, i_r) \in B \right]$

where $P.I_p = \bigcup_{C \in P} C.I_p$ and $P.I_r = \bigcup_{C \in P} C.I_r$.

In terms of this system model, a simulation is an execution of a valid system in which one or more components of the plant are simulated components.

3   Methodology

In this section, we present our methodology that consists of the introduction of two (special) components to be inserted at predefined locations into the architecture of our approach. First, we state the objectives that must be achieved by these components. Next, we discuss the individual requirements imposed on these components, their locations in the system in the architecture, and typical usage in simulation.

The main consequence of our approach is to enable the executions of a variety of valid systems at various stages of a MES development, resulting in in-the-loop simulations at various levels of abstraction.

The first component we introduce is called the *Simulation Wrapper (SW)*. It will be inserted between the control software S and the plant P of a MES that has the capability of both tracing all traffic between S and P and redirecting or duplicating that traffic. Each system will contain a single SW, but its appearance will depend on the system in which it is inserted.

The second component we introduce is called the *Simulator Coordinator (SC)*. It bridges the gap between the executable simulation models (a.k.a., simulators) and interfaces of a component of the plant simulated by these models. Moreover, since most MESes are real-time systems, a simulator coordinator is also responsible for aligning the simulator's notion of time with the system time. In principle, we consider one SC per simulated component. Figure 2 depicts the general architecture of an in-the-loop system using this approach.

In the rest of this section, we discuss the components SW and SC in more detail.

3.1   Simulation Wrapper (SW)

As indicated above, the simulation wrapper is inserted between the control software S and the plant P. The rationale for this placement, as well as other possibilities for placement, has been discussed in [6]. Since the simulation wrapper is a component, i.e., $SW = (SW.n, SW.I_r, SW.I_p, SW.m)$, we need to specify both

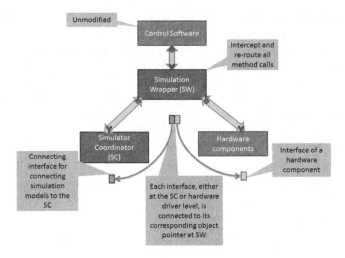

Fig. 2. Overall architecture. Our solution's components are highlighted in red. (Color figure online)

its interfaces and its implementation. Its interface sets are determined by the interface sets of S. For each required interface $i \in S.I_r$, it has three interfaces i_1, i_2, and i_3 that all have the same signature as i. Of these interfaces, i_1 is a provided interface that is intended to be bound to i. The other two are required interfaces that forward method invocations by S along with i to either a driver of a hardware component of the plant (i_2) or to the interface of the simulated version of that component (i_3). Similarly, there are three interfaces for each provided interface of S. Note that the provided interfaces of S correspond to call-backs from the plant. Thus, we have:

$$SW.I_p = SW.I_{p1} \cup SW.I_{p2} \cup SW.I_{p3}$$
$$SW.I_r = SW.I_{r1} \cup SW.I_{r2} \cup SW.I_{r3}$$

where

$$S.I_p \equiv_{sig} SW.I_{r1} \equiv_{sig} SW.I_{p2} \equiv_{sig} SW.I_{p3}$$
$$S.I_r \equiv_{sig} SW.I_{p1} \equiv_{sig} SW.I_{r2} \equiv_{sig} SW.I_{r3}$$

The implementation of SW is more difficult to specify in a formal manner. Therefore, we merely hint at the realization of its functional requirements. In addition, we mention non-functional requirements that such a realization should meet.

Functional Requirements:

– *Interception:* An important aspect of interception is that any invocation of a method from a provided interface $i_1 \in SW.I_{p1}$ needs to be forwarded to its destination under simulation. For this, $SW.m$ must maintain references to its corresponding signature-equivalent interfaces $i_2 \in SW.I_{r2}$ and $i_3 \in SW.I_{r3}$. Listing 1.1 contains a code snippet that shows how this can be done by encapsulating such references in objects that possess the same interface. For the sake of simplicity, various details, such as how to deal with parameters that are themselves objects, or which object to return in case both the real and the simulated methods are invoked are left unspecified.

- *Traceability:* The same code snippet in Listing 1.1 illustrates how forwarding can be augmented with logging of invocation data.

Listing 1.1. Conceptual forwarding by the simulation wrapper

```
Interface1 :: MethodA(p) {
    if (Object2) { // forwards to i2
        RtnObj2 = Object2->MethodA(p);
    }
    if (Object3) { // forwards to i3
        RtnObj3 = Object3->MethodA(p);
    }
    if (Tracing_On) { // invoke custom logging
        LogInvocationData();
    }
    return ( ReturnFrom2() ? RtnObj2 : RtnObj3);
}
```

Non-functional Requirements:

- *Transparency:* To ensure that no modification in either plant or control software is needed, when running a new valid system, interception of method invocations needs to be transparent, i.e., neither the caller nor the callee should be aware of the existence of SW.
- *Small and Predictable Overhead:* To ensure reliable simulation results, SW must satisfy its functional requirements with small (preferably constant) and predictable overhead in terms of computing resources (e.g., CPU and memory), and must not cause unpredictable delay on method invocations between S and P.
- *Automatic Generation:* To support an efficient development process, generating and inserting the simulation wrapper into the architecture of a MES should be automated as much as possible. Because the interfaces of the components that make up a MES are available, and forwarding follows a standard pattern, this is, to a large extent, feasible.

3.2 Simulator Coordinator (SC)

As indicated, a simulator coordinator is responsible for connecting executable simulation models to the system. More specifically, it must take one or several simulation models as the implementation of a potential simulated component from simulation tools such as Simulink, and attach interfaces to it. By doing so, a simulator coordinator, in fact, transforms one or multiple simulation models into a simulated component of P.

In a nutshell, any $SC = (SC.n, SC.I_p, SC.I_r, SC.m)$ is an access point for available executable simulation models that together simulate a component $C \in P$. Hence, it immediately follows that $SC.I_p \equiv_{sig} C.I_p$. For $SC.I_r$, the situation is more complex. In general, it consists of two sets of interfaces. One set assumes the role of the required interfaces of the plant's component under simulation. The other set of interfaces serves to connect the coordinator to the collection of models. If we assume that $M.I_p$ is the set of interfaces provided by the models, then $SC.I_r = SC.I_{r1} \cup SC.I_{r2}$, where $SC.I_{r1} \equiv_{sig} C.I_r$ and $SC.I_{r2} \subseteq M.I_p$. Figure 2 illustrates the overall architecture of an in-the-loop system in which simulators are connected to the simulation wrapper via a simulator coordinator.

To achieve its expected functionality, $SC.m$ must meet the following requirements:

- *Model Connectivity:* For each interface $i \in SC.I_p$ the methods of i must be implemented using the executable simulation models of $SC.m$ invoked through $SC.I_{r2}$.
- *Synchronization:* In general, a simulator simulates the behavior of a simulated component through a sequence of time-stamped state-transitions and associated events. For this, the simulator keeps track of a notion of logical time. In order to obtain a correct in-the-loop simulation, the logical clocks of the simulation models need to be synchronized with the real system-time. An example of how this can be done in practice is shown in the next section.

As with the simulation wrapper, the automatic generation of $SC.m$ is a desirable property. For the generation of the provided interface, this is, to a large extent, feasible. For the translation of interface methods into model methods, however, this is less likely, since it is highly dependent on the primitives of the simulation language and the plant component under simulation (Fig. 3).

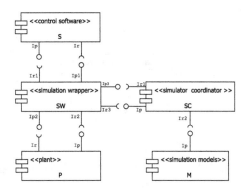

Fig. 3. All the Interfaces of the entire components of our solution. I in this figure actually represents any interface $i \in I$

4   Case Study

In this section, we illustrate the approach introduced in Sect. 3 on an industrial case study from the healthcare domain. More precisely, we explain the procedure required for configuring an SiL simulation for the case study using this approach.

We consider a safety-critical MES, viz., an *Interventional X-Ray (IXR)* machine (See Fig. 4). This is a case in which the control software manipulates quite heavy hardware components, such as a C-ARM and a patient table whose uncontrolled movements may harm patients or medical staff. In view of the cost of the machine and the mentioned safety aspects, there is a strong motivation not only to test the system with simulated hardware, but also to be selective on which hardware components are simulated.

To avoid being overwhelmed by unnecessary details of a complete IXR plant, we focus our attention on the simulation of a single component. In the sequel, we refer to the selected hardware component as C_2 and to its simulating counterpart, connected to the IXR system by means of a simulator coordinator SC and wrapper SW, as C_1.

For $C_2.I$, we selected an EtherCAT network driver, a third-party driver used by the IXR control software to control motors and sensors of an IXR over an EtherCAT network. Therefore, these motors and sensors are the implementation (i.e., $C_2.m$) of the component C_2. Since we intended to configure an SIL, C_2, as a hardware component, is absent.

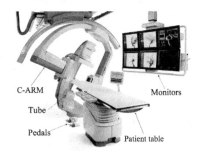

Fig. 4. An Interventional X-Ray (IXR) device

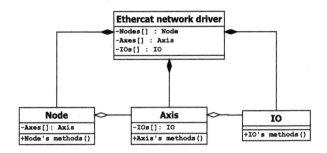

Fig. 5. Class diagram of the EtherCAT driver stub

Figure 5 depicts the structure of the EtherCAT driver's three main provided interfaces, namely, *Node, Axis, IO*. Hence, together they constitute the interface $C_1.I_p$ of the simulated component. For the latter's implementation $C_1.m$, we deployed a Matlab Simulink model that simulates a motor responsible for moving an IXR's patient table up and down and a sensor that measures the pressure on the patient table of an IXR. Both motor and sensor also simulate the original hardware controlled by IXR's S using the EtherCAT network driver.

To enable an SiL, the module of the IXR's control software S responsible for positioning the IXR's patient table, not yet embedded in its dedicated hardware, was used and the following objectives were pursued by this setup:

– To explore which type of motor is appropriate for the patient table, in terms of speed, power and other properties.
– To test whether the control software works properly.

Figure 6 shows the instantiated version of the generic architecture introduced in Fig. 2, for this particular case study.

SW: The main task of the simulation wrapper in this case study is forwarding method calls from S to C_1 through SC. Listing 1.2 shows the implementation of this task for a method named ProduceData() belonging to $C_1.I_p$.

The information determining which components are in P, introducing simulation models, if any, and their input and output parameters along with their critical functions, such as their step functions is obtained through a configuration file fed to each valid system. Using this file, prior to running a valid system, an initialization process is performed to bind relevant components, such as S to SW and SW to (simulated) components of P. For instance, the configuration file created for this case study causes the initialization process to bind C_1 to S via SC via SW. As a consequence, when receiving a method call from S, SW forwards the call to C_1 through SC.

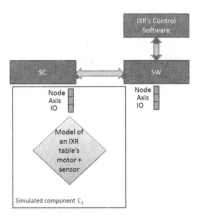

Fig. 6. Architecture solution for an IXR

As mentioned in Sect. 3, in addition to just forwarding calls, *SW* could also record these interactions for a later possible fault analysis (not yet implemented) and for testing purposes.

Listing 1.2. Main functionality of the simulation wrapper

```
if (C2_Object) {
// forwards to the physical component via the driver
RtnObj = C2_Object->ProduceData(p);
}
if (C1_Object) {
// forwards to the simulated component via SC
RtnObj = C1_Object->ProduceData(p);
}
```

SC: Recall that the purpose of the simulator coordinator is to solve two important generic problems: model connectivity, i.e., realizing simulated component interfaces using the methods offered by given simulation models' objects, and synchronization, i.e., aligning the passage of time in the control software with that in the simulation models. In addition, there may be other system specific issues. In this particular case, unit conversion is an example of the latter. We now discuss each of these in some detail.

Model Connectivity: As discussed earlier, the *SC* must expose the same interfaces as the Ethercat driver of the plant component whose simulation it coordinates. In our case, these interfaces are the Node, Axis and IO interfaces, each of which is implemented in *SC* by an object of a corresponding class. The actual implementation of the objects' methods is in terms of Simulink models. For this case study, the entire implementation has been done by hand, but using the configuration file described earlier in the context of the initialization process, a large part of the implementation of these classes, is skeleton code that can be generated automatically.

Furthermore, to have a structured mechanism to import the required Simulink simulation models, we made a design choice to encapsulate them in objects of a single class named *Model*. This class contains attributes and methods of a typical simulation model, like input and output variables, step size and step function. Thus, for every simulation model in $C_1.m$, an object of class *Model* is instantiated in the *SC* to be used by the Node, Axis and IO interface methods for implementation of the simulation proper. The resulting class structure of *SC* is shown in Fig. 7.

Synchronization: This issue addresses the difference in the handling of time between S and simulated components of P (here only C_1). The situation in our case study is as follows. The control software periodically loops through a sequence of control statements, whereas each simulation model steps through a sequence of states. For this, the models provide a function *stepFunc* that determines the next state and a parameter *timeStep* that indicates the advance in time associated with each step. These time steps are much smaller than the period of the control loop and, for the sake of simplicity, we assume in the sequel

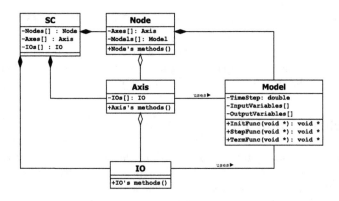

Fig. 7. SC class diagram for this case study

that the period of the control loop T_{ctrl} is a multiple of the time step of every model in $C_1.m$.

Listing 1.3 displays a variant of the actual control loop that captures the essential features, but uses fictional methods to simplify the explanation.

Listing 1.3. Basic control loop with fictional methods and period T_{ctrl}

```
control software loop{
        every (T_ctrl time units){
                readStatus();
                analyze();
                writeStatus();
        }
}
```

Listing 1.4 displays an idealized implementation of method *writeStatus()* $\in$ $C_1.I_p$ whose intended effect is that all models in $C_1.m$ synchronize their state to the moment in time implicitly maintained by the control software state as it iterates through its loop.

Listing 1.4. Synchronization by writeStatus

```
writeStatus(){
for each (model m of C1){
        var dt = 0;
        while (dt < T_crtl) {
                m.stepFunc();
                dt = dt + m.timeStep;
        }
    }
}
```

Unit Conversion: Besides its standard responsibilities *model connectivity* and *synchronization*, in this case study, the *SC* was also responsible for *conversion of values* exchanged between C_1 and S. This responsibility arose because the simulation models in $C_1.m$ only work with the SI base units, whereas the control software S also works with SI derived units, such as volt. To overcome this difference, information about units occurring in both the simulation models and the system was gathered from the configuration file and used to add conversion functionality to the SC, e.g. $V = W/A = m^2 \cdot kg \cdot s^{-3} \cdot A^{-1}$.

5   Conclusion and Future Work

In this paper, we focused on the problem of the development and test of the control software of MESes from a high level perspective of software interfaces such as driver APIs of the under-control plant. The idea is that given the interfaces of the components of a plant, transparently to the control software, engineers have freedom to provide these interfaces using either hardware components of the plant or their simulated counterparts. As a consequence of solving this problem, various in-the-loop simulations, such as SiL and HiL, required for verification and validation of MESes are realized. Note that this paper does not fully solve the problem of mixed simulations (a special interpretation of HiL) where a plant consists of simultaneously hardware components and simulated ones.

It is important to note that our approach's components, especially SW, does not only play an essential role in the development and test of a MES, but it may also exist in the final product for serving different purposes, for example for logging interactions between control software and its plant for fault analysis.

The work in this paper could be extended in three directions. First, more industrial case studies from different domains to be studied for ensuring the applicability of this approach in other domains. Second, investigating the problem of the mixed simulations where there is the freedom of integrating hardware components and simulated ones as a plant using this approach. Third, adding a domain-specific language for this approach in order to extend it and make it as a comprehensive framework with high amount of code generation, especially on the SC side. This is because we believe that the more automated this code generation is, the more valuable the solution is, and it can be easier integrated into current development workflows of MESes.

Acknowledgments. This work was supported in part by the European Union's ARTEMIS Joint Undertaking for CRYSTAL (Critical System Engineering Acceleration) under grant agreement No. 332830.

References

1. Choi, S.B., Young, T.C., Park, D.W.: A sliding mode control of a full-car electrorheological suspension system via hardware in-the-loop simulationg. Dyn. Syst. Meas. **122**(1), 114–121 (2000)
2. Faruque, M., Dinavahi, V.: Hardware-in-the-loop simulation of power electronic systems using adaptive discretization. IEEE Trans. Ind. Electron. **57**(4), 1146–1158 (2010)

3. Hui, L., Steurer, M., Shi, K.L., Woodruff, S., Zhang, D.: Development of a unified design, test, and research platform for wind energy systems based on hardware-in-the-loop real-time simulation. IEEE Trans. Ind. Electron. **53**(4), 1144–1151 (2006)
4. Isermann, R., Schaffnit, J., Sinsel, S.: Hardware-in-the-loop simulation for the design and testing of engine-control systems. Control Eng. Pract. **7**(5), 643–653 (1999)
5. Scippacercola, F., Pietrantuono, R., Russo, S., Zentai, A.: Model-driven engineering of a railway interlocking system. In: Proceedings of the Third IEEE International Conference on Model-Driven Engineering and Software Development (MODELSWARD), pp. 509–519, February 2015
6. Soltani Nezhad, A., Ferreira, L.F.B., van den Heuvel, M.M.H.P., Verhoeven, R., Lukkien, J.J., Mak, R.H., Korff de Gidts, E.: Towards an interoperable framework for mixed real-time simulations of industrial embedded systems. In: Proceedings of IEEE International Conference on Emerging Technology and Factory Automation (ETFA) (2014)
7. Sung Chul, O.: Evaluation of motor characteristics for hybrid electric vehicles using the hardware-in-the-loop concept. IEEE Trans. Veh. Technol. **54**(3), 817–824 (2005)

Gate-Level-Accurate Fault-Effect Analysis at Virtual-Prototype Speed

Bogdan-Andrei Tabacaru[1,2(✉)], Moomen Chaari[1,2], Wolfgang Ecker[1,2], Thomas Kruse[1], and Cristiano Novello[1]

[1] Infineon Technologies AG, Munich, Germany
{Bogdan-Andrei.Tabacaru,Moomen.Chaari,Wolfgang.Ecker,
Thomas.Kruse,Cristiano.Novello}@infineon.com
[2] Technische Universität München, Munich, Germany

Abstract. The cost of efficient fault-effect analysis on gate-level (GL) and register-transfer level models is increasing due to the rising complexity of safety-critical systems on chip (SoCs). Virtual prototypes (VPs) based on transaction-level models are employed to speed-up safety verification. However, VP structures correlate poorly to GL models. This leads to the injection of pseudo-faults into VPs and to the development of suboptimal safety mechanisms for the SoC. To mitigate these drawbacks, in this paper, we propose a safety-verification flow for VPs to maintain 100 % correlation to GL models and to ensure the injection of realistic faults into VPs. Our approach's key aspects are: matching points across abstraction levels and selective abstraction of GL functionality using compiled-code simulation. Measurements show two orders of magnitude speed-up over RTL models and three orders of magnitude over GL models. Moreover, the speed-up increases with design size.

Keywords: Automotive · Fault injection · ISO 26262 · Safety verification · SystemC · TLM · Virtual prototyping

1 Introduction

Safety-critical systems on chip (SoCs) are becoming increasingly larger and more complex as the amount of safety mechanisms within an SoC also steadily increases. To successfully develop optimal safety mechanisms, fault-effect analysis must be conducted on the SoC's hardware models prior to its production release.

Fault injection is an established method within the domain of (functional) safety verification and is a valuable approach to not only determine a system's robustness, but the effectiveness of a system's safety mechanisms as well.

Currently, fault injection is mainly performed on register-transfer level (RTL) models (mostly transient faults) and gate-level (GL) net-lists (stuck-at faults). Parts 5 and 10 of ISO 26262, the standard for safety-critical automotive applications, refer to GL net-lists as "appropriate for fault injection" since they contain sufficient information about a system's structure [1]. Furthermore, RTL models

© Springer International Publishing Switzerland 2016
A. Skavhaug et al. (Eds.): SAFECOMP 2016 Workshops, LNCS 9923, pp. 144–156, 2016.
DOI: 10.1007/978-3-319-45480-1_12

are also "an acceptable approach for stuck-at faults, provided that the correlation with [the] gate level is shown" [1]. Thus, fault injection into lower abstraction levels (e.g., transistor level) is not necessary for safety-critical SoCs.

However, fault injection into GL or RTL models can only take place late in the development cycle (i.e., after the hardware system was modeled and sufficiently debugged). At this time, a change within the SoC becomes expensive and increases the redesign effort. Therefore, a different modeling approach is needed to address the problem of developing optimal safety measures.

One solution for the above mentioned limitations is to perform safety verification on SystemC/TLM-based virtual prototypes (VPs) [2] as they allow safety-architecture exploration early in the design phase [3]. However, the insertion of a sufficient number of realistic faults into such models is an ongoing challenge; for example, VPs are highly abstracted behavioral models and lack many implementation details found in GL or RTL models. For this reason, fault injection into VPs is significantly less reliable than into other abstraction levels. As a consequence, faults injected into VPs may lead to failures (i.e., fault effects at the system's output) which cannot be reproduced at the GL abstraction (i.e., pseudo-faults). Furthermore, this may lead to the development of suboptimal safety mechanisms both qualitatively and quantitatively.

Our focus lies in the insertion of realistic faults into VPs. For this reason, we follow a structured bottom-up approach of fault abstraction (Fig. 1). We start at the transistor level since every fault originates here. Next, we follow the traditional abstraction from transistors to RTL models via the gate level. At this stage, permanent and transient faults conceptually remain the same. However, as we move from RTL models to VPs, fault models become more abstract (e.g., bus-arbitration fault, instruction-decode fault, memory-access fault). Furthermore, complex RTL or GL implementations (e.g., carry-save, carry look-ahead adders) are replaced by a simple mathematical operation within a VP (e.g., addition). These limitations negatively impact the efficient mapping of VP faults to RTL or GL faults. Thus, the results of fault injection into VPs and other hardware models (e.g., RTL, GL) become uncorrelated. Finally, this leads to the reduced capability to define realistic faults on VPs and it makes VPs unreliable as reference models for (functional) safety verification of safety-critical SoCs.

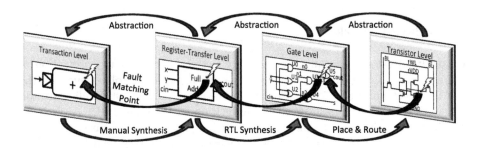

Fig. 1. Fault matching-points on multiple heterogeneous abstraction levels

Currently, the aforementioned limitations are addressed through mixed-level safety-verification flows [4]. Here, VPs and RTL models are co-simulated while faults are injected into the RTL model's interface. Fault effects (i.e., failures) are observed at the VP outputs. However, such approaches require manual implementation of a wrapper to bridge the communication across the two abstraction levels. Additionally, since faults are injected just into the RTL model's boundary, only a suboptimal amount of matching points is added to the VPs.

To address the drawbacks of mixed-level safety verification and to enhance the reliability of VP fault injection, in this paper, we present a method to improve the correlation between SystemC/TLM-based VPs and GL hardware models. We achieve this by automatically enriching VPs with GL information and by executing fault-injection simulations using a compiled-code approach [5]. As a result, the enriched models become structurally identical to their GL counterparts. In other words, the same faults can be injected into both abstraction levels. Therefore, we successfully improve the correlation factor across the two heterogeneous abstraction levels to 100 %. Finally, our approach enables the definition of common fault-injection locations (e.g., module interfaces, internal registers), also called *matching points*, across VPs and GL models (Fig. 1).

To define effective matching points, we developed a safety-verification platform, which automatically transforms GL net-lists into C++ code, integrates the C++ code into existing VPs, and inserts permanent faults (i.e., stuck-at-0 and stuck-at-1) into the enriched VPs using the Monte Carlo approach. After applying our approach on several adders and different components of a MIPS core, all faults injected into the SystemC/TLM models were successfully reproduced on the corresponding GL models. Furthermore, even though our enhanced SystemC/TLM models are more detailed than the original ones, our method's simulation performance is still close to that of the original VPs. Finally, only realistic faults are injected into the enriched VPs using our approach.

The remainder of this paper is structured as follows. Section 2 presents existing contributions related to the topics of fault injection and safety verification into hardware models. Section 3 describes the automatic generation of enriched VPs and the simulation framework used to inject faults into the VPs. Simulation results and measurements made on several adders and a MIPS core are discussed in Sect. 4. Finally, Sect. 5 contains the paper's summary.

2   Related Work

GL fault-injection techniques are highly effective for the safety verification of SoCs [1,6,7]. However, large-scale safety-critical microcontrollers such as the STMicroelectronics SPC5™ [8] or the Infineon AURIX™ [9] families are too large for effective system-level safety verification on the gate level.

Currently, RTL-based fault-injection techniques are widely used in safety-verification flows [10]. However, such frameworks have several drawbacks. First, matching points are not analyzed at all since many techniques inject faults only into RTL systems and exclude comparisons with the corresponding GL models [11,12]. Second, finding matching points between different levels of abstraction (e.g., RTL-GL models) is influenced by the models' implementation details [13]. Finally, fault-injection campaigns on RTL or GL models suffer from slower development, debugging, and simulation speeds compared to VPs.

Formal-based flows employ mathematical properties to exhaustively analyze the reliability and robustness of hardware models (e.g., VPs, RTL, GL) [14,15]. Currently, these methods are becoming more efficient and user friendlier [16]. However, formal methods do not scale for large safety-critical SoCs. Hence, they are mainly used to reduce the effort of simulation-based techniques; for example, in [17], the author formally verified only safety-critical registers.

FPGA (field-programmable gate array) [18,19] and GPU (graphics processing unit) [20] emulation are also widely used for safety verification thanks to their fast execution speed, improved debugging, and higher fault-injection controllability. However, hardware emulation still presents three fundamental drawbacks: (i) high development cost, (ii) complex usability for large net-lists (e.g., AURIX), and (iii) different timing properties between FPGA/GPU and target SoC technologies.

SystemC/TLM-based VPs are created more frequently since they offer faster simulation speeds than RTL and GL models [21]. However, VPs are too abstract for reliable safety verification, which leads to two main problems. First, there is a lack of matching points across the analyzed VPs and RTL models. Second, if matching points are found, distinct fault-propagation effects are observed after injecting the same faults into the different abstraction levels.

VPs are currently mainly employed in mixed-level safety-verification flows [4, 22,23], which co-simulate VPs and RTL/GL models. Thus, faults are injected into the more detailed models and the failures are observed on the VP level. This approach improves fault-effect analysis by providing the highly abstract VPs with missing matching points (e.g., wires, ports), into which to inject faults.

However, faults injected through existing mixed-level safety-verification methods provide suboptimal results compared to fault injection into GL models [24]. As a consequence, this inaccuracy has a considerable negative impact on the efficient design of safety mechanisms in the early SoC development phase. Therefore, an approach is needed to provide better correlation of heterogeneous hardware models across different abstraction levels.

To address the above mentioned limitations of mixed-level safety-verification approaches, in this paper, we present an approach that improves the fault-injection correlation across VPs and GL models. By using SystemC/TLM-based VPs and by aiming to link the results of fault injection across multiple abstraction levels, our work is complementary to [4]. However, we focus on GL models since they contain all implementation details required by the ISO 26262. Additionally, we automated our approach by eliminating the manual wrapper and by enhancing our SystemC/TLM-based VPs with GL information using a compiled-code approach [5]. Moreover, we sped-up fault injection by using a special C++ class instead of mutants. Thus, we inject faults during simulation time without needing to recompile the models and with minimal simulation overhead.

3   Mixed-Level Safety Verification

Matching points rely on structural similarities among different hardware modeling languages to be correctly and efficiently defined. Thus, while RTL and GL models are both functionally and structurally homogeneous (e.g., interfaces, register definitions), VPs and RTL/GL models are mainly functionally similar, but structurally heterogeneous. Furthermore, hardware models are mainly developed manually and the granularity of their implementation is application dependent. As a consequence, the definition of matching points across multiple abstraction levels becomes a challenging task to automate.

Nevertheless, we developed a method to fully automate the definition of matching points across SystemC/TLM-based VPs and GL models. We achieved this by transforming GL net-lists into C++ code using VERITAS [5], an in-house Verilog-to-C++ compiler. Thus, the original VPs are enhanced with GL structural details (e.g., signals, registers, hierarchy levels) (Fig. 2). VERITAS transforms GL wires into instances of special C++ objects (Sect. 3.1) and combinational blocks into C++ functions (e.g., adder_2bit). Furthermore, buses are broken down into boolean variables using **shifting** and **masking** operations.

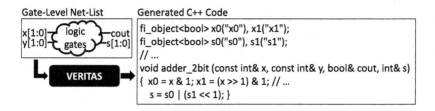

Fig. 2. Transformation of combinational logic gates into C++ code using VERITAS

Next, we replaced basic combinational blocks within VPs with the C++ code generated by VERITAS. We call the resulting VPs *GL-accurate transaction-level (TL) models* since they are SystemC/TLM components with GL granularity (Fig. 3). These models use the socket interface of a SystemC/TLM target module. Furthermore, the C++ code is executed by the module's (non-)blocking transactions.

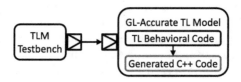

Fig. 3. Integration of gate-level-accurate C++ code into virtual prototypes

Thus, faults can be injected into the same locations (e.g., signals, registers) on the VPs as on the GL net-lists.

The enrichment of VPs with GL information effectively increases the correlation factor across the VP and GL abstraction levels to 100 % while only adding an acceptable simulation overhead (Sect. 4).

To obtain the SystemC/TLM-based VPs and GL models necessary for the definition of matching points, we used a top-down development approach, in which functionally equivalent TL and RTL models are implemented simultaneously from a common hardware specification. After sufficient testing (Fig. 4), the RTL models were synthesized using a commercial tool. Next, the resulting Verilog GL net-list is transformed into C++ code using VERITAS. The generated C++ code is used to replace combinational blocks from the original VP, which only execute one operation (e.g., addition). Finally, we injected permanent faults randomly into the GL-accurate TL models using the Monte Carlo approach.

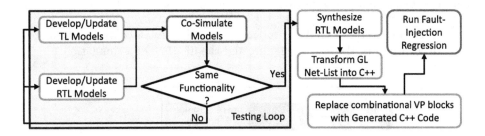

Fig. 4. SoC development flow prior to fault-injection regression

3.1   Fault Injection

Faults were inserted into the enriched SystemC/TLM-based VPs using a fault injector developed as a C++ class. All signals and registers from enriched VPs were instantiated using our fault-injection object (FIO).

Apart from the classic read and write methods of a SystemC signal, our FIO contains extra methods for injecting transient as well as permanent faults. The transient-fault method simply flips a signal's value at a given bit location. This value can be overwritten by the simulator during the FIO's next write cycle. Conversely, the permanent-fault methods effectively block the FIO's value update process during subsequent write cycles. The permanent fault's effect can be removed during a simulation by calling the FIO's release method.

3.2   Fault Models

We focused our fault-effect analysis on the effects of permanent faults (i.e., stuck-at-0 and stuck-at-1) since the effects of transient faults in combinational circuits is still relatively low [25].

We inserted faults into individual bit locations of VPs at the beginning of the simulation. Fault effects persisted until the simulation's end.

We did not inject any logical bugs within our models as we expected them to be bug free during our analysis. Furthermore, the injection of bridging faults, timing faults as well as the modeling of aging effects are out of the scope of this paper.

3.3   Simulation Environment and Flow

The C++ code generated by VERITAS is integrated into existing VPs. Afterwards, the GL-accurate TL models (i.e., enriched VPs) are introduced into a fault-injection simulation environment (Fig. 5) called SaVer. The environment contains a stimulus generator, a transaction monitor, and a fault injector. The stimulus generator drives data either randomly, or targeted (i.e., from a stimulus library) onto the VP's inputs. The fault injector accesses the model's internal signals and injects faults therein from a fault library. The monitor detects changes at the model's output ports. When the output values change, the monitor sends the observed data to an analyzer for processing. Finally, a controller regulates the driven stimulus, the injected faults, and the life time of a simulation.

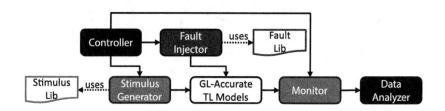

Fig. 5. SaVer's verification environment with fault-injection features

All safety-verification simulations are executed using SaVer's flow (Fig. 6). First, one fault-free reference simulation is executed for each workload as a golden run and the simulation results are dumped into a log file. Next, multiple fault-injection simulations are executed concurrently and the model's outputs are compared to the reference results. Permanent single-bit faults (i.e., stuck-at-0, stuck-at-1) are injected before the start of each faulty simulation. If no mismatch is detected at the model's outputs, the fault is considered masked. Otherwise, the mismatch is a failure caused by the fault's propagation through the system.

4   Case Studies and Results

To comprehensively cover the safety-verification space of our hardware systems, we randomly injected one fault per simulation into the GL-accurate TL models. Additionally, the effects of the injected faults were monitored at the outputs of the TLM verification environment.

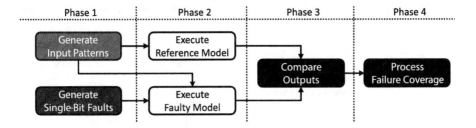

Fig. 6. SaVer's fault-injection regression flow

We injected faults only into internal signals and output ports (i.e., matching points) of GL-accurate TL models. Input ports were excluded since they are already accessible from the stimulus generator.

We simulated all Verilog GL net-lists as well as the MIPS RTL models with a commercial event-driven simulator and all GL-accurate TL models with the SystemC reference simulator [2].

All simulations were performed on a 64-bit machine with an Intel® Xeon® E5 CPU @3.00 GHz, L3 cache 25600 kB, and 264 GB RAM.

We measured the simulation speeds of all our case studies with the UNIX `time` command. We excluded the measurement of compilation and elaboration times of the co-simulated models.

4.1 Adder Architectures

We chose adders with overflow to analyze the relationship among different hardware architectures because the VP model of an adder only represents a call to C++'s '+'-operator, whereas the GL implementation contains multiple logic operations. As a consequence, the only viable matching points between the VP and the GL net-list of the adders are their output ports. Thus, the two abstraction levels are on average only 17 % correlated (Table 1). Furthermore, the correlation factor decreases with the adder's increasing complexity (e.g., carry lookahead).

It is possible to manually improve the correlation across an adder's VP and its GL net-list by implementing a VP structure, which is more similar to the GL net-list. However, such a time consuming and error-prone task renders the VP unusable for early-architecture exploration.

We provide a more adequate solution by automatically transforming the GL net-list into C++ code and integrating it into the existing VP. Hence, the VP is enriched with all signals (i.e., matching points) present in the GL net-list. As a result, the correlation factor increases to 100 % for all analyzed models.

Furthermore, the GL-accurate TL models are on average about 6x slower than the original VPs (Table 1), but also on average about 2x to 5x faster than the original GL models (Fig. 7). Finally, the performance of the enriched VPs increases with the complexity of the simulated model (i.e., the 32-bit adder VP is over 6x faster than the 2-bit adder VP) (Fig. 7).

Table 1. Comparison in number of fault-injection locations and simulation slow-down for several adder architectures

A	B	C	D = B/C	E	F	G = E/F
Model name	Injectable fault-locations (#)		Correlation factor (%)	Simulation time (s)		Slow-down factor
	Original VP	GL-Accurate TL model		GL-Accurate TL model	Original VP	
full_adder	2	6	33.33 %	0.041	0.040	1.03x
adder_2bit	3	9	33.33 %	0.097	0.087	1.11x
nibble_adder	5	31	16.13 %	0.260	0.087	2.13x
adder_4bit	5	35	14.29 %	0.310	0.122	2.54x
addsub_8bit	9	69	13.04 %	0.690	0.194	3.57x
adder_8bit	9	77	11.69 %	1.600	0.194	8.27x
adder_16bit	17	163	10.43 %	3.470	0.405	8.58x
adder_32bit	33	339	9.73 %	13.550	1.142	11.87x
carry_lookahead_32bit	33	523	6.31 %	16.040	1.142	14.05x
Average			16.48 %			5.91x

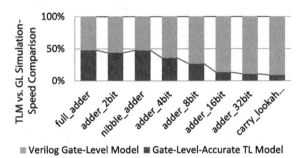

■ Verilog Gate-Level Model ■ Gate-Level-Accurate TL Model

Fig. 7. Simulation-speed comparison between each gate-level and gate-level-accurate TL model

4.2 MIPS CPU Architecture

The MIPS RTL model contains an integer-based instruction set, five pipeline stages, hazard detection, and forwarding. The MIPS VP is a pipelined behavioral model functionally equivalent to the RTL implementation.

We measured the correlation factor of the MIPS VP to its GL counterpart. Similar to the previous case study, we observed on average less than 17 % correlation (Table 2). Nevertheless, after enriching the individual VPs with GL information, the correlation factor increased to 100 %.

To test the performance of our GL-accurate TL models, we replaced individual components from the original MIPS VP with enriched sub-blocks generated by VERITAS (e.g., adder, shift unit, logic unit). Afterwards, we simulated the complete MIPS VP with and without enriched sub-blocks. Finally, we simualted the MIPS RTL and GL models.

Table 2. Comparison in number of fault-injection locations and simulation slow-down for a MIPS CPU

A	B	C	D = B/C	E	F	G = E/F	H	I = E/H
Model name	Injectable fault-locations (#)		Correlation factor (%)	Simulation time (s)		Slow-down factor	Simulation time RTL (s)	Speed-Up factor
	Original VP	GL-Accurate TL model		GL-Accurate TL model	Original VP			
shift	32	931	3.44 %	13.564	0.24	56.51x	70.831	5.22x
hazard_detection	4	73	5.48 %	1.610	0.24	6.71x	70.831	37.01x
id_control	11	116	9.48 %	1.914	0.24	7.98x	70.831	43.99x
ex_forwarding	4	38	10.53 %	1.192	0.24	4.97x	70.831	59.40x
logic_unit	32	266	12.03 %	2.761	0.24	11.50x	70.831	25.65x
adder	33	209	15.79 %	2.593	0.24	10.80x	70.831	27.32x
subtractor	33	174	18.97 %	2.164	0.24	9.02x	70.831	32.73x
jump	3	10	30.00 %	0.408	0.24	1.70x	70.831	173.56x
write_back	38	82	46.34 %	0.380	0.24	1.58x	70.831	186.40x
Average			16.89 %			12.31x		65.70x

Since we used the same original models as reference and only replaced individual VP sub-blocks, the simulation times for the original VP and the RTL models from Table 2 remain the same.

The enriched VPs only suffered an average simulation slow-down of one order of magnitude compared to the original VPs (Table 2). Furthermore, our enriched VPs were on average one to two orders of magnitude faster than the RTL models and over three orders of magnitude faster than the GL models (i.e., simulation time of 14.37 h).

These results offer a conclusive benefit for performing fault-effect analysis and safety-architecture exploration on SystemC/TLM-based VPs early in the development cycle of a safety-critical SoC.

4.3 Fault-Injection Object's Performance

We benchmarked our fault-injection object against C++ boolean variables using 2^{32} read and write accesses over 10 simulations and observed only a 2 % simulation slow-down. After applying the GNU C++ compiler's optimizations, a simulation with our FIO took on average 253.706 ms, compared to the simulation with C++ boolean variables which needed on average 248.639 ms.

4.4 Fault-Effect Analysis

Over 95 % of the faults injected into combinational circuits propagated to the system's output and became failures (Fig. 8). This renders our fault-injection framework highly effective.

The missing failures can be easily triggered by extending the VP's workload and fault libraries with directed input and faulty vectors instead of using Monte Carlo simulations.

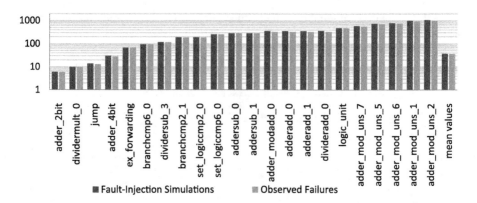

Fig. 8. Accuracy of our fault-injection campaigns based on the ratio of injected faults to observed failures (Color figure online)

5   Summary

In this paper, we presented a comprehensive methodology to completely correlate the results of fault injection across heterogeneous abstraction levels (i.e., SystemC/TLM-based VPs and GL net-lists). The correlation factor across VPs and corresponding GL net-lists was increased from 17 % to 100 % by automatically enhancing the original VPs with complete GL-specific fault-injection locations (e.g., signals, registers).

We also presented a mixed-level framework to automatically inject all realistic single-bit faults as requested by the ISO 26262.

Our method offers faster simulation speeds than equivalent RTL models, GL net-lists, and existing safety-verification flows. Nevertheless, our framework still maintains a simulation speed close to that of traditional VPs.

The effectiveness of implemented safety mechanisms can be tested on the VP abstraction level, at GL accuracy, and at a simulation speed slightly slower than classic VPs. Additionally, fault-effect analyses may be conducted to detect if safety mechanisms are missing, ineffective, or redundant.

Thus, we effectively bridged the safety-verification gap across heterogeneous abstraction levels.

Acknowledgement. This work is partially supported by the German Federal Ministry of Education and Research (BMBF) in the project EffektiV (contract no. 01IS13022).

References

1. ISO, CD. 26262, Road Vehicles-Functional Safety. International Standard ISO/FDIS, 26262 (2011)
2. Open SystemC Initiative et al.: IEEE Standard SystemC Language Reference Manual. IEEE Computer Society (2006)

3. Oetjens, J.-H., Bringmann, O., Chaari, M., Ecker, W., Tabacaru, B.-A., et al.: Safetyevaluation of automotive electronics using virtual prototypes: state of the art and research challenges. In: 51st ACM/EDAC/IEEE Design Automation Conference (DAC), pp. 1–6. IEEE (2014)
4. Baranowski, R., Hatami, N., Kochte, M.A., Prinetto, P., et al.: Efficient multi-level fault simulation of HW/SW systems for structural faults. Sci. Chin. Inf. Sci. **54**, 784–1796 (2011)
5. Tabacaru, B.-A., Chaari, M., Ecker, W., Kruse, T., Novello, C.: Fault-effect analysis on multiple abstraction levels in hardware modeling. In: DVCon, USA, pp. 1–12 (2016)
6. Amyeen, M.E., Nayak, D., Venkataraman, S.: Improving precision using mixed-level fault diagnosis In: IEEE International Test Conference, ITC 2006, pp. 1–10. IEEE (2006)
7. Espinosa, J., Hernandez, C., Abella, J.: Characterizing fault propagation in safety-critical processor designs. In: IEEE 21st International On-Line Testing Symposium (IOLTS), pp. 144–149. IEEE (2015)
8. STMicroelectronics: 32-bit Power Architecture Microcontroller for Automotive SIL3/ASIL-D Chassis and Safety Applications. SPC56 Datasheet. Rev 11 (2014)
9. Infineon Technologies, A.G.: AURIX-TriCore Datasheet. Accessed 22 Feb 2016
10. Leveugle, R., Cimonnet, D., Ammari, A.: System-level dependability analysis with RT-level fault injection accuracy. In: Proceedings of the 19th IEEE International Symposium on Defect and Fault Tolerance in VLSI Systems, DFT 2004, pp. 451–458. IEEE (2004)
11. Schwarz, M., Chaari, M., Tabacaru, B.-A., Ecker, W.: A meta model based approach for semantic fault modeling on multiple abstraction levels. In: DVCon, Europe (2015)
12. Vidrascu, I.-D.: Implementation of a safety verification environment (SVE) based on fault injection. Master's thesis, Fachhochschule Kärnten, Klagenfurt am Wörthersee, Austria (2015)
13. Zarandi, H.R., Miremadi, S.G., Ejlali, A.: Dependability analysis using a fault injection tool based on synthesizability of HDL models. In: Proceedings of the 18th IEEE International Symposium on Defect and Fault Tolerance in VLSI Systems, pp. 485–492. IEEE (2003)
14. Brat, G., Bushnell, D., Davies, M., Giannakopoulou, D., Howar, F., Kahsai, T.: Verifying the safety of a flight-critical system. In: Bjørner, N., Boer, F. (eds.) FM 2015. LNCS, vol. 9109, pp. 308–324. Springer, Heidelberg (2015)
15. Sharma, V.C., Haran, A., Rakamaric, Z., Gopalakrishnan, G.: Towards formal approaches to system resilience. In: IEEE 19th Pacific Rim International Symposium on Dependable Computing (PRDC), pp. 41–50. IEEE (2013)
16. Brinkmann, R.: OneSpin CEO cites 8 "insufficiencies" in Jim Hogan's Formal Guide. Accessed 8 Mar 2016
17. Busch, H.: An automated formal verification flow for safety registers. In: DVCon, Europe (2015)
18. Kastensmidt, F., Rech, P.: FPGAs and Parallel Architectures for Aerospace Applications: Soft Errors and Fault-Tolerant Design. Springer, New York (2015)
19. Bernardeschi, C., Cassano, L., Domenici, A.: SRAM-based FPGA systems for safety-critical applications: a survey on design standards and proposed methodologies. J. Comput. Sci. Technol. **30**(2), 373–390 (2015)
20. Fang, B., Pattabiraman, K., Ripeanu, M., Gurumurthi, S.: GPU-Qin: a methodology for evaluating the error resilience of GPGPU applications. In: 2014 IEEE Inter-

national Symposium on Performance Analysis of Systems and Software (ISPASS), pp. 221–230. IEEE (2014)

21. Chang, K.-J., Chen, Y.-Y.: System-level fault injection in SystemC design platform. In: Proceedings of 8th International Symposium on Advanced Intelligent Systems (ISIS). Citeseer (2007)

22. Kochte, M., Zoellin, C.G., Baranowski, R., Imhof, M.E., Wunderlich, H.-J., Hatami, N., et al.: Efficient simulation of structural faults for the reliability evaluation at system-level. In: 2010 19th IEEE Asian Test Symposium (ATS), pp. 3–8. IEEE (2010)

23. Santos, M.B., Teixeira, J.P.: Defect-oriented mixed-level fault simulation of digital systems-on-a-chip using HDL. In: Proceedings of the Design, Automation and Test in Europe Conference and Exhibition. IEEE (1999)

24. Cho, H., Mirkhani, S., Cher, C.-Y., Abraham, J.A., Mitra, S.: Quantitative evaluation of soft error injection techniques for robust system design. In: 50th ACM/EDAC/IEEE Design Automation Conference (DAC), pp. 1–10. IEEE (2013)

25. Dodd, P.E., Shaneyfelt, M.R., Felix, J.A., Schwank, J.R.: Production and propagation of single-event transients in high-speed digital logic ICs. IEEE Trans. Nucl. Sci. **51**(6), 3278–3284 (2004)

Using SAE J3061 for Automotive Security Requirement Engineering

Christoph Schmittner[1], Zhendong Ma[1(✉)], Carolina Reyes[2],
Oliver Dillinger[3], and Peter Puschner[4]

[1] Austrian Institute of Technology, Vienna, Austria
{christoph.schmittner.fl,zhendong.ma}@ait.ac.at
[2] TTTech Computertechnik AG, Vienna, Austria
carolina.reyes@tttech.com
[3] TTControl GmbH, Vienna, Austria
oliver.dillinger@ttcontrol.com
[4] Department of Computer Engineering,
Vienna University of Technology, Vienna, Austria
peter@vmars.tuwien.ac.at

Abstract. Modern vehicles are increasingly software intensive and connected. The potential hazards and economic losses due to cyberattacks
have become real and eminent in recent years. Consequently, cybersecurity must be adequately addressed among other dependability attributes
such as safety and reliability in the automotive domain. J3061, officially
published in January 2016 by SAE International, is a much anticipated
standard for cybersecurity for the automotive industry. It fills an important gap which is previously deemed irrelevant in the automotive domain.
In this paper, we report our activities of applying J3061 to security engineering of an automotive Electronic Control Unit (ECU) as a communication gateway. As an ongoing work, we share our early experience on
the concept phase of the process, with a focus on the part of Threat
Analysis and Risk Assessment (TARA). Based on our experience, we
propose improvements and discuss its link to ISO 26262.

Keywords: SAE J3061 · Automotive · Cybersecurity · Safety · ISO 26262

1 Introduction

Automobiles have undergone a profound technological shift in recent years. The
automotive industry puts more and more electronics and computational power
into traditionally mechanical systems. Innovations in software and connectivity
enable new features and business models at a stunningly rapid pace. The flip side
of this trend, however, is the increasingly serious cybersecurity concern, mani-
fested in theory and practice [4,6,10] in recent years. The automotive industry
implements the ISO 26262 standard [8] for functional safety of on-board electrical and electronic systems. But cybersecurity is not sufficiently addressed in
any of the previous automotive standards, despite ongoing work to extend ISO
26262 to include cybersecurity [14]. The J3061 [12] Cybersecurity guidebook for

© Springer International Publishing Switzerland 2016
A. Skavhaug et al. (Eds.): SAFECOMP 2016 Workshops, LNCS 9923, pp. 157–170, 2016.
DOI: 10.1007/978-3-319-45480-1_13

cyber-physical vehicle systems, first published in January 2016 by Society of Automotive Engineers (SAE), is a much anticipated standard to fill this gap in security engineering of modern vehicles.

This paper reports our ongoing work to apply J3061 for the secure development of an in-car Electronic Control Unit (ECU) as a communication gateway. Specifically, we share our experience of using the standard for the concept phase in the system development lifecycle. The main focus is to identify threats and assess associated risks in order to derive high-level security requirements. Our main contributions include the experience and lessons learned from applying J3061 to security engineering of an automotive component, the extension of the method for threat identification and the tables for risk assessment from the original standard, and the discussion of the linkage between J3061 and ISO 26262. In the following, we briefly describe the concept phase of J3061 in Sect. 2 and then detail our experiences with the standard in Sect. 3. We discuss the link of J3061 to ISO 26262 in Sect. 4 and conclude the paper in Sect. 5.

2   Overview of J3061

SAE J3061 defines a process framework for a security lifecycle for cyber-physical vehicle systems. It provides high-level guidance and information on best practice tools and methods related to cybersecurity, which can be adapted to existing development processes in an organization. It builds on many existing work on security engineering and secure system development methodologies and has a strong relation to the automotive system functional safety standard ISO 26262. In fact, the security lifecycle defined in J3061 is strongly influenced by the safety lifecycle defined in ISO 26262. Interaction points between the security and safety process are explicitly defined in J3061 to coordinate the two engineering processes. In some sense, it is an information security standard tailored to the automotive safety process. J3061 divides the system lifecycle into concept phase, product development (including system, hardware, and software), production, operation, and service. It also suggests supporting processes such as requirement, change, and quality management.

This paper focuses on the concept phase of J3061. The concept phase consists of 7 steps, illustrated in Fig. 1. The objective of the concept phase is to define high-level cybersecurity goals and strategy. The goals and strategy will then be refined to include technical details in the product development phase. The concept phase starts with the *feature definition* that identifies the physical and trust boundaries of the system, the system under consideration, and the scope of the work. In the *initiation of cybersecurity lifecycle*, the project is planned and documented with respect to the cybersecurity process. The main activity in the concept phase is the *threat analysis and risk assessment* (TARA). As the name suggests, its goal is to identify potential threats, and assess and rate the risks associated with the threats. J3061 provides suggestions of methods and some supporting material for TARA. A sub-activity under TARA is to identify high-level cybersecurity requirements (i.e. *identifying cybersecurity goals*) after

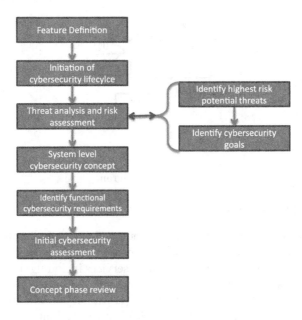

Fig. 1. J3061 concept phase

analyzing the risks. The goals can be stated in terms of what to avoid or the inverse of the threat. The *cybersecurity concept* includes the high-level cybersecurity strategy that satisfies cybersecurity goals for identified threats. The strategy will be refined to a technical strategy later in the production development phase. Based on the high-level strategy, functional cybersecurity requirements are defined in *identify functional cybersecurity requirements*. These requirements are derived from the cybersecurity strategy that satisfies the cybersecurity goals. In perspective, the functional cybersecurity requirements are derived from the strategy. The strategy is derived from the goals based on the outcome of identified threats and risks from TARA.

The last two steps in the concept phase are *initial cybersecurity assessment* and *concept phase review*. Initial cybersecurity assessment conducts an assessment of the level of security of the system. J3061 suggests that the initial assessment contains only the high-level cybersecurity goals, the risks, and open security issues. Concept phase review acts as a quality control gate that reviews the whole concept phase.

3   Application of J3061

In this paper, we apply J3061 to security engineering of an automotive ECU, functioning as a communication gateway. The purpose as follows: first, we follow the guidance in J3061 for automotive cybersecurity in a standard-conform way; second, we are interested to evaluate the guidance specified in J3061 and compare it with our previous experiences of security engineering in other domains.

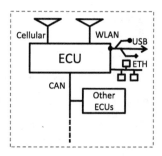

Fig. 2. System diagram

3.1 System Description

The system under development is an automotive ECU including hardware and software installations that offers remote connectivity for the on-board network. It is intended as a gateway for various remote services including data acquisition, remote control, maintenance and over-the-air (OTA) software update. However, it also provides a human-machine interface (HMI) for an operator for certain control actions (e.g. movements of the vehicle) in the cockpit.

The hardware is based on off-the-shelf controller with network interfaces supporting planned features. Illustrated in Fig. 2, it is equipped with cellular and wireless local area network (WLAN) communication interfaces for wireless connectivity. It includes an Ethernet interface for debugging and connecting to local devices (e.g. Ethernet cameras). The USB port is used for local software update and application provision. The CAN interface connects this ECU to other on-board ECUs. The main usage of the ECU is to provide remote connectivity for various access and control activities, previously only possible via the local interface and the HMI. The software for the functionality is based on standard Linux distribution. Note that the example presented in this paper is a simplified version of the actual system.

The first step in the J3061 concept phase is to define physical and trust boundaries and the scope of the features. Based on the system description, the scope is decided to be the remote network access, i.e. access through cellular and WLAN interfaces. Although physical access is a viable attack vector (e.g. from Ethernet or USB port, or physical access to firmware and file system), in our work, we decided to focus on the new attack surface and scenarios emerged from the remote connectivity. Therefore, the physical boundary and trust boundary is the local perimeter of the system, indicated by the dotted line in Fig. 2. In other words, we assume that the cellular and the WLAN interface are the only entry points for an attack.

The next step in the concept phase is the initiation of the cybersecurity process. This is mainly about project planning for cybersecurity. We loosely follow this step by planning and agreeing on the cybersecurity activities in the team and creating a running document to record all steps and corresponding outcomes.

3.2   Threat Analysis and Risk Assessment

The third step in the concept phase is TARA, which includes threat identification, risk assessment/threat classification, and risk analysis. Note that at this stage, we have only partial information about the system, i.e. the "concept" or a vague description of the system architecture and the planned features etc. Therefore, the objectives of the TARA is to identify potential threats and to assess the associated risks, which helps us to prioritize cybersecurity activities in terms of efforts and resources.

J3061 Appendix A provides suggestions for methods and techniques, including the approach originated from the E-Safety Vehicle Intrusion Protected Applications (EVITA) project [1], ETSI Threat, Vulnerability, and implementation Risk Analysis (TVRA) standard [5], Operationally Critical Threat, Asset, and Vulnerability Evaluation (OCTAVE) [3], HEAVENS security model [2], and attack trees [11]. Beside the ones mentioned in J3061, existing approaches also include Cybersecurity HAZOP [16] and STRIDE [17][1]. Cybersecurity HAZOP identifies potential security-caused deviations by combining the functions with specific guide words. While this approach works well for threats to the availability or operational performance of a system, it is challenging to apply it to data-centric assets. STRIDE is another common method for threat identification, e.g. in SAHARA [9]. STRIDE method considers systems with assets and operational performance to reason about threats, based on assets and potential attributes that can be threatened or misused. However, it is based on detailed data flow models among system components and software modules. Our challenge is that the TARA at this preliminary stage is based on incomplete information.

J3061 has not stipulated specific methods and techniques for TARA. In our case, after evaluating existing approaches, based on our experiences we decide to use the Confidentiality, Integrity, and Availability (CIA) analysis. As an established concept in information security, the CIA model is straightforward and the analysis is easy to apply. Confidentiality is concerned with dynamically produced data or static data; integrity is concerned with the manipulation or tampering of software and data; and availability is concerned with the availability of system functions and the communication. CIA considers data in three forms, i.e. in use, in motion, and at rest, in the system and network. Moreover, integrity also concerns the injection of falsified and spoofed data and packets into the system or into the communication channels.

Guided by the CIA model, we conduct brainstorming sessions to go through the identified assets, while considering the following questions:

- What are the threats/attacks on the confidentiality of the asset?
- What are the threats/attacks on the integrity of the asset?
- What are the threats/attacks on the availability of the asset?

The assets are the potential targets of an attacker that are critical for the correct functioning of the system and the stakeholders' interests, i.e. things to

---

[1] Due to page limit and the scope, we refer interested readers to the appendix of J3061 standard or the references for more details.

be protected. In other words, the identification of assets should be aligned with the business goals and mandatory regulatory frameworks such as road safety. We identify and choose three sets of assets: software (software intellectual property and applications), functionality (remote control, remote maintenance, and remote update), and data (measurement and configuration).

For each identified asset, we identify attack scenarios and threats for a fine-granular threat description. The difference between an attack scenario and a threat is that a threat is the goal which an attacker wants to achieve; an attack scenario is the means (attack method) to reach the goal. For example, the same attack scenario (e.g. sniff network traffic) can pose multiple threats (e.g. copy proprietary data or reveal credentials). The brainstorming sessions are conducted by the project team including system developers and security experts. Since the goal is to enumerate as many potential threat scenarios as possible, we do not set limitation on whether a proposed scenario is "realistic enough" during brainstormings. Instead, the scenarios are refined and consolidated afterwards. Although there are currently no criteria on whether attack and threat scenarios are "complete", our approach is to have several brainstorming sessions and reviews and ensure that all publicly known attack scenarios are considered.

Note that we intentionally enumerate the attack scenarios and threats in parallel. This means we use a threat (i.e. the attack goal) to justify the consideration of an attack method. At the same time, the existence of an attack scenario allows us to derive a specific threat or identify the motivation of the attacker. For each identified threat, we identify its corresponding effect, i.e. the consequence or the impact on the system resulting from the attack. Given the nature of automotive when identifying effects, we focus mainly on the safety and security aspects as advocated in [14,15]. The first three columns of Table 1 show examples of our TARA result.

The identified attack scenarios, threats, and effects form the basis for risk assessment, i.e. the assessment and classification of risks associated with a particular threat. In J3061, risk assessment includes the likelihood of a successful attack and the severity of the possible outcome. Several examples are given in the appendix. For instance, in the EVITA method, a similar concept of "attack probability" is used. It is calculated as the sum of the scores of "attack potential", divided into elapsed time, expertise, knowledge, window of opportunity, and equipment required. Whereas for severity, the EVITA method breaks it down into specific terms including financial, operational, privacy, and safety.

In J3061, the supporting materials for making qualitative risk decisions are given as suggestions and examples. We improved their applicability to our specific use case by constructing a slightly different attack probability table (cf. Table 2), based on guidance from the HEAVENS project, which is one of the proposed methods in J3061 and [13]. Attack probability is estimated based on the difficulty to execute an identified attack scenario. Especially during the concept phase, information about the system architecture and hardware/software elements may change or be not yet determined. Focusing on the difficulty instead of vulnerabilities allows a first estimation of the risk. *Capabilities* point to the minimal general knowledge

Table 1. Example threats and risk rating

Attack scenario	Threat	Effect	Attack prob.	Severity	Risks
Asset: Software/Applications					
Exploit known vulnerabilities in OS or applications remotely	Install rootkit, Trojan	Take control of system ECU operations, change parameters, and access data	9 (2 + 1 + 3 + 3)	4	High
Exploit known vulnerabilities in OS or applications remotely	Delete software component	Reduce functionality of ECU	9 (2 + 1 + 3 + 3)	2	Medium
Asset: Remote control functions					
Man-in-the-middle attack on communication	Eavesdropping password used for remote connection	Hijack established connection and disturb normal operation	8 (1 + 1 + 3 + 3)	2	Medium
Brute force or guess remote connection password	Reveal password	Exploit remote connectivity to disturb normal operation	7 (1 + 2 + 2 + 2)	2	Medium
Asset: Remote maintenance functions					
Compromise and control a device in the communication link between ECU and Web server	Eavesdrop communication to intercept maintenance data	Intercept sensitive configuration and maintenance data	7 (1 + 2 + 2 + 2)	3	Medium
Man-in-the-middle attack on communication	Send manipulated maintenance data to Web server	Cause unnecessary maintenance actions by sending crafted maintenance data	8 (1 + 1 + 3 + 3)	1	Low
Asset: Remote update functions					
Send multiple updates to exhaust storage of ECU	Temporarily disable normal function of OS or applications	Partial reduction of system function, storage space exhausted	5 (1 + 1 + 2 + 1)	0	
Compromise server to transmit data to ECU	Change of operating conditions, leading to potential unsafe conditions	Change operating conditions of one or multiple ECUs	8 (1 + 2 + 3 + 2)	4	High
Asset: Measurement & configuration data					
Exploit known vulnerabilities in OS or applications remotely	Unauthorized access to data on ECU	Access to usage or configuration data on ECU	8 (1 + 1 + 3 + 3)	1	Low
Man-in-the-middle attack on communication	Unauthorized access to transmitted data	Access to certain usage data	8 (1 + 1 + 3 + 3)	1	Low

Table 2. Attack probability parameter

Parameter	Score			
	3	2	1	0
Capability	Amateur	Mechanic, Repair shop	Hacker, Automotive expert	Expert team from multiple domains
Availability of information	Information publicly available	Information available for maintenance or for customer/operator	Information available for production, OEM, system integrator	Information available in company of ECU supplier
Reachability	Always accessible via untrusted networks	Accessible via private networks or part time accessible via untrusted networks	Part time accessible via private networks or easily accessible via physical	Only accessible via physical
Required Equipment	Publicly available standard IT devices/SW	Publicly available specialized IT devices/SW	Tailor-made/proprietary IT devices/SW	Multiple Tailor-made/proprietary IT devices/SW

about the product and methods required by an attacker. *Availability* of information describes how easy it is to access the needed information. *Reachability* describes the difficulty to reach the system for an attack. *Required equipment* refers to the needed devices to conduct the attack. Summarizing the scores for each parameter gives an estimation of the attack probability, where a higher scores indicates a higher attack probability. For example, to remotely compromise a system and replace a legitimate software component with a crafted malware that can send messages to the CAN bus, the attacker must at least be a Hacker/Automotive expert with information available for production, OEM, system integrator, with access to the system via private network or "ease" physical interfaces, and equipped with tailor-made/proprietary IT devices/SW. This gives the attack probability score of $1 + 1 + 1 + 1 = 4$. Note that the purpose of the assessment is not to calculate exact numeric values of attack probability, but to generate relative values to cluster and rank the associated the risks.

For the evaluation of the severity we adapt the EVITA severity classes [7]. Due to different usage scenarios, not all ratings are directly applicable. For example, while privacy is an important issue for passenger vehicles, our system is not intended for passenger transportation, thus our focus here is on the confidentiality of critical business data and intellectual property instead of an individual's privacy. Unauthorized changing of data is considered to be operational and safety losses. Table 3 gives the details for determining the severity levels.

The last step of TARA is risk analysis, i.e. threat ranking and the determination of whether a risk associated with a particular threat is acceptable. J3061 provides the example of the HEAVENS security model, which combines the threat and impact level to derive a security level. We adapt the security model to a risk matrix. Shown in Table 4, the range of a particular risk class is based on scores from attack probability and severity class. For example, attack probability of 4 and severity class of 4 will result to a risk of Medium (cf. Table 4). Recall that a high score of attack probability indicates an attack is more likely

Table 3. Cybersecurity severity classes

Severity classes	Safety	Confidentiality	Financial	Operational
0	No injuries	No unauthorized access to data	No financial loss	No impact on operational performance
1	Light or moderate injuries	Configuration data only	Low-level loss	Impact not discernible to operator
2	Severe injuries or moderate injuries for multiple vehicles	Partial data (access to a single update or one application)	Moderate loss	Low losses for multiple vehicles. Operator aware of performance degradation Indiscernible impacts for multiple vehicles
3	Life threatening or fatal injuries Severe injuries for multiple vehicles	Access to complete data	Heavy loss Moderate losses for multiple vehicles	Significant impact on performance Noticeable impact for multiple vehicles
4	Life threatening or fatal injuries for multiple vehicles	Access to data from multiple ECUs in the vehicle	Heavy losses for multiple vehicles	Significant impact on multiple vehicles

Table 4. Risk matrix

Risk	Attack probability				
Severity class	0–2	3–5	6–8	9–11	>11
0					
1		Low	Low	Low	Medium
2		Low	Medium	Medium	High
3		Low	Medium	High	High
4	Low	Medium	High	High	Critical

to occur, e.g. due to lower technical barrier or availability of information. If such attack leads to high severity, then the risk is deemed as high.

The last three columns in Table 1 shows the results of the risk assessment and analysis. Note that for attack probability, we include the sum as well as the individual scores to show how they are calculated based on Table 2.

Through the TARA process, preliminary results are refined to identify "acceptable" risks and to prioritize the risks in order to define the scope of the following work. At this stage, we decide that risks rated with Low are acceptable and focus on Medium and High risks.

J3061 requires the identification of cybersecurity goals in the end of TARA. The goals describe the highest level cybersecurity requirements and goals for achieving cybersecurity. They are a high-level and concise description of what should be avoided, detected or prevented. In our case, the cybersecurity goals include things like:

– Prevent eavesdrop of wireline and wireless communication
– Prevent tampering of wireline and wireless communication

- Avoid unauthorized or wrong (unfinished) software update
- Prevent application of unauthorized or wrong configuration data
- Prevent exploitation of known vulnerabilities
- Prevent and detect attacks on web server for software update

3.3 Cybersecurity Concept and Requirement

The cybersecurity concept describes the high-level strategy for achieving cybersecurity, e.g. the strategy how to satisfy the defined cybersecurity goals. J3061 states that security strategies that address the identified threats need to cover aspects such as embedded system, standard IT, (wireless) communication, and a secure development lifecycle. Some of our cybersecurity concepts include:

- Use secure communication channels whenever possible, e.g. VPN, SSL, or WPA2
- Digitally sign exchanged data, including software update, configure data etc.
- Minimize vulnerabilities and weakness during development and operation (by secure coding practice and review, vulnerability scanning, process and techniques for patching)
- Disable all debugging and maintenance, interfaces, ports, and functions in operation mode
- Leverage build-in security features in hardware and software, whenever possible

The functional cybersecurity requirements are derived from the cybersecurity strategy as well as cybersecurity goals. Therefore, towards the end of concept phase, we derive functional cybersecurity requirements that are clustered into identification and authentication control, secure communication, system integrity, cryptographic keys. Some examples are given below.

- The system shall support different levels of access rights and remote user rights
- The system shall provide the capability to identify and authenticate itself during its life time
- The system shall be able to verify the origin of a software packet in the software update process
- The system shall be able to verify the origin of a remotely issued command
- The system shall provide security communication capability when communicating with external hosts over wireless and wireline
- The system shall provide additional integrity protection for the storage of critical operational data such as configuration data
- If Public Key Infrastructure (PKI) is used, the system shall provide capability to securely store and manage cryptographic keys and credentials, and operate PKI according to common best practices

3.4   Final Steps in Concept Phase

The final steps in the concept phase are an initial cybersecurity assessment and the final concept phase review. The initial cybersecurity assessment contains the assessment of high-level cybersecurity goals identified during TARA, risks associated with the goals, and open issues identified. In the assessment, we conduct a high-level assessment of whether cybersecurity functional requirements are capable of mitigating threats and risks. In the concept phase review, we verify the completeness, correctness and consistency of all the conducted steps in a review workshop and the document review by all project team.

4   Discussion

ISO 26262 is a domain specific instantiation of the generic safety standard IEC 61508 and follows a risk based approach around safety integrity levels, safety goals, and safety concepts [14]. Since J3061 is based on ISO 26262 and envisions a process tightly interwoven with other automotive engineering activities, we start the discussion with a comparison of the concept phase in ISO 26262 and J3061. While J3061 uses the term "feature" and ISO 26262 uses the term "item", both have the same meaning, i.e. system or multiple systems that implement a function at the vehicle level, to which the respective standard is applied.

Currently the guidance regarding safety and security co-engineering (i.e. a combined approach to safety and security engineering) is more extensive in J3061 than in ISO 26262. In 2018 a new version of ISO 26262 should be published which contains guidance for the interaction between safety and security from the safety side. While the number and goal of most process steps in the concept phase is relatively similar between ISO 26262 and J3061, there are differences between Hazard Analysis and Risk Assessment (HARA) in ISO 26262 and TARA in J3061. The most obvious difference is the direction of consideration. HARA focuses on identifying and categorizing of malfunctions in the item which can lead to a hazard, whereas TARA focuses on threats to a feature (cf. Fig. 3).

In addition, the rating of risks differs between HARA and TARA. Both analyzes aim at identifying risks without exact probabilities in the concept phase. For HARA this is due to insufficient information about the system architecture, used hardware components, and how a function will precisely be implemented. For TARA, besides the already mentioned points, in general vulnerability information and threat intelligence is often incomplete without detailed information of the exact design and implementation. HARA focuses on the potential severity of a hazard, probability of exposure to operational situations in which the malfunction leads to a hazard and controllability of the malfunction. Risks are classified in Automotive Safety Integrity Levels (ASILs) and there is a relatively clear guidance on which actions and risk reductions are necessary for certain ASILs. In cybersecurity the guidance is less clear. J3061 suggests different methods for the rating of risks and the usage of controllability as additional parameter only for threats which may impact the safety. While this is done in order to be consistent with ISO 26262 we would suggest to either extend this also to operational

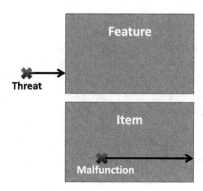

Fig. 3. Direction of consideration for threats and malfunctions

impacts or to remove this parameter. Considering controllability for cybersecurity threats, when the distribution of control between machine and driver is still open and rather difficult. Controllability should rather be considered as a potential cybersecurity control which can be used for risk reduction, after the TARA phase. HARA and TARA are iterative processes throughout the development lifecycle.

In general, the scope of TARA is wider than HARA. HARA focuses on deviation from the intended functionality which are caused by failures and may lead to hazards. TARA focuses, besides functionality, also on the data and extends the scope from safety-related losses to impacts on confidentiality or financial losses. Another related topic under development is the potential extension of the scope of Safety of the intended Functionality (SotiF) and Fail Operational. SotiF describes safety impacts not caused by failures but by insufficient nominal behavior and minimum performance levels for safety critical vehicle functions. SotiF is currently considered as a NWIP (New work item proposal) for a future ISO Standard.

According to the agenda of ISO 26262, the relation between the two standards and how to interact J3061 with ISO 26262 will be included in the upcoming guidance in new versions of ISO 26262.

5   Conclusion

Cybersecurity has becomes a serious concern in the automotive domain in recent years due to the increasing integration of computers and connectivity in modern vehicles. In this paper, we share our experience of applying the guidance in the newly published automotive cybersecurity standard J3061 to a communication gateway ECU in the concept phase. We report our experience of following the standard for identifying threats and risks and derive high-level security requirements. We also show specific methods and techniques used during the process. We compare J3061 with ISO 26262 to discuss their alignment.

We belief that these experiences and lessons learned need to be shared with the automotive safety and security community to push forward automotive cybersecurity and to improve the standard in the long run. For next step, we will continue the application of J3061 to the development phase to gain more insight.

Acknowledgement. This work is partially supported by EU ARTEMIS project EMC^2 (contract no. 621429) and Austrian Research Promotion Agency FFG on behalf of Austrian Federal Ministry of Transport, Innovation and Technology BMVIT. This work also derives from the activities within SCRIPT project (no. 1326126), funded by the Vienna Business Agency under the Call "Pro Industry 2015".

References

1. E-safety vehicle intrusion protected applications (EVITA). http://www.evita-project.org/
2. HEAling Vulnerabilities to ENhance Software Security and Safety (HEAVENS) project. https://research.chalmers.se/en/project/5809
3. Carnegie Mellon University Software Engineering Institute: Operationally Critical Threat, Asset, and Vulnerability Evaluation Framework (OCTAVE)
4. Checkoway, S., McCoy, D., Kantor, B., Anderson, D., Shacham, H., Savage, S., Koscher, K., Czeskis, A., Roesner, F., Kohno, T.: Comprehensive experimental analyses of automotive attack surfaces. In: Proceedings of the 20th USENIX Conference on Security (2011)
5. ETSI TS 102 165-1: Telecommunications and internet converged services and protocols for advanced networking (tispan); methods and protocols; part 1: Method and proforma for threat, risk, vulnerability analysis (2011)
6. Foster, I., Prudhomme, A., Koscher, K., Savage, S.: Fast and vulnerable: a story of telematic failures. In: 9th USENIX Workshop on Offensive Technologies (WOOT 2015) (2015)
7. Henniger, O., Apvrille, L., Fuchs, A., Roudier, Y., Ruddle, A., Weyl, B.: Security requirements for automotive on-board networks. In: Proceedings of the 9th International Conference on Intelligent Transport System Telecommunications (ITST 2009), Lille, France (2009)
8. International Organization for Standardization: ISO 26262 Road vehicles - Functional safety (2011)
9. Macher, G., Sporer, H., Berlach, R., Armengaud, E., Kreiner, C.: SAHARA: a security-aware hazard and risk analysis method. In: Proceedings of the 2015 Design, Automation & Test in Europe Conference & Exhibition, pp. 621–624 (2015)
10. Miller, C., Valasek, C.: Remote exploitation of an unaltered passenger vehicle (2015)
11. Moore, A.P., Ellison, R.J., Linger, R.C.: Attack modeling for information security and survivability. Technical report, DTIC Document (2001)
12. SAE International: J3061 Cybersecurity Guidebook for Cyber-Physical Vehicle Systems, January 2016
13. Schmittner, C., Gruber, T., Puschner, P., Schoitsch, E.: Security application of failure mode and effect analysis (FMEA). In: Bondavalli, A., Di Giandomenico, F. (eds.) SAFECOMP 2014. LNCS, vol. 8666, pp. 310–325. Springer, Heidelberg (2014). doi:10.1007/978-3-319-10506-2_21

14. Schmittner, C., Ma, Z.: Towards a framework for alignment between automotive safety and security standards. In: Koornneef, F., van Gulijk, C. (eds.) SAFECOMP 2015 Workshops. LNCS, vol. 9338, pp. 133–143. Springer, Heidelberg (2015). doi:10.1007/978-3-319-24249-1_12
15. Schoitsch, E., Schmittner, C., Ma, Z., Gruber, T.: The need for safety and cyber-security co-engineering and standardization for highly automated automotive vehicles. In: Schulze, T., Müller, B., Meyer, G. (eds.) Advanced Microsystems for Automotive Applications 2015. Lecture Notes in Mobility, pp. 251–261. Springer, Switzerland (2016)
16. Srivatanakul, T., Clark, J.A., Polack, F.A.C.: Effective security requirements analysis: HAZOP and use cases. In: Zhang, K., Zheng, Y. (eds.) ISC 2004. LNCS, vol. 3225, pp. 416–427. Springer, Heidelberg (2004)
17. Swiderski, F., Snyder, W.: Threat Modeling. Microsoft Press, Redmond (2004)

Dynamic Safety Contracts for Functional Cooperation of Automotive Systems

Sebastian Müller[(✉)] and Peter Liggesmeyer

Lehrstuhl für Software Engineering: Dependability,
Technische Universität Kaiserslautern, 67653 Kaiserslautern, Germany
{sebastian.mueller,liggesmeyer}@cs.uni-kl.de

Abstract. Going along with current research trends like Cyber-Physical Systems it is assumed for future embedded systems to enable a better interconnection of distributed systems. Besides mutual awareness, they should provide a deeper integration on the level of functional cooperation. By today, runtime aspects of system adaptation for functional safety are not sufficiently addressed. As predicted for the near future, especially collaboration scenarios of autonomous driving vehicles like platooning will make it necessary to address safety across the classical boundaries of single automotive systems. Therefore, extending the vehicle safety architecture to an open and adaptive one, implies that there is a need for a runtime assessment of safety. To ensure that the current operational situation based on cooperative functionalities is safe, we propose a safety evaluation with dynamic safety contracts between involved parties. The approach is based on a continuous monitoring, sharing and calculation of safety related quality characteristics of systems at runtime.

Keywords: Cooperative systems · Dynamic safety contracts · Condition monitoring · Safety · Autonomous vehicles · Conditional certificates · Dynamic adaptation

1 Introduction

With concepts like Cyber-Physical Systems or Industry 4.0 a new era of electronic devices is evolving. This evolution was enabled by ever increasing capabilities of embedded computing devices and declining prices. Today´s technical devices contain more and more powerful sensors with the ability to monitor system conditions as well as environmental parameters. Based on that new research areas about connecting those distributed systems evolved. In such networks each system could allocate its limited functionality to a wider context and thus improve the capabilities to reach its own and superordinated system goals. As an illustrative application domain we selected the vehicle domain as it is part of our current research, but as it was outlined the approach is not limited to it. Driven by the current trend towards full autonomous vehicles, cooperation of single vehicles can lead to a safer and more efficient traffic flow. Emerging wireless technologies for vehicle-to-vehicle (V2V) and vehicle-to-infrastructure (V2I) communications have the potential to interconnect these distributed systems of public road users and infrastructure for more coordinated interactions. Higher-level services

© Springer International Publishing Switzerland 2016
A. Skavhaug et al. (Eds.): SAFECOMP 2016 Workshops, LNCS 9923, pp. 171–182, 2016.
DOI: 10.1007/978-3-319-45480-1_14

beyond the ability of isolated vehicles can then be realized. Introducing shared safety related data into the individual vehicle safety architecture paves the way for powerful, but safety critical cooperative functionalities. Concrete applications are manifold like collaboration groups of vehicles driving in a platoon with sharing of sensor data or building master-slave cooperation groups in the commercial vehicle domain (e.g. agriculture) to certify motion of the subordinated driverless slave vehicle. Since the availability of subsumed functionalities from these cooperating systems is changing, we have to establish safety evaluation techniques at runtime.

Ensuring safety for such cooperative functionalities is an essential requirement for getting accepted by the certification bodies. If this is not done, cooperative functionalities have no chance to get introduced to the market. In today's safety standards shifting parts of the safety evaluation to runtime is not considered. The complete safety evaluation for system and environment is done at development time. For cooperating systems this is inappropriate since the "adaptation space" would be too large by assessing all possible operational situations at development time. Related cooperative functionalities could not only vary in available or not but also in a predefined set of intermediate stages. The aggregation of system properties of the collaborating system to safe or unsafe is an additional degree of freedom which depends on the current operational situation. In addition considering always the worst case would degrade the system performance to a large extent. Another aspect is the dynamic behavior of collaborating systems. Cooperative functionalities as considered for safety evaluation are inherently safety critical. If the current operational situation is evaluated to be unsafe an adequate predefined reaction behavior is required to reduce or eliminate potential risks for the collaborating system. Depending on the use case of the cooperative functionality it could be sufficient to deactivate this functionality like for information services in wearables, but it could also be possible that a more situation adapted reaction is required like in the area of cooperative driving. Such situation dependent reactions could only be realized by monitoring safety properties at runtime. Traditional safety engineering approaches have therefore to be enhanced to also address the demands of collaborating systems to establish cooperative functionalities. Consequently, new approaches for ensuring safety are the only feasible path for the introduction of dynamical adaptive systems.

2   State of the Art

In recent years runtime trust assurance [1] and runtime safety certification [2] in open and adaptive systems are upcoming research topics since there is a rising demand for more flexible technical products, which can be adapted to user needs, to dynamic changes in service/device availability or resource situations [3]. The demand for shifting parts of the safety evaluation from development time to runtime results from technical systems which are not fully known at design time. For system concepts like Industry 4.0 a flexible modular architecture is a key factor for a high performance of the assembly line. In such technical systems safety certified modules with predefined functions can be combined in a most flexible way at runtime to adapt the system to rapidly changing customer demands and to accelerate repair times [4]. Ideally diverse previously unknown modules could be added in an easy way like plug and play and the overall system functionality should be evolved at runtime. To ensure safety for such open adaptive systems Schneider introduced the Conditional Safety Certificates (ConSerts) [5], which is the most important contribution for our approach. At runtime it is then possible to evaluate a safety certified higher level static functionality based on available safety certificates and runtime evidences (RtEs) of subordinated systems. Sharing of safety related runtime data for a system cooperation on the functional level was not in the scope of this work. Especially in vehicle domain, but also in other domains as described before, sharing of safety related data seems to be a promising approach for safety and efficiency. In today's safety standards like ISO 26262 [6] it is not considered yet. Oestberg dealt with the question how to integrate shared safety related data of vehicles into standards like AUTOSAR [7, 8]. As a result he suggested to introduce an individual data base to each vehicle, where safety related vehicle sensor data is stored. In the next step the data bases are synchronized between the collaborating vehicles to optimize their safety assessment. Based on that he concluded a safety contract concept for dynamic safety assessment is needed, but he provided no concrete one. Also Priesterjahn introduced a runtime safety analysis for cooperating vehicles based on failure propagation models [9]. But for this only development time knowledge was considered. Cooperation especially demands from participating systems that they are able to adapt themselves to provided services to gain advantage from cooperation. As a conclusion for this section it can be stated that there is at the moment no appropriate approach available which tackles the specific demands of cooperative functionalities for safety assurance and certification.

3 Dynamic Safety Contracts

In the following, the collaboration concept of dynamic safety contracts (DSCs) is explained with the already introduced example of platooning. This application provides various technical optimization opportunities along with a straightforward reaction behavior. In the use-case scenario we demonstrate the evaluation of DSCs for the follower vehicle of a platooning group, which has in case of an accident with the vehicle ahead a higher liability risk. Based on a cooperative autonomous cruise control (CACC) the platooning functionality is integrated into the vehicle. This is shown in Fig. 1. The two important performance parameters are the distance to the front vehicle and the speed, which is prescribed by the speed limit. Driving very close to the vehicle ahead leads to a more efficient highway driving, but at the same time it becomes more dangerous and has to be granted by safety considerations. To access the current operational situation in an optimal way, we consider internal safety related data from the vehicle and external data from the environment together in a unified safety contract, defined at development time and aggregated at runtime. Specifically to each situation, such a contract model should always give the maximum range of possible safety related guarantees. Thinking about continuously changing runtime parameters like speed and distances to objects, we have to consider, next to a qualitative description like 'Function works properly', also a quantitative one for safety contract modeling. Combining qualitative and quantitative runtime data as a safety quality metric leads to

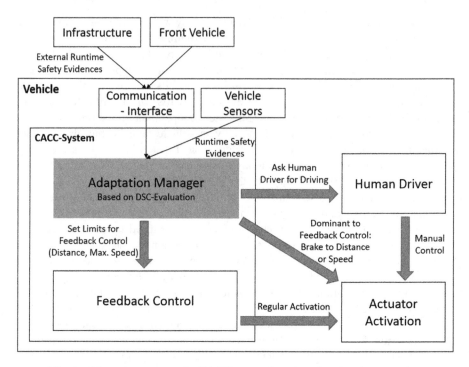

Fig. 1. Adaptation concept for CACC-system based on functional cooperation

safety contract modules with qualitative or quantitative output guarantees, which are described in the following subsections.

3.1   Qualitative Safety Contract Module

A contract module for qualitative safety assessment as shown in Fig. 2 consists of a predefined number of qualitative safety guarantee output ports (at the top of the modules). As a modeling convention they are arranged based on decreasing output guarantees from left to right. This also represents the evaluation order at runtime after the model is transformed into a computable representation. The demand-input ports consists out of qualitative and quantitative demand ports. These input ports are linked to the output ports based on Boolean logic. Qualitative input ports only check for the availability of required RtEs and change to true of false. With quantitative input ports it is checked whether certain continuous parameters fulfill predefined requirements such as lying in specified value range. Based on this module intern check a qualitative runtime proof is derived and forwarded.

Implementation of Qualitative DSCs for CACC Scenario. The qualitative safety contract module "Detection Quality" in Fig. 2 consists of two qualitative output ports. The qualitative output port *Safe Redundant Detection of V1 & V2* represents the maximum output guarantee. It guarantees a successful counterwise detection of the two

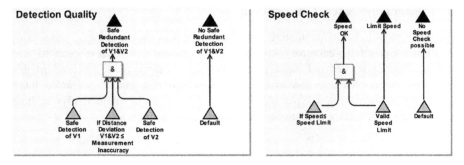

Fig. 2. Qualitative DSC modules: detection quality and speed check

vehicles. The qualitative output port *No Safe Redundant Detection of V1 & V2* represents the default guarantee which actually provides no guarantee level. The first one means that a safe redundant detection between two vehicles could be guaranteed and the second one shows that this is not possible, but at least the module is active. To guarantee a safe redundant detection it is defined in the safety module that from both vehicles a guarantee for a sufficient detection quality of the other one must be available. This means vehicle intern and shared data from the other vehicle have to be combined at runtime based on a qualitative RtE. In addition to this quality metric of detection the derived distance as the most important runtime parameter is checked for plausibility. Accordingly both quantitative current distance parameters are compared as a redundancy check. Another qualitative safety contract module "Speed Check" is shown in Fig. 2 on the right side. The module compares the internal current speed measurement with the external speed limit information. In this scenario a speed limit certificate is shared by the highway infrastructure or the platooning group via wireless communication. Thinking about platooning with regular street signs could have some disadvantages. In such scenarios street signs could be missed caused by the short distances between vehicles or they are not adaptive enough for an efficient platooning in the current operational situation. The speed limit value varies with time and place, consequently the up-to-dateness of the received speed limit has to be guaranteed. In addition the authenticity of the value origin has to be checked. Making this certificate available for safety contract evaluation in the vehicle requires that it has been successfully checked for safety and security consideration in advance, which is expressed by the qualitative input check *Valid Speed Limit*.

Based on the availability of this evidence and the accordance of the current speed value with the speed limit the internal safety property *Speed OK* can be guaranteed. If the certificate for a valid speed limit is available, but the current speed value is outside its specification, at least the internal safety property *Limit Speed* can be provided. The contained valuable information is that although the current speed is outside its boundaries, the system is able to recover the system to the specification, namely due to braking to the speed limit in an automated way. A missing valid speed limit in the vehicular infrastructure would activate the default case, which reports that the system is not able to evaluate this safety relevant aspects by itself. Consequently, the CACC system has to warn the regular driver and ask for assistance.

3.2   Quantitative Safety Contract Module

A contract module for a quantitative safety assessment as shown in Fig. 3 consists of one quantitative safety guarantee output port and an undefined number of qualitative as well as quantitative demand input ports. Quantitative input ports are used in this module to either define a quantitative degradation of the output guarantee more specifically to internal runtime parameters or to build module intern qualitative runtime proofs to check if certain parameters fulfill predefined requirements.

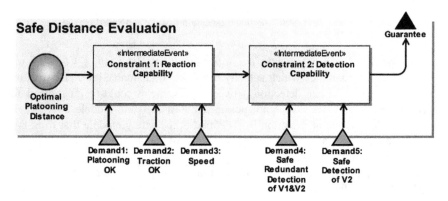

Fig. 3. Quantitative DSC module: safe distance evaluation

To the quantitative safety contract module is an ideal quantitative value assigned, which is visualized as a circle. It represents the best possible output value of the module. The ideal value is only forwarded to the guarantee output if all necessary input demands are fulfilled at runtime. Missing runtime guarantees cause a predefined degradation of the ideal value. The degradation logic is described in the constraint sub modules similar to the qualitative DSC modules based on Boolean decisions. With Boolean algebra the working principle of degradation remains understandable for safety considerations and lightweight for fast computations. Thereby the number of constraints is not limited. In the best case scenario each constraint module, if its optimal input demands are fulfilled, forwards the ideal value remaining constant, otherwise it degrades the ideal value in accordance to the contained degradation logic.

Implementation of Quantitative DSCs for CACC Scenario. In the quantitative safety contract module "Safe Distance Evaluation" in Fig. 3 the maximum quantitative safety guarantee in the sense of the smallest safe distance to the front vehicle is evaluated. The ideal value represents the shortest possible distance to the front vehicle, which is the optimum from process view. To guarantee a safe operation for the shortest distance the highest demands from Constraints 1 and 2 have to be fulfilled. The inner degradation logic from Constraints 1 and 2 for different input guarantees is shown in Fig. 4. Evaluating a safe distance to the front vehicle depends mostly on the reaction (Constraint 1) and detection (Constraint 2) capability of a vehicle, so we divided them accordingly. Such scenario dependent partitions of constraints should support modeling and comprehension of complex dependencies, but should not be considered as mandatory.

In Constraint 1 it is defined that, if the internal *Traction OK* certificate (no traction problems are detected) and the external *Platooning OK* certificate from the vehicle ahead is available, the ideal value of a safe distance is not reduced based on the reaction capability. The availability of the *Platooning OK* certificates should guarantee that there is no hazard detected in the vehicle ahead and confirms that warnings are directly propagated to the follower vehicle. In case of an emergency braking of the leading vehicle the follower vehicle should brake accordingly without substantial time delays. In addition the availability of the safety guarantee *Platooning OK* in the follower vehicle implicitly expresses that there is a working communication link between the collaborating systems and the collaboration was accepted to be trustworthy e.g. based on encryption code. But the authentication process and technical implementation of a communication link is not part of this work. If the *Traction OK* certificate is available and the *Platooning OK* guarantee is missing, there is no direct warning for the follower vehicle. For this case the CACC-system considers a short additional reaction time to detect sudden speed changes of the front vehicle. Depending on the current speed the traveled distance during the reaction time waiting for its own emergency braking varies. In Constraint 1 the reaction time is represented by the degradation of the ideal value with the transformation function *Fusion by Transformation Graph* based on the current speed as an input parameter. A missing *Traction OK* certificate always leads to a maximum degradation. Because of missing grip the CACC-system is not able to give any kind of reliable guarantees for the safe distance. In the Boolean logic the missing *Traction OK* guarantee is described with the *Default* demand, where no input guarantees have to be fulfilled. In Constraint 2 in Fig. 4 it is checked independent of the previous demands, which safety quality certificates are available for the detection of the vehicle ahead. Depending on the detection quality we defined two different safe distances since the variability of the detection quality is limited. One case is the regular detection of the vehicle ahead described with the safety certificate Safe Detection of V2 which degrades the evaluated safe distance slightly (here 20 %). By the use of cooperation the following vehicle can compare its knowledge to the measurement data of the vehicle ahead. If their measurement data about their mutual position can be successfully checked for plausibility, they establish a higher safety integrity level of detection based on redundancy. A more safety critical platooning like smaller distances

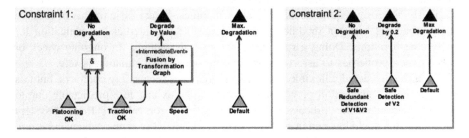

Fig. 4. Constraints 1 and 2 of DSC module "safe distance evaluation"

between vehicles could be granted by safety considerations. In Constraint 2 this is examplified with the *No Degradation* guarantee. Additional information about the working principle of the "Detection Quality" module for redundancy checks was given in the previous section. In this modeled scenario we did the evaluation of the detection quality in a separate module, which supports reuse in different safety evaluation contexts. A missing vehicle intern certificate for a sufficient detection quality of the vehicle ahead makes a determination of a safe distance impossible. This is specified with the maximum degradation of the safe distance in Constraint 2. The degradation of the ideal platooning distance based on missing guarantee certificates for the superordinated modul "Safe Distance Evaluation" is built like the following exemplary equation: Safe Distance = Optimal Value * Constr.1 * Constr.2. In case all input demands of the constraints are fulfilled, the safe distance guarantee is equal to the optimal value. In case the *Platooning OK* certificate is missing, the current speed value is considered for the transformation function. For instance, based on the current speed as input value the transformation function provides 200 % as the degradation output value and the optimal distance was set to 10 m. Besides that only the *Safe Detection of V2* certificate for the detection quality of Constraint 2 is available, which leads to an additional degradation (Safe Distance = 10 m * 200 % * 120 % = 24 m).

3.3 Composition of DSC Moduls and Evaluation Procedure

To guarantee a fast and reliable computation of runtime safety contracts we decided to model their dependencies with direct allocations as shown in Fig. 5. For this reason we arranged the DSC moduls according to their required order of evaluation of runtime guarantees for higher level safety properties and connected them via their module ports to forward qualitative and quantitative safety related data. Thereby, safety related data which requires no preevaluation can be introduced in a flexible way to all levels of DSC evaluation. Considering unsafe situations of cooperation based on degraded DSC modules requires a predetermined reaction concept. At runtime the evaluated safety contracts represent the current valid safety properties of the vehicle cooperation. Based on the remaining safety properties predefined reactions are defined in the "Safe Reaction Manager" Module. This is introduced on the top level of the composed DSC moduls in Fig. 5 as they represent the top level safety properties of the cooperation. In the next section and Fig. 6 the reaction concept is explained more detailed. Since the complete static dependency modeling of DSC evaluation is done at development time, computation time can be minimized due to forwarding runtime guarantees without previously checking requirements from other modules. Direct assignments of runtime safety properties between modules enable a traceable and predictable evaluation for safety considerations. Doing a runtime safety analysis requires an ongoing check of safety related properties to assert that the current operational situation is safe.

We also considered a flexible propagation model between safety contracts, but this would make the evaluation process much more complex and less predictable due to ongoing rearrangements processes. Since evaluation errors always force a system reaction, which could have an impact on safety and availability of the vehicular system, we decided to keep the model as lightweight as possible. Nevertheless the advantages

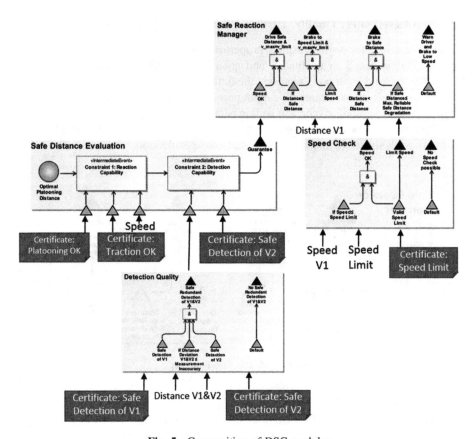

Fig. 5. Composition of DSC modules

of static dependency modeling are reached with a reduction of openness and flexibility. Previously unknown runtime safety guarantees cannot be considered in this evaluation model without further measures. Considering a restricted set of cooperation partners like in a master-slave vehicle cooperation scenario this concept is directly applicable, since all available service types for a cooperation can be taken into account at development time. Whereas, in an open adaptive system approach like the presented platooning scenario, at first a check for a possible certified cooperation between available vehicles has to be done. In this context the ConSerts approach introduced by Schneider fits best to introduce a preliminary check to the DSC evaluation. Based on conditional certificates it evaluates with a demand-guarantee runtime check of related systems a possible integration to a static higher level functionality. We propose to assign an individually adjusted DSC evaluation concept (as presented in Fig. 5) to each functional guarantee definition of a ConSert Tree.

3.4   Top Level Safety Quality Attributes and Reaction Behaviour

To define reactions for degraded safety properties at runtime we use a qualitative safety contract module based on qualitative and quantitative input guarantees as shown in Fig. 6. The demand input ports represent the different facets of degraded runtime safety properties of the system. Quantitative input ports are used again to build module intern qualitative runtime proofs to check if certain parameters fulfill predefined requirements. In addition they can be used to propagate quantitative data, which was evaluated during the safety analysis, to the module for the reaction specification.

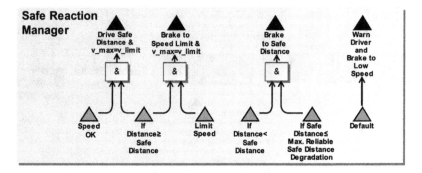

Fig. 6. Safe reaction manager

The "Safe Reaction Manager" Module in Fig. 6 defines how the system should react based on available runtime safety guarantees. The different levels of reaction of the safety analysis in the CACC-system were graphically illustrated in Fig. 1. In the use-case scenario the CACC-system informs the driver that it can be activated in case of a successfully detected front vehicle. In the same way the regular leaving of the vehicles field of vision initializes a deactivation of the CACC-system.

In case the *Speed OK* guarantee in Fig. 6 is available and the current distance to the front vehicle is larger or equal to the evaluated minimum safe distance, the adaptation manager sets the limits for the safe driving distance and the current speed limit for actuator activation for the regular CACC feedback control (Fig. 1). Since the safe distance, unlike the speed limit, is evaluated as part of the runtime safety analysis we have to make sure that the quantitative data is available for the reaction phase. In this case this is done due to forwarding the quantitative value to the reaction phase. If the feedback control is working according the permitted limits of speed and distance, safety of motion for these degrees of freedom can be guaranteed. In case the distance to the front vehicle is sufficient but the vehicle is driving too fast, the adaptation manager initializes a brake command, which is dominant to the regular feedback control. At that moment the vehicle has sufficiently reduced the speed regarding the speed limit the "Speed Check" module switches from *Limit Speed* to *Speed OK*, which shifts also the reaction in the "Safe Reaction Manager" module back from the brake command to the regular driving mode. In case the vehicle is not complying with the evaluated safe distance to the front vehicle, the system initializes a brake command similar to exceeding the maximum allowed speed and brakes until a safe operational state is recovered. Considering both threats at the same time as an exceptional case leads to a prioritized reaction of recovering a safe distance. This is done because we assumed for this scenario that a too short distance to the front vehicle is probably more dangerous than violating the speed limit. The prioritization is reached due to requiring operational safety for current closings as an additional demand for the reaction to threats which are assumed to be less dangerous. At runtime the reaction manager would activate a break command until a safe distance is reached and then it is continued until the speed limit is reached. We use the safe distance evaluation straightforward to establish a reaction, to keep the use case simple. To check if the safe distance evaluation is still reliable we introduced an additional runtime proof in the reaction manager for the reaction case of braking to a safe distance. An evaluated safe distance value, which is greater than the value of maximum degradation determined by a missing *Platooning OK* certificate, a high velocity and a degraded detection capability inside the "Safe Distance Evaluation" module, indicates that either the vehicles reaction or detection capability (or both) is lost.

The worst case scenario means that the vehicle's CACC-system is not able to guarantee a safe autonomous driving anymore, because it cannot check whether the current operational situation is safe. In this case the default reaction case is activated since no input demands from other reaction scenarios can be fulfilled. This can be caused by a total loss of the vehicles reaction capability due to traction problems of the vehicle where no guarantee about the braking distance is possible. Alternatively this can be caused by a total loss of the vehicles detection capability due to sensor problems, where the vehicle is not able to detect the front vehicle or is not able to gather other safety related information like the speed limit. In all of these cases the driver should be warned that the safety of motion cannot be guaranteed and asked to take over control whereby in parallel preventive safety measures like braking should be initialized. Thinking about a platooning group driving on a slippery surface the front vehicle would act like an additional sensor for follower vehicles and detect traction problems first. As a consequence of traction problems, the front vehicle would stop providing the *Platooning OK* certificate, and the follower vehicle would immediately start enlarging the spacing between them. Sharing safety related data has therefore not only the potential to optimize collaboration processes, but also to make them safer due to preventive safety measures.

4   Operationalization of DSC Evaluation

For the modeling of the DSC Moduls we utilized Magic Draw. At the moment we are developing a dedicated Plug-In, which should support automated code generation from the GUI. To adapt the system to current available safety guarantees (Fig. 1) the system has to continuously monitor the available safety guarantees and react in a predefined way. Recently we build a test environment based on the V-REP (Virtual Robot Experimentation Platform) simulation environment and the realtime robot control framework Finroc from RRLab at TU Kaiserslautern. We implemented the platooning scenario according the described use-case. The front vehicle is controlled with a virtual control panel, while the second vehicle is following in an autonomous way by interpreting its environment with sensor networks based on an integrated behaviour based control (iB2C). The two performance parameters (speed and distance) are evaluated inside the Finroc framework at runtime. The different safety contract modules are connected to each other inside the framework. The activation of different safety properties can then be checked due to a runtime visualization of the modules. The correct reaction behaviour can be observed in the V-REP cooperation scene.

5   Conclusion

We believe that building collaboration networks especially in the domain of autonomous vehicles based on concepts like dynamic safety contracts will make mobility safer and more efficient. DSCs could help to assess safety in a more formalized way at runtime and enable new cooperative functionalities. In our future work we want to integrate scenarios with a stronger dependency of cooperation like driverless vehicles in a master-slave configuration as they could be used for harvester scenarios in the agricultural domain. Furthermore we want to investigate how the validity period of the involved runtime safety guarantees can be determined properly.

References

1. Trapp, M., Schneider, D.: Safety assurance of open adaptive systems – a survey. In: Bencomo, N., France, R., Cheng, B.H., Aßmann, U. (eds.) Models@run.time. LNCS, vol. 8378, pp. 279–318. Springer, Heidelberg (2014)
2. Rushby, J.: Runtime certification. In: Leucker, M. (ed.) RV 2008. LNCS, vol. 5289, pp. 21–35. Springer, Heidelberg (2008)
3. Schneider, D., Becker, M., Trapp, M.: Approaching runtime trust assurance in open adaptive systems. In: Proceedings of the 6th International Symposium on Software Engineering for Adaptive and Self-managing Systems, pp. 196–201. ACM (2011)
4. Lee, J., Bagheri, B., Kao, H.-A.: A cyber-physical systems architecture for industry 4.0-based manufacturing systems. Manufact. Lett. **3**, 18–23 (2015)
5. Schneider, D., Trapp, M.: Conditional safety certification of open adaptive systems. ACM Trans. Auton. Adapt. Syst. (TAAS) **8**(2), 8 (2013)
6. ISO/CD26262. Road vehicles, functional safety part 6: Product development at the software level, part 10, guidelines (2011)
7. Östberg, K., Bengtsson, M.: Run time safety analysis for automotive systems in an open and adaptive environment. In: SAFECOMP 2013-Workshop ASCoMS (Architecting Safety in Collaborative Mobile Systems) of the 32nd International Conference on Computer Safety, Reliability and Security (2013)
8. Östberg, K., Johansson, R.: Use of quality metrics for functional safety in systems of cooperative vehicles. In: Ortmeier, F., Daniel, P. (eds.) SAFECOMP Workshops 2012. LNCS, vol. 7613, pp. 174–179. Springer, Heidelberg (2012)
9. Priesterjahn, C., Heinzemann, C., Schäfer, W., Tichy, M.: Runtime safety analysis for safe reconfiguration. In: 2012 10th IEEE International Conference on Industrial Informatics (INDIN), pp. 1092–1097. IEEE (2012)

Time-of-Flight Based Optical Communication for Safety-Critical Applications in Autonomous Driving

Hannes Plank[1]([⊠]), Gerald Holweg[1], Christian Steger[2], and Norbert Druml[1]

[1] Infineon Technologies Austria AG, Graz, Austria
Hannes.Plank@infineon.com
[2] Institute for Technical Informatics, Graz University of Technology, Graz, Austria
http://www.infineon.com/

Abstract. The automotive field has seen tremendous research effort in the past years to increase safety by using vehicle to vehicle (V2V) communication. There are however several issues in RF based V2V communication impairing the safety applications requiring hard-reality communication. Channel congestion, latency and the vulnerability to denial of service attacks demand for an alternative solution to transmit time-critical safety messages.

In this work, we discuss the security and safety aspects of free-space optical communication solutions for line-of-sight V2V communication. We show scenarios to demonstrate the high demand of a reliable low-latency communication link between cars and evaluate the requirements in communication security.

Image sensor based communication is widely accepted as the most promising optical communication link for V2V. This work offers a detailed discussion on how it is possible to increase speed and robustness by using Time-of-Flight 3D image sensors for communication. Finally, we show how communication partners can be localized and how location-aware communication can greatly benefit secured communication by mitigating relay and denial-of-service attacks.

1 Introduction

As long lasting field tests like Google's self-driving car project [9] prove, autonomous cars have a significant lower accident rate, compared to human drivers. In fact, cars operated by humans and pedestrians are the main threat for autonomous cars, due to their sometimes irrational or unpredictable behavior. In certain scenarios, autonomous cars are unable to prevent accidents, when the front view is occluded by other cars. An example is shown in Fig. 1, where a pedestrian steps on the road between two subsequent cars. The accident might be preventable by a reliable communication link between the cars. The car in the front can sense the pedestrian and can detect the fatal movement in the moment of passing by. The front car can send a warning message to the back car, which can take immediate action.

© Springer International Publishing Switzerland 2016
A. Skavhaug et al. (Eds.): SAFECOMP 2016 Workshops, LNCS 9923, pp. 183–194, 2016.
DOI: 10.1007/978-3-319-45480-1_15

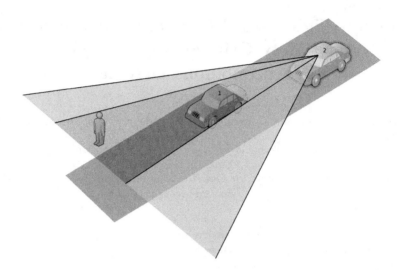

Fig. 1. Example for the need of low delay V2V communication: if vehicle 1 detects a movement of the pedestrian towards the street, it can warn vehicle 2.

Such scenarios require reliable real-time and low latency V2V communication. In this work, we show how recent RF based V2V communication is unable meet these requirements and how optical communication can tackle this problem.

In V2V communication, vehicles in a certain area form an RF ad hoc network. Since they share the same channel, a delay is introduced due to collision avoidance protocols. While RF based V2V communication is successfully used to transmit accident warnings over a longer range, problems appear in close domain, where time requirements are more critical.

Optical line-of-sight communication between subsequent cars has the huge advantage that the communication is limited between two partners and no collisions can appear. Messages can be transmitted directly with very low delay and without the risk of channel congestion. Such free-space optical communication has been traditionally conducted by narrow field of view photo detectors. In a dynamic environment like between moving cars, image sensor based detectors are better suited. Image sensor based communication systems offer a wide field of view and the ability to locate the communication partner, separating the source of information from other interfering light sources creating a robuster communication link. A rather unexplored aspect of image sensor based communication is location-awareness, where the information source during communication can be assigned to a position.

Time-of-Flight sensors are image sensors, originally designed for capturing depth images. However as we show in this work, they are a promising technology enabling robust image sensor based communication with a novel, more efficient modulation method. While traditional image sensors measure an induces charge, proportional on the amount of incoming photons, Time-of-Flight cameras apply a modulation to each pixel and are able to measure phase shift differences of pulsed incoming light. The signal of non-pulsed light is drained from the pixel, eliminating all background interference.

Security is a crucial aspect in V2V communication and certain attack scenarios exist, which can impact the safety of vehicular networks. The nature of image sensor based optical communication offers the significant advantage of localizing the communication partner. Even if the distance cannot be determined by the image sensor itself, localization data is available from other sensors, such as RADAR, LIDAR, or other depth sensing systems. We propose a V2V communication concept, enriching state-of-the-art cryptographic security protocols with localization information, which mitigates relay attacks.

This work is structured the following way: Sect. 2 discusses V2V communication with focus on its limitations in safety and security in low-delay applications. Recent image sensor based free-space optical communication approaches in the automotive domain are then introduced in Sect. 3. In Sect. 4, we provide insight about the workings of Time-of-Flight sensors, and how it can be used for robust image sensor based communication links. Finally we introduce our own concept for a secure and location-aware optical communication link.

2 Problems of RF Based V2V Communication

Vehicular ad hoc networks (VANET) are going to make huge contributions to the safety and convenience of assisted and autonomous driving. Using the RF channel for communication however is not the ideal solution for applications which require very low latency and high reliability. In the RF domain, the communication medium is shared among multiple entities and thus requires collision avoidance protocols. According to Cailean et al. [5], channel congestion is the main reason for unreliability of otherwise properly configured VANETs. Even if a channel is reserved for high priority emergency warnings, a certain delay is always introduced by collision avoidance mechanisms. As shown by Bilstrup et al. [3], current V2V can experience large channel access delays and can not be considered a real-time communication protocol. Mass events like large car crashes can event trigger a broadcast storm [21], where many nodes in a VANET broadcast messages at high frequencies. Agarwal et al. therefore emphasize the need of directional communication for safe and reliable message exchange in dense environments [1].

Crash prediction and avoidance mechanisms are the most common applications, requiring low latency communication. Even if a crash is unavoidable, crash prediction can improve passenger safety by airbag pre-triggering [10]. Crash scenarios as presented in Sect. 1 exemplify the requirement of low latency in V2V communication.

Optical communication between subsequent cars is a promising technology which is congestion free and can offer a very low communication delay. Cailean et al. [5] propose a combination of visible light communication and RF based solutions, being the key to meet modern demands of safety critical V2V communications systems.

2.1   Security

The dynamic environment of VANETs introduces certain security threats, which are not easily countered by cryptographic methods. VANETs based on RF are vulnerable to denial of service (DoS) attacks, which are simple to execute by RF jamming. Different countermeasures are discussed by Hasbullah et al. [11], however they are based on switching to different channels, RF transmission technologies or the utilization of multiple transceivers. While these countermeasures can mitigate the severity of a DoS attack, a sophisticated jamming attack can also block evasion channels.

False accident warnings [22] can impair the traffic flow, as they cause a slow down of the surrounding vehicles. In a network where all cars are authenticated and communication packets are signed, the warnings could be matched with the driver. This however compromises privacy, since vehicles could be tracked by an attacker or authority.

3   Image Sensor Based V2V Communication

The problems in the RF domain of V2V communication can partially be solved by additionally connecting vehicles with an optical line-of-sight based communication system. A line-of-sight connection will limit the communication to two cars and thus prevent channel congestion issues and therefore also reduce latency.

The dynamic environment of V2V communication is a special application of visible light communication, which requires a wide field of view. If a traditional optical communication system with a single photo detector is used, the wide field of view would bundle all lightsources onto the sensor, which would result in a comparatively low SNR. It is therefore necessary to separate lightsources, which is conveniently archived with cameras. The incoming light is projected by the lens onto the sensor, separating the lightsources. When the pixels on the image sensor are used to sample the communication partner's light source, it is possible to only select suitable pixels.

In the past years, various image sensor based communication approaches for V2V communication appeared [5]. The first advances were driven by the fact that cars usually already frequently encounter lightsources [24]. Road, tunnel, traffic or brake lights are increasingly driven by LEDs, which can be modulated. Modulation schemes have been proposed, enabling to modulate visible lightsources without inducing perceivable flickering [4].

Originally most image sensors are designed to produce video streams with typically 30 fps and thus lack of sampling speed for communication. Since most sensors require a full readout of all pixels, the frame rate is severely limited, and dedicated high speed hardware is required to reach feasible speeds for V2V communication [15].

An approach to boost the bandwidth of mostly conventional image sensors are multiple input, multiple output (MIMO) approaches where information is emitted by multiple LEDs in parallel [18]. MIMO approaches rely on the separability of lightsources which however limits the distance. Increasing the resolution of image sensors could counteract the distance problem, but either requires a larger camera or smaller pixels reducing the light sensitive surface area.

A general problem of free-space visible light communication are atmospheric turbulences, which are discussed further in Sect. 3.1. These turbulences are a severe problem for MIMO communication approaches. When light is scattered by small particles like raindrops or fog, the different light sources in MIMO approaches are mixed and can no longer be separated by the receiver.

The demand for fast image sensor based communication lead to the development of dedicated optical communication image sensors (OCI). The sensor of Takai et al. [19] features dedicated communication pixels which are interleaved with imaging pixels. The imaging pixels directly provide a flag image, using comparator circuits. This flag image is used to detect the position of high intensity objects such as LEDs. The communication pixels are designed to be very sensitive to illumination changes, and can be read out separately using an address generator.

3.1   The Influence of Atmospheric Turbulences

A challenge for free-space optical communication are atmospheric turbulences which involve all kinds of obstructions such as fog, rain, snow or dust. Kim et al. [12] simulate rainy conditions on an optical communication channel. They use on/off keying for transmission and measure a SNR loss of 60 %. They show that using modified fixed decision thresholding (MFDT) reduces the bit error rate dramatically.

Fog is the most challenging obstruction, since it absorbs, scatters and reflects light. This means that the sender might also sense a reflection of his own signal. Kim et al. also investigate the influence of fog on visible light V2V communication [13]. Experiments with a fog chamber show massively decreased SNR, which could be compensated to a certain degree by focusing more light on the sensor with an additional lens. Interestingly, their experiments also show that red light exhibits the lowest attenuation coefficient. This confirms the use of red taillights or (invisible) near infrared light (NIR) for optical communication under foggy conditions.

4   Time-of-Flight Sensors

Time-of-Flight cameras are designed to measure the distance on each pixel between the camera and the scene. The basic principle, as illustrated in Fig. 2, is to measure the time it takes emitted light to travel from the camera to the scene and back to the sensor.

During a measurement, an active illumination unit next to the sensor emits pulsed infrared light. The ToF image sensor registers the phase difference between emitted and reflected light. Each pixel is equipped with a photonic mixture device (PMD) [14], capable of converting a phase shift to a measurable voltage. The basic principle of a PMD is illustrated in Fig. 3. When photons

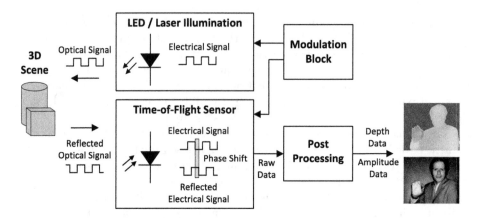

Fig. 2. The principle of Time-of-Flight depth sensing, obtained with changes from [6].

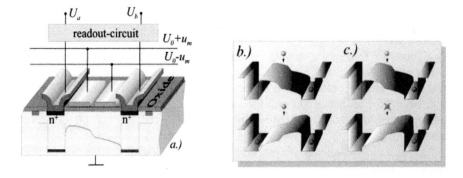

Fig. 3. The working principle of a ToF pixel. A: a pixel is supplied with a modulation signal u_m. B,C: charges are sorted into bucket A or B, depending on the modulation signal. Obtained with changes from [20].

arrive at the sensor, they induce charges in the sensor. Each PMD is equipped with two buckets to store the charges. A reference signal decides into which bucket the charges are transferred. The reference signal is a pulsed signal with the same frequency as the signal emitted by the illumination unit. After a certain integration time, the contents of the buckets are read-out and digitized. The charge difference between the buckets is proportional to the phase-shift of these signals and thus proportional with distance between camera and scene. Because ToF sensors are designed to measure the phase shift of pulsed light signals, ToF sensors can be used as novel visible light receivers for optical communication.

Captured raw images are usually severely biased by different amount of light being reflected by different surface materials. It is common to capture multiple raw images with different phases shifts of the illumination signal and use post-processing methods to reconstruct depth images. Most ToF cameras feature therefore an integrated phase shifting unit (PSU) for emitting phase shifted signals. This enables phase shift modulation of the emitted signal without additional hardware.

Conventional free-space optical communication suffers from background light. Direct lightsources like the sun and a bright environment will reduce the SNR of direct detection based systems. A significant advantage of Time-of-Flight based optical communication is that the pixels are exclusively sensitive to pulsed light. The reason is that PMD pixels of a ToF sensor measure charge differences between two buckets. If non-pulsed light arrives at the pixels, the photons are evenly distributed into both buckets with no change of the charge difference. The pulse frequency of ToF cameras depends on the intended application and is typically in the range between 1 and 100 MHz.

The sender and the receiver must use the same frequency, otherwise the signal is suppressed. This enables to establish multiple non interfering VLC connections in a close environment by using different frequencies.

Each pixel has a limited capacity to store charges during exposure. The ToF sensor we use in our work features a suppression of background illumination (SBI) circuit on each pixel [20]. The SBI circuit actively drains the buckets of the PMD element during exposure. This prevents the pixels from saturating from background illumination, and enables to use ToF sensors for robust depth sensing and communication in bright environments (Fig. 4).

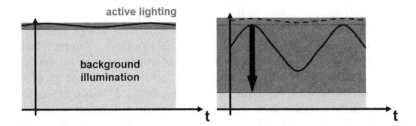

Fig. 4. Pulsed signal detection characteristics of a PMD pixel with (right) and without (left) suppression of background illumination. Obtained from [8]. (Color figure online)

4.1   Optical Communication with Time-of-Flight Sensors

Phase shift keying (PSK) of pulsed light has not been widely considered as viable modulation method in visible light communications [16]. The first and to our knowledge only approach to use Time-of-Flight cameras for optical communication has been accomplished by Yuan et al. [25]. They established a one-way MIMO communication link, using a ToF camera in depth sensing mode as receiver. Photodiodes are used to sense the pulsed illumination signal of a ToF camera. This signal is amplified and phase shifters are used to modulate information using PSK. The modulated signal is then emitted back to the ToF camera with an LED array. The signal is received by the ToF camera and the encoded information is extracted by analyzing the depth image.

In our approach, we use two ToF cameras for mutual communication, serving as receiver and sender. Capturing depth data is optional, and raw images are used for communication. Limiting the exposure time to a minimum enables high frames. The integrated phase shifting unit is used for PSK modulation and the illumination unit is used as emitter.

Compared to on-off keying, pulse position or pulse shift keying based modulation schemes, phase shift keying offers certain advantages. At first, phase shift keying is more robust to signal intensity variations. In a dynamic environment, modulated light does not arrive homogeneously on a set of pixels. During the exposure time, a moving lightsource illuminates an undefined number of pixels with varying intensity. This motion blur might prevent to recover the intensity and consequently causes an information loss. A phase shifted pulsed signal however will have a consistent phase shift, independent of the number of photons arriving at the sensor. The SNR suffers from less sensed photons, but can be compensated by averaging all influenced pixels.

Image sensors produce a relative large amount of data, which takes significant time to read and digitize, limiting the frame rate. Using a high speed camera for optical communication counters this problem, but requires powerful hardware. Phase shift keying however increases the symbol size per transmitted frame. On-off keying is able to transmit one bit per frame on a synchronized system, while it is possible to transmit multiple bits per frame using PSK.

While lightsources are separated by projection onto image sensors, there might be the possibility of interference from other optical communication systems. Usually, the signal strength from a direct connection is so significantly stronger than light from indirect paths, that interference is not problematic. Fog might however reflect sufficient light from other ToF lightsources. Optical interference can be avoided with ToF sensors, by using different pulse frequencies for communication. Unlike RF, pulsed optical communication does not need channel permissions and can be used without limitations over a wide spectrum. Time-of-Flight cameras are also designed to use a wide range of modulation frequencies. Due to the requirement of unambiguous range extension in depth sensing, ToF cameras are able to alternate between multiple modulation frequencies. Our experiments and simulations show that a frequency difference of hundred Hertz is sufficient to effectively suppress a signal.

5   Secured and Robust Communication with Time-of-Flight Sensors

While a lot of attack risks are mitigated by the nature of optical line-of-sight communication, location and context-awareness can further enhance security. In this Section we analyze how the position of a communication partner can be determined and how this localization benefits secure communication.

5.1   Context and Location-Aware Communication

Despite the separation of lightsources, camera based optical communication has the advantage that the sensor can help to provide valuable information about the communication partner. When a line-of-sight connection is established between two subsequent cars for crash prevention, it is important that the cars are located in the same lane.

When image sensors are used for communication, it is not always the case that the produced images are recorded. High sampling speeds, optical filters or active suppression of background light can be the reason that 2D images cannot be used to classify communication partners directly. It is however feasible to fuse data from the communication sensor with other sensors such as LIDAR, 2D or 3D stereo cameras, which are increasingly available in modern cars. The position of the projected lightsource on the image sensor can be used to determine the 3D direction of the communication partner. To determine the direction vector $\overrightarrow{d}$, the camera is approximated with the common pinhole model. The pixel position of the projected light source $x_{i,j}$ is multiplied with the pseudo inverse of the camera calibration matrix $\tilde{P}_D$.

$$\overrightarrow{d} = \tilde{P}_D x_{i,j} \tag{1}$$

The relative direction between camera and communication partner can be transformed to the global coordinate system of the car, when the position of the camera to the origin of the global coordinate system is known. The result is a line-of-sight vector, starting at the center of the camera. This vector can be used to localize the partner's illumination source by combining it with data from other sensors. It is possible to calculate the intersection between the optical line-of-sight and the sensed 3D pointcloud from on-board depth sensors. The intersection point is the 3D position of the communication partner's illumination source.

The line-of-sight can also be directly projected onto 2D images. The projected line can be used as search space to determine the exact source of information using 2D information. Given the fact that car models can be robustly determined by 2D cameras [2], it is possible to use a database to determine and verify the expected lightsource position. Then it is also possible to use triangulation between the communication image sensor and the 2D camera to determine the distance.

5.2   Benefits for Secured Communication

When two subsequent cars communicate over a line-of-sight connection, the transmitted data is already hard to manipulate. Denial of service attacks take a lot more effort, as the line-of-sight connection needs to be either blocked, or overridden by a stronger signal. When using Time-of-Flight sensors, blocking a line-of-sight connection is even harder, as overriding a lightsource need to be done with modulated light at the same pulse frequency. While message manipulation and eavesdropping is hard, state-of-the-art encryption is highly recommended. Wasef et al. [23] propose a public key infrastructure for ad hoc vehicular networks, which can be extended to line-of-sight connections. The security of state-of-the-art encryption, authentication and key exchange protocols can be further be enhanced by location-awareness.

A problem that still impairs secured connections of all kinds are relay attacks. These attacks forward unaltered encrypted connections between two unsuspecting parties. Francillion et al. demonstrate the severeness of these attacks in passive keyless car entry systems [7]. In the application of line-of-sight communication between cars, an adversary could for instance relay the signal of the front car to the car in the back, allowing a potential appearing road hazard to be undetected.

As we previously showed [17], location-aware communication can mitigate relay attacks by the exchange of localization information. Each communication partner forwards the sensed relative position of the other partner over a secured connection. The exchanged localization information has to correspond to the measured position of the communication partner. During a relay attack, the origin of information is not identical with the communication partner. Using GPS position data as localization information is simple, but vulnerable to spoofing attacks. A more reliable way is to use localization information determined by using an additional depth sensing system as described in Sect. 5.1. The mutual relative distance is sufficient for a successful localization verification.

6   Conclusion and Future Work

In this work, we discussed the issues of RF based V2V communication with applications demanding low latency. We showed why camera based optical communication is a viable solution for location-aware communication. Our own approach is based on Time-of-Flight depth sensing technology, which has the novel ability to use phase shifted pulsed light signals for communication. Along with suppression of background illumination and robustness against interference, this makes it a promising technology for optical communication in the V2V domain. Location-aware communication benefits communication security as it can mitigate relay attacks.

For our future work, we will implement a reliable communication solution, using Time-of-Flight cameras and an FPGA based processing system. We will implement a secured communication protocol, using state-of-the-art hardware security anchors. Interfaces are going to be added, so our solution can be integrated into a diversity of embedded systems and can serve as a reliable secured communication solution.

References

1. Agarwal, A., Little, T.D.C.: Role of directional wireless communication in vehicular networks. In: Intelligent Vehicles Symposium (IV), 2010 IEEE, pp. 688–693, June 2010

2. Arzani, M.M., Jamzad, M.: Car type recognition in highways based on wavelet and contourlet feature extraction. In: 2010 International Conference on Signal and Image Processing (ICSIP), pp. 353–356, December 2010

3. Bilstrup, K., Uhlemann, E., Strm, E.G., Bilstrup, U.: On the ability of the 802.11p MAC method and STDMA to support real-time vehicle-to-vehicle communication. Eurasip J. Wirel. Commun. Netw. **2009** (2009)

4. Cailean, A.M., Cagneau, B., Chassagne, L., Dimian, M., Popa, V.: Miller code usage in visible light communications under the PHY I layer of the ieee 802.15.7 standard. In: 2014 10th International Conference on Communications (COMM), pp. 1–4, May 2014

5. Cailean, A.M., Cagneau, B., Chassagne, L., Popa, V., Dimian, M.: A survey on the usage of DSRC and VLC in communication-based vehicle safety applications. In: Proceedings of the 2014 IEEE 21st Symposium on Communications and Vehicular Technology in the BeNeLux, IEEE SCVT 2014, pp. 69–74 (2014)

6. Druml, N., Fleischmann, G., Heidenreich, C., Leitner, A., Martin, H., Herndl, T., Holweg, G.: Time-of-flight 3D imaging for mixed-critical systems. In: 13th International Conference on Industrial Informatics (INDIN), pp. 1432–1437, July 2015

7. Francillon, A., Danev, B., Capkun, S.: Relay attacks on passive keyless entry and start systems in modern cars. In: Network and Distributed System Security Symposium (NDSS), February 2011

8. Frey, V.: PMD cameras for automotive and outdoor applications (2010)

9. Google. Google self-driving car (2016)

10. Gstrein, G., Sinz, W.: Improvement of airbag performance through pretriggering

11. Hasbullah, H., Soomro, I.A., Manan, J.-L.A.: Denial of service (DOS) attack and its possible solutions in VANET. World Acad. Sci. Eng. Technol. **4**(5), 411–415 (2010)

12. Kim, Y.-H., Cahyadi, W.A., Chung. H.Y.: Experimental demonstration of LED-based vehicle to vehicle communication under atmospheric turbulence. In: ICTC (2015)

13. Kim, Y.H., Cahyadi, W.A., Chung, Y.H.: Experimental demonstration of VLC-based vehicle-to-vehicle communications under fog conditions. IEEE Photonics J. **7**(6), 1–9 (2015)

14. Lange, R., Seitz, P.: Solid-state time-of-flight range camera. IEEE J. Quantum Electron. **37**(3), 390–397 (2001)

15. Nishimoto, S., Nagura, T., Yamazato, T., Yendo, T.: Overlay coding for road-to-vehicle visible light communication using LED array and high-speed camera. In: ITSC (2011)

16. Pathak, P., Feng, X., Hu, P., Mohapatra, P.: Visible light communication, networking and sensing: a survey, potential and challenges. IEEE Commun. Surv. Tutor. **17**(c), 2047–2077 (2015)

17. Plank, H., Steger, C., Ruprechter, T., Holweg, G., Druml, N.: Survey on camera based communication for location-aware secure authentication and communication (2016)

18. Roberts, R.D.: A MIMO protocol for camera communications (CamCom) using undersampled frequency shift ON-OFF keying (UFSOOK). In: 2013 IEEE Globecom Workshops, GC Wkshps 2013, pp. 1052–1057 (2013)
19. Takai, I., Ito, S., Yasutomi, K., Kagawa, K., Andoh, M., Kawahito, S.: LED and CMOS image sensor based optical wireless communication system for automotive applications. IEEE Photonics J. **5**(5) (2013)
20. Tobias, M., Holger, K., Jochen, F., Martin, A., Robert, L.: Robust 3D measurement with PMD sensors. Range Imaging Day **7**, 8 (2005). Zürich Section 5
21. Tonguz, O.K., Wisitpongphan, N., Parikh, J.S., Bai, F., Mudalige, P., Sadekar, V.K.: On the broadcast storm problem in ad hoc wireless networks. In: 2006 3rd International Conference on Broadband Communications, Networks and Systems, pp. 1–11, October 2006
22. Tyagi, P., Dembla, D.: Investigating the security threats in vehicular ad hoc Networks (VANETs): towards security engineering for safer on-road transportation. In: Proceedings of the 2014 International Conference on Advances in Computing, Communications and Informatics, ICACCI 2014, pp. 2084–2090 (2014)
23. Wasef, A., Lu, R., Lin, X., Shen, X.: Complementing public key infrastructure to secure vehicular ad hoc networks [security and privacy in emerging wireless networks]. IEEE Wirel. Commun. **17**(5), 22–28 (2010)
24. Wook, H.B.C., Komine, T., Haruyama, S., Nakagawa, M.: Visible light communication with led-based traffic lights using 2-dimensional image sensor. In: 2006 3rd IEEE Consumer Communications and Networking Conference, CCNC 2006, vol. 1, pp. 243–247, January 2006
25. Yuan, W., Howard, R., Dana, K., Raskar, R., Ashok, A., Gruteser, M., Mandayam, N.: Phase messaging method for time-of-flight cameras. In: IEEE International Conference on Computational Photography (ICCP), May 2014

Limitation and Improvement of STPA-Sec for Safety and Security Co-analysis

Christoph Schmittner[1]([✉]), Zhendong Ma[1], and Peter Puschner[2]

[1] Department of Digital Safety and Security, AIT Austrian Institute
of Technology, Vienna, Austria
{christoph.schmittner.fl,zhendong.ma}@ait.ac.at
[2] Department of Computer Engineering, Vienna University
of Technology, Vienna, Austria
peter@vmars.tuwien.ac.at

Abstract. Safety-critical Cyber-physical Systems (CPS) in vehicles are becoming more and more complex and interconnected. There is a pressing need for holistic approaches for safety and security analysis to address the challenges. System-Theoretic Process Analysis (STPA) is a top-down safety hazard analysis method, based on systems theory especially aimed at such systems. In contrast to established approaches, hazards are treated as a control problem rather than a reliability problem. STPA-Sec extends this approach to also include security analysis. However, when we applied STPA-Sec to real world use cases for joint safety and security analysis, a Battery Management System for a hybrid vehicle, we observed several limitations of the security extension. We propose improvements to address these limitations for a combined safety and security analysis. Our improvements lead to a better identification of high level security scenarios. We evaluate the feasibility of the improved co-analysis method in a self-optimizing battery management system. We also discuss the general applicability of STPA-Sec to high level safety and security analysis and the relation to automotive cybersecurity standards.

Keywords: Cyber-physical systems · Safety and security co-analysis · STAMP · STPA-Sec · Automotive cybersecurity

1 Introduction

Safety-critical cyber-physical systems (CPS) become increasingly complex and interconnected. For example, the future transportation system is envisioned to be intelligent and interconnected, in which heterogeneous Information and communications technologies (ICT) and physical elements, from vehicular systems (e.g. hybrid vehicles) to energy provider and infrastructure components, interact with each other and the physical environment to be self-organizing for an optimized multi-modal mobility strategy for drivers, passengers, and goods. Such an interconnection introduces cybersecurity risks which might threaten the safety of the system. As a results, system analysis must consider safety and security in order to define system goals and a concept for a safe and secure system.

© Springer International Publishing Switzerland 2016
A. Skavhaug et al. (Eds.): SAFECOMP 2016 Workshops, LNCS 9923, pp. 195–209, 2016.
DOI: 10.1007/978-3-319-45480-1_16

One of the challenges is to identify potential safety and security risks at the beginning of a system's development lifecycle where only high level information is available for the analysis (i.e. the "concept phase"), in order to reduce and mitigate the risks to an acceptable level. As one of the new approaches, STPA-Sec [1] is an extension of the System-Theoretic Process Analysis (STPA) [2,3] that extends the safety analysis method with security considerations. In STAMP, systems are modeled as hierarchical structures in which higher level controllers control processes at lower levels via actors. The lower levels send feedback to the higher levels via sensors. The output of STPA-Sec is a list of system-level scenarios which can lead to losses. In this paper, we identify several limitations of STPA-Sec and propose improvements when applying STPA-Sec for safety and security co-analysis. Specifically, we improve the annotated control loop used in STPA for causal analysis for identifying unsafe control actions due to security attacks. We evaluate and demonstrate the improved STPA-Sec by applying it to a connected and self-optimizing battery-management system (BMS) for hybrid vehicles.

In the following, Sect. 2 gives an overview of the State of the Art, Sect. 3 introduces and discusses STAMP (Systems-Theoretic Accident Model and Processes), STPA and STPA for Security (STPA-Sec). Section 4 presents our improvements to STPA-Sec for safety and security co-analysis. Section 5 applies the improved STPA-Sec to the case studies and a real-world scenario. Section 5.3 discuss the general applicability of STPA-Sec to safety and security co-analysis and its relation to automotive cybersecurity standards, followed by the conclusion in Sect. 6.

2   State of the Art

The automotive safety standard ISO 26262 [4] divides the system lifecycle into Concept, Development (System, Hardware, Software) and Productions, Operation and Maintenance phase. In each phase specific activities and work results are defined. The main goal during the concept phase is to define functional safety requirements and functional safety concept. Both are based on the safety goals which result from the hazard and risk analysis (HARA). During HARA, hazards and risks are identified and rated. Based on this rating, an automotive safety integrity level (ASIL) is defined, which denotes the required risk reduction. Recently the first automotive cybersecurity standard SAE J3061 [5] was published, proposing a security engineering process in parallel or joint with the safety lifecycle. Regarding the application of a cybersecurity process in conjunction with a safety process tailored to ISO 26262, the standard proposes the following:

> The integration of these activities may be done by keeping the Cybersecurity and safety activities separate, but performing these activities in conjunction with each other and with the same team, or parallel activities may be done by developing an integrated technique that covers both safety and Cybersecurity at the same time. An example of this is to develop a technique to perform both a hazard analysis and risk assessment, and a threat

analysis and risk assessment at the same time using a single integrated template and method. A tightly integrated process for Cybersecurity and safety has the advantage of a common resource set, thus, requiring fewer additional resources [5].

In recent years, multiple methods for safety and security co-analysis have been developed, aiming at a combined approach towards safety and security. SAHARA (A Security-Aware Hazard and Risk Analysis Method) [6] extends the classical Hazard and Risk analysis with security related guide words and an evaluation of risks. FMVEA (Failure Mode, Vulnerabilities and Effects Analysis) [7] extends the Failure mode and effects analysis with threat modes and vulnerabilities. CHASSIS (Combined Harm Assessment of Safety and Security for Information Systems) [8] is a methodology for safety and security assessments and formulation of mitigation measures, based on use case and sequence diagram modeling. Other approaches focus less on the identification of security related hazards but more on a detailed analysis via extended Fault Trees [9–11].

In this paper, we will investigate STPA-SEC [1], a top-down safety and security analysis method, to the concept phase of an automotive use case and evaluated the results according to the requirements provided by ISO 26262 and SAE J3061.

3   Review of STPA-Sec

System-theoretic Process Analysis for Security (STPA-Sec) [1] extends the safety-focused System-theoretic Process Analysis (STPA) method for security analysis. Both methods are based on the theory of STAMP (Systems-Theoretic Accident Model and Processes) [2]. In STAMP, systems are modeled as hierarchical structures in which higher level controllers control processes at lower levels via actors. The lower levels send feedback to the higher levels via sensors. STAMP views safety accidents as a result of a lack of control, instead of a chain or sequence of events. Since modern systems are increasingly complex with multiple interacting elements, it is difficult to identify root causes for accidents. STPA-Sec examines each control action under different possible conditions and guide words and identifies loss scenarios. Losses are interpreted as insufficient or missing controls or safety constraints.

Step 1: Establishing the Systems Engineering Foundation. STPA-Sec takes a top-down approach focusing on identifying unacceptable losses and vulnerable states in order to locate essential system services and functions to be protected and controlled. The first step identifies such unacceptable losses.

Step 2: Creating a Model of the High Level Control Structure. In this step the control model of the system is generated. A control model consists of the controlled processes, controller, sensors and actors and relevant control actions and sensed process variables.

Step 3: Identifying Unsafe/Insecure Control Actions. All control actions from the control model are reviewed. Unsafe or unsecure control actions or control actions leading to hazards (or vulnerable system states) are identified, based on four guide phrases (i.e. "control action not given", "control action given incorrectly", "wrong timing or order of control action", and "control action stopped too soon or applied too long").

Step 4: Developing Security Requirements and Constraints/Identifying Causal Scenarios. In this step, unsafe/insecure control actions are extended to unsafe/insecure scenarios in order to identify missing high level safety/security constraints. An unsafe/insecure scenario consists of an unsafe/insecure control action, context and potential causes. Intentional causal scenarios, e.g. attack scenarios, are identified by analyzing the physical and logical infrastructure similar to established security analysis. An annotated control graph (cf. Fig. 1) supports the identification of potential causes for unsafe control action.

During our application of STPA-Sec, we identified two limitations in the co-analysis of safety and security. First, guidance for the identification of intentional causal scenarios is challenging to apply. While some terms in Fig. 1 can be interpreted in an intentional and security related way (e.g. "incorrect or no information provided" could be interpreted as result of a Denial of Service), we found it helpful to explicitly include such guidance. Second, another restriction of the control loop model is the exclusion of security relevant elements. The control loop describes the control process for the system in the intended

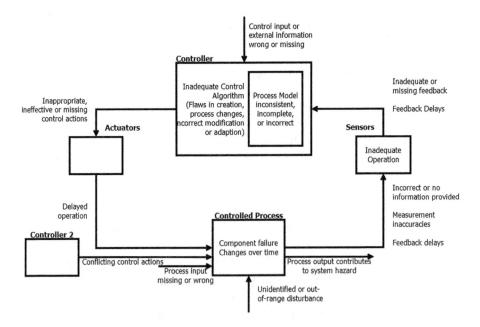

Fig. 1. Control loop annotated with potential starting points for the identification of unintentional causes for unsafe control actions [3]

configuration. However, attackers, undesired influences from elements outside the intended control model, and the exchange of sensitive information not relevant for the control model are not included. While the control model is an important view on the system and its behavior, it does not adequately capture the view of a potential attacker.

4 Extension of STPA-Sec

We propose the following extensions to improve the aforementioned limitations.

4.1 Alignment of Terminology

The safety and security community have developed their own terminologies. Safety and security co-analysis and interaction require clear and correct communication between the two communities. Some of the STPA-Sec terms are safety-oriented, leading to ambiguity and misunderstanding for security analysis. The problem is aggravated because some terms in STPA even deviate from standard safety terminology.

We address this issue by aligning important terms used in STPA-Sec in a safety and security context. First, we identify the terms in STPA-Sec that cause ambiguities. When possible, we use STPA terms as anchors and align the security terms to them. Second, we provide definitions for these terms that are valid for both safety and security. Third, we resolve potential differences between safety and security terminology, and add security-oriented terms that are necessary for co-analysis. We also add definitions to terms in STPA-Sec that are different from common safety terminology. We base our security definition on [12], commonly accepted in the security community. Table 1 shows the resulting terminology. Note that our intention is not to define a comprehensive vocabulary, but rather to establish a common understanding, helpful for safety and security co-analysis.

Table 1. Safety and security terminology

Terms	Definition
Attack	Attempt to gain unauthorized access to or make unauthorized use of an asset
Accident	Event which causes undesired losses of life, availability etc.
Control	In general, alter the operation condition of a system; in security, measure that is modifying risk
Control loop	Model describing the control flow of a system or process. The model consists of one or more controllers, controlled processes, sensors and actuators
Event	Occurrence or change of a particular set of circumstances, also refers to an incident or accident
Hazard	Dangerous system states which can lead to accidents
Threat	Potential cause of an unwanted incident, which may result in harm to a system
Unsafe control action	Control action which can cause, under certain circumstances, hazards
Unsafe control scenario	Scenario which describes context and potential causes for the execution of an unsafe control action
Loss event	Accident
Vulnerability	Vulnerable system state, STPA-Sec uses it to refer to hazard; in security, weakness of an asset or control that can be exploited by one or more threats

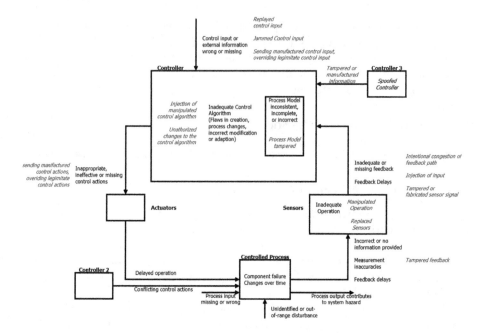

Fig. 2. Control loop with starting points for the identification of malicious scenarios (Color figure online)

4.2   Guidance for the Elicitation of Intentional Scenarios

In order to improve the guidance for the identification of intentional unsafe control scenarios (e.g. attack scenarios leading to the activation of an unsafe control action), we propose an extension to the security approach in STPA. The control model is reviewed by a team of experts for potential causal scenarios for the intended and malicious activation of unsafe control actions. We extend the annotated control graph as a starting point for the investigation of intentional scenarios. This guidance should not be seen as a checklist which covers all possibilities. It is intended as a starting point for further thoughts and the investigation of unsafe and insecure scenarios.

Figure 2 shows the classic guidance for the investigation of unintentional scenarios and, in red and cursive, our extensions for the investigation of intentional scenarios. In addition to the annotations, we add a spoofed controller in order to note the potential that conflicting control actions are intentionally introduced in the system. It is important to consider external unplanned interactions during the investigation of potential causes.

5   Case Study

We evaluate our extended approach by reviewing a number of already identified scenarios in order to backtest if these scenarios are identifiable with the improved guidance for identifying intentional scenarios. In addition, we demonstrate the application to a real-world complex and connected automotive system.

5.1   Backtest of Existing Scenarios

The first reviewed scenario is from the automotive domain. Miller and Valasek identified the missing authentication of control actions in automotive on-board networks as a major vulnerability [13]. If there is no control over the source of a control action, the safety and security depend completely on the insulation of the control system. Guaranteeing that a system is completely free from undesired control actions is much harder than restricting the allowed sources for control actions. Injecting manufactured control actions in an otherwise unaltered system will cause conflicts between legitimate and illegitimate control actions and the consequences and system reactions are not predictable. Such intentional scenarios for unsafe control actions are identifiable with the new guidance *sending manufactured control actions/input, overriding legitimate control actions/input*.

Kundur *et al.* [14] presented a typical cyber attack scenario for smart grids. The scenario includes fabricating or tampering sensor information which causes incorrect decision for the controller regarding necessary control actions for the load management. Such incorrect decisions or unsafe control actions could result in generator trip out. This scenario and similar are covered with the extended guidance for the control path between sensor and controller, especially with *Tampered of fabricated sensor signal*, in the extended annotated control graph from Fig. 2.

Dadras *et al.* [15] presented an interesting attack scenario on vehicular platooning. An adversary vehicle is able to exploit the control logic and destabilize the platoon or influence position and velocity of other vehicles through local changes. By accelerating and braking in a certain frequency range they caused the control algorithm of other vehicles to become instable and oscillating. This manipulation is aimed at the sensor input and exploits known weaknesses in the control algorithm to cause unsafe control algorithm. Such attacks are difficult to perform and require knowledge of the internal workings of the attacked system. Since they are also very difficult to detect and defend against there is some interest to explore such threats. Krotofil *et al.* [16] demonstrated similar behavior in an industrial context, the process in a chemical plant was attackable by manipulating the input of a few sensors. Such scenarios are identifiable with the extend guidance for considering *tampered feedback* from the controlled process.

Although not comprehensive, the backtesting of existing scenarios shows that our approach is better at identifying unsafe and unsecure scenarios using limited and high level information in the system development concept phase.

5.2   Analysis of Battery Management System

We apply our extended STPA-Sec approach to the analysis of a Battery Management System (BMS) for hybrid vehicles [6]. A BMS optimizes the driving strategy, e.g. usage of the electrical engine or combustion engine, based on multiple factors (including the goal for the driving experience chosen by the driver, e.g. minimizing energy consumption, maximizing acceleration and external factors like chosen route, charging opportunities, temperature). Besides, the BMS also directly controls the high-voltage battery system that provides power supply for the electrical engine, and charges the battery from external or internal sources. The different charging scenarios include charging from an external source, the plug-in charging, or charging from internal sources, regenerative braking and the usage of the on-board (internal) combustion engine as generator.

Step 1 - System Description and Hazard and Accident Identification.
Figure 3 gives an overview of the architecture of the BMS and the on-board network. The BMS estimates the state of the battery system by monitoring total and cell voltage, cell temperature and current. Based on the measured values and an internal model of the battery behavior, it calculates the state of charge and state of function(health). It controls discharging and charging of the battery and ensures the safe operation, ensured by restricting the system to its safe operating area. The BMS can partially control the environment (heating or cooling) and request a restricted usage of the battery by sending a message via the CAN-Bus to other control units. The complete high-voltage system can also be de-energized. The CAN communication is utilized for the communication with other control units and to receive information about external parameters which influence the control strategy. External communication and remote connectivity is accessed via the Telematic Unit. In addition, the BMS is directly connected to the outside via the charging interface [17].

Figure 4 shows the control model for the Battery Management System. This control model is the result of an iterative process of extending and refining.

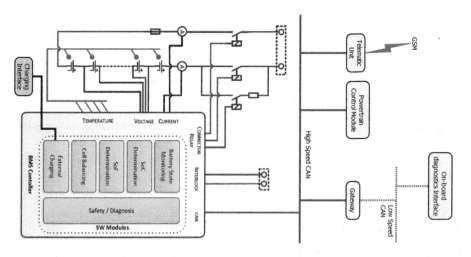

Fig. 3. Architecture of the battery management system [6]

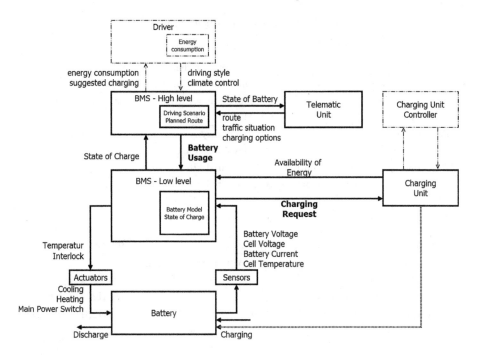

Fig. 4. Control Loop of the battery management system

We started with a rather simple model of the battery as a controlled process and the BMS as controller and refined it.

The low level BMS estimates the state of charge, based on the internal process model of the battery, e.g. how voltage and current relate to the overall charge in the battery. It influences the energy consumption of the vehicle and maintains safe operation of the battery. This is done by controlling the environment and restricting or influencing the discharge of the battery. It is responsible for the short term control strategy for the battery.

The high level BMS is responsible for the long term control strategy for the battery. The goal is to optimize the battery usage. This system relies on the state-of-charge and state-of-health data from the low level controller and combines this information with external data about charging options, costs, route and traffic situation. It interconnects with other vehicles and the infrastructure and optimizes the driving strategy for each vehicle based on the overall traffic flow and energy consumption.

While the driver is not directly involved in controlling the battery, most hybrid vehicles tend to give feedback to the driver on whether he or she is driving ecologically [18]. In some vehicles this information is also available via mobile apps [19]. These apps also allow some level of remote control of the Battery Management System.

Table 2. Table of identified hazards

ID	Hazard	Comment
H1	Over current	Different for charging or discharging
H2	Over voltage	Only relevant during charging
H3	Under voltage	May permanently damage battery performance
H4	Over temperature	May damage battery
H5	Under temperature	Temporary reduces battery performance
H6	Over pressure	May damage battery
H7	Ground fault or leakage current	Undesired flow of power
H8	Reduced Control over vehicle speed	Undesired acceleration or deceleration

Table 3. Table of identified accidents

ID	Accident	Related Hazards
A1	Electric Shock for vehicle passengers or persons touching the vehicle	H7
A2	Battery causes a vehicle fire	H1, H2, H4, H6
A3	Collision with object or other vehicle	H1, H2, H4, H6, H8

In Table 2, we list some of the possible hazardous scenarios for the battery management system.

Based on the list of identified hazards, the following accidents are related to the BMS (Table 3). We focused on safety related loss events and excluded other losses like financial or operational losses.

Step 2 - Identification of Unsafe Control Action. Due to the high number of unsafe control actions generated by STPA-Sec we present only an excerpt of all identified unsafe control actions. In order to identify unsafe control actions all control action from the control loop model of the system Fig. 4 are reviewed, using the guide phrases Sect. 3. Identified unsafe control actions are then linked to the hazards.

Control Action: Charging Request

1. Control Action not given
   (a) Battery is not charged (non-hazardous)
2. Control Action given incorrectly
   (a) Excessive charging request[1] is transmitted to charging unit during plug-in charging (H1, H2, H4, H6)
3. Wrong timing or order of Control Action
   (a) Charging request to charging unit for plug-in charging is transmitted before battery system is ready to charge (H4)

---

[1] Depending on the phase in the charging cycle and the battery there are limits to voltage and current which, when exceeded, may damage the battery.

(b) Charging curve is transmitted to charging unit in wrong order for plug-in charging, constant current and constant voltage phases are swapped (H1, H2, H4, H6)

4. Control Action stopped too soon or applied too long
   (a) Charging Request to charging unit for plug-in charging is transmitted after battery has been fully charged (H1, H2, H4, H6)
   (b) Transmission of charging request to charging unit for plug-in charging has been stopped too soon (non-hazardous)

Control Action: Battery Usage

1. Control Action not given
   (a) Battery usage strategy is not transmitted to low-level BMS, State of charge or driving strategy is not considered for the discharge of the battery (H3, H8)
2. Control Action given incorrectly
   (a) Command given to charge battery during driving by recuperative braking while battery is fully charged (H1, H2, H4, H8)
   (b) Command given to charge Battery while vehicle is driving in electric mode (H8)
   (c) Command given to use battery for electrical engine is given while battery charge is critically low (H3).
3. Wrong timing or order of Control Action
   (a) Command to charge battery by combustion engine is given during plug-in charging (H1, H2, H4)
4. Control Action stopped too soon or applied too long
   (a) Battery usage requested while Battery voltage is critically low (H3)

Step 3 - Identification of Intentional and Unintentional Scenarios for Unsafe Control Actions. Based on the extend annotated control loop (cf. Fig. 2), we identified intentional and unintentional causal scenarios for the unsafe control actions. The identification of the causal scenarios is done via an review of the unsafe control actions, the control model and the annotated control model by experts from the safety, security and automotive domain.

Excessive Charging Request is Transmitted to Charging Unit (H1, H2, H4, H6)

– An excessive charging request can be caused by a modified charging request from the BMS to the charging unit due to tampered process model in the BMS software to enable fast charging for non-fast chargeable batteries. Potential motivation for the owner is that he is interested in faster charging and does not care about longevity of battery due to leasing contract for battery.
– A wrong charging request from BMS to charging unit may be caused by a failure/design error in the temperature sensor for a battery. Due to financial reasons a malicious manufacturer could reduce the number of sensors per battery cells below the number required for a reliable reading.

– Even when the vehicle BMS requests the correct power level a manipulation on the communication between BMS and charging unit could lead to an unsafe charging request. Such a manipulation could be directed at the charging unit or the central charging management system at the backend.

Command Given to Use Battery for Electrical Engine is Given While Battery Charge is Critically Low (H3, H8).

– Battery usage strategy is "optimized" and replayed battery messages are injected into the CAN Bus via the On-board diagnostics interface while the battery charge is critically low. This increases vehicle performance while decreasing life time of the battery and may cause permanent damage to the battery or even the vehicle. Owner is interested in maximized battery usage and does not care about longevity of battery due to leasing contract for battery.
– The battery is replaced with a different model with a changed behavior. The corresponding process model in the controller is not changed which leads to a mismatch between physical process and assumed process behavior. A mechanic shop could do this in order to save money or because they have no access to the internal process models in the controller.
– A compromised telematic unit could be used to send messages which impersonate the high level BMS. This is easy in a CAN Network since messages only carry a receiver ID and no sender ID. Therefore any compromised Electronic Control Unit (ECU) could be used to send commands which trigger unsafe control actions. The telematic unit is especially vulnerable, because most of the external communication is done via this ECU.

5.3 Evaluation and Discussion

STPA-SEC is strongly focused on the considered and intended control model to identify deviations. While this is sound for the identification of safety related effects, it does not cover more information-security centric considerations such as privacy, as recommended in SAE J3061 to apply cybersecurity engineering to all elements including Personally Identifiable Information (PII). Hence losses related to privacy and confidentiality are currently not considered in STPA-Sec or in the control model. STPA-Sec excludes the flow and exchange of data not directly connected to the control of a process, e.g. battery usage information collected for insurance reasons. Connections not directly related to the control flow but can be misused might be difficult to identify within STPA-Sec. An analysis based on an architectural or dataflow model would be better suited for the identification of such risk scenarios.

In addition the general approach of STPA, applying the four guide phrases to all control actions from the control loop model of the system to identify multiple unsafe control actions and then developing multiple unsafe scenarios leads to a very high number of unsafe scenarios which need a strict filtering.

With respect to the automotive cybersecurity guideline SAE J3061 [5], we have the following opinions. The list is divided according to the lifecycle steps in SAE J3061, which are modeled after the lifecycle presented in ISO 26262 [4].

Item Definition. Step 1 in STPA-Sec requires similar information about the system as the item definition. There is a stronger focus on potential interactions and interfaces with systems outside the control model in the existing standard guidance. This is probably based on the fact that even if there is no direct intended influence on a considered control process, there could be an influence due to a manipulation or malfunction in an adjacent system. This extends to the consideration of the system and the system architecture and the distribution and allocation of functions among the involved systems and elements.

Initiation of the Safety/Security Engineering. The initiation of the safety lifecycle is missing from the activities required by STPA-Sec. This step is used to clarify responsibilities and tailor the safety/security lifecycle for the development and is therefore in our opinion outside of the scope necessary for a analysis method.

Hazard and Threat Analysis and Risk Assessment. Automotive safety and security engineering follows a risk based approach. The objective of the hazard and threat analysis and risk assessment is to identify and categorize hazards and threats, determine potential causes and formulate the safety and security goals for preventing or migrating them. The safety and security goals are based on the concept of avoiding unreasonable risks and reducing risks to a tolerable level. SAE J3061 requires additionally a identification of threats to Personally Identifiable Information (PII), this is currently not contained in STPA-Sec.

After the identification and classification of hazards and threats scenarios, STPA-Sec can be used to derive a set of constraints for a system to avoid such scenarios. Constraints, which restrict the system behavior, are only a part of the safety goals. Other concepts which ensure safe and secure operation like a transition to a safe state with reduced functionality or connectivity or fault/intrusion tolerant solutions are not directly mappable to constraints.

Functional Safety/Security Concept. The functional safety and security concept defines the functional safety and security requirements necessary to fulfill the safety and security goals. While a subset of the requirements can be derived from the constraints defined in STPA-Sec, there are additional aspects addressed in a functional safety and security concept. This is partially caused by different approaches towards safety and security engineering currently pursued in the standards and in STPA-Sec. The standards follow the strategy of fault or vulnerability prevention and fault or vulnerability tolerance [20]. This includes more than trying to limit a system to only execute safe actions, the STPA approach. There are some overlaps between fault prevention and constraining a system to safe actions but this is currently a rather unexplored area.

6   Conclusion

In this paper we discussed the limitations of STPA-Sec and proposed several improvements for using it for top-down identification and analysis of unsafe and insecure scenarios for the concept phase in CPS design and development. We applied our proposed improvements in an automotive Battery Management System case study. Despite the improvements suggested in this paper, there are still open issues and it is very likely that a single approach will not be sufficient to satisfy all needs during the safety and security engineering of CPS. In general, STPA-Sec is suitable in the concept phase for safety & security co-engineering, but the results could be improved by combining the method with other approaches that focus more on the network and system architecture. In addition, STPA-Sec requires additional methods for the identification of potential hazards and the rating of risks. It is also still unclear if STPA-Sec is capable of handling large systems with a higher complexity and size.

There are some issues in STPA-Sec that do not align completely with current safety and security standards and activities. This requires extensions and the use of additional methods when developing a system in a standard-conform way. This is also addressed in ISO26262 with the requirement to use both, top-down and bottom-up analysis techniques. Addressing the aforementioned issues will be our research activities in the immediate future.

Acknowledgement. This work is partially supported by EU ARTEMIS project AMASS (contract no. 692474) and Austrian Research Promotion Agency FFG on behalf of Austrian Federal Ministry of Transport, Innovation and Technology BMVIT.

References

1. Young, W., Leveson, N.: Systems thinking for safety and security. In: Proceeding ACSAC 2013, pp. 1–8. ACM Press (2013)
2. Leveson, N.: A new accident model for engineering safer systems. Saf. Sci. **42**, 237–270 (2004)
3. Leveson, N., Thomas, J.: An STPA Primer. Cambridge, MA (2013)
4. ISO: ISO 26262-Road vehicles-Functional safety (2011)
5. SAE: J3061 Cybersecurity Guidebook for Cyber-Physical Vehicle Systems (2016)
6. Macher, G., Sporer, H., Berlach, R., Armengaud, E., Kreiner, C.: SAHARA: a security-aware hazard and risk analysis method. In: 2015 Design, Automation and Test in Europe Conference and Exhibition (DATE), pp. 621–624. IEEE (2015)
7. Schmittner, C., Gruber, T., Puschner, P., Schoitsch, E.: Security application of failure mode and effect analysis (FMEA). In: Bondavalli, A., Di Giandomenico, F. (eds.) SAFECOMP 2014. LNCS, vol. 8666, pp. 310–325. Springer, Heidelberg (2014)
8. Raspotnig, C., Karpati, P., Katta, V.: A combined process for elicitation and analysis of safety and security requirements. In: Bider, I., Halpin, T., Krogstie, J., Nurcan, S., Proper, E., Schmidt, R., Soffer, P., Wrycza, S. (eds.) EMMSAD 2012 and BPMDS 2012. LNBIP, vol. 113, pp. 347–361. Springer, Heidelberg (2012)

9. Steiner, M., Liggesmeyer, P., et al.: Combination of safety and security analysis-finding security problems that threaten the safety of a system. In: Computer Safety, Reliability, and Security (2013)
10. Masera, M., Nai Fovion, I., De Cian, A.: Integrating cyber attacks within fault trees. Reliab. Eng. Syst. Saf. **94**(9), 1394–1402 (2009)
11. Bouissou, M., Bon, J.-L.: A new formalism that combines advantages of fault-trees and markov models: Boolean logic driven Markov processes. Reliab. Eng. Syst. Saf. **82**(2), 149–163 (2003)
12. ISO/IEC: ISO/IEC 27000 Information technology - Security techniques - Information security management systems - Overview and vocabulary
13. Miller, C., Valasek, C.: Adventures in Automotive Networks and Control Units, Las Vegas (2013)
14. Kundur, D., Feng, X., Liu, S., Zourntos, T., Butler-Purry, K.L.: Towards a framework for cyber attack impact analysis of the electric smart grid. In: 2010 First IEEE International Conference on Smart Grid Communications (SmartGridComm), pp. 244–249. IEEE (2010)
15. Dadras, S., Gerdes, R.M., Sharma, R.: Vehicular platooning in an adversarial environment. In: Proceedings of the 10th ACM Symposium on Information, Computer and Communications Security, pp. 167–178. ACM (2015)
16. Krotofil, M., Larsen, J., Gollmann, D.: The process matters: ensuring data veracity in cyber-physical systems. In: Proceedings of the 10th ACM Symposium on Information, Computer and Communications Security, pp. 133–144. ACM (2015)
17. Chynoweth, J., Chung, C.-Y., Qiu, C., Chu, P., Gadh, R.: Smart electric vehicle charging infrastructure overview. In: Innovative Smart Grid Technologies Conference (ISGT), pp. 1–5 (2014)
18. Goodwin, A.: 2011 Kia Optima Hybrid review: 2011 Kia Optima Hybrid, June 2011. http://www.cnet.com/products/2011-kia-optima-hybrid/
19. Goodwin, A.: 2015 Ford Focus Electric review: Ford keeps its electric car in Focus by lowering the price, November 2014. http://www.cnet.com/products/2015-ford-focus-electric/
20. Ye, F., Kelly, T.: Component failure mitigation according to failure type. In: 2004 Proceedings of the 28th Annual International Computer Software and Applications Conference. COMPSAC 2004, pp. 258–264. IEEE (2004)

Security Services for Mixed-Criticality Systems Based on Networked Multi-core Chips

Thomas Koller[1]([envelope]) and Donatus Weber[2]

[1] Chair for Data Communications Systems, University of Siegen, Siegen, Germany
thomas.koller@uni-siegen.de
[2] Chair for Embedded Systems, University of Siegen, Siegen, Germany
donatus.weber@uni-siegen.de

Abstract. Modern cyber-physical systems are designed to execute safety-critical applications with different criticality levels on the same platform. Security is an emerging topic in this domain and gains more and more importance since security vulnerabilities in the systems are accompanied by the risk of malicious attacks. Targeting these vulnerabilities allows an attacker to manipulate the system which results in a decrease of dependability and safety. Therefore, security mechanisms are required to ensure an adequate protection against malicious attacks. The European FP7 project DREAMS introduces a service-based architecture to implement mixed-criticality systems on networked multi-core chips. The architecture is a cross-domain architecture and is based on core services for communication, execution, time synchronization and resource management. The security services extends these core services to provide secure communication, time synchronization and resource management for the architecture. This paper defines the required security properties to harden the DREAMS architecture against malicious attacks. The security properties are mapped to concrete security services that serve as basis for the implementation of the architecture. These services are categorized into different security levels and applied to the core services of the DREAMS architecture.

Keywords: Mixed-criticality · Security · Service-based architecture · Cyber-physical systems · Embedded systems

1 Introduction

Mixed-criticality systems that execute applications of different criticality levels, come into use in a steadily growing number of application areas such as avionics, industrial control or health care systems. These systems are often used for safety critical applications requiring precisely defined levels of dependability and safety. But security vulnerabilities can lead to a decrease of dependability and safety. To avoid this decrease, security in mixed-criticality systems is becoming a major topic.

© Springer International Publishing Switzerland 2016
A. Skavhaug et al. (Eds.): SAFECOMP 2016 Workshops, LNCS 9923, pp. 210–221, 2016.
DOI: 10.1007/978-3-319-45480-1_17

Today's mixed-criticality systems are often defined to operate in trusted environments without direct physical access from outside as for instance in the avionics domain. Nevertheless, future use cases for mixed-criticality systems build on sharing data with systems of the outside world that are not part of the trusted environment. Examples are applications in the internet of things or the smart factory (industry 4.0) domain that need to exchange data with other systems over potentially insecure networks. In the wake of the recent information leakages and cyber attacks, information security has become an integral part of modern systems.

The European FP7 research project Distributed Real-time Architecture for Mixed Criticality Systems (DREAMS) introduces a distributed real-time architecture for networked multi-core chips executing applications of different criticality levels. This paper defines the security requirements for the service-based architecture executed on networked multi-core chips including the communication on network as well as application level and explains the security solution.

The remainder of the paper is organized as follows. Section 2 presents an overview of related work. Section 3 describes the DREAMS architecture and its system structure. The architecture and its system levels are analyzed with regard to security in Sect. 4. Afterwards, Sect. 5 defines the appropriate security properties. In Sect. 6, the required security services for the DREAMS architecture are defined. These services are categorized into different security levels in Sect. 7. Section 8 introduces core services of the DREAMS architecture that are using the security services and classifies them into the security levels. Finally, Sect. 9 concludes the paper and outlines future work.

2   Related Work

The importance of security in mixed-criticality systems is not only given by the request for data privacy, but also by the fulfillment of safety and dependability requirements since these systems are often operated in safety critical domains. Furthermore, a direct relation exists between security and safety, therefore security vulnerabilities can affect the safety of the overall system. More detailed information on the relationship between safety and security is available in [4].

Two levels of communication need to be distinguished in systems with networked multi-core chips. Communication on chip level comprises all communication between the processor cores via the network-on-chip (NoC), while cluster level communication targets the interconnectivity between the multi-core processor nodes.

There are several approaches for securely transferring data on a NoC. [7] proposes a NoC firewall to protect the NoC from malicious instructions. Similar solutions to secure the NoC are described in [3,5,6].

Security aspects of time-triggered system-on-chip (TTSoC) architectures have been elaborated in [13]. [8] describes a security architecture using partitioning with secure channels for the ACROSS [11] multi-processor system-on-a-chip (MPSoC).

Communication on cluster-level can be secured with techniques, such as MACsec [1] including [2], if Ethernet is used, or IPsec [12], if IP is used.

The DREAMS architecture combines different integration levels of mixed-criticality systems (i.e., cluster, chip and software execution environment) and offers real-time capabilities. Since this kind of architecture is new for the this domain, security solutions have not yet been investigated. The research work presented in this paper presents the ongoing research on security in mixed-criticality systems to close the gap.

3   DREAMS Architecture

The system structure of a mixed-criticality system executing on networked multi-core chips based on the DREAMS architecture can be described by a combination of physical and logical view as defined in [10] (Fig. 1).

The physical view consists of nodes interconnected by an off-chip network which in turn forms a cluster. The system can consist of a set of clusters. In a node, different tiles are interconnected using a network interface (NI) by a NoC. These tiles can be comprised of one ore more processor cores, they can be a memory or they are formed by other resources, e.g., an I/O resource. In the former case, a processor core can run a hypervisor which in turn provides partitions. These partitions, which are separated by time and space partitioning, executes software components.

In the logical view these software components form application subsystems which are part of different criticality domains. Application subsystems are assigned to criticality levels. Application subsystems with the same criticality level can form a criticality domain. Components communicate through message-based interfaces with messages using virtual links. These virtual links are realized as end-to-end simplex multicast channels.

Applications located in the partitions of a tile use these virtual links to exchange data with communication partners, such as memories, peripherals or other applications. These communication channels consist of on-chip and off-chip parts. The different parts are connected via gateways as depicted in Fig. 2.

An example of these applications is the resource management in DREAMS. The components of the resource management, i.e., global resource manager

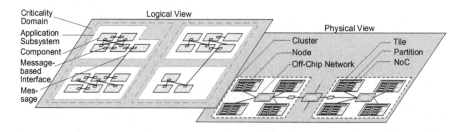

Fig. 1. DREAMS system architecture as defined in [10]

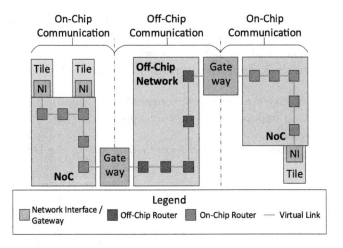

Fig. 2. On-chip/off-chip network

(GRM), local resource managers (LRMs), local resource schedulers (LRSs) and resource monitors (MONs), are placed in different locations of the system which cause that the communication between the components includes the on-chip and the off-chip network.

DREAMS defines a waistline structure of domain-independent platform services. Towards the bottom, a variety of implementation choices is supported to instantiate these services on different platforms. The waistline services comprise a secure and fault-tolerant global time base as well as timely and secure communication, execution and integrated resource management services for time and space partitioning. Optional services with increased functionality and flexibility are built upon this waistline.

More detailed information on the DREAMS architecture is available in [9,10].

4   Security in the DREAMS Architecture

Security needs to be considered at different levels of the DREAMS architecture. This includes security of data in the memory, on the chip, off the chip, transmission of data from the chip to the off-chip network, in the hypervisors and in the software design of the applications running on the DREAMS architecture.

The focus for securing the physical communication is laid on the off-chip network which connects the different chips. The off chip network is for a attacker one of the easiest accessible parts of the system. Approaches to secure the NoC are presented in [3,5–7].

Depending on the view on these secure communication services, there are different end points for the communication services. This means that end-to-end communication is seen differently as described in the following. Based on the classification of the communication at the physical level and the logical level (Sect. 3), there are two classes of secure communication services.

End-to-end security for the off-chip network (physical level) means that the communication between the two communication end points, the gateways between the on-chip and the off-chip network, is secured and provides the requested security services. In this case, the NoC is treated as a secure trusted zone.

End-to-end security for the logical communication refer to the secure communication from an application to another application (Fig. 3). This includes the entire virtual link.

Based on this classification, three security domains for the DREAMS architecture can be distinguished:

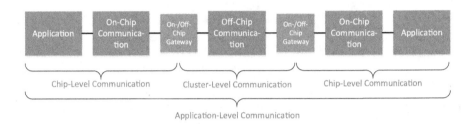

Fig. 3. Communication levels

- **Chip-level security** covers the requirements for on-chip security, e.g., protection against an attacker having access to the chip and tries to attack components on the same chip.
- **Cluster-level security** covers the requirements of off-chip security, i.e., the communication between different chips to prevent attacks such as man-in-the-middle attacks, replay attacks, spoofing attacks, denial-of-service (DoS) attacks and data masquerading attacks. The requirements in this section also concern secure communication between the GRM, LRMs, LRSs and MONs, as instantiations of these components can be located on different nodes.
  In addition, a global time base is essential for predictable virtualization of resources and time and space partitioning in DREAMS. The time distribution and synchronization is performed on network level and needs to be protected against active attacks.
- **Application-level security** covers the complete end-to-end communication channel (virtual link) between two applications. This includes the on-chip (chip-level) and off-chip (cluster-level) parts.

In all of these security levels an adjusted key management is required. The key management for chip-level, cluster-level and application-level security has different requirements, since symmetric key or asymmetric key techniques can be used.

5 Required Security Properties

First step in the process of defining the DREAMS security services is the identification of required security properties. The following set is the result of a security analysis performed on the DREAMS architecture.

- **Integrity** is required on application level for applications such as the resource management. Configuration messages must not be modified unnoticeably. Every intended and unintended modification of the message should be detectable. The same applies for the cluster-level communication between the off-chip components and the off-chip gateways.
- **Authenticity** is required on application level to ensure that data is genuine and that the actual origin of the data is the same as the claimed origin. Especially for the resource management it has to be ensured, that only a valid GRM can reconfigure the system.
  On cluster level, authenticity ensures that two components in the off-chip network are able to verify each other, e.g., two nodes including the components in between.
- **Confidentiality** is required in use cases like health care applications where private data must not be exposed. In this case, confidentiality is requested on application level.
  On cluster level, confidentiality is required for messages that are exchanged between the different nodes through the off-chip network. Applications that do not implement the confidentiality services on application level can use the cluster-level service of off-chip communication.
- **Access Control** is required to restrict access to a component.
  On application level, not every application should be able to use a service provided by another application.
  On cluster level, only authorized nodes and off-chip components should be able to access the system.

6 Definition of Security Services

The majority of the security services and mechanisms is integrated transparently into the DREAMS architecture. Applications use them implicitly, e.g., by using the network level communications without knowing that the communications take place with integrated security services. The security services for application-level security have to been used explicitly by the applications.

The security services for the DREAMS architecture are defined by mapping the security properties of Sect. 5 to the system levels of Sect. 4.

6.1 Integrity

The integrity service generates a cryptographic checksum for a message, which is transmitted together with the message. The integrity check service verifies the integrity of a message by recalculating the cryptographic checksum on the received message and comparing it with the received checksum. The checksum is realized by a message authentication code (MAC). With this checksum, any modification in the message is detectable.

Using the integrity check service for off-chip communication, the receiver of the message detects changes in the data that occur in the off-chip communication.

The integrity service for end-to-end communication ensures that all changes are noticeable and that not only the changes during the off-chip communication are detectable. For example, this service can be used by the resource management components (GRM, LRMs, LRSs and MONs) to ensure the integrity of the communication.

6.2 Authenticity

The authentication code generation service generates a MAC tag (symmetric algorithms) or a digital signature (asymmetric algorithms) on the message for ensuring the data origin as well as to verify the communication partner.

The authentication code verification service verifies the data origin or the communication partner by verifying the received MAC tag or digital signature along with the message. It is used by the on-chip/off-chip gateways and the switches for authenticating the off-chip communication and by the applications to verify the authenticity of the application-level end-to-end communication.

6.3 Confidentiality

To provide confidentiality, encryption and decryption services are required. The encryption service encrypts data with a given cryptographic key. It transforms a plain text into a cipher text. The decryption service in turn transforms a cipher text into a plaintext. If the key is correct and there was no transmission error, the plaintext is correctly recovered.

The encryption and decryption service for off-chip communication is used for confidential communication between two components, e.g., between on-chip/off-chip gateways and switches, respectively.

The encryption and decryption service for end-to-end communication is used for a confidential communication between two applications. Even the system components between the two applications, e.g., gateways and switches, cannot interpret the content of the communication.

On both levels, attackers and the unintended recipients, such as malicious applications cannot construe the messages because they do not possess the key to decrypt the exchanged messages. Only the legitimate communication partners, owning the correct cryptographic key, can decrypt the exchanged data.

6.4 Access Control

The access control service verifies, if a system resource is allowed to access the requested object.

For off-chip communication the access control service checks, if a component has the permission to communicate through the on-chip/off-chip gateway. The gateway checks both directions, the on-chip/off-chip communication and the off-chip/on-chip communication.

For end-to-end communication it checks the permission if an application is allowed to communicate with another application or a component, e.g., with the secure memory or a different partition.

6.5 Additional Services

To provide the main security services, additional security services are required. These includes the key management comprising the key storage.

Key Generation and Destruction Service. The key generation and destruction service generates cryptographic keys needed for secure communication and destructs (securely removes) the keys that are note longer needed. The service can generate both symmetric keys and asymmetric key pairs. Symmetric keys are used for encrypted communication. Asymmetric keys are used for the sharing of the symmetric keys or with some additional effort, they can be used to authenticate a communication partner or the origin of the data. If a cryptographic key is no longer needed by the application for which it was created, the service destructs the key which is usually stored in the secure storage.

Key Exchange Service. The key exchange service exchanges cryptographic keys between the communication partners. Considering the threat assumptions for the on-chip and the off-chip network (Sect. 4), this service is mainly used for the off-chip communications. For application-level communication, there are two different options: Using symmetric algorithms, the key exchange can be performed in a similar way as for the cluster-level. Using asymmetric algorithms (or a hybrid combination with symmetric and asymmetric algorithms), a public key infrastructure (PKI) has to be established. The key exchange is performed in a secure way so that an adversary cannot get hold of the keys transferred through the network.

Secure Storage Service. The secure storage service saves important data, such as cryptographic keys, in a secured part of the memory. Applications can use it to save sensitive data in the storage. No other application has access to this part of the memory and so, it cannot interpret the sensitive data. The access to the storage is controlled by an access control list. The secure storage service can be used by the key generation and destruction service for managing the cryptographic keys for the application-level security.

7   Security Service Classification

The security properties and the resulting security services can be used jointly. The common usage of the security properties are classified into four categories as presented in Table 1. A classification into different categories allows an selection of a security level that is required by a concrete service or application in the DREAMS architecture. Not every combination is reasonable, just the same as an independent usage of confidentiality. In the latter case, an attacker can manipulate the encrypted data and, depending of the content of the plain data, the receiver cannot recognize the manipulation.

Table 1. Classification of security properties

Security level	Security property
0	No security property
1	Integrity
2	Integrity & Authenticity
3	Integrity & Authenticity & Confidentiality

On security level 0, no security property is used. Security level 1 provides integrity that allows to recognize manipulation of the data. In addition to integrity, security level 2 provides authenticity. A manipulation of data is detectable and the data origin as well as the communication partner can be verified. Confidentiality is provided on security level 3. It is always used in combination with integrity and authenticity. As described above, using confidentiality without integrity would not protect against data manipulation. Authenticity is included because of the usage of the authenticated encryption (AE) or authenticated encryption with associated data (AEAD) mode of operation. This saves the necessity to provide a fifth security level providing only integrity and confidentiality.

Access control is a security service which is independent of the described security levels and is not listed in the table. If the service is required, it can be used in parallel to the selected security level.

The security services are provided by security mechanisms described in Sect. 6. Table 2 summarizes the security mechanisms used for the different security levels. No security mechanism is required on level 0. A MAC provides integrity on level 1. On level 2, depending of the usage of symmetric or asymmetric algorithms, MACs or digital signatures can be used. Using the symmetric MAC, the authenticity is proved by applying the correct common key. To provide confidentiality on level 3, encryption and decryption mechanisms are used. Integrity and authenticity are provided in the same way as on level 2.

Table 2. Classification of security mechanisms

Security level	Security mechanism
0	No security mechanism
1	MAC
2	MAC or Digital signature
3	MAC or Digital signature & Encryption/Decryption

8   Use Cases in the DREAMS Project

The communication between resource management components and the time synchronization are two examples of DREAMS core services that use the security services and mechanisms.

8.1   Resource Management

The resource management is located on application level. Attacks on the resource management can lead to wrong configurations of the system or of individual resources, e.g., an attacker could masquerade himself as a GRM and select an inappropriate configuration. One aspect that has to be secured are the messages that are exchanged between the resource management components. These messages may contain sensitive data. Additionally, the messages must not be manipulated and the origin of the message has to be verifiable. These requirements demands the security level 3 and the security services have to be provided on application level.

8.2   Time Synchronization

The time synchronization service is located on cluster level. Each node of the system possess a clock that has to be synchronized. Attacks on the time synchronization service can lead to wrong time values in the entire system or in individual components. If the time values are wrong in the entire system, this can cause an incorrect behavior regarding the real time and time triggered measurements can be taken at the false point in time. If individual components are attacked, they will perform actions at the false point in time. This causes an untimely behavior, e.g., untimely messages. Confidentiality is not important for time synchronization messages. But the integrity and the authenticity have to be guaranteed. Security level 2 fulfills the requirements for the time synchronization service. This security service has to be provided on cluster level. As the security services of the cluster-level communication are integrated transparently into the off-chip communication, the time synchronization service does not have to implement them explicitly.

9   Conclusion

Security services have been identified as mandatory part of the DREAMS architecture when it comes to hardening it against vulnerabilities. The set of required security properties comprises authenticity, integrity, confidentiality and access control that need to be guaranteed on different system levels, namely chip, cluster and application. The security services for the cluster-level have been defined in a way that their use is transparent for the applications. Security services for the application-level provide end-to-end security for the communication between two applications. The security services have been classified into different security levels. For the core services and applications, it allows an easy selection of the required security level. An exemplary classification has been introduced for the resource management service and the time synchronization service. Next step is the implementation of the security services for the DREAMS architecture, namely for the DREAMS core services communication, execution, time synchronization and resource management.

Acknowledgement. The research leading to these results has received funding from the European Union's Seventh Framework Programme FP7 2007-2013 under grant agreement 610640.

References

1. IEEE 802.1AE-2006 Standard for Local and Metropolitan Area Networks-Media Access Control (MAC) Security, June 2006. http://ieeexplore.ieee.org/stamp/stamp.jsp?arnumber=1678345
2. IEEE 802.1X-2010 Standard for Local and Metropolitan Area networks Networks - Port-Based Network Access Control, February 2010. http://ieeexplore.ieee.org/servlet/opac?punumber=5409757
3. Ancajas, D.M., Chakraborty, K., Roy, S.: Fort-NoCs: mitigating the threat of a compromised NoC. In: Proceedings of the 51st Annual Design Automation Conference, DAC 2014, pp. 158:1–158:6. ACM, New York (2014). http://doi.acm.org/10.1145/2593069.2593144
4. Avizienis, A., Laprie, J.C., Randell, B., Landwehr, C.: Basic concepts and taxonomy of dependable and secure computing. IEEE Trans. Dependable Secure Comput. **1**(1), 11–33 (2004). http://ieeexplore.ieee.org/stamp/stamp.jsp?arnumber=1335465
5. Fiorin, L., Palermo, G., Lukovic, S., Catalano, V., Silvano, C.: Secure memory accesses on networks-on-chip. IEEE Trans. Comput. **57**(9), 1216–1229 (2008). http://ieeexplore.ieee.org/stamp/stamp.jsp?arnumber=4492766
6. Fiorin, L., Palermo, G., Lukovic, S., Silvano, C.: A data protection unit for NoC-based architectures. In: Proceedings of the 5th IEEE/ACM International Conference on Hardware/Software Codesign and System Synthesis, CODES+ISSS 2007, pp. 167–172. ACM, New York (2007). http://doi.acm.org/10.1145/1289816.1289858

7. Grammatikakis, M., Papadimitriou, K., Petrakis, P., Papagrigoriou, A., Kornaros, G., Christoforakis, I., Tomoutzoglou, O., Tsamis, G., Coppola, M.: Security in MPSoCs: a NoC firewall and an evaluation framework. IEEE Trans. Comput. Aided Des. Integr. Circuits Syst. **34**(8), 1344–1357 (2015). http://ieeexplore.ieee.org/stamp/stamp.jsp?arnumber=7131504

8. Isakovic, H., Wasicek, A.: Secure channels in an integrated MPSoC architecture. In: IECON 2013 - 39th Annual Conference of the IEEE Industrial Electronics Society, pp. 4488–4493 (2013)

9. Obermaisser, R., Weber, D.: Architectures for mixed-criticality systems based on networked multi-core chips. In: 2014 IEEE Emerging Technology and Factory Automation (ETFA), pp. 1–10 (2014). http://ieeexplore.ieee.org/stamp/stamp.jsp?arnumber=7005228

10. Obermaisser, R., Owda, Z., Abuteir, M., Ahmadian, H., Weber, D.: End-to-end real-time communication in mixed-criticality systems based on networked multicore chips. In: 2014 17th Euromicro Conference on Digital System Design (DSD), pp. 293–302. IEEE, August 2014. http://ieeexplore.ieee.org/stamp/stamp.jsp?arnumber=6927257

11. Salloum, C., Elshuber, M., Hoftberger, O., Isakovic, H., Wasicek, A.: The ACross MPSoC - a new generation of multi-core processors designed for safety-critical embedded systems. In: 2012 15th Euromicro Conference on Digital System Design (DSD), pp. 105–113 (2012). http://ieeexplore.ieee.org/stamp/stamp.jsp?arnumber=6386877

12. Seo, K., Kent, S.: Security architecture for the internet protocol, December 2005. https://tools.ietf.org/html/rfc4301

13. Wasicek, A., El-Salloum, C., Kopetz, H.: A system-on-a-chip platform for mixed-criticality applications. In: 2010 13th IEEE International Symposium on Object/Component/Service-Oriented Real-Time Distributed Computing (ISORC), pp. 210–216, May 2010

Analysis of Informed Attacks and Appropriate Countermeasures for Cyber-Physical Systems

Francesca Saglietti[✉], Matthias Meitner, Lars von Wardenburg,
and Valentina Richthammer

Software Engineering (Informatik 11), University of Erlangen-Nuremberg,
Martensstr. 3, 91058 Erlangen, Germany
{francesca.saglietti,matthias.meitner,
lars.wardenburg}@fau.de,
vs.richthammer@studium.fau.de

Abstract. Based on considerations about the knowledge required to carry out different types of network attacks, this article discusses the logical demands posed to the attacker in order to circumvent the most classical checks for message trustworthiness. In view of the limitations of existing avoidance and detection techniques, the article stresses the need for targeted testing strategies aimed at the identification of exploitable code vulnerabilities. For this purpose, it proposes a paradigm for the generation of intelligent test cases meant to maximize the chances of anticipating challenging scenarios during early verification phases.

Keywords: Cyber-attack · Informed attack · Level of knowledge · Communication constraints · Confidence constraints · Control constraints · Arithmetical overflow · Buffer overflow · Testing

1 Introduction, Motivation and Intention

It is well-known that the threat of IT attacks is continuously increasing and provoking high losses due to non-productivity and maintenance costs [1]. In case of safety-relevant information the effect of IT threats goes beyond economic concerns as soon as they may severely affect the possibility of timely intervention on physical entities requiring urgent support – be it the case of hospital patients crucially requiring medical treatment or of critical technical processes subject to appropriate automatic control, as is the case in industrial plant control or car-to-car communication.

For several reasons, including distance, distribution and logistics, the communication between controlling and controlled entities typically makes use of increasingly complex networks joining sensors with computer nodes via corresponding terminals over which the operators may need to update relevant plant configuration data. Even in case of proprietary networks the connection complexity and the user facilities of such architectures complicate the task of analysing the risk of potential misuse and of excluding severe IT attacks [2].

The intention of the present article is to address this problem in a systematic way by considering the chances and the impact of attacks dependent on the amount of

A. Skavhaug et al. (Eds.): SAFECOMP 2016 Workshops, LNCS 9923, pp. 222–233, 2016.
DOI: 10.1007/978-3-319-45480-1_18

application-specific knowledge available to potential attackers and on the complexity of the underlying logical constraints. With respect to the expertise required in the application and control domain considered, the following levels of application- and control-specific knowledge resp. information may be distinguished:

- a mere network-specific insider knowledge is likely to suffice in order to identify the location of communication media, to perceive the transfer of bit streams, or to access protocol meta-data (in the following denoted as "*low level*", see Sect. 2);
- additional insight concerning the technical process to be controlled and the envisaged control system behaviour is required in order to allow for a meaningful interpretation of messages (in the following denoted as "*medium level*", see Sect. 3);
- full information is available to insider attackers in case they additionally know the software-based control system including potential code vulnerabilities (in the following denoted as "*high level*", see Sect. 4).

The levels considered are summarized in Table 1.

Table 1. Levels of knowledge with corresponding domains of knowledge

Levels of network, application, control knowledge			Knowledge/information domains
High	Medium	Low	Cable location
			Bit streams
			Protocol and protocol meta-data
		Process behaviour and data	
		Control system behaviour and specification	
	Control system code and potential vulnerabilities		

Especially in view of the classes of insider attacks involving the highest level of insight, the present article aims at evaluating strengths and weaknesses of existing avoidance and detection counter-measures. Based on the identified limits of the state-of-the-art, the article will successively focus on the need and on the chances of developing dedicated intelligent testing strategies targeted at optimizing the chances of anticipating informed attacks during a preliminary security-based verification phase (see Sect. 4).

2 Network Attacks Based on Network Knowledge

Evidently, the term "*cyber-physical systems*" refers to a wide range of applications which may vary in terms of several attributes. Common to them is the inclusion of one or more physical processes communicating via sensors and actuators with one or more logical units. Depending on several attributes, among them number, distribution and distance of communicating entities, networking complexity and criticality this may give rise to a wide range of patterns. In order to ease the analysis of attacks, the following considerations will focus on a simplified, low-sized scenario consisting of the following entities (see Fig. 1):

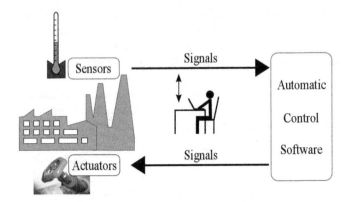

Fig. 1. Attack scenario considered

- a *physical process* (e.g. the production process of an industrial plant) sending information on its current physical state via *sensors* and subject to changes initiated by *actuators*;
- a *computer-based control system* receiving and processing the process information sent by the sensors to identify whether an intervention is needed; in this case, a corresponding message is sent to the process actuators;
- a *communication network* supporting message passing between the physical process and the control system;
- one or more *human(s)* able to influence the communication between the senders and the receivers.

Even if it limits the following considerations to a mere quadruple of communicating agents, the proposed analysis does not restrict generality to an unacceptable degree, as any network attack over a – however complex – net topology will involve misuse along at least one communication edge; this makes it reasonable to consider such a "*one-edge-attack*" in more detail.

The potential of communication misuse depends on the level of knowledge of the attacker(s): evidently, very simple attack scenarios not requiring any plant knowledge nor network access, e.g. cable disruption or magnetic influence on communication cables, typically result in permanent or temporary communication disturbances usually resulting in service interruption. As such actions may jeopardize operation and even safety, they must be prevented by physical protection measures.

More subtle than the physical attacks just considered are actions attempting at the simulation of regular communication between process and software. Attackers enabled to access the network and familiar with protocol meta-data, for example, may gain further knowledge regarding communication frequency and topology by educated guesses. The resulting information may enable them to remove, insert or modify relevant messages without violating the protocol. For example, by copying relevant message portions and resending them at regular frequency, the attackers may falsify process information for the purpose of preventing the control system from taking appropriate decisions.

Such attacks go beyond threatening classical information security values [3], as they target inappropriate, possibly highly unsafe physical states by mere intervention on the communication medium and without necessarily jeopardizing stored data or service availability.

On the other hand, whether interfering by physical action or by ad hoc message manipulation, the uninformed attacks considered so far are usually easily recognizable by standard control software capable of identifying missing or semantically irregular message streams. Depending on the reliability and availability demands of the application considered, such control systems have to initiate upon detection proper reactions like operator alerts or plant shutdowns.

3 Network Attacks Based on Application/Control Knowledge

3.1 Classification of Constraints on Attacks

As mentioned in the previous chapter, intelligent control systems must be designed to analyse data trustworthiness in order to identify message manipulation. This section is devoted to an analysis of this attack under the additional assumption that the attacker(s) are application experts fully informed

- on the technical process under control, as well as
- on the behaviour of the digital control system in use.

More precisely, in this section the attacker is not (yet) required to know about the details of the internal logic of the digital control system, but possesses knowledge about the control system specification, i.e. about the software response to the messages it receives. In addition to this expertise, the attackers are also assumed to be able to

- legally access the network over which the technical process under control communicates via sensors with its control system to inform about its current physical status and on the need of intervention via actuators;
- interpret the semantics of the message(s) sent over the network;
- read, remove, modify and insert messages.

In this case the attacker may try to influence the control system behaviour by manipulating the stream of messages such as to simulate a world different from the real one and thus to trigger a controlling intervention different from the one really required. In order to achieve this goal, the attacker is forced to make sure that neither the network nor the control system is able to identify the manipulation of the message stream as such (be it by copies, deletion or modification of single messages).

To achieve this, the sequence of messages sent over the network has to fulfil three different requirements coincidentally:

- first, it must not violate any of the constraints posed by the network to ensure regular communication (in the following denoted as *communication constraints*);
- moreover, it must not violate any of the constraints required by the control software in order to consider the input data as trustworthy measurements (in the following denoted as *confidence constraints*);
- finally, it must fulfil data constraints [2] (in the following denoted as *control constraints*) such as to impose to the control system the incorrect behaviour envisaged by the attackers, either by simulating the occurrence of relevant fake events or by masking the occurrence of relevant real events.

In the following, the three classes of constraints just introduced are further analysed and refined in more detail:

Communication Constraints. Usually, regular message communication between real-world and computer is subject to constraints of various nature which may be further classified as follows:

- *constraints on protocol meta-data* refer to information characterizing the transport of process data over a communication medium, like message origin (sender), message destination (receiver), action intended to be carried out on message data upon reception (e.g. read/write), communication correctness (redundancy bits);
- *constraints on message stream* refer to information characterizing legal message sequences and may concern time intervals between the arrivals of serial messages as well as the order of consecutive messages;
- *constraints on message structure* refer to information characterizing the syntax of messages as defined by the input specification of the control software.

As soon as one or more communication constraints are ostensibly violated, the underlying message-passing can be regarded as affected by intentional or accidental events reducing or annulling the trustworthiness of the information transported. In such cases, the control system will initiate a predefined countermeasure like an operator warning or an automatic shutdown.

Confidence Constraints. A further category of constraints addresses the actual process data contained in the message(s); the following constraint classes can be distinguished:

- *validity constraints* relate to information characterizing the acceptability of sensor measurements in terms of their lying within predefined physical ranges corresponding to the instrument accuracy;
- *consistency constraints* refer to information characterizing the level of agreement between redundant sensor measurements required to consider them as sufficiently accurate;
- *plausibility constraints* refer to information related to the quantitative relationship between valid measurements of different process variables connected by inherent physical dependencies.

As soon as one or more confidence constraints are violated, the process measurements received can be regarded as irregular; this indicates that some anomalous event takes place which requires a timely counteraction. On the other hand, as long as all communication constraints are fulfilled, there is no reason for the control system to mistrust data accuracy.

Control Constraints. As already mentioned, upon fulfilling communication and confidence constraints, the attack target may be two-fold:

- on the one hand, attacker(s) may intend to simulate *anomalous process behaviour* such as to initiate countermeasures which under regular circumstances may reveal wasteful at the best, but potentially hazardous by contributing to destabilize the balance of the technical application supervised;
- on the other hand, they may want to simulate *regular process behaviour* while manipulating or even sabotaging the technical process such that any safety-related intervention required to be immediately initiated by the automatic control system may be crucially delayed or jeopardized for an indefinite time.

In both cases the attackers need to consider so-called control constraints whose fulfilment characterizes regular process behaviour and whose violation characterizes anomalous process behaviour. Typical examples of control constraint classes are:

- *constraints on the value of a single process variable* refer to information characterizing the range of a particular process variable during regular operation;
- *constraints on a tuple of values of different process variables* refer to information characterizing the combined ranges of several process variables; combined constraints may be more stringent than individual ones as they address the coincidental approach of boundaries by different process indicators;
- *trend constraints* refer to information characterizing regular time-dependent evolution of any process variable as indicated by consecutive messages.

3.2 Examples

The constraint classes and types are summarized in Table 2 together with a few typical examples illustrating them.

3.3 Avoidance and Detection Techniques

Among the major countermeasures classically applied for the purpose to avoid network attacks is *encryption* which undoubtedly can significantly contribute to reduce the chances of cyber-criminal actions in general. Signing signals at their source can increase data integrity as far as the encryption technique can be considered as secure. With respect to informed attacks, however, encryption is likely to find its limits in the need to allow insider network users to intervene on communication by legal updating of relevant process parameters. This may require to allow them access to encryption information.

Table 2. Constraint classes and types illustrated by examples, partly inspired by [4]

Constraint classes	Constraint types	Examples
Communication	*Protocol meta-data*	Profibus meta-data referring to source and destination address, function code (e.g. request or send/request, station type)
	Message stream	Minimal time/maximal time between consecutive messages; sequence number of previous message incremented by 1 modulo memory size of the counter
	Message structure	Header, sequence number, sensor_data_1, ... sensor_data_n, checksum, trailer
Confidence	*Validity* of measurement S	$S_{min} \leq S \leq S_{max}$ where $[S_{min;} S_{max}]$ denotes the accuracy range of the sensing instrument
	Consistency of valid redundant measurements S_1, S_2, S_3 with $S_1 \leq S_2 \leq S_3$	IF $S_1 \geq 0.95 \cdot S_3$: average $\{S_1, S_2, S_3\}$ IF $S_1 \geq 0.975 \cdot S_2 \wedge 1.05 \cdot S_1 \leq S_3$: aver.$\{S_1, S_2\}$ IF $S_2 \geq 0.975 \cdot S_3 \wedge S_1 \leq 0.95 \cdot S_3$: aver.$\{S_2, S_3\}$
	Plausibility of relations between non-redundant measurements	Thermodynamic dependencies between steam level and pressure
Control	*Single boundary* on pressure P	$P \leq P_{max}$ where $[0; P_{max}]$ denotes the pressure range for regular operation
	Combined boundary on (pressure P, steam level L)	$P \leq 0.9 \cdot P_{max}$ and $L \leq 0.9 \cdot L_{max}$
	Trend of pressure P	$\Delta P \leq \Delta P_{max}$ where ΔP denotes the rate of change of P by quadratic interpolation

The *constraints* considered and classified above contribute to filtering the communication messages in order to identify corrupt communication and sensing. The more complex and extensive the constraints and corresponding filtering techniques, the more difficult it is for the potential attacker(s) to carry out unidentifiable attacks. In addition, *network decentralization* also contributes to prevent attacks by restricting the access of potential attackers to only a part of the relevant message information. In this case the scope of attack of each attacker would be limited such that the fulfilment of consistency and plausibility constraints would require the synchronized action of several attackers.

4 Network Attacks Based on Code Knowledge

In this section it is assumed that – in addition to the levels of knowledge considered so far – the attacker(s) also possess *full information* about the code inside the control system. This applies for example in case the network users have been previously involved in code development when they may have had opportunities to identify or insert code portions potentially increasing system vulnerability.

4.1 Overflow-Based Network Attacks

Typical sources of code vulnerability are *overflows* occurring when data is greater than actually storable or data size is greater than supported by a given buffer; typical examples are the following cases:

Arithmetic Overflow. Arithmetic overflows occur when (intentionally or unintentionally) computer calculations result in values which are out of the permitted range. The effects are false values for relevant variables possibly resulting in dramatically incorrect behaviour. On the other hand, arithmetic overflows must not be banned in general, as they may provide suitable solutions for specific problems like the management of circular buffers.

Stack Buffer Overflow. In case of a stack buffer overflow a program stores part of its data inside the call stack, but outside of the specified memory area reserved. This may result in overwriting

- a *variable* residing close to the buffer, or
- the *return address* by a new pointer. This is particularly critical if the new pointer leads to the execution of *malicious code* previously inserted, possibly after traversing no-op instructions intended to close the gap between the jumping point and the start of the shellcode.

  Further overflow variants involve similar considerations for heap buffers or for combinations of overflow types, e.g. in case of arithmetic overflows of an integer variable meant to determine the size of the free buffer space left.

4.2 Overflow Avoidance, On-Line Checks and Static Analysis

Overflow effects such as those mentioned above are meanwhile well-known; for the purpose of their avoidance and detection, a number of existing techniques reveal different strengths and weaknesses.

Avoidance Techniques. During development, constructive techniques can help avoid the problem by making use of particular languages like Java or C# which prevent buffer overflows from occurring by providing mechanisms for checking buffer boundaries. For performance and licensing reasons, however, programming language prescription may represent an unacceptable restriction. Buffer overflows can also be avoided by exclusive use of safe library functions including boundary checking instead of unsafe functions like *strcpy*() or *gets*().

Online Detection Techniques. Countermeasures preventing the execution of code residing on a stack are supported by some operating systems based on so-called *executable space protection* (ESP). A further countermeasure for online overflow detection is provided during compilation by tools which, like StackGuard [5], reorganise the stack by including a so-called *canary value* just before the return address. After any function call, this value is checked for any modification. Attackers aiming at overwriting the return address must also overwrite the canary value. If a modification is detected, the program is usually terminated. This and all other countermeasures based on dynamic checks are evidently limited by the execution time overhead involved.

Static Analysis Techniques. During early verification phases, different analysis techniques may be applied. Among the static ones, there are techniques targeted at the early identification of unsafe functions by means of appropriate tools [6]. More sophisticated techniques analyse the data flow for the purpose of identifying overflow hazards; among them, *integer range analysis* [7] maps the problem of buffer overflow identification onto an integer constraint problem. Although beneficial, such approaches are doomed to incompleteness, as they can only address statically identifiable overflow causes.

4.3   Overflow Detection by Testing Techniques

The limitations of the state-of-the-art identified above reveal the need for novel testing techniques targeted at the early detection of exploitable vulnerabilities like overflows. Depending on the control and data flow complexity of the program considered such testing techniques may rely on analytical reasoning or require heuristics-based approaches. Their potential is the focus of the authors' ongoing investigations.

Whether systematic or random-based, such approaches are aimed at the simulation of intelligent attackers operating under an application- and network-specific profile. Intelligent test data must be generated such as to maximize the chances of activating code vulnerabilities under the given profile conditions.

The underlying mathematical problem to be addressed involves multi-objective optimization pursuing the following targets:

- target 1: in order to prevent an early attack detection, test data must fulfil all network-specific communication constraints as well as all application- and control-specific confidence and consistency constraints (see Sect. 3.1); this target may be systematically achieved by means of constraint-based test data generation techniques;
- target 2: in order to provoke an overflow, test data must maximize the chances of enabling writing operation(s) outside of the allocated memory space (see Sect. 4.1);
- target 3: in order to support both search width w.r.t. target 2 and test confidence in case of unsuccessful search, test data must maximize a predefined control or data flow coverage measure.

On the whole, a solution to this multi-criteria optimization problem would provide either a meaningful message stream actually capable of exploiting a code vulnerability or at least significant quantitative evidence against the potential of such a class of attacks by means of objective measures reflecting the amount and the coverage of secure behaviour observed.

Concerning testing targeted at reliability- rather than security-based properties, similar test data generation problems were successfully approached by genetic algorithms. Such heuristics revealed as useful in many testing contexts, including unit testing based on control and data flow coverage [8], integration testing based on component interaction coverage [9], statistical testing based on operationally representative coverage of component interactions [10] as well as testing of cooperating robots based on agent interaction [11] and operational coverage [12].

It is well-known that genetic algorithms consist of stepwise generating successive populations of individuals based on a given initial population. Successive generation are derived by

- evaluating each individual of the current population by means of a fitness function reflecting the degree of fulfilment of the target-based criteria;
- applying genetic operators (like selection, recombination and mutation) on the current individuals based on the fitness values obtained as well as on predefined probabilistic parameters.

This iterative process is concluded as soon as the criteria are considered as acceptably met, at the latest after a maximum number of iterations or even after a given number of iterations lacking any meaningful improvement. Genetic algorithms involve a wide range of variants, e.g. concerning elitism strategies applied to transfer the fittest individuals to the next generation in order to support monotonic improvement, while ensuring at the same time the enrichment of genetic material by mutation.

For the particular case of security-targeted testing considered in this section, the fitness of an individual, i.e. of a message stream, is captured by a measure reflecting the degree of its meeting the target criteria. Target 1 addresses a must criterion which may be constructively enforced such as not to require any particular fitness evaluation procedure. Target 3, on the other hand, addresses maximal code coverage; depending on the coverage metric considered, this may allow for an absolute fitness measurement, or at least for an evaluation of the relative improvement of a population when compared with the previous one. Finally, target 2 addresses the exploitation of a potential vulnerability, i.e. the fulfilment of a condition of unknown satisfiability. Therefore, the definition of an appropriate fitness measure is not straightforward. An option currently under investigation consists of measuring the distance of the current buffer fill level to a (lower or upper) buffer boundary and in rewarding individuals approaching such a boundary.

5   Conclusion

This article analyzed the impact of network attacks classifying them in terms of the level of network, application, control or code knowledge required; hereby, it focused on the highest levels of knowledge which assume extensive expertise in the application-specific domain, in process control and, in particularly challenging situations, even in the details of the logic residing in the control system code.

On the basis of a variety of informed attacks, the article elaborates on the logical demands posed to the attacker in order to circumvent the most classical checks for message trustworthiness.

Finally, the article considers the state-of-the-art in prevention and detection techniques by comparing strengths and weaknesses of a selection of existing constructive and analytical approaches. As a result, it stresses the need for more targeted testing techniques aimed at an early detection of exploitable vulnerabilities; for this purpose, it proposes a paradigm for the generation of intelligent test cases meant to maximize the chances of anticipating challenging scenarios during early verification.

Acknowledgment. The authors gratefully acknowledge that a major part of the work presented was supported by the German Federal Ministry for Economic Affairs and Energy (BMWi), project SMARTEST. The project is carried out in cooperation with the partner institutions University of Magdeburg, University of Applied Sciences of Magdeburg-Stendal and AREVA GmbH. In particular, the authors thank Robert Fischer und Robert Clausing for inspiring discussions.

References

1. Zetter, K.: Countdown to Zero Day. Stuxnet and the Launch of the World's First Digital Weapon. Crown, New York (2014)
2. Krotofil, M.: Rocking the pocket book: hacking chemical plants for competition and extortion, white paper, Black Hat Conference (2015)
3. Bundesamt für Sicherheit in der Informationstechnik (BSI): IT-Grundschutz-Standards, BSI-Standards 100-1, 100-2, 100-3, 100-4 (2008)
4. Quirk, W., Wall, D.N.: Customer functional requirements for the protection systems to be used as the DARTS example. In: European Project "Demonstration of Advanced Reliability Techniques for Safety Related Computer Systems" (DARTS), Research Programme ESPRIT II, Project Final Deliverable (1990)
5. Cowan, C., Pu, C., Maier, D., et al.: StackGuard: automatic adaptive detection and prevention of buffer-overflow attacks. In: 7th Conference on USENIX Security Symposium, USENIX Association (1998)
6. Viega, J., Bloch, J.T., Kohno, T., McGraw, G.: ITS4: a static vulnerability scanner for C and C++ code. In: 16th Annual Conference on Computer Security Applications (ACSAC 2000). IEEE Xplore (2000)
7. Wagner, D., Foster, J.S., Brewer, E.A., et al.: A first step towards automated detection of buffer overrun vulnerabilities. In: Network and Distributed System Security Symposium (NDSS 2000). The Internet Society (2000)

8. Oster, N., Saglietti, F.: Automatic test data generation by multi-objective optimisation. In: Górski, J. (ed.) SAFECOMP 2006. LNCS, vol. 4166, pp. 426–438. Springer, Heidelberg (2006)

9. Saglietti, F., Pinte, F.: Automated unit and integration testing for component-based software systems. In: Workshop on Dependability and Security for Resource Constrained Embedded Systems. ACM Digital Library (2010)

10. Meitner, M., Saglietti, F.: Target-specific adaptations of coupling-based software reliability testing. In: Fischbach, K., Krieger, U.R. (eds.) MMB & DFT 2014. LNCS, vol. 8376, pp. 192–206. Springer, Heidelberg (2014)

11. Saglietti, F., Winzinger, S., Lill, R.: Reconfiguration testing for cooperative autonomous agents. In: Koornneef, F., van Gulijk, C. (eds.) SAFECOMP 2015. LNCS, vol. 9338, pp. 144–155. Springer, Heidelberg (2015)

12. Saglietti, F., Spengler, R., Meitner, M.: Quantitative reliability assessment for mobile cooperative systems. In: Skavhaug, A., Guiochet, J., Bitsch, F., Schoitsch, E. (eds.) SAFECOMP Workshops 2016. LNCS, vol. 9923, pp. 118–129. Springer, Heidelberg (2016)

Advanced Security Considerations in the Arrowhead Framework

Sándor Plósz[1]([✉]), Csaba Hegedűs[2], and Pál Varga[3]

[1] Department of Safety and Security, Austrian Institue of Technology,
1220 Vienna, Austria
sandor.plosz.fl@ait.ac.at
[2] Telecommunications Division, AITIA International Inc., Budapest 1039, Hungary
hegeduscs@aitia.ai
[3] Department of Telecommunications and Media Informatics,
Budapest University of Technology and Economics, Budapest 1117, Hungary
pvarga@tmit.bme.hu

Abstract. The Arrowhead Framework aims to create collaborative automation using networked embedded devices by establishing a service oriented approach to govern them. Various cyber-physical Systems can provide and consume Services from one another in closed automation clouds. These System-of-Systems has been introduced by the Arrowhead framework as Local Clouds. These clouds – being high value targets – can then be subject to an extensive amount of threats. This paper is dedicated towards revising the Arrowhead framework to further enhance its security solutions. A certificate-based architecture is presented to solve authentication and authorization tasks not just within, but in-between Local Clouds by using a token concept applied for services. This schema also allows the integration of resource constrained devices in coexistence with different levels of security.

Keywords: Internet of Things · Collaborating system of systems · Authorization · Authentication · Certificates · Ticketing

1 Introduction

The Arrowhead project defines a framework for creating distributed industrial systems by collaborative networked embedded devices [2,12]. This framework intends to integrate popular application layer protocols using a unique Service Oriented Architecture (SOA).

In an Arrowhead automation cloud environment, communications can be subject to an extensive amount of threats. These include i.e. spoofing, tampering or Denial of Service attacks, and can compromise the security and integrity of the whole infrastructure. These System-of-Systems still possess a general infrastructural vulnerability, despite its decentralized architecture [11].

In order to prevent such threats, the Arrowhead Framework has to provide strict authentication and authorization capabilities (AA). These functionalities

© Springer International Publishing Switzerland 2016
A. Skavhaug et al. (Eds.): SAFECOMP 2016 Workshops, LNCS 9923, pp. 234–245, 2016.
DOI: 10.1007/978-3-319-45480-1_19

are indispensable, considering the involved cyber-physical Systems and business processes. Furthermore, the framework targets the collaboration and interoperability of embedded, and often resource-constrained devices using proprietary or industrial protocols. In many cases the devices have limited capability of performing security tasks such as advanced encryption and decryption utilized by modern secure transmission protocols such as Transport Layer Security (TLS) or the Internet Protocol Security (IPSec) [10]. For such cases, a ticketing-based approach has been developed in [7], which works with CoAP. For MQTT and REST – which use the Transmission Control Protocol (TCP) –, security based on TLS would be desirable.

In this work we present the certificate-based security concept for the Arrowhead multi-cloud environment. We investigate how this can co-exist for the other ticket-based security concept within Arrowhead, and how translation between the protocols can work, while keeping security transparent.

2 The Elements of the Arrowhead Framework

2.1 Local Automation Clouds

It is a great challenge to get heterogeneous systems (or architectures) work together – especially in the automation domain, which has very specific real-time, and security requirements. Legacy protocols, commercial off-the-shelf products and monolithic architectures often cripple interoperability and dynamic reconfigurability. The Arrowhead Framework uses the approach of Service Oriented Architectures (SOA) [4] to tackle this problem: it aims at providing interoperability by facilitating the service interactions within closed or at least separated automation environments.

Fig. 1. Arrowhead Local Clouds deployed in different domains

These *Arrowhead Local Clouds* might fulfill various tasks and can have their own sets of appointed stakeholders (e.g. their operators or developers). These Local Clouds all have their operational boundaries, let those be functional, geographical or network-segmented. Nevertheless, they must be governed through their own instances of the *Arrowhead Core Systems*, as Fig. 1. suggests. These are clouds in the sense that they use common resources: the Core Systems of that domain. These common Core System resources (e.g. related to Service Registry, Authorization or Orchestration) are used by all kinds of other entities – applications – in the network, and can also be implemented in a distributed way. This means that the scalability of the Local Cloud mostly depends on the scalability of the Core Systems (e.g. by implementing them using virtualization and Web Services [1] technologies).

2.2   Systems and Services

In the Arrowhead Local Clouds there can be an arbitrary number of *Systems* that can provide and consume *Services* from one another: they create and finish *servicing instances* dynamically in run-time. Services are defined so that loose-coupling, late binding, and service discoverability can be realized. Here, Arrowhead-compatible Systems must use the mandatory *Core Systems and their Core Services* provided by the Framework, to realize their operational targets (as shown in Fig. 2.). These Core Services also support to set up the initial field for information-exchange. There are two main groups of the Core Systems: the mandatory ones that need to be present in each Local Cloud, and the automation supporting ones that further enhance the capabilities of a Local Cloud.

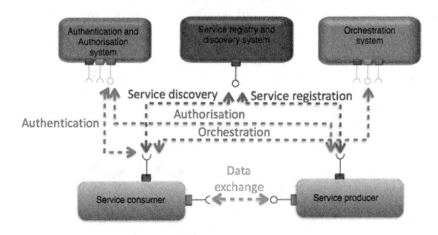

Fig. 2. Arrowhead Core Systems and their use

2.3   Core Systems and Services

In accordance with [12], this work attributes the same functionality to each of the Core Systems. There are three mandatory Core Systems:

- The Service Registry stores all the Systems (that are currently available in the network) and their service offerings. Systems have to announce their presence, and the services they can offer. The registry takes note of this information when systems come online, and might have to revoke them when they go offline.

- The Authorization System – as its name suggests – manages authentication and authorization (AA) tasks.
- The Orchestrator is responsible for instrumenting each System in the cloud: where to connect. It instructs Systems so by pointing towards specific Service Providers to consume specific Service(s) from. This has to be done by a simple request-response sequence, which ends with the requester System receiving a Service endpoint. After these, the System is obligated to consume from that Service instance.

There are further automation supporting Core Systems available, in order to provide additional core services such as event handling, system configuration, factory description, or inter-cloud orchestration, which should otherwise be implemented within many of the systems. This way these services are available for any of the systems, without consuming their local resources.

2.4 Inter-cloud Servicing

Arrowhead Local Clouds are generally autonomous and independent from each other, since they are deployed separately for various reasons. However, there are specific cases, where Systems from different clouds need to consume Services from one another. To this end, an inter-Cloud servicing architecture was introduced in [13]. This comes up with two additional Core Systems to the framework: the Gatekeeper, and the Network Manager.

The Gatekeeper provides essentially two services for the mandatory Core Systems:

- the Global Service Discovery (GSD) process, that aims at locating adequate service offerings in neighboring Clouds;
- the Inter-Cloud Negotiations (ICN) process, in which mutual trust is established between two Clouds and the actual connection between endpoints is then built up.

The concept is depicted by Fig. 3. After these processes, the Network Manager is responsible for creating the data path between the Service Provider and the Consumer.

This setup includes some security considerations taking place, e.g. declaring inter-Cloud access rights (from and to other Local Clouds) in the Authorization Systems, or setting up the trusted neighborhood domains.

3 Security in the Arrowhead Framework

3.1 Issues to Tackle

Assuring security in distributed architectures is not as trivial as in centralized systems: the roles for authentication and authorization are not bounded to one

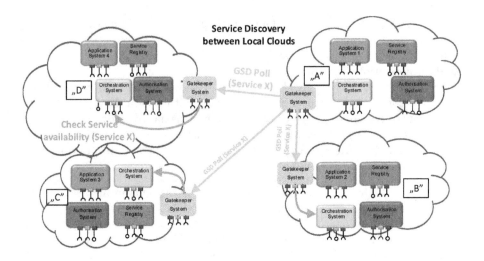

Fig. 3. Inter-cloud service discovery between Gatekeepers

single entity but are to be taken up by everyone. We need to define a novel security solution in order to fulfill the strict security requirements of the automation world. A threat analysis methodology elaborated in [8,9] suggests that the following possible vulnerabilities have to be tackled here:

1. Confidentiality: Data is only to be available for those who were intended to access it. This objective needs to be assured by proper authorization paired with authentication. Threats like spoofing and information disclosure can violate this objective.
2. Integrity: Data and system resources are only to be changed in appropriate ways by the appropriate people. This can be assured by proper encryption (or digest) and can be exploited by tampering type of attacks.
3. Availability: Systems should be ready when needed and perform acceptably. Denial of Service (DoS) attacks can endanger this objective.
4. Authenticity: The identity of users is to be verified (unless it is acceptable to service anonymous users). Spoofing type of threats aim to violate this.
5. Accountability: Users should not be able to deny performing their earlier actions. Proper and verifiable logging needs to be implemented to prevent this.

It is worth noting that while authentication should be mandatory for all communications, at least three further levels of application security should be acceptable for Application Systems within Arrowhead (even in co-existence). Besides having no additional security, there can be cases where only integrity is required and cases where both integrity and confidentiality is essential.

3.2 A Ticketing Approach

Resource-constrained (but Arrowhead-compatible) Systems might not be capable of implementing advanced security measures. A lightweight authentication solution has been developed for such Systems, based on the Constrained Application Protocol (CoAP), and the Kerberos protocol [7]. It uses a centrally issued ticket as a token of identity but does not contain any identity information directly. To authenticate Application Systems within a Local Cloud one must contact the AA server to verify its identity and privileges.

Besides its protocol-restricted implementation (supporting merely CoAP), the weak points of this authentication method make it vulnerable to a number of attacks. Firstly, the challenge-response nature on an insecure channel implies that the ticket itself does not verify the authenticity of the sender – and can be exploited with a man in the middle approach. Secondly, since the service provider has to request the local ticketing AA server to validate the ticket (and therefore authenticate the consumer), it is also easy to bypass this control loop. Thirdly, this validation process is requested at every inbound connection and therefore the AA server is vulnerable to a DoS attack.

On the other hand, this approach is advantageous for a number of reasons. The service providers are relieved from the processing burden of identifying and verifying the consumers: it is done by the central AA entity. It also bears the future capability of integrating it with admission control functions: service providers can assert whether the inbound connection is ratified by the Core Systems – and can be serviced – or not.

3.3 The Public Key Infrastructure

Public Key Infrastructure (PKI) [5] defines how to create certificates that can be used to achieve authentication, message integrity and confidentiality. PKI builds on Public-key cryptography (PKC), which employs an asymmetric encryption scheme. This means that it uses different keys for the encryption and the decryption processes, compared to symmetric key encryption methods, where the same key is used for the encryption and decryption.

There are two type of keys in a PKI architecture: these are called the public and the private keys. As their name suggests, they differ in their confidentiality level. While private keys belong to its owner and must be kept as a secret, whereas the public key can be freely distributed. Information encrypted by the public key can only be decrypted using the private key – and vice versa. Therefore, the validity of the information can be assured both ways (inbound and outbound) when the recipient/sender possesses one of the keys. However, predesignated trust is still required in certificate-based authentication and encryption methods that build on the features of the PKI. In order to achieve the mutual trust between entities, a Certificate Authority (CA) must be appointed in the system. The role of a CA is basically to sign certificates (and thereby to validate their identity and content). All entities in the system trust (and know) their CA and can only validate the received certificates that contain information about its counterpart (its public key) and is signed by the local CA. Certificates can be used to both verify the authenticity of the parties, as well as to check the integrity of messages in the communication. Therefore, parties that have signed certificates from the same CA can communicate securely.

As a consequence, if an entity A wishes to communicate with another entity (B), it will need to get the signed certificate of B containing the public key of B.

In the new Arrowhead Service, the functionality of a CA is realized and combined with an authorization methodology embedded in the orchestration process.

4   Enhancements in the Arrowhead Framework

4.1   Creating a Certificate Hierarchy

To fulfill the security requirements set in Sect. 3.1., we propose an application level AA architecture based on the X.509 [5] PKI infrastructure. Each capable Arrowhead System should be provided with a certificate and should therefore have its identity binded to its public key. Every Local Cloud has a Certificate Authority that issues and signs these System certificates. This CA is the root of the trust chain within its Local Cloud and has its own certificate signed by a parent CA. This entity also possesses the Certificate Revocation List defined in the standard: certificates that have been invalidated and therefore not to be accepted.

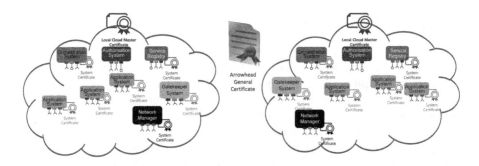

Fig. 4. Arrowhead certificate hierarchy

This chain of trust model fits well into to System hierarchy concept of the Arrowhead framework, as depicted in Fig. 4. A general, master Arrowhead certificate can be signed by a well-known trusted CA (such as Comodo or GlobalSign) and issued to the the Arrowhead domain owner (e.g. the project consortia). This administrator entity then can issue and sign Local Cloud certificates for operators in its own application process for establishing new Local Clouds. Within these new Clouds then the Authorization System realizes the CA tasks and owns the cloud certificate. The benefits of this approach:

- The Arrowhead community has oversight over new Local Cloud establishments
- Inter-Cloud interactions are secured by the certificate hierarchy
- Local Cloud owners can issue and revoke certificates for Systems in a deployment procedure
- System bootstrapping and authentication is certificate-secured within its Cloud (can also be bounded to tamper-proof hardware)
- All communications can be signed and/or encrypted with SSL/TLS.

If an Application System in a Local Cloud requires a certificate (e.g. during its deployment procedure), it will have to generate a private-public key pair and submit a Certificate Signing Request (CSR) containing the pair and its identity. There are other fields in a CSR used to verify the identity of the requester. This way the Arrowhead bootstrapping procedure can be automated [14], and augmented with certificate generation.

```
Subject: C=HU, L=Budapest, O=Manufacturer1,
OU=Fleetcloud1,
CN=TempSensor1.Car1.FleetCloud1.Manufacturer1.arrowhead.eu
```

Fig. 5. Identity and hierarchical information stored in certificates

We propose a certificate structure to implement the above discussed hierarchy, as depicted on Fig. 5. This format is a customization of the general X.509 certificate and it bounds the identity of the system specifically to a Local Cloud (which makes spoofing attacks more difficult). This approach might seem l'art pour l'art, but is a very convenient way of providing authorization, as discussed in the following section.

4.2   Managing Access Rights

Building on the PKI infrastructure and the certificate distribution capabilities described in Sect. 4.1, a new level of security can be added at the servicing level. Since message decryptability only lies with the party owning the appropriate keys, the Core Systems can supervise and provide authorization for Application Systems in a Local Cloud.

There are a number of fundamental questions that describe an automation scenario regarding authentication, authorization or data ownership. The Arrowhead Framework defined Local Clouds that are governed through their own instances of the Core Systems, as described in Sect. 2. However, full centralization is not desired for multi-stakeholder scenarios.

When Application Systems are introduced in a Local Cloud, there are further bootstrapping tasks besides certificate distribution and the establishment of general trust, a process has been examined in [6]. Such automated bootstrapping procedures require that the operators of the Cloud have properly configured the Core Systems about the new Application System's to-be deployment. These include the followings:

1. Orchestration rules: how it can be orchestrated (e.g. whether it has static servicing connections).
2. Authorization status: where it might be allowed to consume Services from.
3. Further deployment descriptors also have to be configured: e.g. in the QoS Manager or Plant Description Systems.

In Arrowhead, Application Systems generally give up certain autonomy and are to be instructed by the Core Systems on how to operate [14]: which Services they have to consume from which Service Providers. This centralization of control helps managing the System-of-Systems via the Arrowhead Core Systems. However, there are certain cases where Application Systems should retain parts of their autonomy and have the possibility to reject connections even though they have been properly orchestrated. In such exception handling cases re-orchestration will be required.

Moreover, Systems acting as Service Providers should also be able to verify that inbound servicing requests are properly authorized and verified by the Core Systems. To this end, an orchestration process was introduced in [3] and described in Sect. 2 to include process and resource-allocation based restrictions when composing Services.

To this end, we introduce an authorization token building on the ticketing schema that will provide application-level security. A such token is only valid for *one servicing instance*: one Service Consumer is authorized one-time to consume a specific Service from the Service Provider at hand. This information (Consumer-Service-Provider) can be stored in a string and should be decryptable and parseable by Application Systems that require such advanced admission control functionalities. These tokens have the following characteristics:

– It builds on the certificate hierarchy introduced in Sect. 4.1;
– Generated by the Authorization System based on access rights during the orchestration process, see Fig. 6;
– This token is then passed on to the Consumer by the Orchestrator;
– It is only decryptable by the Service Provider and its private certificate key;
– It assures that proper orchestration took place and the Consumer is verified to access the Service;
– Based on this, the Service Provider can either accept or reject the connection.

This methodology reduces Provider-side authorization and admission control to a string-based validation of the Consumer's identity declared in its certificate based on the contents of the encrypted token. Although this requires that Application Systems implement and evaluate this process at every single inbound Service request.

4.3   Integration with the Ticketing Schema

Extending the works of [7], we propose to integrate the authorization token approach with the ticketing based authentication service in order to provide

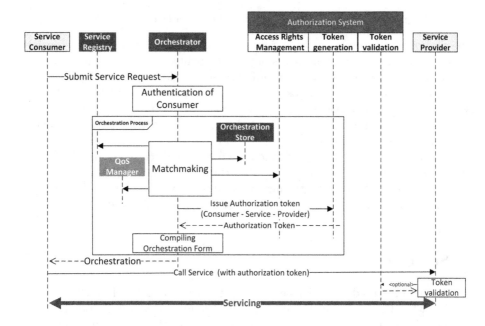

Fig. 6. Authorization tokens generated in the orchestration process

admission control for all Systems in a Local Cloud: let those be certificate or ticket based.

This requires that the ticket issued for a System should not only authenticate but authorize it as a Service Consumer. In this case, the orchestration response message does not contain a token. Instead, we propose the following process for cases where resource-constrained Consumers only possess the authentication ticket:

1. The orchestration process instructs the ticket-owner Consumer to connect to a specific Service Provider.
2. The Consumer tries connecting with its authentication ticket on an insecure channel instead of using certificates and the token.
3. The Service Provider will try to verify the ticket with the Authorization System.
4. The Authorization System will only respond positively if the Consumer was orchestrated properly before.

This methodology does not rely on the Service Provider's authentication method. It only requires that the Authorization System stores the result of the last orchestration process for the Consumer (with a validity period) and its currently active authentication ticket. However, when mutual identity verification is required (the Consumer validating a ticket-based Provider), it will require an other round of verification with the Authorization System, but the roles reversed.

4.4   Integration with the Inter-cloud Architecture

The authorization token approach is also an adequate solution to the security issues arisen with inter-Cloud servicing requirements, as discussed in Sect. 4.1. This token is generated by the Service Provider's Cloud in cooperation with the Consumer's Cloud Core Systems. Therefore, this token is valid even if it was issued for a "foreigner" Consumer in an inter-Cloud orchestration process: it is completely transparent from the Provider's point of view (it is still issued by its own Authorization System).

For scenarios where the inter-Cloud data path is realized via tunneling (using the services of the Network Manager [13]), this token can also help to establish it. This is achieved by orchestrating every System on the data path properly with its own authorization token that validates the partners along the tunneling chain.

5   Summary

This paper presented an enhancement for the security-related capabilities of the Arrowhead Framework. Since any Local Cloud of this automation-specific Internet of Things domain can be subject to extensive threats, providing proper security mechanisms for them is of major interest. After a brief recap on the Arrowhead Framework, we described some security requirements and related issues. The currently used ticketing approach for authorization and authentication has some drawbacks. We can overcome them by using a certificate-based approach.

In order to solve authentication and authorization issues not just within, but in-between Local Clouds, we introduced a few enhancements. First, we applied the concept of certificate hierarchies. In this, every Local Cloud has a Certificate Authority that issues and signs its System certificates. This CA is the root of the trust chain within its Local Cloud, and has its own certificate signed by a parent CA. Second, we described how the certificate and the ticketing approaches can co-exist, and even be translated to one another (within some limitations).

Moreover, we described how to manage access right within Local Clouds by using this approach. For this, we introduced an authorization token, building on the ticketing schema – but being valid only for one servicing instance. Another advantage of this token approach is that it naturally fits in the inter-Cloud servicing scenarios: the token is valid even if it was issued for a "foreign" cloud.

Future work includes creating a reference implementation of the proposed concept which can be used by any distributed system of systems to manage inter-cloud authentication and authorization.

Acknowledgment. This work is supported by the EU ARTEMIS JU funding, within project ARTEMIS/0001/2012, JU grant nr. 332987 (ARROWHEAD). The authors would like to thank all the Arrowhead partners for the discussions, and would also like to acknowledge the efforts of the Hungarian team who participated in this work: from evopro Hungary and from Budapest University of Technology.

References

1. Alonso, G., Casati, F., Kuno, H., Machiraju, V.: Web Services. Springer, Heidelberg (2004)
2. Blomstedt, F., Ferreira, L.L., Klisics, M., Chrysoulas, C., de Soria, I.M., Morin, B., Zabasta, A., Eliasson, J., Johansson, M., Varga, P.: The arrowhead approach for soa application development and documentation. In: IECON 2014–40th Annual Conference of the IEEE Industrial Electronics Society, pp. 2631–2637, October 2014
3. Hegedus, C., Daniel Kozma, G.S.P.V.: Enhancements of the arrowhead framework to refine inter-cloud service interactions. IEEE IECON 2016 (2016)
4. Erl, T.: SOA Principles of Service Design (The Prentice Hall Service-Oriented Computing Series from Thomas Erl). Prentice Hall PTR, Upper Saddle River (2007)
5. International Telecommunication Union, Telecommunication Standardization Sector (ITU-T), X.509: Information technology Open Systems Interconnection The Directory: Public-key and attribute certificate frameworks. Recommendation 509, October 2012. http://www.itu.int/rec/T-REC-X.509-201210-I/en
6. Carlsson, O., Csaba Hegedus, J.D.P.V.: Organizing iot systems-of-systems from standardized engineering data. IEEE IECON 2016 (2016)
7. Pereira, P.P., Eliasson, J., Delsing, J.: An authentication and access control framework for coap-based internet of things. In: IECON 2014–40th Annual Conference of the IEEE Industrial Electronics Society, pp. 5293–5299, October 2014
8. Plosz, S., Farshad, A., Tauber, M., Lesjak, C., Ruprechter, T., Pereira, N.: Security vulnerabilities and risks in industrial usage of wireless communication. In: Proceedings of the 2014 IEEE Emerging Technology and Factory Automation (ETFA), pp. 1–8, September 2014
9. Plósz, S., Tauber, M., Varga, P.: Information assurance system in the arrowhead project. ERCIM News **2014**(97), 29 (2014). http://ercim-news.ercim.eu/en97/special/information-assurance-system-in-the-arrowhead-project
10. Ravi, S., Raghunathan, A., Kocher, P., Hattangady, S.: Security in embedded systems: design challenges. ACM Trans. Embed. Comput. Syst. **3**(3), 461–491 (2004). http://doi.acm.org/10.1145/1015047.1015049
11. Roman, R., Zhou, J., Lopez, J.: On the features and challenges of security and privacy in distributed internet of things. Comput. Netw. **57**, 2266–2279 (2013). http://www.sciencedirect.com/science/article/pii/S1389128613000054
12. Varga, P., Blomstedt, F., Lino Ferreira, L., Eliasson, J., Johansson, M., Delsing, J., Martinez de Soria, I.: Making system of systems interoperable - the core components of the arrowhead technology framework. J. Netw. Comput. Appl. (2016)
13. Varga, P., Hegedus, C.: Service interaction through gateways for inter-cloud collaboration within the arrowhead framework. In: 5th International Conference on Wireless Communications, Vehicular Technology, Information Theory and Aerospace and Electronic Systems (Wireless VITAE) (2015)
14. Wiki, T.A.F.: https://forge.soa4d.org/plugins/mediawiki/wiki/arrowhead-f/index.php/

The Role of the Supply Chain in Cybersecurity Incident Handling for Drilling Rigs

Aitor Couce-Vieira[✉] and Siv Hilde Houmb[✉]

Secure-NOK AS, Grønnegata 142, 2317 Hamar, Norway
{aitorcouce,sivhoumb}@securenok.com
http://www.securenok.com

Abstract. This paper presents a characterisation of the oil and gas drilling supply chain in the context of cybersecurity incident handling. Coordination and collaboration between stakeholders are critical factors in incident handling. However, the number of organisations and stakeholders involved in drilling is high and, thus, it is relevant to understand better their interactions during incident handling. This paper provides a high-level overview of these stakeholders interactions during cybersecurity incident handling, as a basis for future research. This characterisation shows the suitability of modelling the supply chain from the incident perspective to understand, more clearly, the ramifications of incidents and the coordination needs.

Keywords: Oil and Gas · Drilling · Cybersecurity · Incident response · Supply chain · Value chain

1 Introduction

Digital systems have become critical in oil and gas drilling. In the last decade, most of the equipment has been integrated with control systems, automating tasks that decades ago were performed manually. In addition, information systems became more integrated with remote operation centres, improving drilling knowledge and decision-making.

The digitalisation of drilling installations paved the way to cybersecurity incidents, which are events that involve malicious or unwarranted actions in information or control systems, such incidents might escalate causing incidents in business or engineering operations. Cybersecurity in drilling shares with other sectors a series of challenges at securing information and control systems in industrial facilities. First, the importance of having full control of the status of the equipment and the industrial process. Second, the potential operational and physical consequences of cybersecurity incidents in industrial control systems. Third, the need for making decisions in real time to handle incidents as quick as possible and avoid escalation. And fourth, the incorporation, in risk analysis, of the uncertainties of operational risks.

In the last decade, cyber attackers moved the focus towards industrial control systems (ICS) and critical infrastructure such as oil and gas (O&G) [1]. In 2008,

© Springer International Publishing Switzerland 2016
A. Skavhaug et al. (Eds.): SAFECOMP 2016 Workshops, LNCS 9923, pp. 246–255, 2016.
DOI: 10.1007/978-3-319-45480-1_20

hackers blew up a Turkish oil pipeline. In the control room, the operators console showed that everything was running as planned before a phone call from the field triggered the alarm. In 2009, a disgruntled former employee remotely disabled the safety controls of an offshore rig in the US. During 2012, a virus infected an Iranian oil facility, shutting down the terminals of the control system. In 2012, the worlds largest oil company, Saudi Aramco, was the victim of an attack disabling 30.000 computers for 11 days. Overall, reports from the U.S. ICS-CERT show that the energy sector, which includes O&G, is one of the mayor targets, reaching 56 % of the incidents reported in 2013 [2]. Major incidents in control systems are unlikely but possible: around 7 % of cyber attacks to critical infrastructure penetrate into critical systems [3].

The harsh and uncertain conditions during drilling represent a serious safety and environmental risk. The major risk in offshore platforms is a blowout, which poses a risk of explosion in the installation [4,5]. Incidents with heavy equipment on the rig also represent a serious safety risk, as well as the risk of ruining the drilling operation if the equipment breaks [4]. The harsh conditions might also affect the integrity and viability of the well, affecting extraction costs or reducing the amount extracted during production. The value of the reservoir is in the range of millions of Euros. An injection of drilling fluids in the reservoir might difficult the construction of the well or the future extraction of the hydrocarbons.

These actions are extremely difficult to trigger from a cyberattack, however, a poor security status of the control system might facilitate incidents or difficult their handling. In addition, operational incidents involving the control systems might cause loss of time in the drilling operations and difficult and costly recoveries. Offshore drilling rigs are isolated and bringing specialists or equipment requires a helicopter trip. In fact, given the high cost of these platforms, a delay of even a few hours could represent ten of thousands of Euros. Drilling can cost more than € 250,000 per day, representing an important cost aspect in producing oil and gas offshore.

This paper deals with an additional challenge in this domain: the relative complexity of the stakeholder map. This is specially relevant during incident handling, because coordination and collaboration are critical factors for a successful response. The goal of the paper is to characterise this stakeholder map in the context of cybersecurity incident handling of the main system of the installation, namely, the drilling control system (DCS). This characterisation might serve as a high-level starting point for further research on the topic.

The rest of the paper is structured as follows: Sect. 2 introduces the reader to the drilling supply chain; Sect. 3 characterises the drilling supply chain during an incident in the drilling control system; and Sect. 4 provides an example stakeholder case characterisation.

2   Background

This section provides an introduction to the drilling supply chain and the general challenges of handling incidents. Section 2.1 introduces the concepts of value and supply chain. Section 2.2 describes the drilling supply chain and the stakeholders present in the drilling installation. Section 2.3 summarises the need for cooperation and coordination during incident handling.

2.1 Value Chain and Supply Chain

The value chain [6] consists in the activities an organisation performs to create and deliver a valuable product. The focus of the value chain is on the business level and its main goal is maximising value. On the other hand, the supply chain consist in the parties involved in producing and delivering that valuable product. In this case, the focus of the supply chain is on the operational level and its general goal is optimising the execution of operations. From the supply chain point of view, incidents disrupt the execution of operations. From the value chain point of view, incidents perturb the secure and safe state of operations, reducing the value creation in those operations.

2.2 The Drilling Sector as Part of the General Supply Chain of the Oil and Gas Industry

The oil and gas or petroleum industry is divided in the following three sectors [7]:

- Upstream: Exploration and extraction of oil and gas from hydrocarbon reservoirs.
- Midstream: Transportation and storage of oil and gas products.
- Downstream: Processing crude oil and raw gas into derived products such as gasoline, petrochemicals, purified sale gas, or propane.

O&G drilling is part of the upstream sector together with exploration and production. The first step in upstream is exploring and analysing hydrocarbon reservoirs and obtaining leases for exploiting them. The purpose of drilling is building a well to tap a reservoir and preparing the well for production. Finally, production involves the extraction of oil and gas and its stabilization for transporting them to downstream refineries and plants.

Figure 1 depicts the general oil and gas supply chain.

Drilling [4] is performed by installations such as immobile platforms, mobile semi-submersible rigs, or drill ships. The drilling operation usually takes two or three months, and requires drilling, casing, and cementing the well. Another important activity is controlling the well to prevent blowouts or fluid exchanges between the well and the reservoir.

Stakeholder relationships in drilling rigs are complex since several companies have different roles in the operations [4].

There are four types of organisations present on drilling rigs:

- The *oil company* owns the reservoir and directs drilling operations as part of the overall upstream process of exploring, drilling, and producing. Therefore, the oil company creates value by maximising hydrocarbon production at a minimum cost and, thus, focuses on the technical and financial viability of the well.

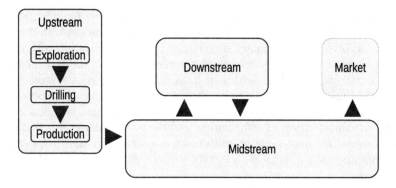

Fig. 1. Oil and gas industry supply chain. The arrows indicate the supply process from the discovery of the reservoir (exploration) to the delivery of refined oil and processed gas to the industries and homes

- The *drilling contractor* owns the drilling rig and carries out the drilling operations under the directions of the oil company. Drilling contractors drill dozens of wells during the 15–20 year lifespan of a rig. Therefore, the drilling contractor creates value by delivering the well with the minimal time delay.
- *Service companies* carry out specialized operations, such as cementing, and create value by delivering their services with minimal time delay.
- *Equipment providers* are not involved in drilling but they provide support for their equipment and, therefore, create value by maintaining the reliability and reputation of their equipment. In the cybersecurity context, there are two relevant equipment providers. The first one is the *system integrator*, which provides control or information systems. The second one is the *product supplier*, which provides components (e.g., servers, PLCs[1], or HMIs[2]) to the system integrator.

An additional goal of all stakeholders is keeping operations safe and with a limited environmental impact.

Our focus is on the relevant stakeholder relations during the handling of an incident in a drilling control system. Drilling stakeholders are directly relevant, however most part of the O&G supply chain does not participate directly in the drilling operations. Therefore, their indirect involvement can be integrated in the oil company (e.g., exploitation costs, production expectations) and into an overall market consideration of the midstream and downstream sectors, regarding the prices and delivery of the oil or gas production.

2.3   The Need for Coordination During Incident Handling

Incidents are dynamic, complex, uncertain, and stressful. Handling an incident requires a balance between meticulous incident preparedness and spontaneous

---

[1] Programmable Logic Controllers.
[2] Human-Machine Interfaces.

incident handling. One of the main challenges during incident handling is having a coordinated response by the stakeholders affected by the incident. In the case of oil and gas, it involves the primary stakeholder with direct relation with the incident, but also secondary stakeholders in the rig operations, directly affected by or affecting the incident. Lessons learnt from emergency response studies [8–10] highlight the importance of achieving a shared vision of the incident preparedness to achieve a consistent incident handling. Another recommendation is avoiding the compartmentalisation of information and decision-making: external collaboration provides incident handlers with more resources and knowledge, whereas good communication is critical to obtain a more global vision of the incident ramifications.

The assessment of the drilling supply chain and their role during cybersecurity incidents is relevant due to the combination of two challenges: the challenge of managing incidents in a multi-stakeholder environment, and the challenge of cybersecurity incidents on drilling rigs. In the next section we present an schematic overview of the drilling supply chain that is used for assessing the role of the stakeholders during a cybersecurity incident.

3   Drilling Supply Chain During Cybersecurity Incidents

This section provides, in Sect. 3.1, a structured characterisation of the supply chain from the point of view of handling an incident in a drilling control system. Section 3.2 provides additional considerations to complement the characterisation.

3.1   Characterisation of the Supply Chain During Cybersecurity Incidents in a Drilling Control System

Figure 2 provides an overview of the supply chain involved in cybersecurity incident handling for drilling rigs. More specifically, the figure shows the supply chain from the drilling control system point of view. This system is in charge of the equipment that drills the well through the earth's surface.

The white boxes represent the supply chain, whereas the grey boxes represent the supply chain activities related with handling an incident in the drilling control system. From the point of view of the incident, the core activity is the drilling system operation, depicted in black.

The activities that precede the drilling system operation are relevant for two reasons. The first one is that they provide support for solving incidents. The second one is that they could be sources of cybersecurity incidents that can affect or infect the drilling control system.

The system integrator provides the drilling system of the rig. Product suppliers, on the other hand, provide the components of the drilling system (e.g., computers, controllers, network devices) to the system integrator. The value of these organisations during incident handling relies on the support, experience, and knowledge about the technologies they provide.

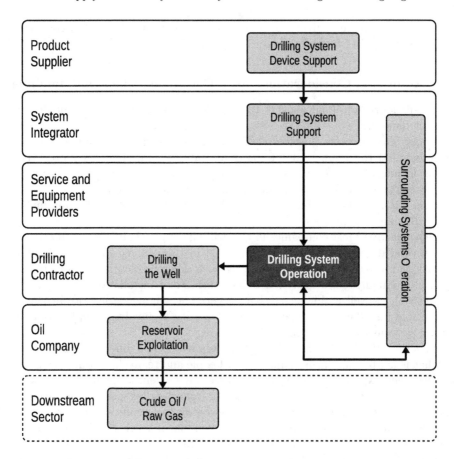

Fig. 2. Drilling supply chain and cybersecurity incident handling activities. White boxes represent relevant stakeholders. Grey boxes represent relevant activities in the context of a cybersecurity incident in the drilling system. Arrows represent which activities are supporting others in the creation and maintenance of value

Surrounding systems might be a source of risks or incidents that can affect the drilling control system. There are multiple systems from multiple stakeholders on the rig: corporate systems of the oil company or the drilling contractor, other control systems of the drilling contractor or service providers, and communication systems to the operational centres onshore.

The activities following the drilling system operation are the major activities supported by the control system, and determine the goals and constraints of the incident handling. The drilling contractor is in charge of the drilling operation, focusing on delivering it without delay. In addition, the oil company is in charge of the overall project of exploiting the reservoir, focusing on optimising the profitability of the reservoir. Finally, the market is the downstream sector of oil and gas where the oil company provides the crude oil or raw natural gas.

Market goals of price, delivery, or market share determine the overall goals that the oil company has for the reservoir exploitation.

3.2 Additional Considerations for a Coordinated Incident Handling

There are four additional aspects to consider when analysing stakeholders in incident handling:

Goals: The previous characterization of activities in the supply chain helps to understand the main goals of the organisations and, thus, their objectives during incident handling. However, it is also important to consider other goals such as safety, environment, reputation, or compliance. In addition, a PESTLE[3] analysis [11] could be helpful to identify the social constraints and requirements of the different organisations.

Departments: Most companies in the drilling supply chain are multinationals with several departments and roles involved in the drilling operation. Drilling operations involve several roles on the rig with different security responsibilities (e.g., oil company's site leader, drilling contractor's installation manager and toolpusher), as well as higher-level managers and engineers onshore in charge of multiple installations. Regarding cybersecurity, it involves people from the control systems domain and IT domain.

Visibility: Parties during incident handling will have a different point of view on what is happening during an incident. People and teams have different goals, activities and experience. Each party will see the incident from the point of view of how it affects their systems or activities, or from their perspective on the entire drilling process. Each party will be more aware of the ramifications of incidents in their domain than in other domains. An example of this is the different points of view of control system teams and IT teams regarding cybersecurity.

Capabilities: Similarly, they will have different resources and abilities for detecting, responding, and recovering from incidents. A control system user might have successfully detected a problem in the system, but she might only be able to respond partially. For example, a system user might be able to respond to a malware by substituting the device or reinstalling the operating system. However, the complete solution will not be in place until the system integrator or product supplier provide a security update for the device.

4   Example Case: Malware Infection of a Controller

In this section, we provide a general example on how the characterization of the supply and value chain is useful for assessing the stakeholder roles. The example is a malware infection in the drilling control system.

This malware infection consists of the following steps:

- Step 1 – Infection: Somebody uses an infected USB stick or laptop within the rig network, i.e., the surrounding systems in our characterization.

---

[3] Political, Economic, Social, Technological, Legal, and Environmental.

- Step 2 – Propagation: The malware propagates to the different systems of the rig including the drilling control system.
- Step 3 – Controller infection: The malware infects a critical component of the drilling control system. For example, the mud pump PLC.
- Step 4 – Digital consequence: The malware shuts down the controller.
- Step 5 – Physical/operational consequence: The mud pump stops operating.

4.1 Supply Chain Characterisation in the Case of Malware Infection of a Controller

The response for steps 1 and 2 involve actions such as eradicating or containing the infected devices, or checking whether other systems are infected. Protections in place (e.g., firewalls) might contain the propagation but they do not offer a complete protection since the malware could bypass the firewall, for example, by exploiting firewall or user-enabled vulnerabilities. Therefore, eradicating the virus or ensuring that it does not expand further involves a coordinated response with the other system owners, potentially all the supply chain stakeholders.

Regarding step 1, in case the person that brings the infected device has no intention of harm, the response actions might involve changing the security policies. This is not really an incident response action but rather a lesson learnt for future risk management. However, whether the insider is malicious or not, response actions might involve activities for identifying who is the insider amongst the people interacting with the first infected system.

Regarding step 3, the malware might be harmless to the drilling operations and, as long as there is no operational risk, it might be a low priority incident. Even so, response options could be actions such as reinstalling the controller software, substituting the device, and checking whether other devices are infected. The priority in these actions is avoiding as much disturbance as possible to the drilling operations. In addition, system integrators and product suppliers might be involved at this level. These suppliers provide support to contain or erase the malware in their devices, or recovery solutions such as the substitution of the device or a software update to eliminate the vulnerability exploited by the malware.

During step 4 it is important to coordinate with the drilling operators. This might also be essential during step 3 in case the risk assessment indicates a relevant operational risk. Furthermore, the coordination might involve the participation of other departments of the drilling contractor or the involvement of the oil company (as the owner of the reservoir being drilled). In this case, the focus of the response is to minimise the impact on operations, as the most likely risk is delaying operations. That said, and depending of the equipment and operations, the shutdown of the controller poses a safety and environmental risk due to the degradation of the drilling operations or the well control. The presence of safety systems and the engineer's oversight reduces the likelihood of any of these risks, but the potential serious impact might require a diligent response. This is the case, for example, for the mud pump, as this piece of equipment injects a fluid that facilitates the perforation of the hole and the stabilisation of the well pressure to a point in which neither collapses nor fluid is injected accidentally in the reservoir. Therefore, any cybersecurity response is conditioned by the overall response strategy from the engineers in charge of drilling and well control.

4.2 Supply Chain Considerations in the Case of Malware Infection of a Controller

From the description of the event, we see that the further the incident escalates, the costlier and riskier the response might be. Therefore, it is important to deal with the incident as early as possible. In our example, an early response at digital system-level, such as containment or substitution of devices would be relatively cheaper and less time-consuming compared to the potential impact of the operational delays, failures, and risk in case the mud pump fails.

A first observation is that the operators of the rig systems might be unaware of the escalation potential of the incident. In this case, a downwards communication in the supply chain, from the drilling engineers to the system engineers, would provide a more complete view of the potential increase in the risk if the malware is not contained. Regarding upwards communication in the chain, it would relevant to check whether the malware would affect the controller in a way that would impact operations. If so, informing drilling engineers would be important for a timely response without perturbing operations.

In the malware example, the best response from the system point of view might be refreshing the system and eradicating the virus. However, this response will probably cause a delay in the drilling operations. In case the malware does not harm operations, waiting to a maintenance time might be a better response than an immediate action, as this could be even worse than the malware, in terms of operational or safety risk if the system is performing a critical operation.

Overall, we emphasise the need for coordination and communication. A coordinated risk response and information flow between stakeholders is advantageous if not critical during incident handling. This recommendation might sound general and obvious, but taking into account the stakeholders role is not a trivial activity during incident handling. Incident or risk handling actions in a rig setting might require or recommend coordination of actions and information flow. Therefore, it is relevant, in a cybersecurity context, to have a characterisation of the stakeholders, their activities, goals, and departments in drilling systems operations.

5 Conclusion

The assessment of the drilling supply chain and its role during cybersecurity incidents is relevant due to the challenge of managing incidents in a multi-stakeholder and high risk environment. It is important to understand the goals, activities, and perspectives of the different stakeholders, because these factors contextualise the coordination and collaboration necessary to handle incidents.

Stakeholder and supply chain assessment has been a relevant topic in O&G drilling for a long time due the need for operational coordination during drilling. However, the traditional characterisation is a top-down approach from the point of view of the entire drilling operation. Therefore, we provide a high-level characterisation that depicts this stakeholder map from the point of view of protecting the main system in the installation - the drilling control system. This might serve as a starting point for understanding, in a structured manner, the ramifications of a cybersecurity incident in the rig systems and for eliciting a more complete picture of relevant threats, countermeasures and impacts during incident or risk analysis.

This paper is part of the innovation project *Cybersecurity Incident Response Framework for the O&G Industry to Optimize Oil Production and Prevent Safety and Environmental Disasters* funded by the Regional Research Fund of West Norway (project 245291). Future work will focus on the development of a stakeholder model for supporting incident and risk analysis during a cybersecurity incident in the control systems on a rig. Our aim is including this model in a risk-based framework for cybersecurity incident handling for drilling rigs. The inclusion of stakeholder considerations will facilitate the evaluation of the risks and potential responses and is critical because of the need for stakeholder coordination.

References

1. Crude Faux: An Analysis of Cyber Conflict within the Oil & Gas Industries. Center for Eduction and Research, Information Assurance and Security, Purdue University (2011)
2. ICS-CERT Year in Review. Industrial Control System Cyber Emergency Response Team (2013)
3. NCCIC/ICS-CERT Year in Review. National Cybersecurity and Commuincations Integration Center/Industrial Control System Cyber Emergency Response Team (2015)
4. Bommer, P.M.: A Primer of Oilwell Drilling. University of Texas at Austin, Austin (2008)
5. Deepwater Horizon Study Group: Final Report on the Investigation of the Macondo Well Blowout. University at California at Berkeley (2011)
6. Porter, M.E., Millar, V.E.: How information gives you competitive advantage. Harvard Bus. Rev. **63**(4), 149–160 (1985)
7. Inkpen, A.C., Moffett, M.H.: The Global Oil & Gas Industry: Management, Strategy & Finance. PennWell Books, Tulsa (2011)
8. Waugh, W.L., Streib, G.: Collaboration and leadership for effective emergency management. Public Adm. Rev. **66**(s1), 131–140 (2006)
9. Allen, L.Y.H.: Organizational collaborative capacities in disaster management: evidence from the Taiwan red cross organization. Asian J. Soc. Sci. **39**(4), 446–468 (2011)
10. Kapucu, N., Garayev, V.: Collaborative decision-making in emergency and disaster management. Int. J. Public Adm. **34**(6), 366–375 (2011)
11. Collins, R.: A graphical method for exploring the business environment. Oxford University Working Paper, vol. 956 (2010)

Control of Cyber-Physical Systems Using Bluetooth Low Energy and Distributed Slave Microcontrollers

Øyvind Netland[1(✉)] and Amund Skavhaug[2(✉)]

[1] Department of Engineering Design and Materials,
Norwegian University of Science and Technology, Trondheim, Norway
oyvind.netland@ntnu.no
[2] Department of Production and Quality Engineering,
Norwegian University of Science and Technology, Trondheim, Norway
amund.skavhaug@ntnu.no

Abstract. In this paper, Bluetooth Low Energy is used for communication between master computers and distributed slave microcontrollers that perform low-level tasks that the master is unable or not suitable to do, e.g. hard real-time and low-level I/O. The wireless communication with the master computer allow slaves to be added, replaced or removed without the need for rewiring. Dependability can be increased as implementation of redundancy, both for masters and slaves, does not require wired connections between them. This concept has been utilized in an industrial prototype and evaluated in an experiment presented in this paper. The experiment evaluated the communication latency with Bluetooth Low Energy, compared to a wired alternative, which is important for reliable operation. The results showed a similar average latency, but the worst case was less favorable for Bluetooth Low Energy. However, since the slaves are intended to manage time critical operations locally, with the master computer in a supervisory role, these delays will be acceptable in many applications, when considering the advantages of a wireless master-slave communication.

Keywords: Bluetooth low energy · Linux · Distributed · Dependability · Real-time

1 Introduction

Bluetooth Low Energy [1] (BLE) is a wireless network technology for low latency and low power consumption transfer of small data packets, with low bandwidth as a tradeoff. This makes it suitable for the transfer of status and command messages within a distributed control system, especially when parts of the system are physically separated from each other, e.g. moving or rotating equipment. In this paper we argue that the flexibility afforded by wireless communication can be beneficial even for communication between devices where wired communication is a viable alternative.

Bluetooth Low Energy is a widely used technology, that has become commonplace over the last years, in computers, phones and Internet of Things devices. Multiple microcontrollers and single-board computers have built in support, or support can in most cases be added.

A. Skavhaug et al. (Eds.): SAFECOMP 2016 Workshops, LNCS 9923, pp. 256–267, 2016.
DOI: 10.1007/978-3-319-45480-1_21

In a previous paper [2], we investigated the use of consumer-grade single-board Linux computers, which have gained in popularity over the last years, for control of cyber physical systems [3, 4]. These computers offer high computational power in small, inexpensive devices, with various capabilities and interfaces. There are also advantages to using Linux, which has large amount of drivers, libraries etc. and easy access to support through active communities. Linux also offer an environment that many developers are familiar with.

However, cyber-physical systems interact with the real-world, where the real-time performance of low-level I/O might be important and necessary for dependable operation. This means they should be guaranteed to react to certain events within specified time constraints or deadlines [5]. Linux is not considered a real-time operating system and in order for it to behave as one, it is common to use a real-time microkernel between the hardware and the Linux kernel [6, 7]. A popular implementation of this today is Xenomai. Extensions as this add a layer of complexity and require significant additional development time and specialized knowledge. Some of the main reasons for using Linux are lost, e.g. drivers and available support. Linux drivers can be used, but will operate in the non real-time context of Linux, not the real-time context of Xenomai. It can even reduce the performance compared to Linux alone, due to unnecessary context switches between real-time and non real-time.

A commonly used alternative to improving the real-time capabilities of a control system is to delegate the real-time tasks and low level I/O operations to one or more slave microcontrollers. Communication between the master computer and slave microcontroller(s) will typically be serial communication using a UART or a bus such as I2C. The master takes a supervisory role and perform the tasks it is most suited for, while the slave(s) perform specialized tasks. With real-time operating systems or no operating system at all, the slaves, can do tasks and local control loops where timing, low-level I/O operation and deterministic behavior are important. However, a limitation is that masters and slaves are hardwired, often with a one to one relationship, which makes it difficult to extend a system with additional slaves or replace faulty slaves on the fly.

Section 2 of this paper describes the use of BLE instead of a wired solution for master-slave communication in a cyber-physical control system, and how this can be used to improve the dependability. Section 3 describes an experiment that was performed to test the real-time capabilities of the proposed solution, in order to evaluate its viability, and gain knowledge about the applications it is suitable for. The results of the experiment are presented in Sect. 4 and discussed in Sect. 5. Section 6 ends the paper with concluding remarks.

2   Bluetooth Low Energy

Bluetooth Low Energy, sometimes referred to as Bluetooth Smart, use the same 2.4 GHz spectrum as classic Bluetooth (and WiFi). However, the protocol is different and not compatible. ZigBee is a competing technology with similar specifications as BLE, and a comparison between classic Bluetooth, BLE and ZigBee is given in [8]. BLE was chosen due to better support on both embedded and general purpose computers and smart phones.

BLE has a star topology, with a BLE central that can connect to multiple BLE peripherals. A BLE peripheral cannot accept connections from more than one central at the time. Connections and advertising of BLE peripherals are performed by the Generic Access Profile (GAP).

When a connection is established, the data transfer is defined with Generic Attribute Profile (GATT). The BLE peripheral acts as a server that has defined one or more services. Each service is intended to represent a function of the peripheral, and can have one or more characteristics, which represents a data value or a part of the service.

Data transfer is performed periodically, with a connection interval (CI). The peripheral suggests a CI between 7.5 ms and 4000 ms, but it is up to the BLE central to decide the period by how often it will attempt to initiate data transfers by sending requests. There is also a slave latency parameter that specify whether the slave should respond to all data transfer requests or ignore some of them. Combined, these parameters set the effective communication period, and therefore the expected latency in the control system. There is a correlation between the communication period and power use [9], thus if low power use is desirable, e.g. battery powered, it could be an alternative to accept longer latency.

Each connection interval, the BLE central can read or write attributes exposed by the GATT server. It can also subscribe to notifications and indications from peripherals, which means that the peripheral can notify the central within the data transfer during a connection interval. The difference between notifications and indications is that indications are acknowledged.

2.1 Description of Solution

The solution presented in this paper uses BLE between master computers and slave microcontrollers, as shown in Fig. 1, instead of more traditional wired solutions as UART or I2C. The master computers can be any computer with a BLE interface, which means most modern laptops, smart phones, some single board computers, or any

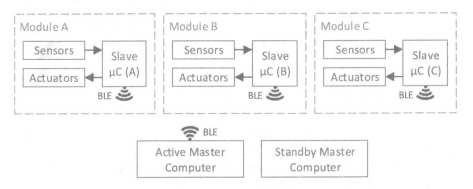

Fig. 1. Description of solution using three redundant BLE slave microcontrollers, and two redundant master computers

computer able to use a BLE USB device. This paper focus on a single board Linux computer, as they have low cost compared to their capabilities and are often useful for embedded and cyber-physical systems. The method is transferrable to other types of masters, and it would be a convenient way to use a mobile phone in a control system, since most modern smart phones have BLE, but few or none wired connectors.

Wireless communication has the obvious benefit of allowing for communication between master and slaves that are separated from each other. In addition, it can be used to make modules, each controlled by a BLE slave that can be added, removed or replaced in a system with minimal hardware changes. BLE and BLE microcontrollers typically have very low power consumption, thus some slave modules would be able to use a battery as a power source, making it entirely wireless.

The reliability and availability aspects of dependability of a control system can be improved by having multiple modules capable of performing the same tasks, i.e. redundancy. There are several ways to implement this, a common type is a K out of N system that uses a central, often complex, voting logic to decide on the result, which could be implemented with a number of BLE slaves. However, this paper focus on another type of redundancy, where two or more modules are able to perform the same tasks. Each module has its own sensors and actuators as shown in Fig. 1, and the master can seamlessly switch between which of them to use. This solution greatly reduces possible common cause failures, as there is no voting logic required and the master slave communication does not require a multiplexer or shared bus to communicate with multiple slaves.

It is assumed that the master is able to detect if one of the slaves fail, either because it fails silently, or with sanity checks. If this occurs, the system can continue using another slave, thus the mean time between repairs can be reduced. This is especially relevant for systems that are deployed at a location where repairs are difficult to perform, such that the cost of repairing a system is significantly higher than the additional cost of redundancy.

Redundancy on the master side can be achieved by having multiple BLE enabled computers. Only one master can be connected to any one slave at a given time, thus, one of the masters will be active and the rest are standby masters ready to take over if needed. Multiple, inexpensive computers can be deployed together for high dependability. None of the masters has to be wired to the slaves, thus changes to the system or replacement of masters are easy, which is beneficial to the maintainability of the system.

The dependability aspects of security and safety, which often can be of concern for wireless communication. Potential problems include eavesdropping to the communication, impersonation of either a master or slave and vulnerability to radio jamming. BLE have built in encryption and frequency modulation to prevent these problems, but this have not been investigated in detail in this paper.

2.2 Implementation

The presented solution has been implemented in an instrumentation platform prototype, intended for remote inspections of industrial plants at locations that are difficult to visit, e.g. offshore wind turbines. The remote location of the system means it should be able to operate unattended with a minimum of repairs. One of the strategies that have been used to achieve this is to have two master computers, and four slaves (two able to operate each of the two separated parts of the system). Since the communication between the masters and slaves is wireless as shown rightmost in Fig. 2, both masters are able to communicate directly to all slaves. A wired solution would not allow this, unless an additional component that would be a single point of failure. It is also possible to extend the capabilities of the system by adding more slaves.

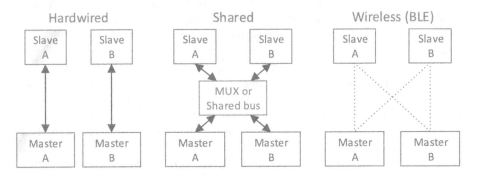

Fig. 2. Variants of master/slave communication

Master Computer. For the master computers we used Variscite VAR-SOM-DUAL CPU modules [10], with integrated BLE interfaces. This CPU module has a dual core ARM 1 GHz CPU and 512 MB RAM, similar to what you can find on consumer-grade ARM computer boards. However, it does not have the typical connectors, as USB, Ethernet, HDMI etc., instead it has a SO-DIMM socket and connects to a motherboard customized for a specific application.

The master computer used a Linux system created with Yocto Fido [11], an embedded Linux build system. The Linux system was configured to be command-line only. The Linux kernel version was 3.14.38 and BlueZ version 5.28 [12] was used for Bluetooth communication.

Slave Microcontroller. The NRF51822 microcontroller [13] from Nordic Semiconductor was used as slaves. It is a 32-bit ARM M0 microcontroller with a built-in BLE interface, running at 16 MHz. It was programmed using the Nordic NRF51 SDK version 10.0.0 and built with GCC on Windows 10, using the S110 SoftDevice [14] for BLE communication.

3   Testing the Communication Delay

Traditional wireless communication, as WiFi and classic Bluetooth, would not be suitable in the concept presented here, both due to high and unpredictable latency and because it is difficult to implement on low-powered slave microcontrollers. BLE, on the other hand, has specifications that could make it a viable alternative. We performed an experiment to evaluate how a master/slave BLE communication performed compared to a UART communication that we consider to be a typical alternative.

The results from the experiment provide a better understanding of how BLE communication would work, and which limitations the solution would have. It is not expected that the BLE communication would be suitable to be a part of real-time control loops that run with a very short period, as this should be handled by the slave by itself. Thus the communication latency would affect how quickly the slave would react to commands from the master, and how updated the information the master received from the slaves are, which are important for the performance and reliability of the system.

3.1   Test Device

The same VAR-SOM-DUAL CPU module and Linux system described in 2.2 were used in the test, but on a VAR-SOLOCustomBoard, which serves as a generic development board for the platform, instead of our custom board. Two small BLE Nano development boards, with NRF51822 devices, were used as slaves.

An Arduino Pro board [15] was used to make a test program that measured the time from sending a signal to a slave, until a response was received. Arduino was used for convenience, and since the test program was relatively simple. It uses the 16 bit TIMER1 of the AVR microcontroller on the Arduino to measure the time, and the value was converted to milliseconds. The resolution of the measurement was 4 µs.

The test program performs a test, print the result and wait for a random number of milliseconds between 40 and 100 before starting a new test. The delay was chosen to be at least 40 ms, to allow at least a few connection intervals to pass before the next test. It also has to be random, with a range of multiple connection intervals, to make sure that each test is started at a random point within the intervals.

3.2   Experiment Description

This experiment compared wireless BLE and wired UART roundtrip communication between a slave microcontroller and a Linux master computer. A minimal application was developed for the master that would listen for and respond to either UART or BLE messages. This was the only user application that was running on the minimal Linux system during the test. The test equipment is shown in Fig. 3, with the master, two slaves and the test program running on an Arduino. Three different methods, shown in Fig. 4, were tested. For each method, 50000 individual tests were performed.

UART Response. In this case, the response time of a signal sent from a slave, to the master and back again using UART was measured. When the tester sends a signal, it triggers an interrupt in the slave that will immediately sends a short message on the UART connection to the master. The master will receive this, and return another short message. When the slave receives this, it will send a response pulse back to the tester. A baud rate of 38400 was used, and a total of 4 bytes were transferred during each roundtrip, which corresponds approximately 100 µs.

Fig. 3. Test system with master board (right), two slaves (bottom left) and test program running on Arduino (upper left)

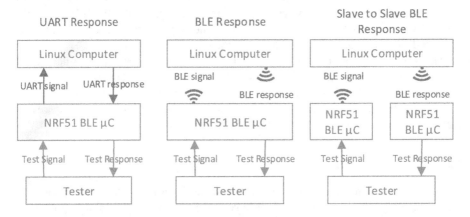

Fig. 4. Different communication methods used in the experiment

BLE Response. In this case, the response time of a signal sent from a slave, to the master and back again using BLE was measured. When the tester sends a signal, it triggers and interrupt in the slave that will immediately sends a short message on the BLE connection to the master. The master will receive this, and return another short message. When the slave receives this, it will send a response pulse back to the tester. The BLE response test was performed with both the minimal 7.5 ms connection interval and a larger interval of 20 ms.

Figure 5 show the expected timeline for the roundtrip communication. Since it will be impossible for the master to respond within the same period as it receives, there will be a minimum latency equal to the connection interval. The slave response time (both to the start test signal and to the response from the master), the actual transfer time and the time the slave has to wait for a BLE period to start the transfer are all adding to the total time. Of these, the waiting time for BLE period is expected to be the most significant, and it will be a random time between 0 and the connection interval, depending on when in the BLE period the slave is ready to transmit.

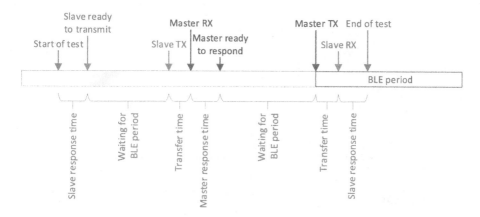

Fig. 5. Expected BLE roundtrip communication.

Slave to Slave BLE Response. In this case, the response time of a signal sent from one slave, to the master and back to another slave using BLE was measured. This was tested because BLE slaves are not able to communicate directly.

4   Results

The measurements are summarized in Table 1. The distribution of the BLE tests are illustrated in Fig. 6, with a line indicating the average (very stable) response time from the UART test.

Table 1. Summary of results in communication delay test.

	UART	BLE CI = 7.5 ms	BLE CI = 20 ms	BLE slave to slave CI = 7.5 ms
Mean	11.40	14.12	25.60	12.69
Min	11.36	9.17	17.15	2.72
Max	13.91	64.62	79.31	47.75
St.dev	0.03	4.35	6.25	5.9

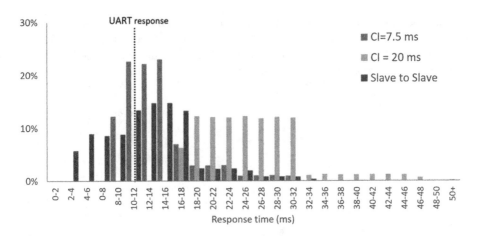

Fig. 6. Distribution of results in communication delay test.

5   Discussion

The average UART response was 11.4 ms, which is somewhat longer than expected, and much longer than the time required to transmit the data. The overhead is assumed to originate from the Linux system. An advantage with the UART response is that there is very little difference between the samples.

The average BLE response was slightly higher than the UART response, and also varied more. This was expected due to the periodic nature of BLE communication. For connection intervals of 7.5 ms, the minimum response time was lower than for UART. The majority of the samples was within approximately one connection interval (7.5 ms) of the minimum value, which is as expected by a periodic communication method. We did not observe any significant unexpected overhead in the communication, as with the UART communication. However, we can also see a group of values that is between 1 and 2 connection intervals of the minimum value, and an even smaller group that is between 2 and 3. These are samples where one or two connection intervals were "missed". This could be due to the master response time shown in Fig. 5 was longer than the time available before the next BLE period, or that there was a problem with the wireless data transfer. Both of these problems would result in the response getting delayed by one (or more) periods. A similar effect is observed for the longer connection interval, but there are fewer "misses", possibly due to more time being available for the master to respond.

If the minimum connection interval is used, then the average master-to-slave communication delay for BLE is comparable to UART, while the worst case was 4–5 times longer. A less predictable communication latency is not favorable, but since the most time critical tasks are performed by the slave, the relatively small difference between BLE and the wired alternative means that BLE would be a viable alternative in many applications.

BLE communication between two slaves, via the master, was actually faster than the communication from a slave to the master and back to the same slave. The reason for this is explained in Fig. 7, where the connection intervals of the two slaves are shown to be out of phase with each other, which allow the master to respond to the second slave at an earlier time than it would have been able to respond to the first. The minimal latency of 2.72 ms was surprisingly low, and would have required a nearly "perfect" timing, where both data transfers were ready to be sent just before the BLE data transfer was initiated.

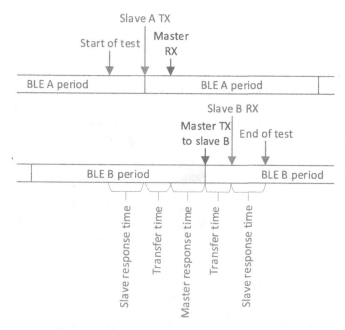

Fig. 7. Expected best-case slave to slave communication, where it is assumed no waiting time for BLE period.

6 Concluding Remarks

The solution proposed in this paper is a variant of the commonly used concept of having slave microcontrollers to do specific, often low-level I/O or real-time, tasks on behalf of a master computer. This has many applications, e.g. in embedded systems or cyber-physical systems. Bluetooth Low Energy (BLE) is used instead of a typical wired communication method between the master and slave. An obvious advantage with wireless communication is that slaves can be distributed without having to consider how it should be wired. In addition, the wireless communication makes it easy to add, change and remove slaves without rewiring or even shut down the system.

Improved dependability could be achieved, since both redundant masters and slaves are possible, and communication between all masters and all slaves is possible without a multiplexer or a shared bus that would be single-points of failure.

The specifications of BLE makes it more suitable for use within a control system compared to earlier wireless communication methods, as WiFi and classic Bluetooth, due to low latency. This was evaluated in an experiment that compared BLE master/slave communication with UART based communication. The results showed that the latencies of BLE communication were more varied to that of UART. However, due to the advantages to using BLE, as presented in the paper, it could be advantageous in many applications.

7   Future Work

The experiment could be extended to include simultaneous communication between two or more slaves with a common master, to determine how BLE communication scale compared to wired alternatives. Another possibility is to perform a similar test that compare BLE with other similar technologies, as ZigBee.

References

1. Whitepaper Bluetooth Low Energy, Technical report, Stallmann, Release r03
2. Netland, Ø., Skavhaug, A.: Dependable cyber-physical systems with redundant consumer single-board linux computers. In: Koornneef, F., van Gulijk, C. (eds.) SAFECOMP 2015 Workshops. LNCS, vol. 9338, pp. 224–234. Springer, Heidelberg (2015). doi: 10.1007/978-3-319-24249-1_20
3. Shi, J., Wan, J., Yan, H., Suo, H.: A survey of cyber-physical systems. In: 2011 International Conference on Wireless Communications and Signal Processing, pp. 1–6 (2011)
4. Sha, L., Gopalakrishnan, S., Liu, X., Wang, Q.: Cyber-physical systems: a new frontier. In: 2008 IEEE International Conference on Sensor Networks, Ubiquitous, and Trustworthy Computing. IEEE (2008)
5. Burns, A., Wellings, A.: Real-Time Systems and Programming Languages: Ada 95, Real-Time Java, and Real-Time POSIX. Addison Wesley, New York (2001)
6. Lehrbaum, R.: Using Linux in embedded and real-time systems. Linux J. **2000**(75es), Article No. 10 (2000). Belltown Media
7. Barabanov, M., Yodaiken, V.: Real-time Linux. Linux J. **23**(4.2), 1 (1996)
8. Georgakakis, E., Nikolidakis, S.A., Vergados, D.D., Douligeris, C.: An analysis of Bluetooth, Zigbee and Bluetooth low energy and their use in WBANs. In: Lin, J. (ed.) MobiHealth 2010. LNICST, vol. 55, pp. 168–175. Springer, Heidelberg (2011)
9. Gomez, C., Oller, J., Paradells, J.: Overview and evaluation of Bluetooth low energy: an emerging low-power wireless technology. Sensors **12**(9), 11734–11753 (2012)
10. VAR-SOM-SOLO/DUAL v1.X Datasheet Freescale i.MX6-based System-on-Module, Technical report, Variscite Ltd, Revision 1.04 (2016)
11. Yocto Project 1.8 – Fido. https://www.yoctoproject.org/yoctoproject/fido. Accessed 17 May 2016
12. BlueZ Official Linux Bluetooth Protocol Stack. http://www.bluez.org. Accessed 17 May 2016

13. nRF51822 Multiprotocol Bluetooth low energy/2.4 GHz RF System on Chip Product Specification v3.1, Technical Report, Nordic Semiconductor, Revision 3.1 (2014)
14. S110 nRF51 Bluetooth® low energy Peripheral SoftDevice, Technical report Nordic Semiconductor, v2 (2015)
15. Arduino Web Site. https://www.arduino.cc. Accessed 14 Mar 2016

5th International Workshop on Next Generation of System Assurance Approaches for Safety-Critical Systems (SASSUR)

SASSUR 2016: The 5th International Workshop on Next Generation of System Assurance Approaches for Safety-Critical Systems

Alejandra Ruiz[1], Jose Luis de la Vara[2], and Tim Kelly[3]

[1] TECNALIA, Spain
alejandra.ruiz@tecnalia.com
[2] Universidad Carlos III de Madrid, Spain
jvara@inf.uc3m.es
[3] University of York, UK
tim.kelly@york.ac.uk

SASSUR 2016 is the 5th edition of the International Workshop on Next Generation of System Assurance Approaches for Safety-Critical Systems. With this edition we have tried to consolidate and to keep the main objective of the workshop while we introduce the new challenges and trends in the assurance domain. This is in line with our intention to explore new ideas on compositional, evolutionary, and efficient approaches to assurance and certification.

Systems and scenarios such as the wider use of autonomous air vehicles and its regulation, recent incidents with autonomous cars, regulation changes for medical devices, national authorities' request for information and comments on new assurance standards, and potential security threats in safety-critical systems, all motivate the need for new and cost-effective forms of assurance. The topics of interest in the workshop include, among others, cross-domain product certification, integration of process-centric and product-centric assurance, compliance management, evolutionary approaches for safety and security assurance, metrics for safety assurance and certification processes, safety and security co-assurance, assurance case-based approaches, seamless development tool chain for safety-critical systems, evolution of standards and practices, human factors in assurance and certification, COTS and management of third-party assurance evidence, mixed-criticality system assurance, and safety assurance on new types of systems (e.g. adaptive systems).

The program of SASSUR 2016 consists of eight high-quality papers. We have divided the papers into three categories based on their focus and the topics that they cover:

- Safety Concept and Requirements Definition

    1. "Automotive Safety Concept Definition for Mixed-Criticality Integration on a COTS Multicore", by Irune Agirre, Mikel Azkarate-Askasua, Asier Larrucea Ortube, Jon Perez, Tullio Vardanega and Francisco J Cazorla.

2. "Defining Autonomous Functions Using Iterative Hazard Analysis and Requirements Refinement", by Fredrik Warg, Martin Gassilewski, Jörgen Tryggvesson, Viacheslav Izosimov, Anders Werneman and Rolf Johansson.
3. "ASIL Tailoring on Functional Safety Requirements", by Markus Fockel.

- Assurance Approaches

1. "AMASS: Architecture-driven, Multi-concern, Seamless, Reuse-Oriented Assurance and Certification of CPSs" by Alejandra Ruiz, Barbara Gallina, Jose Luis de La Vara, Silvia Mazzini and Huascar Espinoza.
2. "Towards the Adoption of Model-based Engineering for the Development of Safety-critical Systems in Industrial Practice" by Marc Zeller, Daniel Ratiu and Kai Höfig.
3. "Goal-Oriented Co-engineering of Security and Safety Requirements in Cyber-Physical Systems", by Christophe Ponsard, Gautier Dallons and Philippe Massonet.
4. "Practitioners' Perspectives on Change Impact Analysis for Safety-Critical Software – A Preliminary Analysis" by Markus Borg, Jose Luis de La Vara and Krzysztof Wnuk.

- Tool support

1. "Seamless integrated Simulation in Design and Verification Flow for Safety-Critical Systems" by Ralph Weissnegger.

Acknowledgements. We are grateful to the SAFECOMP organization committee and collaborators for their support in arranging SASSUR. We also thank all the authors of the submitted papers for their interest in the workshop, and the steering and programme committees for their work and advice. We are grateful to DNV GL staff for accepting our invitation to give the keynote presentation. Finally, the AMASS project supports the workshop (H2020-ECSEL grant agreement no. 692474; Spain's MINECO reference PCIN-2015-262).

Workshop Committees

Organization Committee

Alejandra Ruiz	TECNALIA, Spain
Jose Luis de la Vara	Universidad Carlos III de Madrid, Spain
Tim Kelly	University of York, UK

Steering Committee

John Favaro	Intecs, Italy
Huascar Espinoza	TECNALIA, Spain
Fabien Belmonte	ALSTOM, France

Programme Committee and Reviewers

Markus Borg	Swedish Institute of Computer Science, Sweden
FaGereon Weiß	Fraunhofer ESK, Germany
Mehrdad Sabetzadeh	University of Luxembourg, Luxembourg
Paolo Panaroni	INTECS, Italy
Gaël Blondelle	Eclipse Foundation, Germany
Kenji Taguchi	AIST, Japan
Paolo Barbosa	Universidade Estadual da Paraiba, Brazil
Ibrahim Habli	University of York, UK
Jose María Álvarez	Universidad Carlos III de Madrid, Spain
Stefano Tonetta	Fondazione Bruno Kessler, Italy
Sunil Nair	Institute for Energy Technology, Norway
Barbara Gallina	Mälardalens University, Sweden
Thomas Olsson	Swedish Institute of Computer Science, Sweden
Ulrik Franke	Swedish Institute of Computer Science, Sweden

Automotive Safety Concept Definition for Mixed-Criticality Integration on a COTS Multicore

Irune Agirre[1]([✉]), Mikel Azkarate-askasua[1], Asier Larrucea[1], Jon Perez[1],
Tullio Vardanega[2], and Francisco J. Cazorla[3,4]

[1] IK4-Ikerlan Technology Research Centre, Mondragon, Spain
{iagirre,mazkarateaskasua,alarrucea,jmperez}@ikerlan.es
[2] University of Padua, Padua, Italy
tullio.vardanega@math.unipd.it
[3] Barcelona Supercomputing Center, Barcelona, Spain
francisco.cazorla@bsc.es
[4] Spanish National Research Council (IIIA-CSIC), Barcelona, Spain

Abstract. Mixed-criticality systems integrating applications subject to different safety assurance levels into the same multicore embedded platform can provide potential benefits in terms of performance, cost, size, weight, and power. In spite of this evidence, however, several hard challenges related to the safety certification of multicore approaches must be considered before endorsing their unrestrained adoption. This paper describes an ISO-26262 compliant safety concept for an automotive mixed-criticality case-study on top of a multicore platform. To this end, key aspects such as time and space partitioning are evaluated and enforced by means of hardware protection mechanisms.

Keywords: Mixed-criticality · Safety · Certification · Multicore

1 Introduction

Mixed-criticality systems integrate applications subject to different certification assurance levels into the same embedded platform. Their integrated nature can provide to the Critical Real-Time Embedded Systems (CRTES) outstanding benefits over traditionally-followed federated architectures. These advantages include reduction in the cost, size, weight and power factors, as well as, in the amount of wiring and connectors. Nevertheless, the ever increasing demand of CRTES for integrating a higher number of embedded functionality with higher levels of performance requirements cause the traditionally-used single-core processors hit their limit in terms of performance, complexity, power consumption and heat dissipation. As a result, CRTES industries have started to transition to multicore processors as an alternative to the infeasibility of further increasing clock speeds and the limits of Moore's law on single-cores.

© Springer International Publishing Switzerland 2016
A. Skavhaug et al. (Eds.): SAFECOMP 2016 Workshops, LNCS 9923, pp. 273–285, 2016.
DOI: 10.1007/978-3-319-45480-1_22

Unlike conventional computing systems, where multicores are well established, CRTES and mixed-criticality systems are bound to be certified given the possible destructive effects that a failure in these systems can cause. Mixed-criticality CRTES have been successfully integrated on single-core processors while fulfilling the requirements posed by certification standards [3]. On the contrary, there are no established approaches to achieve the safety certification on existing multicore architectures yet. The main concerns result from their inherent complexity, reduced temporal predictability, interferences coming from shared resources, the lack of previous experience and the weak support on safety certification standards [6]. To reduce this gap, this paper contributes with the definition of a safety concept for an integrated mixed-criticality automotive case-study on top of a Commercial Off-The-Shelf (COTS) multicore processor. The core matter of the safety argumentation is based on a set of hardware protection mechanisms integrated on the automotive state-of-the-art AURIX processor family [10]. Thanks to the protection mechanisms implemented at the hardware layer, we show how to safely integrate mixed-criticality applications on a multicore complying with industrial safety standards (ISO-26262 [2]) without the need of a hypervisor.

The rest of this paper is structured as follows. Section 2 gives overall background information and Sect. 3 describes the mixed-criticality requirements posed by safety standards. Section 4 introduces the case-study and the main safety features of its common-practice federated implementation. The federated approach is transformed into an integrated mixed-criticality safety concept in Sect. 5. Section 6 analyses the related work. Finally, Sect. 7 draws the main conclusions.

2   Background and Problem Statement

The ever increasing demand for additional embedded functionality leads to a considerable complexity growth [12]. As a consequence, the continued viability of the federated architecture paradigm conventionally followed by industry is challenged, due to the large number of required Electronic Control Unit (ECU)s, cables, electrical parts and connectors [18]. In the automotive domain this has resulted in vehicles with up to 100 ECUs, 400 connectors with 3000 individual terminals and over 3 thousand meters of cables that make the wiring the third most expensive and heaviest part of a car [5,15].

The improved performance of multicore processors make them true enablers for mixed-criticality systems, enabling the integration of a high number of applications on a single computing platform and overcoming, to a big extent, the limitations of the traditional federated paradigm. Yet, mixed-criticality systems must follow strict certification processes before they are allowed to be put in operation. To aid in this process, there are several certification standards to cover different needs, often written to cover specific domain applications (e.g., IEC-61508, Automotive ISO-26262, Railway EN-50128, Avionics DO-178). Standards provide some guidance for mixed-criticality integration based on the concept of partitioning [19], but unfortunately, they have not been updated yet to cover the new challenges involved by novel multicore architectures.

The most common approach to attain mixed-criticality requirements is to rely on the use of a software separation layer (e.g., hypervisor) that provides the required level of independence among the different applications. However, the use of a hypervisor adds additional complexity to the software stack and it needs to be certified according to the highest integrity level present on the system. Additionally, the multicore versions of the hypervisors are not mature enough yet and they lack in-service experience. In this paper we aim to overcome this limitation by proposing a safety concept for mixed-criticality integration on a multicore COTS architecture based on a set of hardware mechanisms without the need of integrating a hypervisor.

3   Safety Requirements for Mixed-Criticality Integration

Standards provide two options for the certification of mixed-criticality systems: (1) certify all components of the system - including the non safety-related software - for the highest criticality level present on the system, or (2) provide enough evidence of independence among the applications and certify each application according to its criticality level in a composable manner (e.g., ISO-26262-6 p.7.4.10 [2]). Considering the highest integrity level for the entire system is generally cost and effort prohibitive. Therefore, a means to guarantee that the co-existing applications do not endanger the functional behaviour and timing correctness among each other is required.

This is commonly achieved by partitioning techniques that provide functional separation and design fault containment among the applications. The goal of partitioning is to achieve the same level of functional isolation as a federated implementation [3]. This is commonly achieved by demonstrating freedom from interference (i.e., independence) in both spatial and temporal domains as defined in different safety standards (e.g., IEC-61508-3 Annex-F, ISO-26262-6 Annex-D, DO-175 paragraph 6.3.3f):

- *Spatial independence* must ensure that one application cannot alter the code, private data or command the peripherals of another application.
- *Temporal independence* must ensure that the execution of one application does not obstruct, in the temporal domain, the execution of other applications (e.g., by taking too much processor execution time or by locking shared resources).

Based on the definition of partitioning, the particular strategy followed for defining the automotive safety concept consists on transforming a federated architecture with common-practice safety techniques and solutions into an integrated mixed-criticality approach. To this end, in Sect. 4 we briefly review the main safety properties of the federated implementation of an automotive use case. Using the federated argumentation as a baseline, in Sect. 5 we describe a solution for integrating such case-study on a COTS multicore platform while preserving the required independence.

4   Federated Safety Concept for an Automotive Case-Study

This section defines a federated system level safety concept for an automotive case-study with safety techniques and solutions that are common-practice in industry. This safety concept is not described in detail but it serves as a baseline for developing the integrated mixed-criticality safety concept.

4.1   Case-Study Definition

The automotive case-study defined for the evaluation of the mixed-criticality safety concept has been derived from the CONCERTO European Research project [7], and it is comprised of a safety-critical Cruise Control (CC) system and a non safety-related subsystem. The main job of the CC is to control the speed of a vehicle automatically without human intervention. The system takes control over the throttle of the car to maintain the vehicle's speed as set by the driver. The CC is composed of two safety ECUs that perform the CC functionality:

- Signal Acquisition ECU: Reads the set of input buttons, pedals and speed sensor and transmits the commands to the Engine Control ECU via the car's vehicle bus.
- Engine Control ECU: Based on the received commands the monitor and control functionalities set the required torque value to control car's speed, provide feedback through a lamp and deactivate the CC system when necessary.

To give the mixed-criticality flavour to the case-study, a non safety-related application is also considered (e.g., power window controller). The window controller is usually part of the Body Computer Module (BCM) which implements additional functionalities (e.g., mirror control, central locking). For the sake of simplicity, only the power windows controller is considered in the scope of this case-study and it is considered as a non safety-related subsystem. Figure 1 shows the high level conceptual architecture of the federated implementation of the case-study.

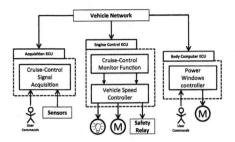

Fig. 1. Federated system architecture for the automotive use case

4.2   Safety Requirements

The CC shall perform a set of Safety Goals (SG) compliant with Automotive Safety Integrity Level (ASIL) D according to the automotive ISO-26262 standard. In this paper, we focus on the following safety goal for the definition of the safety concept:

– SG-1: Avoid the inability to deactivate CC when required (ASIL D)

From this safety goal a number of safety requirements are derived for the CC system (SR_CC). Most relevant safety requirements are gathered in Table 1. It must be noted that the CC is a fail-safe system. This means that in case of failure or whenever a safety goals is not met, the system goes to a safe state as defined in requirement SR_CC_5_A of Table 1.

Table 1. Main safety requirements of the CC system

ID	Description
SR_CC_1_A	The safety goal "**Cruise Control Deactivation**" avoids the inability to deactivate the CC when required. In case of a fault leading to inability to deactivate CC, the engine control unit shall switch to a "safe state" within the Process Safety Time (PST) / Fault-Tolerant Time Interval (FTTI)
SR_CC_1_B	"**Cruise Control Deactivation**"must be provided with **ASIL D** level
SR_CC_2_B	The 'CC commands' transmitted by the Cruise Control Signal Acquisition functional unit shall be consistent with the status of the buttons (set, speed+, speed-, off, resume)
SR_CC_3_B	The "**Cruise Control Monitor**" function shall generate a '**Cruise Control Disengagement**' signal consistent with the input button/pedal requests
SR_CC_5_A	The '**safe state**' shall be achieved by deactivation of the Cruise Control System (by commanding safety digital-outputs connected to external safety-relays)
SR_CC_6_A	The PST (IEC-61508)/FTTI (ISO-26262) is 1 s

4.3   Federated Safety Concept

In the federated implementation each safety ECU has dedicated hardware as depicted in Fig. 1 and executes safety software compliant with the following features:

– *Life-cycle and development Tools*: The system, platform and software are developed following a safety life cycle, using qualified tools and compilers and applying the appropriate Functional Safety Management (FSM) compliant with ASIL D requirements.
– *Independence of execution*: Each ECU has independent resources (i.e., memories, peripheral and clock). The vehicle communication bus is shared among all ECUs.

– *Vehicle communication bus*: Controller Area Network (CAN) based 'safe communication' implemented either with Time-Triggered CAN (TTCAN) or with a CAN based safety communication protocol that provides equivalent safety techniques and attributes of interest:
  • It is compliant with ISO-11898-4 [1].
  • It establishes a global notion of time by means of a Time Master (TM) that transmits a synchronization message to all the nodes (ISO-11898-4).
  • It achieves interference freeness among safety-related (time-triggered) and non safety-related communication (event triggered, rate constrained, best effort, etc.). Safety-related nodes are assigned to time-triggered communication that provides the required temporal and spatial guarantees.
– *External interfaces*:
  • The Signal Acquisition ECU reads safety-related digital inputs for the CC driver interface buttons (SET/SPEED+, SPEED-, OFF, RESUME) and safety-related analogue inputs (break, accelerator and clutch pedals and speed sensor).
  • The Engine Control ECU exclusively manages an external safety-relay through a digital output for the hardware deactivation of the CC (safe state activation).
  • The fail-safe state of the safety digital output is de-energized.
  • The default state of the safety digital output during no-power and initialization is de-energized (inherent fail-safe state).
– *Safe State:* The safe state is defined as the de-activation of the CC system (giving back control to the driver) as defined in the safety requirement SR_CC_5 of Table 1. Whenever there is a violation of a safety goal or if the system, hardware or software diagnosis detect an error, the safe state must be reached and maintained.
  • Safe state is achieved by means of de-energization of the safety digital output connected to an external safety-relay that deactivates the CC.
  • The safety-relay is monitored by means of a digital input to the Engine Control ECU that represents the state of the contact.
– *Diagnosis*: The system includes diagnostic measures with a high coverage (DC >99 %) for ASIL D (ISO-26262-5 Annex D).
  • Diagnosis with a high diagnostic coverage are implemented on all relevant components of each safety-related ECU (e.g., signature of a double word in memories, Power Failure Monitor, watchdog timer, clock monitoring).
  • The safety software application implements additional life-cycle related techniques (e.g., defensive programming), Error correction/detection techniques and complements the diagnosis techniques implemented in the platform (e.g., refresh watchdog timer).

5   Mixed-Criticality Safety Concept on a COTS Multicore

With the aim of overcoming the limitations of the federated approach in this section we integrate the CC system together with the non safety-related application in a single multicore platform.

5.1   The AURIX Platform

The chosen processor family is the AURIX TC27x, a COTS multicore provided by Infineon [11]. The AURIX is a very promising architecture for mixed-criticality for a number of reasons. It embeds many safety features that makes it suitable to host safety-critical applications up to ASIL-D level easing and reducing certification costs. Moreover, unlike most multicore processors, the AURIX is designed with determinism in mind with features that ease the timing analysability of the platform: it includes local scratchpad memories on each core for both instructions and data and does not share cache memories among the cores. In addition, as a result of the research held in [10], a number of hardware mechanisms have been enhanced on its architecture to improve the isolation among the cores at hardware level. The main components of the AURIX are the following:

- *Three processing cores*: Core 0 and Core 1 operate in lockstep mode, where an additional CPU is transparently executing the same code in background for safety comparison purposes. Each core has private instruction and data scratchpad memories and first level instruction and data caches.
- *Shared Memories*: SRAM and Flash common for all cores.
- *On-chip interconnect*: High bandwidth peripherals (i.e., cores, DMA and shared memories) are interconnected through a crossbar called Shared Resource Interconnect (SRI). Those elements are then connected to medium and low bandwidth peripherals through the System Peripheral Bus (SPB).
- *Shared peripherals*: The platform includes a number of peripherals connected to the SPB, such as, timers, several communication interfaces (e.g.,CAN), I/Os, etc.

Partition to Core Allocation: We allocate the different ECUs of the federated approach into three different partitions distributed in the AURIX cores equivalently to the ECU distribution in the federated implementation as depicted

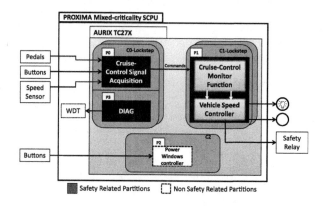

Fig. 2. Partition to core allocation (AURIX TC27X)

in Fig. 2. Partition *P0* encapsulates the CC signal acquisition ECU. *P1* includes both the CC monitor and control functionalities which are executed one after the other in a sequential manner. Finally, the non safety-critical power windows controller is implemented on partition *P2*. One additional partition is introduced to perform software-based diagnostics, configuration and protection activities (*P3*). Safety-related partitions are allocated to the two lockstepped processors to attain increased diagnostic coverage. *P3* has also safety implications and it is therefore executed in core 0 together with partition *P0*. The non safety-related partition is allocated to the remaining core without redundancy.

5.2   Cross-Acceptance of the Federated Safety Concept

Several new challenges arise from the transformation of the federated architecture to an integrated mixed-criticality approach. However, some of the safety properties described in the federated approach of Sect. 4.3 can be maintained. Same safety life-cycle and FSM measures apply for system, platform and software applications. In addition, the external interfaces shall be equivalent to those described in the federated implementation and the fail-safe system requirements shall be maintained to reach the safe state. The definition of required diagnostic techniques can be reused taking into account the properties of the new hardware platform and additional diagnostics shall be implemented to deal with the new hazards that the sharing of a single computing platform involves.

The major difference in the integrated approach is that now the different applications share many on-chip resources and that off-chip CAN based communication

Table 2. Interference Sources in the AURIX platform

ID	Element	Event	Interference
Spatial Interference Sources (SIS)			
SIS 1	Core local data scratchpad	Invalid memory access	Write to the address belonging to the data of another partition running in the same core
SIS 2	Shared SRAM (LMU)	Invalid memory access	Write to the address belonging to the data of another partition running in the same or in a different core
SIS 3	Addressable devices	Invalid memory access	Write to the address belonging to the control/configuration registers of a peripheral device assigned to another partition
Temporal Interference Sources (TIS)			
TIS 1	Core local cache memories	Coherency protocol, cache line eviction, cache pollution	Non-determinism in the system and delays caused due to cache sharing among different partitions on the same core
TIS 2	SRI Crossbar	Simultaneous access by various masters to the same slave	Contention by simultaneous requests arbitrated based on the configuration of the arbiter on each slave (e.g., SRAM memory)
TIS 3	SPB Bus	Parallel transaction requests	Contention by parallel access requests to the bus arbitrated on a priority-based basis
TIS 4	Inter-core communication mechanism	Blocking communication	Partition blocked by a delay in the communication or if the transmission ceases

is replaced by on-chip communication. As a result it is challenging to guarantee independence of execution among the applications. Table 2 gathers the main spatial and temporal interference sources that must be addressed on the AURIX processor and were not present in the federated approach.

5.3   Independence of Execution Among Partitions on the Same Core

Interference sources SIS 1 and TIS 1 of Table 2 arise among partitions assigned to the same core (i.e., *P0* and *P3* in core 0). We address them by following the common practices used on single-core architectures, i.e., memory segregation and cyclic scheduling among partitions:

- Core Local Memory Protection: The CPU local memories on each core can be configured in four memory Address Protection Sets (APS) per CPU with specific permissions for code and data accesses based on the address generated by an application. Figure 3(a) shows the configuration of the different memory regions for the partitions executing on core 0. In this way, in each partition switch or if an interrupt or trap handler is entered, the associated address protection set is selected and accesses from other partitions are not permitted.
- To guarantee temporal independence among partitions *P0* and *P3*, a static cyclic scheduling algorithm is implemented on top of core 0 as shown in Fig. 3(b). This scheduling is defined at design time based on Worst-Case Execution Time (WCET) estimates computed for each partition by an appropriate timing analysis technique.

In each execution time window of core 0 only one of the Address Protection Sets is active (Fig. 3(b)). The Operating System (OS) kernel is the responsible for setting up the address protection correctly on each context switch. This OS service shall be developed according to ASIL D safety requirements.

5.4   Independence of Execution Among Partitions on Different Cores

Apart from the interferences within the cores, the sharing of resources at platform level cause many other sources of interferences (see Table 2). We deal with those interferences by applying the mechanisms provided by the AURIX as follows:

- *Shared memory (SIS 2 and TIS 2 in* Table 2*):* The shared SRAM memory can be configured in eight write protected address ranges. A specific memory range with exclusive write permissions is configured for each safety-critical partition as shown in Fig. 4 (PMR 0 for *P0*, PMR 3 for *P3* and PMR 4 for *P1*). Write accesses are protected by checking the ID used to initiate SRI master transactions (Master TAG ID). Each core has two master interfaces (code and data) to access to the SRI, each of it with an unique ID. For core 0, where two different partitions are executed, the platform gives the option to configure two additional IDs on the same core, by identifying the partitions as safe (C0_DATA_S) or regular (C0_DATA_NS).

Core	Partition / Task	Address Protection Set (APS)	Protection
C0	P0	Data Scratchpad APS 0	read / write
		Program Scratchpad APS 0	Fetch
C0	P3	Data Scratchpad APS 1	read / write
		Program Scratchpad APS 1	Fetch
C0	Interrupt handlers	Data Scratchpad APS 2	read / write
		Program Scratchpad APS 2	Fetch
C0	OS kernel	Data Scratchpad APS 3	read / write
		Program Scratchpad APS 3	Fetch

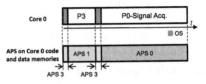

(a) Address protection configuration on Core 0   (b) Scheduling of partitions on Core 0

Fig. 3. Memory and time segregation on Core 0

- *Safe inter-partition communication (TIS 4 in* Table 2*)* is guaranteed by means of shared SRAM memory. Each shared memory is configured as a write protected address range where only one partition has write permissions. Accordingly, inter-partition communication channels are unidirectional with an independent shared memory for each of the required communication channels. Three additional protected memory regions are defined in Fig. 4 for the communication among *P0* and *P1* (PMR 1), *P0* and *P2* (PMR 2) and *P1* and *P2* (PMR 5).
- *Addressable on-chip resources (SIS 3 and TIS 3 in* Table 2*)* are protected by a firewall mechanism where the access to the SRI and SPB slaves is only granted to the masters configured with such rights. The CC monitor and control partition (*P1*) is granted exclusive access to the digital output connected to the external safety relay. Similarly, the diagnostics partition *P3* has exclusive access to the digital output for controlling the external watchdog. Each of these digital output belongs to an independent GPIO port line to ensure separation (Fig. 4(b)).

Regarding the scheduling at system level, in core 0 partitions are arbitrated as shown in Fig. 3(b) but the rest of partitions have all processor time for themselves and they are executed in parallel. Accordingly, sources of temporal interferences caused by the parallel execution of partitions shall be addressed:

- The SRI crossbar supports parallel transactions between different SRI-Master and SRI-Slave peripherals. Still, contention can be caused when two masters simultaneously target the same SRI-Slave (i.e., on-chip memories). To ensure a fair arbitration of the simultaneous requests and prevent one partition from being starved by higher priority requests, a round-robin arbitration is established.
- The SPB is implemented as a shared bus that provides mutual exclusive accesses to the on-chip peripherals. Each master needs to be granted bus ownership to initiate a transfer, which is arbitrated on a priority-based basis. To protect against bus starvation of lower priority masters, the AURIX includes a prevention mechanism that guarantees that all masters are granted bus access in a pre-defined period of time.

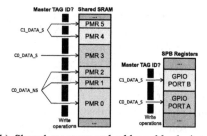

Master TAG ID	Core	Partition	Protected Memory Range (PMR)	Protection	Protected SPB Slave
C0_DATA_NS	C0	P0	PMR 0	write	
	C0	P0	PMR 1	write	
	C0	P0	PMR 2	write	—
C0_DATA_S	C0	P3	PMR 3	write	GPIO PORT A (DO for WDG)
C1_DATA_S	C1	P1	PMR 4	write	GPIO PORT B
	C1	P1	PMR 5	write	(DO for relay)

(a) Access protection configuration   (b) Shared memory and addressable device protection

Fig. 4. Protection mechanisms against spatial interferences

To guarantee that deadline overruns do not jeopardize safety, the system is protected by a watchdog that in such circumstances puts the system into the safe state. Still, not to compromise system's availability a WCET analysis shall be conducted to ensure that all partitions are able to meet their time deadlines under the established design choices.

5.5 Platform Configuration

The configuration of the protection mechanisms described in previous sections shall be static and defined during design stage: partition to core allocation, protection sets, routing of interrupts to cores, scheduling and arbitration policies in the SRI and SPB, watchdog time windows, etc. On the one hand, configuration registers can only be accessed in Supervisor mode and a register protection mechanism is also in place to define which masters may have modification rights on the safety-related registers. In our case, only the diagnostics partition (*P3*) has such rights. On the other hand, after system initialization, whenever the software in Supervisor mode and from an authorized master attempts to modify a safety configuration register, it first needs to unlock a password protected bit. Once this bit is unlocked, the software is allowed to modify the registers within a predefined time period protected by the watchdog (the password protected bit needs to be locked again before watchdog time-out).

6 Related Work

The development, and particularly the certification, of CRTES upon multi-core processors is an ongoing challenge [4,13,16] which is further exacerbated when mixed-criticality applications are involved [17,18,21]. As a result, current research in the field of mixed-criticality has mainly focused on new mechanisms capable to deal with the new demands of multicore architectures. Multiple solutions are directed at virtualization and hypervisor tools [4,20,22]. The usage of time deterministic architectures [9] is also considered, as it could significantly simplify the collection of evidences required for a certification process. However, determinism is compromised in most modern COTS multicore platforms with increasing intrinsic complexity. In this direction, the AURIX processor family, designed for the automotive market, has a number of features (e.g., core local scratchpad memories) that improve such determinism AURIX. Moreover, the research held in the ARTEMIS-JU RECOMP project [10] enhances a number of hardware properties to support mixed-criticality integration making the AURIX a very promising architecture for mixed-criticality. Unfortunately, all those innovative solutions are still not considered common-practice in the CRTES industry and achieving certification of mixed-criticality systems integrating such novel techniques becomes a challenging process. Few works consider the evaluation of real-world mixed-criticality applications running on multicores and their end-to-end certification processes. In this line, the research held in FP7-MultiPARTES contributes with a certification strategy for mixed-criticality systems based on multicore partitioning [17], successfully implemented in a wind power application on top of a certifiable hypervisor [18].

7   Conclusion and Future Work

This paper has contributed with a safety concept definition for an automotive mixed-criticality system integration on a COTS multicore with hardware protection mechanisms. This work tightens the big conceptual gap between multicore and certification, as the assumptions and analysis considered at this design stage have been reviewed and assessed by a certification body. Still, one key open subject in the described safety concept is the method to determine WCET bounds of each software application to ensure temporal independence in an efficient way (without excessive resource over-provisioning). The WCET estimation of multicore processors is highly complicated by the presence of shared resources and the parallel execution of software applications. A common design principle to deal with tming uncertainties rests on adding conservative safety margins to the WCET value. However, in multicore architectures this results in overly pessimistic WCET estimates that lead to an ineffective use of the available resources. From the system architect and system provider perspective, several limitations arise regarding WCET estimation, timing analysis and providing sufficient evidence to confirm that timing requirements are met. This is the main subject of our ongoing work that seeks to overcome the WCET estimation problem in multicores by the inclusion of the novel Measurement Based Probabilistic Timing Analysis (MBPTA) [8,14] technique in the mixed-criticality architecture described throughout the paper.

Acknowledgments. This work has been supported by the European Community's FP7 PROXIMA project under grant No. 611085. The work received precious in-kind contributions including the system model and the corresponding safety requirements, from partner Intecs of the CONCERTO project (ARTEMIS-JU grant nr. 333053), in the context of an active inter-project collaboration with PROXIMA.

References

1. ISO-11898-4: 2004 Road vehicles - Controller area network (CAN) - Part 4: Time-triggered communication (2004)
2. ISO/DIS-26262-10: Road Vehicles - Functional Safety (2009)
3. Aeronautical Radio Inc. (ARINC): ARINC-653: Avionics application Software standard interface part 1 - Required Services (2010)
4. Burger, S., et al.: Implications of multi-core processors on safety- critical operating system architectures. In: ECRTS 2014 (2014)
5. Buttle, D.: Real-time in the prime-time - (keynote talk). In: ECRTS 2012, ETAS GmbH (2012)
6. Certification authorities software team: multi-core processors - Position Paper. Technical report, CAST-32, May 2014
7. CONCERTO: Deliverable Report D1.2, rev. 1.2, December 2013
8. Cucu, L., et al.: Measurement-based probabilistic timing analysis for multi-path programs. In: ECRTS (2012)
9. El Salloum, C., et al.: The ACROSS MPSoC - a new generation of multi-core processors designed for safety-critical embedded systems. In: DSD-2012, pp. 105–113 (2012)
10. Farrall, G., et al.: Hardware and software support for mixed-criticality multicore systems. In: WICERT 2013 (2013)
11. Infineon: AURIX Family - TC27x. http://www.infineon.com/
12. Kopetz, H.: The complexity challenge in embedded system design. In: ISORC 2008 (2008)
13. Kosmidis, L., et al.: Containing timing-related certification cost in automotive systems deploying complex hardware. In: DAC 2014. pp. 22:1–22:6. ACM (2014)
14. Kosmidis, L., et al.: Measurement-based probabilistic timing analysis and its impact on processor architecture. In: DSD 2014 (2014)
15. Leohold, J.: Automotive system architecture. In: Summer School on Architectural Paradigms for Dependable Embedded Systems, pp. 545–591 (2005)
16. Nevalainen, R., et al.: Impact of multicore platforms in hardware and software certification. In: WICERT 2013 (2013)
17. Perez, J., et al.: A safety certification strategy for IEC-61508 compliant industrial mixed-criticality systems based on multicore partitioning. In: DSD 2014 (2014)
18. Perez, J., et al.: A safety concept for an IEC-61508 compliant fail-safe wind power mixed-criticality system based on multicore and partitioning. In: ICRST 2015, pp. 3–17 (2015)
19. Rushby, J.: Partitioning in avionics architectures: Requirements, mechanisms, and assurance. Technical report (1999)
20. SYSGO: SYSGO. PikeOS hypervisor. http://www.sysgo.com/products/pikeos-rtos-and-virtualization-concept/
21. Trujillo, S., et al.: European project cluster on mixed-criticality systems. In: DATE 2014 Workshop, 3PMCES (2014)
22. Trujillo, S., et al.: MultiPARTES: multi-core partitioning and virtualization for easing the certification of mixed-criticality systems. Microprocess. Microsyst. **38**, 921–932 (2014)

Defining Autonomous Functions Using Iterative Hazard Analysis and Requirements Refinement

Fredrik Warg[1]([✉]), Martin Gassilewski[2], Jörgen Tryggvesson[3], Viacheslav Izosimov[4], Anders Werneman[5], and Rolf Johansson[1]

[1] SP Technical Research Institute of Sweden, Borås, Sweden
{fredrik.warg,rolf.johansson}@sp.se
[2] Volvo Cars, Göteborg, Sweden
martin.gassilewski@volvocars.com
[3] Comentor AB, Göteborg, Sweden
jorgen.tryggvesson@comentor.se
[4] KTH Royal Institute of Technology, Stockholm, Sweden
izosimov@kth.se
[5] Qamcom AB, Göteborg, Sweden
anders.werneman@qamcom.se

Abstract. Autonomous vehicles are predicted to have a large impact on the field of transportation and bring substantial benefits, but they present new challenges when it comes to ensuring safety. Today the standard ISO 26262:2011 treats each defined function, or item, as a complete scope for functional safety; the driver is responsible for anything that falls outside the items. With autonomous driving, it becomes necessary to ensure safety at all times when the vehicle is operating by itself. Therefore, we argue that the hazard analysis should have the wider scope of making sure the vehicle's functions together fulfill its specifications for autonomous operation. The paper proposes a new iterative work process where the item definition is a product of hazard analysis and risk assessment rather than an input. Generic operational situation and hazard trees are used as a tool to widen the scope of the hazard analysis, and a method to classify hazardous events is used to find dimensioning cases among a potentially long list of candidates. The goal is to avoid dangerous failures for autonomous driving due to the specification of the nominal function being too narrow.

Keywords: ISO 26262 · Functional safety · Autonomous vehicles · Hazard analysis · Safety goals · Item definition

1 Introduction

Fully autonomous cars are expected to bring substantial benefits both to society at large and the individual car users. Examples are fewer accidents due to elimination of human driving errors, better traffic flow management leading to increased road capacity and reduced pollution, and relieving the drivers from the task of driving.

However, automation also introduces new sources of error, including insufficient understanding of the environment and failure to take proper action in all situations that

© Springer International Publishing Switzerland 2016
A. Skavhaug et al. (Eds.): SAFECOMP 2016 Workshops, LNCS 9923, pp. 286–297, 2016.
DOI: 10.1007/978-3-319-45480-1_23

can arise. In the case of manual driving, and even with advanced driver assistance systems (ADAS), the human driver is always responsible for controlling the vehicle, which means, for instance, that omission errors for an ADAS function can be acceptable. In this paper we consider autonomous driving (AD) with a level of automation where the system has full responsibility for the driving task in at least some situations (level 3 or above in the NHTSA definition [11]). This level of automation has a profound effect on how to ensure functional safety, as the human driver (HD) no longer can be expected to take over in an emergency situation. It is not only very difficult to maintain the required level of vigilance as a passive overseer [10], but such a requirement would be contradictory to one of the basic promises of AD: to free up the drivers' time. As a consequence, it becomes necessary to make sure an AD vehicle can reach a safe state on its own in all relevant situations when AD is activated.

In the functional safety standard for road vehicles, ISO 26262:2011 [7], the scope and requirements of an electrical/electronic (E/E) function are parts of the *item definition*, which is an input to the functional safety process and the hazard analysis. This means only situations and hazards that affect the already defined function need to be taken into account. In this work we argue that, in the context of AD functions, the hazard analysis should have the wider scope of making sure the proposed function itself is adequately specified so that it, possibly in conjunction with other functions contributing to the AD functionality, covers all hazardous events (HEs) relevant to the goal of autonomous operation. The result of this extended analysis may, in addition to safety goals, be necessary changes to the scope and requirements of the proposed function. While there is ongoing work on how to manage violations of safety goals due to limitations in nominal functionality called '*Safety of the Intended Functionality*' (SotIF), we claim that the problem is rather a consequence of improper item definition and/or safety requirement refinement (see also discussion in [4]).

In this paper, we propose a new structured iterative work process and analysis techniques where the hazard analysis is used not only to ensure functional safety, but also as an aid when defining the scope of the function. Working iteratively is a natural choice since the scope of the function affects the hazard analysis and vice versa in this process. Input is an initial description of the goals and benefits of the proposed function. We call it the *preliminary feature description* in order to make it clear that it is not a final work product, but rather a starting point that will be refined and improved upon. The item definition, which describes the final scope and requirements of the function, is an output of the process, together with the item's safety goals. The main goal of the approach is to avoid dangerous failures due to the specification of the nominal function being too narrow. To that end, generic situation and hazard trees are used as a tool to widen the scope of the analysis beyond the limits of the initially proposed feature. The process also integrates rules from [3] which are used to classify hazardous events and can find omissions or overlaps in the set of HEs; i.e. finding the dimensioning HEs that will result in unique safety goals.

Section 2 of the paper discusses related work. Section 3 describes the proposed process in detail, with an integrated example. Finally, Sect. 4 concludes the paper.

2   Related Work

There are a number of techniques that address the problem of identifying candidate hazards. Methods such as Preliminary Hazard Analysis, HAZOP and FMEA are often recommended. Other methods include one described by Jesty et al. in [8]; this method is based on a state machine model of the transitions between a failure occurring in a system and a hazardous event. While useful, these techniques are not aimed at aiding the process of defining the scope of a function, which is our goal in this work.

One technique in our process is the use of generic situation and hazard trees to help the safety engineers find all relevant situations and hazards. There is some previous work on classifying generic situations. Jang et al. [1] decompose a situation into hierarchical categories of properties where the top level properties *vehicle*, *road*, and *environment* are followed by three levels of sub-factors. Situations are constructed by selecting properties from the last level, called state. The purpose is to make situation analysis more efficient, but how the classification is used is only discussed superficially. However, the way situations are constructed from our situation tree is similar. Another effort, even more related to our use of trees, is the situation classification described by Kemmann [5] in the context of the SAHARA framework for structured hazard analysis and risk assessment (note that this is not the same method as the safety/security-oriented SAHARA described by Maher et al. [12]). The SAHARA framework is ontology-based, and the situation analysis part, OASIS, organizes situation properties in trees which can be reused and extended with increasing experience. The situations created by combining the properties are meant for reuse between projects, together with their attached exposure class which therefore only have to be assessed once. While we have opted for a less formal, more light-weight way to construct and use situation trees in this work, the option to integrate the SAHARA approach in our iterative process would certainly be feasible, and could bring additional benefits for reuse and automation. The aim of OASIS, to create a knowledge base and make sure important situations are not missed in the situation analysis, is the same as ours. Neither the approach of Kemmann nor that of Jang has the purpose of being part of the function definition process however. The German organization VDA has created a standardized list of situations with the purpose of harmonizing the use of exposure factors [2]. However, this list is not structured into properties or useful for determining completeness of analysis like a situation tree.

Agile and lean development methods have gained in popularity during the last decade. Although nothing in ISO 26262 explicitly forbids agile methods it can be difficult to understand how to apply them, as the standard uses a conceptual V-model more similar to traditional sequential development processes. Stålhane et al. [6], propose *SafeScrum* to combine agile software development and safety according to IEC 61508. SafeScrum is based on the assumption that safety requirements are rather static, and refers to traditional processes for the safety lifecycle outside the agile software development. Another investigation into how to combine agile methods with safety standards has been done by Vuori [9]. While our approach to conduct hazard analysis and requirements elicitation in a semiformal and iterative process is partly inspired by agile ideas and concepts, its usefulness is not limited to agile organizations.

3   Iterative Hazard Analysis and Function Refinement Process

The upper part of Fig. 1 illustrates the proposed work process. It starts with a preliminary feature description from which hazard analysis and risk assessment (HA&RA) and function definition are iteratively refined (solid arrows). These steps are repeated until they are mature enough to create both item definition and safety goals. This differs somewhat from ISO 26262 (lower part of the figure), where the item definition is an input to HA&RA, and the safety goals are the output. Even if not shown in the figure, it is implicit that hazard analysis might be revisited and updated later in the design process due to changes to function requirements or discovery of additional hazards. The following subsections describe each of the steps in more detail.

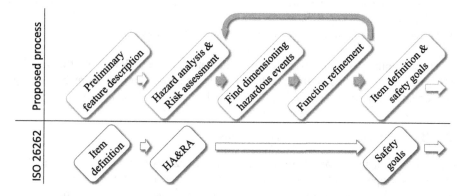

Fig. 1. Proposed hazard analysis and function refinement process compared to ISO 26262.

3.1   Preliminary Feature Description

The aim of the preliminary feature description is to describe the expected (end customer) benefits and define the initial scope of the proposed feature. The format for such input (market research, input from previous projects, use cases, initial requirements etc.) can be freely selected to fit the organization. For our example we borrow the concept of user stories common in agile methodologies; a user story describes benefit from an end user perspective, but is usually not written by end users. It should be noted that these user stories will be at a higher level of abstraction than for their typical use in software projects. The format of a story is: *"As a <role>, I want <goal/desire> so that <benefit>"*. A full feature is described as a collection of user stories (sometimes called a theme). This simple format allows for easy modification and expansion of the theme as needed, and can be easily understood by all stakeholders, not only safety engineers.

Throughout Sect. 3, we will consider an example where an automated emergency braking (AEB) feature for an autonomous vehicle is analyzed. This envisioned feature has the purpose of avoiding accidents in the face of obstacles that appear suddenly and therefore are not part of the tactical plan of a likewise envisioned AD function handling normal autonomous operation. Keep in mind that the example is simplified to fit into this paper, and therefore covers a much smaller number of situations than a real such feature would likely do. Table 1 shows the initial user stories, which describe some conditions when the emergency brake must work. The level of detail for the initial input is not critical since the subsequent steps have the purpose of bringing up questions regarding the scope of the function. However, it is supposed to guide the hazard analysis as to which situations and hazards are relevant for the feature. Very general stories are less likely to be useful in that respect, making the process more difficult than it needs to be. For instance, a single story saying simply *"I want emergency braking"* would be more difficult to work with than the stories in Table 1.

Table 1. AEB example: initial user stories.

As a driver, I want AEB for crossing animals so that my automated car doesn't run into animals
As a driver, I want AEB for other motor vehicles so that my automated car doesn't hit vehicles making unexpected maneuvers
As a driver, I want AEB for tricycles so that my automated car doesn't hit children on tricycles

The preliminary feature description may also include other relevant information, for instance limitations imposed if the feature includes or expands upon an already existing component, or if part of the solution for some other external reason is given.

3.2 Hazard Analysis and Risk Assessment

The objective of the hazard analysis is to identify hazards that may occur in the E/E function and operational situations where the occurrence of these hazards may be dangerous; operational situations and hazards are combined to form hazardous events. In order to reduce the risk of missing relevant operational situations and hazards in the analysis we use tree structures representing a knowledge base of potential situations and hazards to investigate. By systematically going through the trees, one can avoid omissions resulting from the anchoring bias that is likely to occur based on the initial idea of the scope of the function. Furthermore, the trees both act as a tool to keep track of covered aspects when performing hazard analysis for a new function, and make sure gained experience is preserved for future projects.

Situation Analysis. An operational situation tree is shown in Fig. 2. The root of the tree is the operational situation. Each successive level breaks down the situation in different aspects of increasing detail, where the goal is that siblings on any given level are mutually exclusive and collectively exhaustive with respect to their parent. The tree in the figure does not fulfill the exhaustive property for space reasons; only selected aspects are shown to illustrate the principle. Even given unlimited space, however, a tree is unlikely to ever be perfect, instead it is meant to be continuously updated to reflect current best understanding of potentially relevant situations.

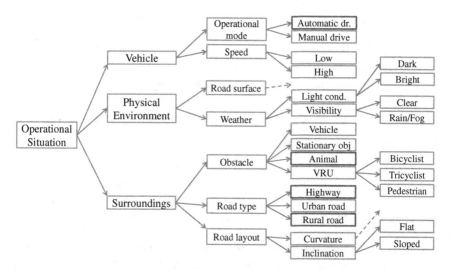

Fig. 2. Example of a generic situation tree.

Operational situations for use in the hazard analysis are composed by selecting and combining leaves (properties) from the tree; the combination is what defines the unique operational situation. Leaves sharing the same parent are of the same kind (aspect) but describe mutually exclusive properties of a situation. If no leaf at all is selected from a particular aspect, the situation is considered to be valid for all properties of that aspect. For instance, the situation *"automatic drive on highway or rural road with animal obstacle"*, using the highlighted properties in Fig. 2, would implicitly include *"in all physical environments, road layouts, and speeds"*. In this way, we have a semi-formal description of the situation that can be used to classify situations and find gaps in the analysis, i.e. combinations that have not yet been considered.

It should be noted that any reference to "completeness of analysis" means with respect to the currently used situation tree. Since the tree constitutes the known universe of situations for the analysis, making sure the tree contains an adequate representation of reality is also imperative. This is discussed further at the end of this section.

The initial selection of operational situations is guided by the preliminary feature description. However, this selection does not have to be perfect. If relevant situations or hazards have been omitted, or selected despite being out of scope for the feature, this will be corrected as the iterative process progresses. For the AEB example, the specific obstacles mentioned in the user stories are obvious candidates: vehicle, animal and tricycle. The operational mode is also given: automatic drive. Beyond that, it is up to using one's best knowledge to add properties that may affect the way safety goals and function requirements will look like. Table 2 includes some operational situations that may result from such a process. When selecting situations and hazards, adding a rationale to explain why certain aspects in the tree are not relevant for the function will strengthen the argument of completeness of the hazard analysis and could be used as evidence in a safety case.

Table 2. AEB example: hazardous events and risk assessment.

HE	Operational Situation	Hazard	E	C	S	ASIL
1	AD on highway/rural road with animal obst.	Undetected object	2	3	2	A
2	AD with tricycle obstacle	Undetected object	2	3	3	B
3	AD with other vehicle obstacle	Loss of braking	4	3	3	D
4	AD in bright light with other vehicle obst.	Loss of braking	4	3	3	D
5	AD in high speed with stationary object obst.	Mode confusion	2	3	2	A

Hazard Identification. Hazards are handled similarly to operational situations. Figure 3 shows an example of a generic hazard tree. Again, for space reasons, the number of hazards shown is limited. The basic structure is similar to the situation tree with the hazard at the root, and several levels of subcategories. As opposed to the situation tree, however, there is no combination of leaves. Each leaf by itself represents one possible hazard that can be included in the hazard analysis if relevant for the function being defined. For AD vehicles, where the E/E system moves beyond the operative level and is also responsible for tactical decisions, we have included a class of tactical level hazards to capture events where avoiding the tactical mistake may be the only way to prevent an incident. Potential driver/operator interference for AD functions is included as foreseeable misuse hazards. In Table 2, a hazard is combined with each operational situation to form hazardous events for our AEB.

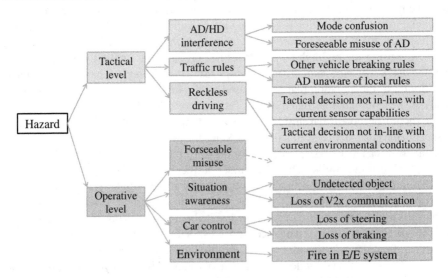

Fig. 3. Example of a generic hazard tree with operational and tactical hazards.

Risk Assessment. In ISO 26262, the result of risk assessment is assignment of an automotive safety integrity level (ASIL) to each hazardous event. ASILs range from A to D, where D is the most critical and hence requires the most elaborate measures in order to avoid failures. ASIL is assigned by first evaluating the exposure (E0 to E4), controllability (C0 to C3) and severity (S0 to S3) for occurrence of the hazard in the given situation. Based on the value of those factors, the standard prescribes a certain ASIL. All these values are shown in Table 2 for the example HEs. For an autonomous function, we generally assume controllability, i.e. the driver's ability to mitigate the effect of a failure in the E/E system, to be C3 (difficult to control or uncontrollable) since the driver is out of the driving loop. The risk assessment has to be updated in every iteration as new or modified situations and hazards are added.

Iteration and Extending the Trees. New hazardous events will be created in the same manner in each iteration. It should be stressed that the generic situation and hazard trees are only a starting point since generic trees cannot cover the needs for all items and all contexts. As the function description matures and more known detail about the context is taken into account, the generic trees should be extended with context-aware specializations and additions. Such context information can be, for instance, functionality or performance characteristics of the target vehicle or environment. The properties should be selected by finding limits where one of the risk assessment factors (E, C, S) in the resulting hazardous events is affected. Such changes may go into a context-aware tree created for a specific project. Furthermore, new general aspects can be added to the generic tree, thus contributing to the situation knowledge base to be reused in future projects. Such additions can be made at any level of the generic tree below the root.

The *"speed"* property in Fig. 4 shows how more generic properties (*"high"* and *"low"* in Fig. 2) are replaced with context-aware and more specific properties of the same kind. For instance, 40 km/h might be a speed limit where the severity factor of a collision is reduced. The *"animal"* property under obstacles is also extended with a new level containing more detailed context-specific information. These are changes that may go into a context-aware tree created for a specific project. Another addition shown in the figure is *"maneuver"* with its own sub-properties. This is a more general aspect, where extending the generic tree would be suitable.

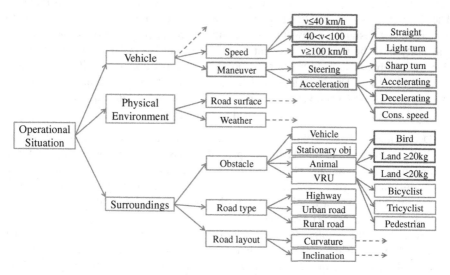

Fig. 4. Situation tree extended with new general and context-specific properties.

3.3   Categorizing and Finding Dimensioning Hazardous Events

The previous step may easily give rise to a very large number of hazardous events (HEs). While the situation and hazard trees are helpful in classifying HEs, they will not directly show which ones are dimensioning, that is, which HEs are sufficient to cover all the safety goals. In order to understand the relationship between HEs, we use the method described in [3], which enables an arbitrarily long list of HEs to be reduced to only contain the dimensioning ones by applying a set of rules. There are eight rules of which four are to identify dominance, and four for non-dominance. In [3] it is shown that this set of rules is consistent and complete. This means that by comparing each pair of HEs in the list and applying these eight rules, the HEs which are sufficient to identify all safety goals of concern can be identified.

The rules depend upon the ability to categorize situations and hazards using set theory, i.e. determine if two situations are mutually exclusive, subsets, identical or overlapping. An advantage of using the trees is that the situations and hazards are already clearly defined making this trivial. For instance, one of the dominance rules state that from the three HE table columns situation, hazard, and integrity (ASIL): *Dominance exists if two columns show relation 'identical' and the third one has the relation '$\subset$' or '<'*. With this rule, one can show that HE4 in Table 2 can be removed since it is dominated by HE3; the situation in HE4 is a subset of that in HE3 and the other properties are identical.

This method enables a fine-grained approach when categorizing hazards and situations, which mean the safety margins can be designed more precisely, avoiding unnecessarily conservative ASIL implications on the entire E/E architecture.

3.4   Function Refinement

In this step requirements elicitation for the intended nominal functionality is performed. The requirements should define a function that fulfills the user stories, and as is always the case when designing a new function, additional concerns such as cost and technical feasibility must be taken into account. The provisional list of HEs from the previous step will complement the user stories by providing information of what it takes to maintain safe operation. This knowledge will be used when defining the scope of the function in more detail. The hazardous events are considered as part of the requirements elicitation, and one of three actions is performed for each HE:

1. Decide that the HE is within the scope of the function and add requirements to reflect this. For instance, in our AEB example, HE5 considers what should happen when encountering stationary objects on the road, which was not covered in the user stories. In this case it may make sense to include stationary objects in the scope of the function, since a braking function that reacts to i.e. moving vehicles but not stationary would probably not be useful.
2. Break down the problem further since the HE is too general or abstract to classify as within or outside scope. For instance, look at the HE on emergency braking for animals. It may be the case that it will be technically difficult to design a sensor system that detects birds and small fast animals like a rabbit. On the other hand, these

are not likely to pose a threat to the passengers of the car, i.e. the severity factor is low. Therefore, the situation tree is expanded with a new subclass for different types of animals (see Fig. 4), and the HE updated to reflect what is within the scope of the function. Table 3 shows that for the next iteration the original HE1 is marked as out of scope and a new HE1b that deals with *"land animal ≥ 20 kg"* is added to the list. It will also be necessary to update the classification as exposure should be lower but severity higher compared to a collision with any animal.

Table 3. AEB example: changes to hazardous events for second iteration.

HE	Operational Situation	Hazard	E	C	S	ASIL
~~1~~	~~AD on highway/rural road with animal obst.~~	~~Undetected object~~	~~2~~	~~3~~	~~2~~	~~A~~
1b	AD on highway with land animal ≥20 kg obst.	Undetected object	1	3	3	A
~~2~~	~~AD with tricycle obstacle~~	~~Undetected object~~	~~2~~	~~3~~	~~3~~	~~B~~
~~2b~~	~~AD on highway with tricycle obstacle~~	~~Undetected object~~	~~0~~	~~3~~	~~3~~	~~QM~~
3	AD on highway with other vehicle obstacle	Loss of braking	4	3	3	D
5	AD on highway in high speed with stationary object obstacle	Mode confusion	2	3	2	A

3. Restrict the scope of the function in order to find a feasible solution. Consider a case where the analysis shows that constructing a function that works in any surrounding poses too many technical or cost obstacles. Instead, it is decided to build an AD that can only be used on highways. In the AEB example, this would likely change the exposure for tricycles to E0, since highways are restricted areas where it is extremely unlikely a tricycle would ever be. Table 3 shows how HE2 is updated to HE2b to reflect this; but in fact, HE2b shows that the integrity level drops to QM, so even if the user story about tricycles is kept, it will not result in any safety requirement that needs to comply with ISO 26262. The other HEs are also updated to reflect that the function is only available on highways.

After the first iteration, the function is delimited by a number of HEs, but the exact scope may still be uncertain. For each subsequent iteration of refinement, it becomes clearer what the capabilities of the function should be. Note that if more than one function/item is involved in AD operation, it should be considered that the relevant HEs may fall within the scope of any of those functions, so the aim of the analysis is to make sure all HE are taken care of by these functions together.

The preliminary feature description is of less importance once we have an initial list of HEs and requirements to continue refining in subsequent iterations. However, the user stories could still serve a purpose, especially in an agile organization, if they are kept updated. While HEs and function requirements are more detailed, they may not be as suitable for e.g. prioritization and communication with a product owner. In the AEB case, one would add stories reflecting that we have restricted AEB to highways and added stationary obstacles after the first iteration.

HEs considered outside the scope are removed from the dimensioning list, but retained separately together with a rationale why it was not included. Where relevant, these scope restrictions will become part of the user manual for the vehicle, e.g. *"The AEB function of this vehicle can only be used on highways"*.

Sufficiency Checklist. After this step the iterative process continues with a new round of situation analysis and hazard identification given the new decisions made during function refinement. Iteration should continue until the list of HEs and function requirements are stable, complete, and useful. Below is a checklist to help determine when this is fulfilled, which also requires some engineering judgment:

- Sufficient situation and hazard coverage:
  - The generic trees should be fully covered (i.e. all properties are used in the analysis or have a rationale why they are not relevant for the function).
  - It must be clear whether the remaining HEs are within or outside scope.
  - Rules for dominance and non-dominance (see [3]) have been used to find potential gaps among the identified HEs.
- Clarity for continued design process:
  - Function requirements are useable for next steps of refinement.
  - HEs have a suitable level of abstraction to make safety goals which will not result in overly conservative ASIL assignment.

3.5   Item Definition, Safety Goals and Further Refinement

When the HEs and requirements are sufficiently elaborated, the final step of the process is to create safety goals from the dimensioning HEs, and an item definition which includes the functional requirements. This is input to the functional safety concept in ISO 26262, and from this point on the standard can be followed without modification.

The further work is likely to be iterative as well. For instance, the item's refinement will need to be complemented with prototyping of the item's elements, in correlation with preparation of the system architecture work. This work will provide feedback to item definition, functional safety concept and technical safety concept. It is possible that both prototyping and system architecture work will effectively call for modification of the item definition. It can be a result of, for example, not fulfilling physical constraints, too much cost, or too much of development effort needed. Hence, the item will evolve during the whole development process. In addition, in a constantly changing environment for autonomous vehicles, such as new rules and regulations introduced and new methods discovered, the item will likely have to be kept open to modifications even after the product is released to the market. Whenever such modifications are called for, the hazard analysis needs to be revisited to capture any necessary changes to the safety goals.

4   Conclusions and Future Work

In this paper we argue that completeness of safety goals is a new challenge for autonomous vehicles. When no driver is available to fill in potential gaps, under-specified functions can pose a danger. We propose a method that can help reach completeness of safety goals for the entire AD functionality by using hazard analysis as an aid when defining the scope of the function. Since the scope of an advanced function will likely make it difficult to perform all the steps manually while still keeping everything consistent, a suitable future improvement would be tool support, including further work to make the process itself more suitable for automation.

Acknowledgements. The research has been supported by the Swedish government agency for innovation systems (VINNOVA) in the FUSE project (ref 2013-02650).

References

1. Jang, H.A., Hong, S.-H., Lee, M.K.: A study on situation analysis for ASIL determination. J. Ind. Intell. Inf. **3**(2), 152–157 (2015)
2. VDA: Situationskatalog E-parameter nach ISO 26262-3. VDA 702, Verband der Automobilindustrie e.V. (2015)
3. Johansson, R.: Efficient identification of safety goals in the automotive E/E domain. In: Proceedings of 8th European Congress of Embedded Real-Time Software and Systems (ERTS²) (2016)
4. Bergenhem, C., Johansson, R., Söderberg, A., Nilsson, J., Tryggvesson, J., Törngren, M., Ursing, S.: How to reach complete safety requirement refinement for autonomous vehicles. In: Critical Automotive Applications: Robustness and Safety workshop (CARS) (2015)
5. Kemmann, S.: SAHARA - A structured Approach for Hazard Analysis and Risk Assessments, Technische Universität Kaiserslautern (2015)
6. Stålhane, T., Myklebust, T., Hanssen, G.: The application of safe scrum to IEC 61508 certifiable software. In: Proceedings of ESREL 2012, Helsinki, Finland (2012)
7. ISO: International Standard 26262:2011 Road vehicles – Functional safety (2011)
8. Jesty, P.H., Ward, D.D., Rivett, R.S.: Hazard analysis for programmable automotive systems. In: Proceedings of 2nd International Conference on System Safety, IET (2007)
9. Vuori, M.: Agile development of safety-critical software. Technical report 14, Tampere University of Technology, Department of Software Systems (2011)
10. Bainbridge, L.: Ironies of automation. Automatica **19**(6), 775–779 (1983). Pergamon Press
11. National Highway Traffic Safety Administration (NHTSA): Preliminary Statement of Policy Concerning Automated Vehicles. http://www.nhtsa.gov/staticfiles/rulemaking/pdf/Automated_Vehicles_Policy.pdf
12. Maher, G., Sporer, H., Berlach, R., Armengaud, E., Kreiner, C.: SAHARA: a security-aware hazard and risk analysis method. In: Proceedings of 2015 Design, Automation and Test in Europe Conference and Exhibition (DATE) (2015)

ASIL Tailoring on Functional Safety Requirements

Markus Fockel[(✉)]

Software Engineering, Fraunhofer IEM, Paderborn, Germany
markus.fockel@iem.fraunhofer.de

Abstract. Cyber-physical systems like self-driving cars are highly complex and safety-critical. This results in a great number of safety requirements that have different levels of criticality. In automotive, the criticality is categorized in Automotive Safety Integrity Levels (ASIL). As a high ASIL causes high development effort, the goal is to develop most subsystems with lower ASIL requirements. To achieve this ASIL tailoring, subsystems need to be separated or redundantly implemented. These safety measures are usually integrated late in the development process and thus cause costly development iterations. In this paper, we present a systematic, tool-supported ASIL tailoring process for the requirements analysis phase. It is applied on formal safety requirements and automatically generated fault trees for a functional view of the system. The process supports early planning of safety efforts for mixed-criticality systems and avoids costly late development iterations.

Keywords: ASIL tailoring · ASIL decomposition · Fault tree generation

1 Introduction

The safety requirements engineering dilemma [3] states, that possible failures and hazards can best be found late in the development process where all the system details are known (e.g., the software code is existing). But changing the system to prevent or mitigate a failure then causes expensive development iterations (changing requirements, changing architecture, changing code, . . .). Thus, failures ideally would be found early, already in the requirements analysis phase. Because then, required safety measures and resulting effort and cost can be planned from the start.

The complexity of mechatronic systems is rapidly increasing. In the automotive industry, driver assistance systems start to perform automatic emergency braking or emergency steering maneuvers – paving the way towards cyber-physical systems (CPS) like self-driving cars. The control of brakes and steering is highly safety-critical. To make safe decisions, the systems need to have a solid understanding of the vehicle's surroundings. For that, they use numerous sensors, cameras, navigational data and Vehicle-to-X communication [19]. Furthermore, the development of such systems requires a strong interplay of different engineering disciplines

© Springer International Publishing Switzerland 2016
A. Skavhaug et al. (Eds.): SAFECOMP 2016 Workshops, LNCS 9923, pp. 298–310, 2016.
DOI: 10.1007/978-3-319-45480-1_24

(i.e., mechanical, electrical and software engineering). This complexity makes it difficult to find all possible failures early and plan safety measures.

The hazards caused by failures of a system have different safety-criticality. A malfunction of a car's infotainment system is less critical than a failure of its brakes. To categorize hazards and safety requirements in terms of safety-criticality, ISO 26262 defines the *Automotive Safety Integrity Level* (ASIL) [13] ranging from ASIL D to ASIL A (in decreasing order) and QM for non-safety-critical elements. The ASIL value represents the degree of rigor that should be applied in development, implementation, and verification of a requirement in order to avoid unreasonable risk in the final product [18].

As a high degree of rigor implicates high development effort, there naturally is a demand to reduce the amount of high ASIL requirements and subsystems. To achieve this goal, so-called *ASIL tailoring* [13] is applied to separate subsystems (and their safety requirements) with different ASIL and to decompose safety requirements into redundant safety requirements with lower ASIL. The increasing system complexity and interconnection hinders finding solutions for separation and redundancy. Thus, many subsystems have to be developed with a high degree of rigor causing high development effort. Furthermore, if ASIL tailoring solutions are found in late phases of development, high effort has already been spent in previous phases to meet the degree of rigor required for the original ASIL. To decrease the development effort for safety measures, system complexity should already be addressed in the early discipline-spanning requirements analysis phase. Since that is the earliest possibility to plan safety measures and tailor the ASIL values of subsystems.

The contribution of this paper is a systematic, tool-supported ASIL tailoring process for the system requirements analysis phase. It is embedded in a Model-based Systems Engineering method to deal with the interdisciplinary development of CPS. To cope with complexity, it uses a functional abstraction of the system under development. The tool-support automatically generates failure propagation models from formal requirements to reduce the effort for early planning of safety measures and ASIL allocation. In this paper, we focus on the process steps rather than on the algorithms used.

The following Sect. 2 presents related work. Section 3 describes the ASIL tailoring approach using an automotive example. Section 4 concludes the results and lists future work.

2   Related Work

To assist in the process of ASIL tailoring, automated approaches to calculate possible ASIL allocations to technical system and software architectures have been developed [2,15]. These approaches require the set of hazards with their ASIL and the system or software architecture with given failure propagation models as input. The failure propagation models stem from the structure and behavior of the system. So these approaches help in finding a cost-efficient allocation of ASIL values to subsystems after their technical structure and behavior was defined. They do not consider the requirements that led to those work products. If a change of structure or behavior would result in a better ASIL allocation, this leads to costly development iterations because the requirements have to be changed as well. To reduce development iterations, we apply ASIL tailoring already during system requirements analysis based on automatically derived failure propagation models. One of the named ASIL allocation approaches could be integrated into our ASIL tailoring process in future work.

3   ASIL Tailoring Process

The development of automotive systems is characterized by the cooperative work of different engineering disciplines (i.e., mechanical, electrical and software engineering). Development processes like Automotive SPICE [1] thus include discipline-spanning system level development phases (cf. System Requirements Analysis and System Architectural Design in the top of Fig. 1). In these phases, Model-based Systems Engineering (MBSE) methods are used to bring together disciplines and foster a common understanding of the system under development (SUD) [12]. Based on the discipline-spanning System Architecture, the disciplines start with their specific work products (cf. phases Mech., E/E and SW in Fig. 1).

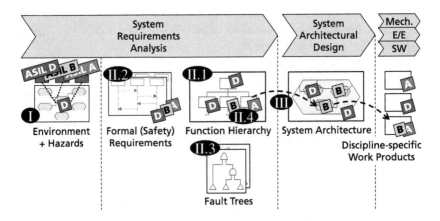

Fig. 1. Dev. phases and work products annotated with ASIL tailoring process steps.

The ASIL tailoring process presented in this paper is embedded into the MBSE method CONSENS (CONceptual design Specification technique for the ENgineering of complex Systems) [7, Sect. 4.1]. Figure 1 shows the used work products and associated process steps.

An automotive OEM (original equipment manufacturer) typically orders subsystems of a vehicle from different suppliers. Each supplier is provided with information about the environment of their subsystem (i.e., other subsystems in its context that it has to interact with) and the hazards (incl. ASIL determined by the OEM) that its failures could cause (cf. Environment + Hazards in Fig. 1). The environment model is the first work product specified in the ASIL tailoring process (Step I).

To cope with complexity, MBSE methods include different abstraction levels. A functional level is introduced between the system requirements and the technical system architecture [5][7, Sect. 4.1][17, Chap. 5]. In CONSENS, the functional level is specified by means of a function hierarchy (cf. Fig. 1). Before specifying technical elements of the system architecture, the functional level is used to abstract from technical realization details and broaden the design space. A function specifies how its inputs are transformed into outputs, aiming at fulfilling a particular task. To reduce complexity, the overall functionality of the system, represented by a root function, is broken down into sub-functions (Step II.1) until technical realizations can be found.

To plan safety measures and required effort in the system requirements analysis phase, we apply ASIL tailoring on the function hierarchy. The first tailoring option is separation: Functions (and their safety requirements) with different ASIL are separated, such that functions with lower ASIL do not interfere with higher ASIL functions. The second option is introducing redundancy: A safety requirement is decomposed into redundant safety requirements with lower ASIL whilst making sure that the corresponding functions do not interfere with one another (there are no cascading nor common-cause failures). The second option is commonly referred to as ASIL decomposition.

To find possible ASIL tailoring solutions and to verify that an applied tailoring meets the non-interference requirements, safety analyses have to be performed. As requirements are iteratively refined while developing the function hierarchy and applying ASIL tailoring, the safety analyses should require only reasonable effort. Thus, we automatically generate a failure propagation model in form of fault trees (Step II.3) to be used for safety analysis. For that, the requirements (esp. the safety requirements) are specified with a formal, scenario-based language in Step II.2. The failure propagation model is used to allocate tailored ASIL values to the functions of the function hierarchy in Step II.4.

The steps II.1 to II.4 are iterated until the detail level of the functions is sufficiently trivial to be realized by technical elements of the system architecture. In the final Step III the functions are thus allocated to their realizing system elements.

In the following we describe the ASIL tailoring process in detail. To illustrate the approach, we use the example of a rear door system. It is responsible for electronic opening, closing, locking and unlocking the rear door of a vehicle. It receives signals from electronic control units (ECUs) and mechanically moves the rear door through an actuator. For all following diagrams we use the SysML [16] which is based on the UML and designed to specify interdisciplinary models.

Step I: Specify Environment and Hazards. To start the ASIL tailoring process, first the technical environment of the SUD (esp. the interfaces) and the hazards with their ASIL values have to be specified. The top of Fig. 2 shows the environment of the RearDoorSystem and an ASIL B hazard RearDoorOpeningCommission. The SUD is identified by the CONSENS stereotype «SystemTemplate» and the systems that interact with the SUD are marked with the stereotype «EnvironmentElementTemplate». Ports are typed by interfaces or blocks. Sending ports are specified as conjugated (∼).

The environment element BodyControlModule is an ECU that receives the inputs of the remote key and accordingly sends opening/closing or locking/unlocking commands to the RearDoorSystem. The environment element ElectronicStabilityControl represents the ECU that is responsible for brake maneuvers and measuring the

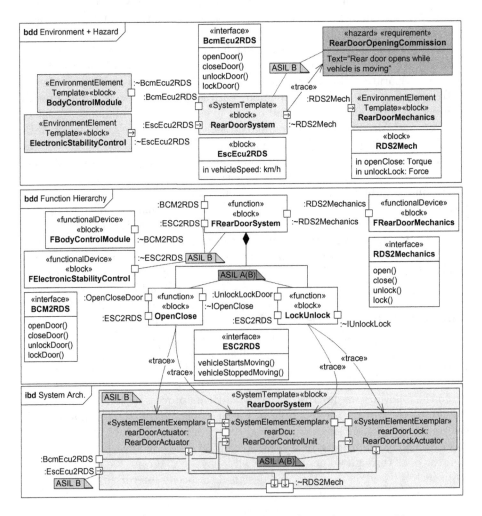

Fig. 2. Environment with hazard, function hierarchy, and system architecture.

vehicle speed by wheel speed sensors. It sends the vehicle speed in km/h to the Rear-DoorSystem. The environment element RearDoorMechanics describes the mechanics of the rear door. The RearDoorSystem moves the mechanics by applying torque and locks/unlocks the mechanics by applying force to a bolt.

The SysML requirement RearDoorOpeningCommission with the stereotype «hazard» represents the hazard that occurs when the rear door mechanics open the rear door while the vehicle is moving. As the RearDoorSystem would apply opening torque to the mechanics for this hazard to occur, it is connected to the port:~RDS2Mech via a trace-link. In this example, the hazard has a safety-criticality of ASIL B and thus the RearDoorSystem has to be developed compliant to ASIL B.

Step II.1: Derive Functions. In this step, functions of one level of the function hierarchy are derived based on the parent level or initially based on the environment model from Step I.

The topmost level of the example function hierarchy (cf. middle of Fig. 2) is derived from the environment model. Environment elements are transformed into a functional representation marked with the stereotype «functionalDevice». The SUD is transformed into the top-level function of the function hierarchy.

To be able to specify information flow and failure propagation in the function hierarchy, we extended CONSENS to also specify ports and interfaces for functions. The ports on the top-level of the function hierarchy are the same as in the environment model. The only difference is, that we solely use interfaces (no blocks) as port types and abstract from technical details. In the example, the fact that mechanical torque or force is applied to the mechanics is irrelevant on the functional level (cf. interface RDS2Mechanics). Also, the exact value and unit (e.g., km/h, mph, wheel speed) of the vehicle's speed do not matter. On the functional level, event information that shall trigger certain behavior is required. So in this example only the moments in which the vehicle starts or stops to move are important (cf. interface ESC2RDS).

Step II.2: Specify Requirements for Functions. In this step, requirements are specified and refined for the functions introduced in Step II.1.

To specify formal requirements on the functional level, we use *Modal Sequence Diagrams* (MSDs) [10]. They extend UML sequence diagrams via a profile to distinguish provisional and mandatory behavior. Furthermore, they are applicable for hierarchical architectures like a function hierarchy [11]. Requirements specifications modeled via MSDs can be validated by simulation with the so-called play-out algorithm [4]. Furthermore, they can be formally verified for consistency by synthesizing global controllers [9]. We use the formal semantics of MSDs to automatically generate fault trees for the function hierarchy in Step II.3.

In the example, the requirements R-1 to R-4 and the safety requirement FSR-1 from Fig. 3 are specified in the first iteration of Step II.2. The MSD R-1 describes the requirement that as soon as the body control module requests the rear door to be opened, the rear door system shall open the rear door via the rear

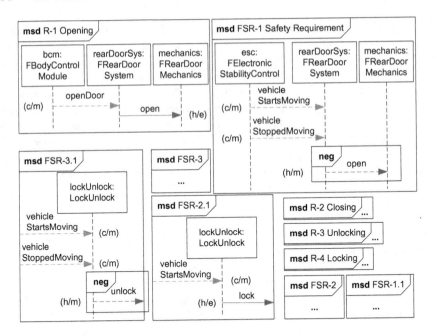

Fig. 3. Requirements specified as MSDs. (Color figure online)

door mechanics. Each lifeline of the MSD represents an instance of a function or functional device in the function hierarchy.

Each message in an MSD has a temperature describing its modality (i.e., whether it is provisional or mandatory). It can be hot (h) or cold (c). If it is hot, then there must not be another message from the same MSD occurring while the system is waiting for the hot message. Otherwise the specified requirement would be violated. If it is cold and another message from the same MSD occurs instead, the MSD is aborted but the specified requirement is not violated. A hot message has a red color and a cold message is blue. Each message also has an execution kind. It can be executed (e) or monitored (m). If it is executed the system has to make sure the message occurs eventually. If it does not occur, the requirement is violated. Executed messages are shown with a solid line and monitored messages with a dashed line.

The cold and monitored (c/m) message openDoor in the MSD R-1 may occur but does not have to. If it occurs, the hot and executed (h/e) message open gets active and has to occur eventually and before the message openDoor occurs again.

The MSD FSR-1 in Fig. 3 specifies the safety requirement that as long as the electronic stability control signals that the vehicle is moving, the rear door system shall not open the rear door. A negative fragment in the bottom of an MSD contains the messages that shall not occur while the diagram is active. So if the hot message open occurs between the cold messages vehicleStartsMoving and vehicleStoppedMoving, the requirement is violated.

Step II.3: Generate CFT for Function Hierarchy. In this step, the failure propagation model for the function hierarchy is generated from the requirements specified as MSDs in Step II.2. To model failure propagation with the same language and tooling as the function hierarchy, we use a SysML profile for so-called *Component Fault Trees* (CFTs) [14][17, Chap. 8]. CFTs consist of sub-tree components that can be mapped to functions of the function hierarchy. This fosters traceability between the function hierarchy and its failure propagation.

The top diagram in Fig. 4 shows two connected CFTs. The top CFT (gray) describes the correlation of the incorrectly sent message open that leads to the hazard RearDoorOpeningCommission describing that the rear door mechanics open the rear door while the vehicle is moving. This CFT is manually specified based on the textual description of the hazard. The bottom CFT (white) describes the failure propagation of the top-level function FRearDoorSystem. It is automatically generated from the structure of the function hierarchy and the behavior described in the requirements specified as MSDs.

Failures propagate over connectors that link fault tree events (rectangles), basic events (circles), OR/AND-gates and input/output failure modes (triangles). To distinguish between different types of failures, we type the input/output failure modes and basic events by a failure type hierarchy based on Giese et al. [8]. In this paper, we distinguish **O**mission, **C**ommission and **Cr**ash failures. To distinguish input from output failure modes, output failure modes are specified as conjugated (e.g., open:∼C).

The CFT :FRearDoorSystemCFT in the top diagram of Fig. 4 was generated from the requirements in the MSDs R-1 to R-4 and the safety requirement FSR-1 in Fig. 3. The message open could have a commission failure if one of three failures occurs: In the MSD R-1, if the message openDoor is wrongly sent by bcm. In the MSD FSR-1, if the message vehicleStartsMoving is not sent or the message vehicleStoppedMoving is inadvertently sent by esc (because in both cases open is not forbidden). The failure unlock:∼C is caused by an input failure caused by the body control module (R-3). The omission failure of the lock message is also caused by an input failure from the body control module or by a crash of the rear door system itself (R-4).

Step II.4: Calculate ASIL Allocation. In this step, the ASIL value of the hazards is propagated through the functions of the function hierarchy based on the generated CFTs from Step II.3. The CFTs show how failures propagate through the functions based on the (safety) requirements. As failures lead to hazards, they inherit the maximum ASIL of the hazards they are connected to. As the CFTs represent functions, the functions inherit the maximum ASIL allocated to an output failure mode of their corresponding CFT.

The hazard RearDoorOpeningCommission has the ASIL value ASIL B (cf. Fig. 2). In the top diagram of Fig. 4 the hazard is directly caused by the output failure mode open:∼C of the CFT :FRearDoorSystemCFT. Thus, ASIL B propagates over the failure modes to that CFT. The CFT represents the failure propagation through the top-level function FRearDoorSystem, so that function has to be developed compliant to ASIL B.

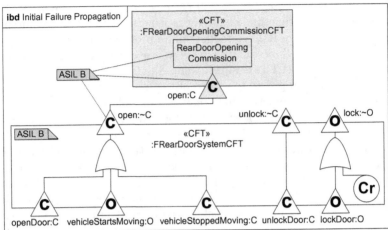

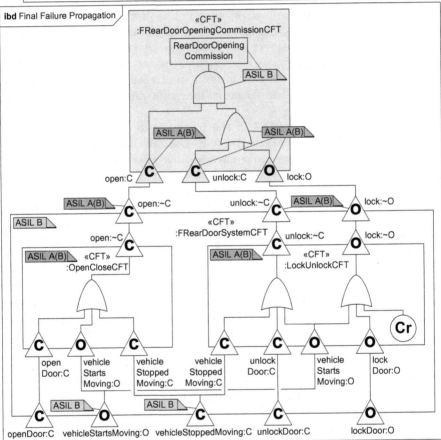

Fig. 4. Initial and final failure propagation consisting of manually specified hazard CFTs (gray) and automatically generated function CFTs (white).

As a hazard with ASIL B exists, there is no way to reduce the ASIL for the system as a whole nor its overall top-level function below that ASIL value. But to reduce effort and cost, the parts of the system that have to be developed with the degree of rigor required for ASIL B should be as minimal as possible. Thus, the top-level function should be decomposed into sub-functions in such a way, that a lower ASIL allocation is allowed for some of them. This is realized by ASIL tailoring through separation or redundancy.

Iteration of Steps II.1 to II.4: Refine Function Hierarchy and Requirements. The functions of one level of the function hierarchy are decomposed into sub-functions by iterating the steps II.1 to II.4. The MSDs of each function are refined for their sub-functions. In addition, new or refined safety requirements are introduced to tailor the ASIL of sub-functions.

The top-level function FRearDoorSystem can be decomposed into a function OpenClose for opening and closing and a function LockUnlock for locking and unlocking (cf. middle of Fig. 2). This obvious decomposition is underpinned by the generated CFT in the top diagram of Fig. 4. It shows that failures of the messages lock and unlock do not interfere with the failure open:~C that causes the hazard. So the separated function LockUnlock could be developed with a lower ASIL.

To also reduce the ASIL of the function OpenClose, that can directly cause the ASIL B hazard, redundancy needs to be added. If the hazard no longer is caused by a single-point-failure (i.e., open:~C), but by a two-point-failure of two separate, non-interfering functions, then those two functions may be developed with a lower ASIL [13].

In the example, this is done by adding safety requirements to automatically lock the rear door when the vehicle starts moving and to prohibit its unlocking while the vehicle is moving (cf. MSDs FSR-2, FSR-2.1, FSR-3, and FSR-3.1 in Fig. 3). If the door is mechanically locked, it cannot open even if the rear door system applies opening torque to the mechanics.

To check if the function decomposition and the added requirements lead to a safe system and the ASIL of the sub-functions can be reduced, the steps II.3 and II.4 are repeated. The bottom diagram in Fig. 4 shows the regenerated CFT. The gray top CFT was manually changed to reflect the added redundancy. The hazard now only occurs if the open message is inadvertently sent and either the unlock message is inadvertently sent as well or the lock message is omitted.

The CFT for the rear door system is automatically generated based on the refined function hierarchy and the requirements specified as MSDs. The CFTs for each sub-function are contained in the CFT for the parent function and failure modes are connected according to the function ports and MSDs.

The CFT shows that there is no failure of the function OpenClose leading to a failure of the function LockUnlock and vice versa. So they are free from inter-ference. The CFT also shows, that the two input failure modes vehicleStartsMov-ing:O and vehicleStoppedMoving:C of the top-level function lead to failures of both sub-functions. This means that both sub-functions can fail for a common cause (i.e., a single-point-failure). It is still allowed to reduce the ASIL of both sub-functions if the common-cause failures are handled with the rigor of the original ASIL [13].

The ASILs annotated in the bottom diagram of Fig. 4 show the result of the ASIL calculation step. The ASIL of the two sub-functions was reduced to ASIL A because the two sub-functions are free from interference and their common-cause failures are handled according to their original ASIL B. This puts a requirement on the electronic stability control that may cause the according input failures. The example assumes that the vehicle movement information is needed by other more safety-critical ECUs anyway such that the ASIL B requirement causes no additional effort.

The sub-functions could be refined into further hierarchy levels but in this example we assume that they are sufficiently trivial to be realized in the system architecture. The final function hierarchy shows that a decomposition of the rear door system's functionality into separate functions with lower ASIL than the original ASIL of the hazard is generally possible. The system architecture can thus be developed aiming at this goal.

Step III: Allocate Functions to System Architecture. Once the function hierarchy is finished, it is used as a basis to develop the system architecture in the following development phase. The sub-functions of the function hierarchy are allocated to their realizing system elements via trace-links. The ASIL values allocated to the system elements are taken from the ASIL allocation of the function hierarchy and need to be verified by a safety analysis on the system architecture.

In the bottom of Fig. 2 the system architecture of the rear door system is depicted. The final system consists of three elements that can be developed compliant to ASIL A and only for the integration phases need to be compliant to ASIL B (which is specified by the B in parentheses). This is realized by technical safety measures that were already planned in the system requirements analysis phase on the basis of an ASIL tailoring on the abstract function hierarchy.

4   Conclusion

The safety requirements engineering dilemma states, that failures can best be found late in the development process but ideally would be found early, already in the requirements analysis phase. Because then, required safety measures and resulting effort and cost can be planned from the start. In the automotive domain, safety-criticality is categorized in Automotive Safety Integrity Levels (ASIL). To reduce the effort for safety measures, subsystems shall be assigned with a low ASIL. This can be achieved by so-called ASIL tailoring that separates subsystems or introduces redundancy.

In this paper, we presented a systematic, tool-supported ASIL tailoring process for the system requirements analysis phase. It is embedded in the Model-based Systems Engineering method CONSENS to deal with system complexity introduced by interdisciplinary development. The tool-support automatically generates Component Fault Trees (CFTs) from formal requirements specified with Modal Sequence Diagrams (MSDs).

The approach supports early planning of safety measures during requirements analysis and thus avoids costly late development iterations. It provides a broad design space for ASIL tailoring because it abstracts from technical details and instead uses a functional view of the system based on the requirements. The time and effort spent for safety analyses to verify applied ASIL tailorings is reduced by automatically generating the CFTs.

For future work we plan to reduce the effort of specifying requirements as MSDs by adapting an approach that combines natural language and model-based requirements [6]. In addition, we want to evaluate the approach with further examples from industry.

Acknowledgments. We thank the students of the project group Aramid for developing the tool-support for CFT generation and ASIL allocation.

References

1. Automotive Special Interest Group (SIG): Automotive SPICE: Process Reference Model, v4.5 (2010)
2. Azevedo, L.S., Parker, D., Walker, M., Papadopoulos, Y., Araujo, R.E.: Assisted assignment of automotive safety requirements. IEEE Softw. **31**(1), 62–68 (2014)
3. Berry, D.M.: The safety requirements engineering dilemma. In: Proceedings of the Ninth International Workshop on Software Specification and Design, pp. 147–149, April 1998
4. Brenner, C., Greenyer, J., Panzica La Manna, V.: The ScenarioTools play-out of modal sequence diagram specifications with environment assumptions. In: 12th International Workshop on Graph Transformation and Visual Modeling Techniques (2013)
5. EAST-ADL Association: EAST-ADL Domain Model Specification, v2.1.12 (2013)
6. Fockel, M., Holtmann, J.: A requirements engineering methodology combining models and controlled natural language. In: 4th International Model-Driven Requirements Engineering Workshop (MoDRE). IEEE, Karlskrona, August 2014
7. Gausemeier, J., Rammig, F.J., Schäfer, W.: Design Methodology for Intelligent Technical Systems. Lecture Notes in Mechanical Engineering. Springer, Heidelberg (2014)
8. Giese, H., Tichy, M., Schilling, D.: Compositional hazard analysis of UML component and deployment models. In: Heisel, M., Liggesmeyer, P., Wittmann, S. (eds.) SAFECOMP 2004. LNCS, vol. 3219, pp. 166–179. Springer, Heidelberg (2004)
9. Greenyer, J., Brenner, C., Cordy, M., Heymans, P., Gressi, E.: Incrementally synthesizing controllers from scenario-based product line specifications. In: 9th Joint Meeting of the ESEC/FSE, pp. 433–443. ACM, New York (2013)
10. Harel, D., Maoz, S.: Assert and negate revisited: modal semantics for UML sequence diagrams. Softw. Syst. Model. **7**(2), 237–252 (2008)
11. Holtmann, J., Meyer, M.: Play-out for hierarchical component architectures. In: 11th Workshop Automotive Software Engineering. GI-Edition - Lecture Notes in Informatics (LNI), vol. P-220. Bonner Köllen Verlag (2013)
12. INCOSE: Systems engineering handbook: A guide for system lifecycle processes and activities (version 3.2.2) (2011)
13. ISO: ISO 26262:2011(E): Road vehicles - Functional safety (2011)

14. Kaiser, B., Liggesmeyer, P., Mäckel, O.: A new component concept for fault trees. In: 8th Australian Workshop on Safety Critical Systems and Software (2003)
15. Mader, R., Armengaud, E., Leitner, A., Steger, C.: Automatic and optimal allocation of safety integrity levels. In: Proceedings of the Annual Reliability and Maintainability Symposium, RAMS 2012, pp. 1–6. IEEE (2012)
16. OMG: OMG Systems Modeling Language (OMG SysML) (2012)
17. Pohl, K., Hönninger, H., Achatz, R., Broy, M. (eds.): Model-Based Engineering of Embedded Systems: The SPES 2020 Methodology. Springer, Heidelberg (2012)
18. Ward, D.D., Crozier, S.E.: The uses and abuses of ASIL decomposition in ISO 26262. In: 7th IET International Conference on System Safety, Incorporating the Cyber Security Conference 2012, pp. 1–6, October 2012
19. Winner, H., Hakuli, S., Lotz, F., Singer, C. (eds.): Handbook of Driver Assistance Systems. Springer, Cham (2016)

Architecture-driven, Multi-concern and Seamless Assurance and Certification of Cyber-Physical Systems

Alejandra Ruiz[1(✉)], Barbara Gallina[2], Jose Luis de la Vara[3], Silvia Mazzini[4], and Huáscar Espinoza[1]

[1] ICT Division, TECNALIA, Derio, Spain
{alejandra.ruiz,huascar.espinoza}@tecnalia.com
[2] MDH University, Västerås, Sweden
barbara.gallina@mdh.se
[3] Universidad Carlos III de Madrid, Madrid, Spain
jvara@inf.uc3m.es
[4] INTECS, Pisa, Italy
silvia.mazzini@intecs.it

Abstract. Unlike practices in electrical and mechanical equipment engineering, Cyber-Physical Systems (CPS) do not have a set of standardized and harmonized practices for assurance and certification that ensures safe, secure and reliable operation with typical software and hardware architectures. This paper presents a recent initiative called AMASS (Architecture-driven, Multi-concern and Seamless Assurance and Certification of Cyber-Physical Systems) to promote harmonization, reuse and automation of labour-intensive certification-oriented activities via using model-based approaches and incremental techniques. AMASS will develop an integrated and holistic approach, a supporting tool ecosystem and a self-sustainable community for assurance and certification of CPS. The approach will be driven by architectural decisions (fully compatible with standards, e.g. AUTOSAR and IMA), including multiple assurance concerns such as safety, security and reliability. AMASS will support seamless interoperability between assurance/certification and engineering activities along with third-party activities (external assessments, supplier assurance). The ultimate aim is to lower certification costs in face of rapidly changing product features and market needs.

Keywords: Assurance · Safety · Security · Certification · System architecture · Reuse · Seamless interoperability

1 Introduction

Embedded systems have significantly increased in number, technical complexity, and sophistication toward open, interconnected, networked systems (such as "the connected car"). This has brought a "cyber-physical" dimension with it, exacerbating the problem of assuring safety, security and reliability in the presence of human, environmental and technological risks. Furthermore, the products into which these Cyber-Physical Systems (CPS) are integrated (e.g. aircrafts) need to respect applicable standards for assurance and in some areas they even need certification.

© Springer International Publishing Switzerland 2016
A. Skavhaug et al. (Eds.): SAFECOMP 2016 Workshops, LNCS 9923, pp. 311–321, 2016.
DOI: 10.1007/978-3-319-45480-1_25

Unlike practices in electrical and mechanical equipment engineering, CPS do not have a set of standardized and harmonized practices for assurance and certification that ensures safe, secure and reliable operation with typical software and hardware architectures. As a result, the CPS community often finds it difficult to apply existing certification guidance. Ultimately, the pace of assurance and certification will be determined by the ability of industry and the certification and assessment authorities to overcome technical, regulatory, and operational challenges. Another key difficulty appears when trying to reuse CPS products between projects and even from one application domain to another. Product evolutions become costly and time consuming because they entail regenerating the entire body of evidence or their certification can be constrained by different standards. This may imply that the full assurance and certification process is applied as for a new product, thus reducing the return on investment of such reuse decision.

This paper presents a recent initiative called AMASS (Architecture-driven, Multi-concern and Seamless Assurance and Certification of Cyber-Physical Systems) [1] to promote harmonization, reuse and automation of labour-intensive certification-oriented activities via using model-based approaches and incremental techniques. Section 2 describes the main challenges faced by AMASS in the light of current state of the art and Sect. 3 summarizes the proposed directions to solve those challenges.

2   Current State and Challenges

AMASS builds upon two large-scale past projects, OPENCOSS [2] and SafeCer [3], which dealt with the problem of certification of safety-critical systems in multiple domains using model-based approaches and incremental techniques. Among the main targeted tangible results, AMASS will produce a Reference Tool Architecture (ARTA). The ARTA (Fig. 1) represents a virtual entity that embodies a common set of tool

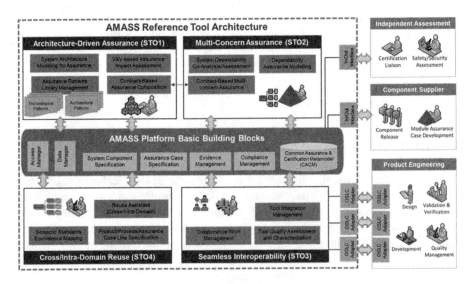

Fig. 1. AMASS high-level tool architecture

interfaces/adaptors, working methods, tool usage methodologies and protocols that will allow any stakeholder of the assurance and certification/qualification activities to seamless integrate their activities (e.g., product engineering, external/independent assessment, component/parts supply) into tool chains adapted to the specific needs of the targeted CPS markets, such as industrial automation, automotive, space, railway, avionics or air traffic management.

Figure 1 also shows the AMASS Platform Basic Building Blocks, which are the result of merging existing technologies from OPENCOSS and SafeCer. These building blocks include tools for specification of system components, specification of assurance cases as structured argumentation trees, evidence management, and compliance management. In addition to these, the basic building blocks include user access management and data management tools, as well as the Common Assurance and Certification Metamodel (CACM). CACM is an evolution of the OPENCOSS and SafeCer metamodels. Using a common metamodel for different application domains and assurance activities will also enable management of assurance/certification assets in a common format, sharing patterns of technology and architecture, and cost-effective reuse between different domains and standard frameworks.

Supported on the basic building blocks, AMASS will work on four pillars, which corresponds to specific challenges and Scientific and Technical Objectives (STO):

- **Architecture-Driven Assurance**. The standard architectures (such as AUTOSAR in the automotive industry and IMA in avionics) needed to handle these new large, networked systems are only now being equipped with mechanisms to handle dependability-related aspects. OPENCOSS and SafeCer approaches are agnostic regarding system architectural and engineering choices. This is an intentional feature to meet key requirements about cross-domain harmonization and flexibility. The architecture-agnostic approach is in the right direction since it permits to benchmark industrial case studies and demonstrate the feasibility of using a common framework for multiple application domains. However, the need for more cohesively integrated approaches (assurance/certification versus engineering activities) requires further research and industrial validation with standard and modern engineering practices (e.g., AUTOSAR-driven model-based development).
- **Multi-concern Assurance.** OPENCOSS and SafeCer were oriented to safety aspects. The synergies between safety and security (among other dependability properties) seem to offer clear opportunities for the reuse of assurance assets, although prior research in this area has suggested that the domain-specific standards do not always support such reuse. Also, the contract-based approaches to compositional assurance developed in OPENCOSS and SafeCer depend, in some respects, on precise mechanisms associated with safety characteristics. There is a need to refine this approach to support the management of trade-offs between various system characteristics (including safety, security, reliability and the like).
- **Seamless Interoperability**. Providing a seamless interoperability between assurance/certification activities and engineering activities (e.g., design, implementation, validation and verification- V&V), along with third-party activities (e.g., external assessments and supplier assurance) is of prime importance to lower the threshold of product assurance and certification in face of rapidly changing product features

and market needs. The challenge is to be able to gather evidence from different types of tools by means of standardized and well-defined adapters or exchange tools.

- **Cross and Intra-domain Reuse**. The OPENCOSS and SafeCer approaches aim to reduce the assurance effort when reusing products, by promoting flexible and systematic reuse approaches that are fully cognizant of the similarities and differences between approaches to safety assurance across the main safety-critical system domains. While these approaches are a first proof of concept of cross- as well as intra-domain reuse and many safety-critical industries are convinced of the benefits to share some development with other industries, one obstacle to the cost-effective reuse of cross-domain assets is the fact that the terminology and semantics used to describe and manage assurance across different application domains are not consistent.

3 Approaches

3.1 Architecture-Driven Assurance

The architecture represents a major aspect for ensuring dependability of a CPS and for meeting assurance and certification needs and requirements. It describes the realization of the system and consists of the components and all the mechanisms necessary to fulfill, among others, safety, security, reliability, and availability requirements.

The architecture components shall have specific dependability characteristics. These characteristics impose constraints on component reuse, that can refer to both technical aspects (e.g., a component can only be deemed safe for a given operational context) and economical (e.g., component reuse will have an impact on CPS cost). In addition a CPS' architecture must conform to the applicable standards so that a system can be effectively certified according to them.

The AMASS architecture-driven reuse will build on the results of the OPENCOSS and SafeCer projects, and address the additional architecture-related features that can greatly increase the opportunities of cost reduction and of reuse for CPSs, as well as facilitate the analysis for assurance and certification.

System Architecture Modelling for Assurance. Architecture-driven reuse will build on the component model and contract-based verification facilities developed in the SafeCer project. The OPENCOSS CCL metamodel for assurance will be extended with a more detailed formalism for the definition of the system architecture and for analysis of the system dependability with the inclusion of the SafeCer component and contract models, enriched with "white box" information (e.g., fault, error, and failure), "black-box" annotations, and all the other concepts that would allow to improve the analysis of all the aspects that affect assurance activities.

We plan to study the relation of the OPENCOSS and SafeCer assurance models with different system modelling languages (e.g. UML, SysML, AADL, EAST-ADL, etc.), safety modelling profiles, and specific platform models and architectures like AUTOSAR for automotive and IMA for avionics. A finer-grained analysis of a CPS and its assurance and certification information will allow industry to make more informed decisions regarding what can be reused between systems (including different versions of systems) and reuse consequences.

Assurance Patterns Library Management. OPENCOSS and SafeCer have straightforward mechanisms to specify assurance patterns for argumentation and for compliance with standards. However, further research and case studies are necessary to cohesively integrate these patterns in specific assurance and certification activities. This includes safety/security architectural patterns definition and application (e.g. 3-level-monitoring, E2E protection, and partitioning, among others), and auto-generation of platform models and configurations based on these patterns (e.g. for AUTOSAR and IMA). The use of patterns speeds architecture specification and facilitates the (re)use of components, especially if developed to be used in such patterns. Moreover, it enables the reuse of models and associated analysis results, e.g. guarantees of tolerance on failure communication associated with E2E protection [4] or security-related non-interference associated with partitioning [5].

Assurance of Specific Technologies. AMASS will consider technology trends such as the use of new multi-core hardware platforms, the introduction of middleware solutions (such as AUTOSAR in the automotive domain), deterministic communication technologies, and new networked functionalities such as remote diagnosis, software upgrading, towards vehicle and aircraft autonomy. Since OPENCOSS and SafeCer results are technology-agnostic, they do not directly support the assurance and certification of many characteristics of the new technologies for CPS. However, these characteristics have a great impact on how CPS assurance and certification has to be managed for highly-critical CPSs. Therefore, the characteristics thus must be carefully taken into account as part of the technology patterns, and benchmarked in case studies to determine the circumstances under which they can be reused, assured, and certified.

Contract-Based Assurance Composition. The concepts of contracts in OPENCOSS and SafeCer will be integrated in AMASS. In particular, the AMASS approach for the argumentation that a system architecture is compliant with the system properties will follow the contract refinement defined in the system model. Therefore, the guarantees of the system will be ensured by the composition of the components contracts, while the assumptions of a component will be ensured by the context provided by the system architecture. In case contracts are specified and analyzed with formal methods, evidence for the contracts refinement argument will be provided by verification tools such OCRA [6], developed in the SafeCer project. Safety analyses based on the contract specification will enrich the assurance case with fault trees showing the dependency of system failures on the component failures.

V&V-based Assurance Impact Assessment. Automatic V&V-oriented techniques will enrich the OPENCOSS and SafeCer assurance approaches. These techniques include automated search of compliant arguments in a set of components to define a new safe application that conforms to a set of safety/security requirements, search of adequate component candidates for a project (e.g. in railway: segregated safety controller, reduce footprint of hardware, safe communication protocol) starting with several functional and safety requirements (or safety patterns), formal techniques to validate that the requirements specification is complete, correct, and unambiguous, and automated support of assurance decisions by provision of what-if scenarios when changing any engineering feature.

3.2 Multi-concern Assurance

The OPENCOSS project has developed an approach for mapping safety assurance artefacts, techniques and requirements across domains, using the OPENCOSS CCL, to resolve the inconsistencies in terminology across the target domains and to support informed reuse of assurance assets. Also, the compositional certification approaches developed in OPENCOSS and in SafeCer further support reuse by encapsulating assurance concerns for individual components into reusable assurance argument modules and by providing a mechanism to configure these modules to form an overall system assurance case. In order to fully leverage the benefits of development methodologies based on the informed reuse of components, however, it is important to consider other aspects of the system's design as part of the assurance framework: characteristics such as reliability, availability, maintainability, durability, performance and security also have an impact on safety, and need to be considered in the assurance of critical CPS.

In the AMASS project, we aim to exploit the existing OPENCOSS and SafeCer approaches and extend them to provide a tool-supported methodology for the development of assurance cases which address multiple system characteristics. There are three aspects to this work.

Dependability Assurance Modeling. The OPENCOSS CCL metamodel is relatively generic, and its extension to support the reuse of assurance data relating to other dependability-related requires considerable further domain modelling, but no fundamental re-engineering of the approach. Similarly, the CCL vocabulary will require the addition of further concepts, but the vocabulary-based and model-based techniques for using mappings between concepts are readily transferable. From a methodological point of view, the SafeCer Safety-oriented Process Line Engineering remains valid. However, its modeling means may require to be extended (through the AMASS CACM metamodel) to explicitly address additional dependability-related attributes.

Contract-Based Multi-concern Assurance. The contract-based approaches to compositional certification developed in OPENCOSS and SafeCer depend, in some respects, on precise mechanisms associated with safety characteristics. AMASS proposes to refine this approach to support the management of trade-offs between system characteristics.

System Dependability Co-Analysis/Assessment. The synergies between safety and security (among other dependability properties) seem to offer clear opportunities for the reuse of assurance assets, although prior research in this area has suggested that the domain-specific standards do not always support such reuse [7]. The AMASS project will focus initially on extending the OPENCOSS and SafeCer approaches to address those aspects of security which impact on safety issues for critical CPS, where the potential to save costs through reuse is high. The project will then integrate and extend existing architecture-driven approaches to the assurance of system and security, such as the D-MILS approach [8], where the system architecture is the key element for hinging the assurance of both safety and security aspects such as partitioning and redundancies, or the SESAMO [9] component-oriented design methodology, based on model-driven technology and jointly addressing safety and security aspects and their interrelation for networked embedded systems in multiple domains. The interplay between security and safety will also be considered in terms of process requirements. The recently introduced notion of Security-informed Safety-oriented Process Line [10] will be further investigated in AMASS in order to enable the alignment of safety and security standards.

3.3 Seamless Interoperability

This area aims at guaranteeing the interoperability of the AMASS tool framework with other tools used in the lifecycle of CPS, such as design and V&V tools, whereby assurance evidence can be generated either manually or automatically by the tools themselves (code generators, testing tools, safety analysis tools, etc.). The challenge is to be able to gather evidence from different types of tools by means of standardized and well-defined adapters or exchange tools. There are some axes in this direction that can considerably improve the opportunities of AMASS adoption.

Tool Integration Management. AMASS will deal with the problem that (1) assurance information is present at each lifecycle phase (e.g. concept, design, implementation, and V&V) and (2) multiple different tools can be involved at each phase, so the AMASS tool framework needs to interwork with each of these tools. One promising approach is to use OSLC [11], by extending it to assurance aspects (safety, security, etc.). As part of this work, the AMASS consortium plans to reuse existing results from the Crystal (http://www.crystal-artemis.eu/) and MBAT projects (http://www.mbat-artemis.eu/) for OSLC-based tool interoperability, since many of their partners are also in AMASS. The data models for tool integration will be also part of the AMASS CACM metamodel. In addition, further assurance and certification needs for the integrated information must be considered, e.g. traceability requirements and analysis of information completeness and consistency according to the applicable standards.

Collaborative Work Management. We mean supply chain and collaborative issues when developing, assuring and certifying CPS. AMASS needs to address aspects and needs such as DIA definition (ISO 26262 OEM-Supplier interaction definition), the development of a platform to exchange safety related information (potentially as cloud-based collaboration services, and private), issues related to information composition, versioning and update, security and scalability problems, and provision of server side services, e.g. intelligent search, cross project consistency checks.

Tool Quality Assessment and Characterization. The engineering of CPS increasingly relies on the use of tools that automate, replace, or supplement complex development and V&V tasks. CPS safety can be compromised if the tools fail. To mitigate this risk, safety standards (e.g. DO-178C/DO330, IEC 61508, EN 501258, and ISO 26262) define tool qualification processes, including tool characterization. Compliance with these processes can be required for (re-)certification purposes, thus a system supplier can need to collect information about tool qualification and to provide this information as assurance evidence for the overall system certification process. Within SafeCer, a tool qualification process line was investigated in order to reduce time and cost via reuse. Within AMASS, this exploratory work will be deepened and broadened to consider also AMASS-related tool-chains.

3.4   Cross/Intra-domain Reuse: The Ubiquitous Need for Reuse

The higher complexity and size of CPS products combined with the growing market demand requires the industry to redefine its core and non-core activities, and to implement a coherent and systematic reuse strategy instead of relying exclusively on in-house-developed applications. For example, if the engine control computer from the automotive industry is to be reused in aerospace industry, the full certification process is applied as for a new product, thus reducing the return on investment of such decision. In such circumstances, systematic cross-domain reuse would be crucial to reduce the cost of re-certification. In circumstances where a new version of a product comes from a previously certified version of that same product, systematic intra-domain reuse would be crucial. Systematic intra-domain reuse would also be crucial in case of incremental certification (e.g., from a generic product to a specific one, obtained via addition of functionalities).

The OPENCOSS and SafeCer approaches aimed to reduce much of this repeated assurance effort, by promoting a flexible and systematic reuse approach that is fully cognizant of the similarities and differences between approaches to safety assurance across the main safety-critical system domains. In particular, on the one hand the CCL allows OPENCOSS tool users to model "equivalence maps" between different standards and regulations (including intra- and cross-domain) in order to facilitate reuse decisions between assurance projects from different application domains. On the other hand, safety-oriented process lines allow users to model process commonality and variability enabling systematic reuse.

While these approaches are a first proof of concept of cross- as well as intra-domain reuse and many safety-critical industries are convinced of the benefits to share some development with other industries, it first and foremost requires a common and strongly validated assurance and certification platform. This way, the certification results for a system or component originally developed for a different domain or for a different criticality level can be carried over to other domains. Also, a number of open technical aspects need further research:

Semantic Standards Equivalence Mapping.   One obstacle to the cost-effective reuse of cross-domain assets is the fact that the terminology and semantics used to describe and manage assurance across different application domains are not consistent. For example, there is some degree of overlap between concepts such as 'fault', 'hazard' and 'mishap' and what constitutes a 'component' or a 'subsystem', but there are also gaps between the definitions of these concepts across the standards. OPENCOSS started to solve this issue by using the CCL Vocabulary approach. The CCL Vocabulary is a structured and harmonised way to store and communicate knowledge about assurance artefacts and concerns. However, no complex, real cases were explored with this approach. Within SafeCer, an ontology-based method for process elements reuse was explored [12]. AMASS shall extend the CCL Vocabulary (though the AMASS CACM metamodel) approach by automating its creation and usage via deepened usage of the SafeCer ontology-based method. An automated CCL Vocabulary approach will also allow us to perform informed gap analysis on the standards and mitigate against the danger of inappropriate reuse where a given assurance asset does not appropriately match the requirements of the reuse context.

Cross-concern Reuse. In addition to mappings between standards related to the same concern, we need to identify mappings between standards that focus on different concerns in order to enable cross-concern reuse. It is well known for instance that the safety and security communities could be merged within a unified terminological framework under the dependability umbrella. This potential merge could foster the identification of commonalities and thus reusable artefacts.

Reuse Assistant (Cross/Intra-Domain). In addition to semantic mappings, we need to understand how the concepts work in terms of their relationship with one another to define the objectives of the standards – i.e. the intent which informs requirements and process activities, and the artefacts they result in -, in order to come to a clearer understanding of the role played by each activity and artefact in the overall assurance effort. AMASS will support users to understand whether reuse of the assurance assets is reasonable or determine what further analysis is required to justify claims of compliance. For example, AMASS will provide tool assistance to highlight the reasons why fault analysis is performed and the point in the development of the system at which it is applied (and hence the degree of detail involved). The compositional argument approach developed by SafeCer and OPENCOSS will evolve to get the ability to characterise pre-existing argument modules in terms of the intent of the applicable standards. This characterisation will rely on a clear understanding and statement of the assurance objectives of each standard, and of the assurance assets used to evince the claims made to demonstrate their satisfaction.

Product/Process/Assurance Case Line Specification. Variability management creates a pain in the industry. Various methods have been developed to manage variability and thus relieve industry from such a pain. For software, subversion and git are already an improvement to manage variability due to product evolution. Subversion, however, does not satisfy the management of all sources of variability. A systematic approach is needed to deal with software/hardware variability management, but also process and assurance case-related variability. The AMASS project will focus on extending and integrating the current methods in order to manage for instance ripple-effects that changes on product requirements might have on processes as well as assurance cases. The objective is to promote a fully integrated approach addressing the fundamental dimensions for certification purposes.

4 Conclusion

Despite the wide adoption of the concept of cyber-physical systems (CPS), its entrance in critical domains such as automotive, medical or aerospace is not advancing at the pace that the designers and producers would want in order to exploit the many benefits brought to these domains. While CPS can more efficiently react to changing requirements and adapt to different environments, these properties are challenging for the adoption in critical domains. Connectivity and complexity introduce new risks and extend potential risk causes towards security threats.

The validation and certification of the new-implemented solutions is the main barrier preventing this adoption. Critical domains present a long tradition of certification procedures and standards since the very early stages of software and systems engineering history. Unfortunately, this long history translates into complex validation procedures that require extensive testing and long certification campaigns, increasing the associated costs and preventing fast adoption of new concepts. In addition due to the isolation of critical systems validation, the certification focus was mainly restricted to safety and not threats from malicious causes. Furthermore, the increase in the complexity of the systems has been handled by extending exponentially the validation test campaigns.

The AMASS project brings a new vision into these assurance and certification procedures where extensive testing and validation and black box models are replaced by an intelligent approach based on the underlying architecture of the CPS system. The procedures will profit not only from previous certification results of pre-existing modules, but also from equivalent or similar architectures already validated.

This process of learning from similar architectures is performed more or less unconsciously by all the designers during early architectural design phases. All the designers and companies rely on a series of architectures that are well known "to work properly". AMASS project will provide a systematic methodology and tooling to pass from this qualitative and intuitive approach into a formal validation procedure where the underlying architecture of the CPS to be certified plays a key role in defining and executing the validation process. AMASS will extend this approach to architectures with inherent safety and security properties. AMASS will bridge between safety and security validation and certification, and ease both.

AMASS will shape this approach in a complete toolset that will integrate all the experience and developments of previous projects such as OPENCOSS and SafeCer and extend it towards cybersecurity. The AMASS approach should allow to handle the changing system security over the product lifetime. A safe system is designed once and is not changed over the product lifetime. A secure system can change massively due to e.g. software updates and therefore also the security has to be ensured in these changing lifetime process. This toolset approach is a key element in the impact strategy, as it will reduce dramatically the entry barriers of new actors in the CPS business by providing them with a consistent and easy-to-use validation toolset that shall reduce their learning curves and increase their chances to perform a "right-first-time" validation of new CPS architectures.

To obtain the maximum impact from this new approach it is necessary that the proposed methodologies and tooling are perfectly aligned with both the industrial validation procedures and standards, and with the emerging architectures derived from cutting edge cyber-physical systems. Here is where the full potential of AMASS will develop. The project includes the complete value chain of actors involved in CPS validation procedures, from tool providers to industrial end users, including top-notch technological providers. This allows AMASS to identify the most commonly used architectures and those new emerging ones identified by the industry as the most promising ones, adapting the tools and procedures to them and therefore guaranteeing the applicability of the results in the domains included in the project, as well as easing its fast extension into those domains not included in the project.

References

1. AMASS: ECSEL Project (Architecture-Driven, Multi-concern and Seamless Assurance and Certification of Cyber-Physical Systems). http://www.amass-ecsel.eu/
2. OPENCOSS: FP7 Project (Open Platform for EvolutioNary Certification of Safety-Critical Systems). http://www.opencoss-project.eu/
3. SafeCer: ARTEMIS Project (Safety Certification of Software-Intensive Systems with Reusable Components). http://www.safecer.eu/
4. Denney, E., Pai, G.: A formal basis for safety case patterns. In: Proceedings of the 32nd International Conference on Computer Safety, Reliability and Security (SafeComp 2013), Toulouse, France, September 2013
5. Rushby, J.: Noninterference, transitivity, and channel-control security policies. Technical report SRI-CSL-92-02, December 1992
6. Cimatti, A., Dorigatti, M., Tonetta, S.: OCRA: A tool for checking the refinement of temporal contracts. In: ASE 2013, pp. 702–705 (2013)
7. Bock, H.-H., Braband, J., Milius, B., Schäbe, H.: Towards an IT security protection profile for safety-related communication in railway automation. In: Ortmeier, F., Lipaczewski, M. (eds.) SAFECOMP 2012. LNCS, vol. 7612, pp. 137–148. Springer, Heidelberg (2012)
8. http://www.d-mils.org/
9. Born, M., Favaro, J., Winkler, M., Heidt, L., Boulanger, A.: Integrated design and evaluation of safety and security in automotive system development. In: Proceedings of VDA SYS 2015, 15–16 July 2015, Berlin (2015)
10. Baldovin, A., Zovi, A., Nelissen, G., Puri, S.: The CONCERTO methodology for model-based development of the avionics software. In: Proceedings of the ADA Europe Conference 2015, June 2015, Madrid (2015)
11. Open Services for Lifecycle Collaboration (OSLC). http://open-services.net/
12. Gallina, B., Szatmári, Z.: Ontology-based identification of commonalities and variabilities among safety processes. In: Abrahamsson, P., et al. (eds.) PROFES 2015. LNCS, vol. 9459, pp. 182–189. Springer, Heidelberg (2015). doi:10.1007/978-3-319-26844-6_13

Towards the Adoption of Model-Based Engineering for the Development of Safety-Critical Systems in Industrial Practice

Marc Zeller[(⊠)], Daniel Ratiu, and Kai Höfig

Siemens AG, Corporate Technology, Otto-Hahn-Ring 6, 81739 Munich, Germany
{marc.zeller,daniel.ratiu,kai.hoefig}@siemens.com

Abstract. Model-based engineering promises to boost productivity and quality of complex systems development. In the context of safety-critical systems, a traditionally highly regulated and conservative domain, the use of models gained importance in the recent years. In this paper, we present a set of practical challenges in developing safety-critical systems with the help of several examples of development projects that belong to different application domains. Following this, we show how could the adoption of model-based engineering for the development of safety-critical systems cope with these challenges.

1 Introduction

Model-based development is currently one of the key approaches to cope with increasing development complexity in general. Particularly the development of todays safety-critical systems underlies a series of legislative and normative regulations making safety the most important non-functional property of embedded systems. Applying model-based approaches during the development of complex products means the use of adequate models for different aspects of the system. Such models ease the development, increase the quality and enable a systematic reuse. This has the potential to help the industry to meet even tighter deadlines for new products and decrease the costs.

Along with the growing system complexity the effort needed for safety assessment is increasing drastically in order to guarantee the high quality demands. However, this trend is contrary to industry's aim to reduce development costs and time-to-market of new products. The use of models would help along two directions. Firstly, it makes safety engineering as a standalone sub-task of system development more efficient. Secondly, and even more important, this is an essential step towards a holistic model-based development approach which closes the gap between functional development and safety assessment. Reusing development models for safety analyses and feeding back the results of safety analyses in the development models is a key step for reaching synergies.

Although a large body of research results about using model-based development for safety-critical system already exists, they did not found their way into the industrial practice yet. In this paper, we outline the current practice in

A. Skavhaug et al. (Eds.): SAFECOMP 2016 Workshops, LNCS 9923, pp. 322–333, 2016.
DOI: 10.1007/978-3-319-45480-1_26

developing safety-critical systems and derive a set of challenges. Based on this, we describe how would the adoption of Model-Based Engineering (MBE) in the development of safety-critical systems cope with these challenges. Therefore, we present how can models help to assess that a system is sufficiently safe (models for safety) and how models can be applied for the development of safety-critical systems (safety for models).

2   Safety Assessment at a Glance

The goal of the safety assessment process is to identify all failures that cause hazardous situations and to demonstrate that their probabilities are sufficiently low. In the application domains of safety-relevant systems, the safety assurance process is defined by the means of safety standards (e.g. IEC 61508 [1]). Although each domain has its own standards and regulation, the safety assessment includes a generic set of activities which are related to the system engineering process (see Fig. 1).

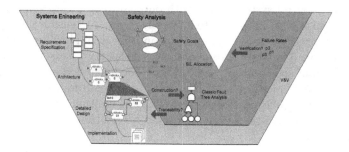

Fig. 1. Development of safety-critical systems in current industrial practice

As a first step, safety goals are defined according the system requirements. Based on the system requirements the architecture of the system is designed. After performing a hazard and risk analysis, *Safety Integrity Level (SIL)* information is obtained and allocated to the elements in the system architecture (e.g. the components of the systems). In the next step, the detailed design of the system is built which is the basis for the implementation of the system. Based on the detailed system design, the safety engineer is developing a safety analysis for the specified system. Traditionally, safety analysis consists of bottom-up safety analysis approaches, such as *Failure Mode and Effect Analysis (FMEA)*, and top-down ones, such as *Fault Tree Analysis (FTA)*, to identify failure modes, their causes, and effects with impact on the system safety. The result of a (quantitative) analysis is a set of failure rates for the hazardous events which are used for the verification of the safety requirements defined in the safety case.

3   Current Practice in Developing Safety-Critical Systems

In the following, we present four examples which illustrate the current practice of developing safety-critical systems in different domains at Siemens.

3.1   Example 1: Modular Certification for Trains

Traditionally, trains have high requirements in terms of safety. Modern trains are built using a modular platform concept. Such a platform concept enables the manufacturer to build various train configurations in a flexible way and reuse certain parts.

Currently, a *clone and own* strategy is used in order to build a new trainset based on the existing platform. However, every new trainset developed based on the same platform requires an individual certification. Even more, the certification needs to be granted by different certification authorities of the countries in which the trains will run. Furthermore, in the railway domain, there is a substantial legacy and constraints imposed by the existing infrastructure. For instance, there are different train protection systems in use by railways across Europe. These control systems have both on-board components and side-track components which must interoperate flawlessly in order to ensure safe operation.

In current practice, model-based development is applied to isolated subsystems of trains. The system development and safety assessment are mainly based on multiple specification and analysis documents. However, the modularization of specific parts of a train enables their reuse for multiple trainsets. But changing one specific part of the train impacts multiple analysis documents. Thus, the adjustment of the safety analysis is a very time-consuming and complex manual task.

3.2   Example 2: Reusable System for Industry Automation

In the industry automation domain, compositional system development fosters individual solutions for customers with high potential for modular certification. Thereby, every specific system consists of an individual set of solvers, sensors as well as actuators of different types and vendors. Each system is an individual combination of parts according to the customer's requirements. The architecture of industry automation systems is very flexible in terms of involved sensors and actuators. Moreover, the system is composed by reusing standardized components from a repository.

In current projects use, safety assessment is based on reusable certificates for the quality of the process. Process-based certification involves organization aspects, qualification of involved personnel and proof of quality goals for system elements. However, with the growing system complexity process-based certification is becoming more and more expensive. Moreover, it does not support the compositional and flexible way current systems in industry automation are built.

To enable efficient product-based certification of the individual system, modular safety assessment as well as the systematic reuse of safety artifacts must be possible. Moreover, the safety assessment processes of the industry automation system should be embeddable into customers' certification processes for the overall manufacturing system.

Model-based development is solely applied for describing the components functionality of PLCs by using domain specific modeling languages (e.g. Continuous Flow Charts, CFCs).

3.3   Example 3: Medical Devices

Modern medical devices realize complex safety-critical functionalities due to multiple system states, placing of the machinery within the clinical environment and high sensitivity requirements. Requirements for healthcare systems in terms of safety are single-fault protection and partial fail-operational by two options: First, risk avoidance by bringing the system in a safe state. Second, providing independent redundancy.

In the current industrial practice, manually maintained tables are used to calculate failure rates, separate failure classes and to guide the safety analysis process and show that a medical system is sufficiently safe. The reuse of individual component or sub-systems is managed manually by copy-and-paste and cell references.

However, with the growing complexity of the functions of medical devices, which involve even larger circuits with increased reuse, more sophisticated methods and tools are needed for safety assessment in order to fulfill high quality demands in this domain and meet fail-operational requirements in the future.

3.4   Example 4: Future Automotive ICT Platform

Today's vehicles are filled with more information and communication technology (ICT) than ever before. A paradigm shift from the array of control units used today to a flexible set of software-implemented features stored on just a few central platform computers enables a cost-effective way to implement current as well as novel functionalities. Such an architecture, e.g. developed in the German national funded project RACE[1], provides a central platform computer concept with fail-operational behavior. Moreover, the platform aims to offer plug-and-play capabilities to easily enhance or integrate new features and components while the car is in the field. Therefore, run-time (re-)qualification of the system w.r.t. safety is the central future business case to ensure that the impact of the extension has no negative results.

In current practice, a fault containment region-based analysis provides reusable hardware failure rates for a later qualification of specific functionalities planed to run on the central ICT platform w.r.t. safety [2].

However, this approach for system qualification is solely used during the development to assess the system in terms of safety. Run-time (re-)qualification based on the current approach is not yet possible.

---

[1] http://www.projekt-race.de/en/.

4   Challenges

The current practice in developing safety-critical systems in the context of industrial projects faces the following challenges w.r.t. safety assessment:

4.1   Efficient Construction of Safety Analyses

In current practice, constructing a safety assessment (e.g. using fault trees or FMEAs) and maintaining its quality through the development is a challenging and time-intensive manual task (see Sect. 3). With the increasing system complexity the manual construction of a safety analysis model for an entire system is becoming very hard or even unfeasible. Moreover, incremental and iterative development processes used in industry require safety analyses to be performed along the complete design process and provide immediate feedback to the system engineers about the safety aspects of the systems being developed.

To perform safety analysis efficiently in large-scale industrial projects, methods are required to construct safety analysis models in a structured way based on the information available in the detailed system design.

4.2   Evolution of the System Design

During most industrial development projects, change requests can come from various stakeholders such as the client, certification authorities or development teams of the different sub-projects. But changes can also be a part of a development strategy, if an existing product can be evolved in a new system in an incremental manner with small changes and adjustments (e.g. in the development of trains based on a platform concept, see Sect. 3.1). In case of modifications of the system design during the development process, the safety analysis must be adapted accordingly to guarantee that the results of the safety analysis are still valid. Since traceability between the artifacts in the system design and the safety assessment is solely achieved manually in current practice, each change within the system design results in time-consuming manual adjustment performed by the safety engineer. For instance, after each modification all FMEA tables or fault trees of the system must be completely reviewed and all parts affected by the modification must be adapted.

In order to decrease the time-consuming adaptation of the safety analyses, traceability between the elements in the safety analysis and the related elements in the system design must be established [3]. Moreover, automated synchronization of the safety analysis model with changing system design in a continuous manner is needed.

4.3   Systematic Reuse of Safety Artifacts

In industrial practice, developers often have existing development artifacts which are reused to compose a system (see Sect. 3.1 or 3.2). Such development artifacts are for instance stored within a repository and put together as a new configuration for a product. This compositional development strategy allows automated system construction from preexisting building blocks. With the motivation for reusing the results of safety analyses of existing development artifacts, the safety assessment needs to be aligned with compositional system design. Hence, safety artifacts on the granularity of component-level must be exchangeable within the safety analysis model.

To enable systematic reuse the safety artifacts related to system components should be stored within a repository and used to compose a system-wide safety analysis model. The composition of the safety artifacts should be performed at best in an automated way.

4.4   Seamless Traceability

In practice, the results of the safety analysis process cannot be mapped easily with the systems' safety goals, since their relation is often not clearly traceable and maybe ambiguous. Therefore, the verification of the systems' safety goals with the results of the safety analyses is a complex task itself. This is a challenge in the development of safety-critical systems in large-scale industrial projects across all domains within Siemens (see Sect. 3). In order to enable an unambiguous mapping between the safety goals and the safety analyses results, seamless traceability between the safety goals, system specification, and safety analyses must be established.

For an efficient connection of different artifacts (e.g. specification, high-level design, and low-level design) within the system engineering process, information should be integrated automatically without the manual establishment of traceability links.

4.5   Automated (Re-)Qualification

Adaptations and modifications of an embedded system are traditionally performed solely during the development. However, there is a strong trend to build open and adaptive system platforms (see the example of a future automotive ICT platform in Sect. 3.4). These systems can be enhanced during run-time with novel functionalities and may be coupled temporary with other systems which dissolve and give place to other configurations. The key problem in assessing the safety of such systems is that the configurations over its lifetime are unknown and potentially infinite. State-of-practice safety analysis techniques are currently applied during development and require an a priori knowledge of the configurations that provide the basis of the analysis of system. Such techniques are not applicable to open, adaptive systems that build up a new configuration at run-time. Therefore, safety analyses must be applicable to assess novel system configurations ad-hoc during run-time in an automated way. Such that the adaptation or modification of the system in the field can be assessed in terms of safety.

5   Leveraging Models in the Development of Safety-Critical Systems

In this section, we show how to cope with the previous mentioned challenges by using models for the assessment that a system is sufficiently safe (Sect. 5.1) as well as using models in the development of safety-critical systems (Sect. 5.2).

5.1   Models for Safety

The idea of model based safety assessment is to support automatic generation of classical safety artifacts such as fault trees or FMEA tables from system models [4–6]. Therefore, the system models are often annotated with failure propagation models to construct the safety artifacts. Examples for such an approach are HiP-HOPS (Hierarchically Performed Hazard Origin and Propagation Studies) [7] or Component Fault Trees (CFTs) [8]. These failure propagation models are commonly combinatorial in nature thus producing static fault trees. This is also driven by the industrial need to certify their system with static fault trees or FMEA tables. Only rarely more advanced safety evaluation models, such as Dynamic Fault Trees (DFTs) [9], Generalized Stochastic Petri Nets (GSPNs) [10], State-Event Fault Trees (SEFTs) [11], or Markov models [12], exist in practice. Besides annotating the architecture specification, there are also approaches in current research to synthesize safety artifacts via model checking techniques (e.g. FSAP/NuSMV-SA [13]). However, such approaches have not found the way yet in the current industrial practice.

5.2   Safety for Models

Model-based development aims to address the high complexity of current systems by the use of adequate and rich models through all development phases from requirements engineering, to design, implementation, integration and deployment. Models are envisioned to be used at different granularity levels: Abstract models describe the entire system, and subsequently more concrete models are used at sub-system level until finest granular models are used at the component level. Thereby, the high-level models are kept in sync with lower level models. In an ideal world, the entire development is supported by a seamless and deeply integrated set of adequate models that address development concerns [14].

However, the adoption of model-based development in practice varies strongly between different industrial application domains. In general, the current adoption and benefits of using model-based development is by far not reaching the promises given by the research community (see also [15]):

Requirements are very weakly modeled if at all – they are written using plain natural language text or they are captured in a hierarchical tree-like structure like that provided by DOORS. Besides the natural language text, requirements should be associated to meta-data such as the "safety integrity level" (for safety requirements).

Architectures are described informally with the help of "boxes and lines" pictures drawn in tools like MS Visio. When the architecture is modeled, it is done with SysML tools, like MagicDraw or Enterprise Architect. Many times the architecture is described in a hierarchical manner like systems consisting of subsystems, etc. The behavior specification of system-level abstract components is not a common practice (e.g. annotating interfaces of components with invariants, specifying pre/post conditions in a machine readable form). After the initial design, keeping the architecture consistent with the system implementation during the life-cycle and across product families requires a huge manual effort and long review cycles.

Behavior of atomic components is implemented using models or code, such as C/C++. When control- or state-based-like algorithms are being developed, then one of the mostly used tools is Simulink/Stateflow. For more hardware-close functionality however like device drivers or communication protocols, the plain code is used instead of models. Different domains already use domain specific modeling languages for describing the components functionality like SIBAS (railway), Simulink (controls) or PLC (industry automation) in large-scale projects.

However, besides the control algorithm modeling activities, which are current practices across different Siemens business units, the use of models for the system development is rather sporadic. Furthermore, most of the times ad-hoc toolchains are used which comprise and extend commercially available tools with specific customizations.

5.3 Integrating MBE with Safety-Critical Systems Development

Using both models to analyze a system in terms of safety and models for the development of safety-critical systems, the practical challenges in industry, as previously described in Sect. 4, can be addressed as follows:

Efficient Construction of Safety Analyses. Models used in safety analysis, such as CFTs or HiP-HOPS, annotate the system models with failure propagation models. This enables the construction of the safety analysis model in a structured way. Due to the use of models in the assessment of functional safety, advances of MBE such as providing traceability, tool support and consistency checks can be utilized. Moreover, model-based safety engineering approaches allow the (semi-)automated generation of safety artifacts such as Fault Trees or FMEAs, if the system design is specified by using models (e.g. [4,5]). Hence, the use of models for development improves the efficient construction of safety analysis models, since they reuse the information available in the system design and offer a sound methodology. As a result, safety analyses may be applied more frequently during the entire product development process.

From industrial adoption viewpoint, the construction of safety analysis models from the information in the system design models must be clearly traceable and understood by developers. Moreover, system and safety engineers must still be able to work with methodologies and models, with which they are familiar.

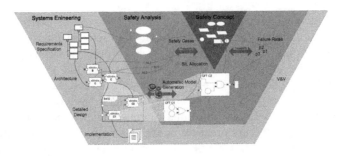

Fig. 2. Adaption of MBE in the development of safety-critical systems

Evolution of the System Design. When a model-based development strategy is used, traceability between system design and safety analysis artifacts is established. Thus, the impact of changes in the system design is narrowed to encapsulated parts in the safety analysis model. The validity of the unchanged parts of the safety analysis is preserved. For example, the modification of a specific system component does only affect the corresponding component within a CFT model. Instead, in classic fault tree analysis, each fault tree must be reviewed manually whether to adjust certain sub-tress or not.

Also the information within both kinds of models must be consistent during the complete development process. For instance, if a certain system element is deleted or renamed, the safety analysis model must be adjusted accordingly. By using models in system design and safety assessment the synchronization can be performed (semi-)automatically to guarantee that the safety as well as the system engineers always work on consistent data. Since the time-consuming maintenance of the safety analysis model is reduced significantly and safety analysis is kept in sync with the system design, safety analyses may be repeated during the complete development process. Thus, iterative development processes as used currently in industry can be supported in terms of safety assessment [16].

Systematic Reuse of Safety Artifacts. Since the models used in model-based safety assessment interlink safety with the system design artifacts, it is possible to reuse these safety artifacts in the safety assessment of different contexts. Hence, it is possible to construct a safety analysis model based on the reuse of preexisting parts and the specification of the newly created parts (compositional safety assessment). In terms of top-down safety analysis, one possible direction is to use the CFT methodology and to establish a framework to synchronize with the system design model and to store and exchange specific CFT elements [17]. Another direction is to enable reuse in bottom-up safety analysis, e.g. by introducing model-based FMEA techniques [18]. However, in order leverage compositional safety assessment in industrial practice, techniques for the automated composition of safety artifacts are need [19]. First, as a preliminary approach, to give system engineers a first feedback w.r.t. system's safety in the early stages of the development. Second, to automate the system qualification in terms of functional safety.

Seamless Traceability. By the use of model-based approaches for safety analysis, traceability between system design elements (e.g. components) and safety artifacts (e.g. the failure propagation within a component) is established [7,8]. Hence, it is possible to synchronize system design and safety artifacts and prevent inconsistencies during the development. However, to be able provide an unambiguous relation of the results of the safety analyses and the systems' safety goals, we need to make the argumentation explicit by describing the safety goals and providing links to the analysis results which prove that the goal is fulfilled. Model-based approaches for constructing safety argumentation, such as the Goal Structuring Notation (GSN) [20], close this gap by providing links between safety goals, system design elements, safety analysis, and their results (see Fig. 2). Thus, seamless traceability in the development of safety-critical systems is achieved by combining models for development, safety analysis and building safety concepts in a pragmatic way. However, this is an intermediate step on the way towards the use of a *holistic product model* which provides deep, coherent and comprehensive integration of requirements, specification, implementation, test/verification & safety models [14].

Automated (Re-)Qualification. The safety of upcoming embedded systems cannot be fully assured prior to deployment (see Sect. 3.4). In order to assure the safety of such reconfigurable system, the degree of automation in safety assessment must be further increased. Using models for the system design and the safety analysis provides a relation of system design elements and safety artifacts and enables the reuse of safety artifacts. By providing techniques to compose safety analysis automatically from preexisting building blocks, the (re-)qualification of the system in terms of safety can be automated. Moreover, to enable the in-the-field safety assessment of a system, the methodology must be able to deal with system parts which provide no or incomplete information about its failure propagation. This is because upcoming embedded systems may interact spontaneously during operation including parts which are produced by different companies. Therefore, methods are needed to automatically fill up empty safety analysis artifacts [21] in order to be able to perform a safety assessment of a system configuration, which is not know a priori.

6 Related Work

Many papers (e.g. [22,23]) discuss the challenges in MBE from an industrial practice. However, the specific characteristics in the development of safety-critical systems are not considered.

The use of models in safety assessment processes has gained increasing attention in research within the last decade [24–27]. But to our knowledge this is the first work which deals with the actual challenges that model-based safety engineering faces in industrial practice.

7   Conclusion

In this paper, we outline the current practice in developing safety-critical systems with the help of several examples of different business domains of Siemens. Based on this experience, we derive the challenges in the industrial practice. Moreover, we describe how the adoption of MBE for the development of safety-critical systems can cope with these challenges from a practitioners viewpoint. Therefore, we advocate that there is a dual perspective of the use of models in the context of safety-critical systems development. First, by using models for the assessment, that a system is sufficiently safe (models for safety). Second, using models for the design of safety-critical systems (safety for models). Only if these two perspectives are addressed jointly, models can leverage the development of safety-critical systems efficiently.

References

1. Int. Electrotechnical Commission (IEC): IEC 61508: Functional safety of electrical/electronic/programmable electronic safety related systems (1998)
2. Höfig, K., Armbruster, M., Schmid, R.: A vehicle control platform as safety element out of context (2014) (presentation held at HiPEAC Computing Systems Week)
3. Schultz, M., Meyer, L., Langer, B., Fricke, H.: Model-based safety assessment as integrated part of system development. In: International Workshop on Aircraft System Technologies (AST) (2011)
4. Rauzy, A.: Mode automata and their compilation into fault trees. Reliab. Eng. Syst. Saf. **78**(1), 1–12 (2002)
5. Papadopoulos, Y., Parker, D., Grante, C.: Automating the failure modes and effects analysis of safety critical systems. In: International Symposium on High-Assurance Systems Engineering (HASE), pp. 310–311 (2004)
6. Majdara, A., Wakabayashi, T.: Component-based modeling of systems for automated fault tree generation. Reliab. Eng. Syst. Saf. **94**(6), 1076–1086 (2009)
7. Papadopoulos, Y., McDermid, J.A.: Hierarchically performed hazard origin and propagation studies. In: Computer Safety, Reliability, and Security (1999)
8. Kaiser, B., Liggesmeyer, P., Mäckel, O.: A new component concept for fault trees. In: Proceedings of the 8th Australian Workshop on Safety Critical Systems and Software, pp. 37–46 (2003)
9. Bechta Dugan, J., Bavuso, S.J., Boyd, M.: Dynamic fault-tree models for fault-tolerant computer systems. IEEE Trans. Reliab. **41**(3), 363–377 (1992)
10. Ajmone Marsan, M., Conte, G., Balbo, G.: A class of generalized stochastic petri nets for the performance evaluation of multiprocessor systems. ACM Trans. Comput. Syst. **2**(2), 93–122 (1984)
11. Kaiser, B., Gramlich, C.: State-event-fault-trees – a safety analysis model for software controlled systems. In: Heisel, M., Liggesmeyer, P., Wittmann, S. (eds.) SAFECOMP 2004. LNCS, vol. 3219, pp. 195–209. Springer, Heidelberg (2004)
12. IEC: IEC 61165: Application of Markov techniques (1995–2003)

13. Bozzano, M., Villafiorita, A.: Improving system reliability via model checking: the FSAP/NuSMV-SA safety analysis platform. In: Anderson, S., Felici, M., Littlewood, B. (eds.) SAFECOMP 2003. LNCS, vol. 2788, pp. 49–62. Springer, Heidelberg (2003)

14. Broy, M., Feilkas, M., Herrmannsdoerfer, M., Merenda, S., Ratiu, D.: Seamless model-based development: from isolated tools to integrated model engineering environments. Proc. IEEE **98**(4), 526–545 (2010)

15. Florian Fieber, B.R., Regnat, N.: Assessing usability of model driven development in industrial projects. In: 4th Workshop From Code Centric to Model Centric Software Engineering: Practices, Implications and ROI (2009)

16. Zeller, M., Höfig, K.: INSiDER: Incorporation of system and safety analysis models using a dedicated reference model. In: Annual Reliability and Maintainability Symposium (RAMS), pp. 1–6 (2016)

17. Höfig, K., Zeller, M., Heilmann, R.: ALFRED: a methodology to enable component fault trees for layered architectures. In: 41st Euromicro Conference on Software Engineering and Advanced Applications (SEAA), pp. 167–176 (2015)

18. Höfig, K., Zeller, M., Grunske, L.: metaFMEA-a framework for reusable FMEAs. In: Ortmeier, F., Rauzy, A. (eds.) IMBSA 2014. LNCS, vol. 8822, pp. 110–122. Springer, Heidelberg (2014)

19. Möhrle, F., Zeller, M., Höfig, K., Rothfelder, M., Liggesmeyer, P.: Automated compositional safety analysis using component fault trees. In: IEEE International Symposium on Software Reliability Engineering Workshops, pp. 152–159 (2015)

20. Kelly, T., Weaver, R.: The goal structuring notation - a safety argument notation. In: Proceedings of the Workshop on Assurance Cases (2004)

21. Höfig, K., Zeller, M., Schorp, K.: Automated failure propagation using inner port dependency traces. In: Proceedings of the 11th International ACM Sigsoft Conference on the Quality of Software Architectures (QoSA), pp. 123–128 (2015)

22. Baker, P., Loh, S.C., Weil, F.: Model-driven engineering in a large industrial context — motorola case study. In: Briand, L.C., Williams, C. (eds.) MoDELS 2005. LNCS, vol. 3713, pp. 476–491. Springer, Heidelberg (2005)

23. Liebel, G., Marko, N., Tichy, M., Leitner, A., Hansson, J.: Model-based engineering in the embedded systems domain: an industrial survey on the state-of-practice. In: Software & Systems Modeling, pp. 1–23 (2016)

24. McDermid, J., Kelly, T.: Software in Safety Critical Systems: Achievement and Prediction. University of York, UK (2006)

25. Lisagor, O., Sun, L., Kelly, T., The illusion of method: Challenges of model-based safety assessment. In: Proceedings of 28th International System Safety Conference (2010)

26. Lisagor, O., Kelly, T., Niu, R.: Model-based safety assessment: Review of the discipline and its challenges. In: 9th International Conference on Reliability, Maintainability and Safety (ICRMS), pp. 625–632 (2011)

27. Sharvia, S., Kabir, S., Walker, M., Papadopoulos, Y.: Model-based dependability analysis: State-of-the-art, challenges, and future outlook. In: Software Quality Assurance, pp. 251–278 (2016)

Goal-Oriented Co-Engineering of Security and Safety Requirements in Cyber-Physical Systems

Christophe Ponsard$^{(\boxtimes)}$, Gautier Dallons, and Philippe Massonet

CETIC Research Center, Charleroi, Belgium
{christophe.ponsard,gautier.dallons,philippe.massonet}@cetic.be

Abstract. Many safety critical systems are integrating more and more software based systems and are becoming increasingly connected. Such Cyber-Physical Systems require high assurance both on safety and security but also on how such properties affect each other. This covers not only design time aspects but also the run-time: as cyber-security threats evolve constantly, it is necessary to consider how to perform updates of the software without breaking any safety properties. This paper proposes a method to co-engineer them based on sound techniques taken from goal-oriented requirements engineering. The approach is illustrated on a case study from the automotive domain. The case study illustrates the challenges to safety and security co-engineering created by the trend of growing connectivity and the evolution towards more autonomous vehicles in the transportation domain.

1 Introduction

Transportation systems are increasingly relying on software for monitoring and controlling the physical world, including to assist or replace human operation (e.g. drive assistance in cars, automated train operations), resulting in higher safety-criticality. Several such systems are also becoming increasingly connected and are referred to as Cyber Physical Systems (CPS) [20]. Those characteristics expose CPS to security threats that in turn can lead to safety hazards.

Transport domains such as railroad, automotive or aeronautics are heavily regulated to ensure transportation safety. Many transport systems are safety critical and must respect many safety standards such as ISO 26262 [7] (automotive) or EN 50128 [3] (Railways). Cyber-security must deal with a constantly evolving threat landscape. New cyber-security vulnerabilities, attacks and threats appear on a continuous basis, requiring new counter measures to be designed constantly. To maintain the security of safety critical cyber-physical transport systems it is necessary to continuously update cyber-physical system security software and data via their live communication connection. A key research challenge is how to update the security functions and data of cyber-physical systems without breaking any safety properties. This calls for a co-engineering approach of security and safety [26]. Security updates can be made at different times, e.g. during

© Springer International Publishing Switzerland 2016
A. Skavhaug et al. (Eds.): SAFECOMP 2016 Workshops, LNCS 9923, pp. 334–345, 2016.
DOI: 10.1007/978-3-319-45480-1_27

planned system downtime or while the system is running, but can unintentionally lead to outages and unplanned downtime. In some cases security functions and data may be redeployed, reconfigured and verified before the system is returned to operational status. In other cases, where the system must continue running and modifications can only be made via a live update, verification is more complex because you have to consider the cyber-physical system itself as well as the communicating system and its links. So, this calls for co-engineering approaches that can decompose systems into subsystems while preserving some global system safety properties.

In order to develop systems that can deal with such scenarios, it is important to be able to precisely identify and reason about the requirements that are involved and especially the safety and security requirements. Our approach is to take a sound Requirements Engineering (RE) approach on the problem using Goal-Oriented Requirements Engineering (GORE) which has shown very good capabilities for modelling requirements and reasoning about them [10] and which can address the need of decomposition while preserving global properties.

Our contribution on this paper is to illustrate our on-going work on how GORE can cope with the co-engineering of security and safety properties in cyber-physical systems. GORE has already been used to reason both on safety and security but most of the time independently of each other. In this paper we explore how to deal with the interplay of safety and security in GORE. The approach can be used for the initial co-engineering of security and safety requirements, and for specifying under which conditions and assumptions run-time adaptation of security functions and data may be made. The approach allows subtle conflicts between safety and security goals to be identified and resolved. Our work is illustrated with an example from the automotive domain.

This paper is structured as follows. Section 2 presents a state of the art in co-engineering of security and safety requirements. In Sect. 3, we present our goal-oriented co-engineering approach as well as the tool support we developed. Then Sect. 4 illustrates and discusses it on an automotive case study. Finally Sect. 5 draws some conclusions and identifies some future work.

2   State of the Art

2.1   Overview of Alternative Approaches

The problem of addressing the security and safety for CPS is heavily studied both in the literature and both within communities of experts in the fields concerned. A quite exhaustive literature review has been consolidated by the MERGE project [8]. It specifically examines the need to address these two dimensions for the design of CPS [15,18,19] and identified four different approaches to consider the links between security and safety:

1. Security and safety (in particular the processes) are considered totally separately. In this case, only interactions between processes are needed.

2. Security is considered at the service of safety. In this case the Safety engineering processes, methods and tools are updated with concepts and considerations from the security field. Conventional techniques for analyzing Safety risks (HAZOP, FMEA, fault tree, ...) are modified to take into account security giving rise to specialized versions of these methods (e.g. FMVEA, CHASSIS [25]).
3. Safety is considered as a way to improve security practices benefiting from the maturity of safety practices. This leads security to provide a system view.
4. Security and safety are addressed together by co-engineering. This approach is supported by the formal methods community and leads to a unification of processes, methods and tools.

The second approach is the most conservative for safety critical systems like transportation. Because it does not bring much change in current practices to safety procedures, one might expect to see it recommended in those domains. However, the directions taken by the areas of transport are not yet clear or still frozen. For example, in the field of automotive, there is still no specific safety or security standard forcing a direction in the way of considering these two dimensions [18,24]. The changes proposed in the literature are either to push safety methods [25] (approach 2) or to recommend co-engineering (approach 4) [27]. In the railway domain, there is also not yet a clear choice [18].

Despite this situation, the most reasonable choice seems to be the co-engineering for the following reasons:

- The separate approach to security and safety leads to important costs for companies due to the duplication of processes, methods, tools and the need of many synchronization between the approaches. This approach, that can be used at the beginning, cannot remain appropriate for interconnected systems with increasing complexity.
- Considering security at the service of safety might result in wrong priorities. Particularly some security properties are less important in this context (e.g. confidentiality rarely impacts safety). In addition, some components may have security needs disconnected from safety that are not correctly addressed and others may have mixed needs. Making security a mere concern of safety would not address all the necessary dimensions to the specific needs of the components.
- Safety as a means of improving security will not achieve the safety objectives of CPS.

2.2 Requirements Engineering Approaches for Security and Safety

The literature is stressing the need for methods that:

- align security RE and safety RE [15,28]
- decompose systems to separate the safety/security/mixed components and other components while ensuring global properties [15,28]

- support formal methods [2, 15, 28]
- use attack trees as a best practice of security engineering [5, 9, 16].

Requirements engineering (RE) is a key step in all system development. Over the years, very efficient methods have been developed both for dealing with safety and security aspects and among them Goal-oriented requirements Engineering (GORE) [10]. Such methods rely on the central concept of goals in order to capture, at different levels of abstraction, the various objectives the system under consideration should achieve. GORE is concerned with the use of goals for eliciting, elaborating, structuring, specifying, analysing, negotiating, documenting, and modifying requirements [10].

Different goal oriented modelling methods covering security [21] and safety can be considered: SecureTropos [14], KAOS (which means "Keep All Objective Satisfied") [11–13, 30] and secure i* [21].

In the rest of this paper, we will consider the KAOS method because it is quite representative, has well documented approaches both for safety [12] and security [13]. Actually it was initially developed in the safety context and subsequently extended to security [30] proposing a notation close to "attack trees" which makes it particularly suitable to the problem considered in this paper. Some other candidates have some limitations, e.g. secure i* does not support formal methods [6] and SecureTropos does not allow the analysis of threats [6]. This choice can however be transposed to other GORE methods.

3   Background on the KAOS Goal-Oriented RE Methodology

In KAOS, different abstraction levels to express goals can range from high-level strategic goals like "Maintain[Safe Car Operation]" down to operational goals such as "Achieve[Immediate deactivation of cruise control when braking]". High-level goals can be progressively refined into more concrete and operational ones through relationships linking a parent goal to several sub-goals, with different fulfilment conditions using either "AND-refinement" (all sub-goals need to be satisfied) or "OR-refinement" (a single sub-goal is enough, i.e. possible alternatives). The "WHY" and "HOW" questions can be used to conveniently navigate to parent and sub-goals, respectively. This results in a goal tree structure. The goal decomposition stops when reaching a goal controllable by an agent, i.e. answering the "WHO" question about responsibility assignment. These goals are either requirements on the software or expectations on the behaviour of agents in the environment. Domain properties can also be taken into account to justify a refinement. Such properties are intrinsically valid like the law of physics relating car deceleration with its mass.

Although the goal part is central, a KAOS model is actually structured on the following four sub-models (Fig. 1):

- The **goal model** structures functional and non-functional goals of the considered system. It also helps identify potential conflicts and obstacles related to goals and reason about their resolution. It is graphically represented as a goal tree.

- The **object model** defines and interrelates all concepts involved in goal specifications. Its representation is aligned with UML class diagrams and allows structuring entities, relations, events and agents.
- The **agent model** identifies the agents of both the system and the environment as well as their interface and responsibilities. They can be shown as part of goal trees or in more specific diagrams.
- The **operations model** describes how agents functionally cooperate to ensure the fulfilment of the requirements assigned to them and hence the system goals. Functional flow diagrams are used here.

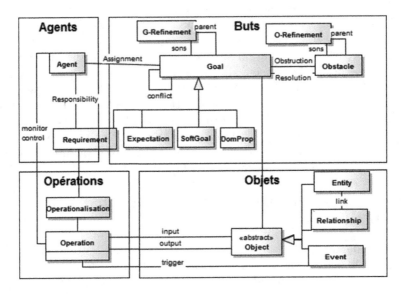

Fig. 1. Overview of the KAOS generic meta-model

3.1 A Goal-Oriented Co-Engineering Approach

The state of the art calls for a deeper study on how GORE-based methods can support co-engineering to address the safety and security dimensions simultaneously. It should be also remain flexible enough to be compatible with other approaches, especially when safety is critical (approach 2).

3.2 Safety vs Security Approach

As a first step, Table 1 shows a side-by-side comparison of how safety and security are addressed. Actually, KAOS allows working on safety and security in a common or separate manner, and allows linking those specific objectives with the overall objectives of the system. In addition, it provides a systemic approach

Table 1. Comparison of safety and security engineering approaches

	Safety Engineering	Security Engineering
Goal Category	Safety Goal	Security goal
Obstacle variant	Hazard	Anti-goal (or Threat)
Finest refinement	Root cause	Vulnerability
Agent	Environment (unexpected)	Attacker (malicious)
Impact	Damage to people and things, priority over all other requirements (e.g. availability)	Measured in business terms, e.g. system availability, reputation
Refinement Methods	Fault Tree Analysis, HAZOP, FMECA	Attack trees, Threat trees
Risk managementtechniques	Obstacle elimination Obstacle reduction Obstacle tolerance (goal restoration)	Vulnerability removal/isolation Attack recovery Attack impact reduction
Analysis Type	Design-time analysis. Update not frequent. But learning from past accident important activity.	Run-time monitoring for discovery of vulnerabilities, suspect behaviours. Frequent updates to patch.
Standards	IEC61508 (generic), ISO26262 (automotive), IEC50128 (railways), DO178B/C, etc	Common criteria

while allowing decomposition into subsystems. Finally, it can be linked with formal methods that can be used to demonstrate some system properties (safety properties, security properties or mixed properties) in a unified way. Two key modelling concepts come into play:

- **In the safety context:** an obstacle can be considered as any undesirable property or **hazards** (e.g. gearbox malfunction) that directly obstructs system goals (e.g. passenger safety) which are desired properties. Obstacles can be refined using obstacle refinement trees that are the dual as goal refinement trees [12].
- **In the security context:** the notion of malicious agents having interest in the realisation of some threats, is used as the dual of normal agents cooperating to the achievement of a system goal [13]. They can be structured using attack trees [30].

Classical risk management techniques are applied both to safety and security aspects. This risk-based approach is formalised for security by referring to SIL and quantifying the residual risks. OECD is also stressing that "Digital security risk should be treated like an economic rather than a technical issue, and should be part of an organisation's overall risk management and decision-making" [17]. Or course both security and safety risks need to be considered together. Tactics like attack recovery can thus also be applied as long as it does not impact safety critical functions.

3.3 Towards Combining Safety and Security

While generally considered separately, we considered combining them for co-engineering purposes, especially given their strong common foundation, including the ability to drive the discovery of hazards/threats and to identify how to address them. The following principles highlighted in the state of the art are key drivers:

- Models are used both for safety and security. Safety impact of security failures are considered, hence making a connection between both kinds of analysis.
- Safety is at the inner core of the system, providing de facto better isolation. Security layers or different criticality levels are deployed around it. Using this principle enables to stay aligned with approach 2. It will also lead to a sound architecture, especially to cope with the conflict between heavy security update procedures and the need for flexible security updates.
- Both security incidents and system failures are monitored to keep evaluating the global system dependability. This enriches the knowledge base on how to update the system and to better design future systems.

The global method can cope both with top-down and bottom-up analysis processes. The top-down process is composed of the following main steps:

- the starting point are safety and security requirements. The requirements are explicitly tagged with their nature. For security requirements, a possible high level attacker can already be identified.
- mixed threats and obstacles are carried out on such high-level goals. For safety requirements, the main driver is a hazard analysis and for security goal, it is an attack analysis. Hazards are marked with a safety nature while threats are marked with a security nature.
- threats may be identified as potential causes of some hazard based on some heuristics such as the ability of an attacker to control the occurrence of an obstacle or the security critical nature of an involved asset.
- hazards may also be identified in threats analysis with other kinds of heuristics. E.g. considering some known failure might enable some attacks and lead attackers to provoke such failure on purpose.
- the refinement process stops when elementary hazard/threats are identified. For hazards it corresponds to root cause while for threats it corresponds to vulnerabilities.

The bottom-up process starts from known vulnerabilities and root-cause, and tries to see how they can challenge security or safety aspects. The global process generally proceeds by a mix of both approaches: refining top goals and trying to match known (class of) hazards and vulnerabilities.

Once the analysis is complete a second stage of resolution can be applied. Such resolution follows the strategies described in the respective methods. However combining the analysis also enables to propose more efficient resolution tactics, e.g. addressing both security and safety issues. This area is still under investigation and part of our future work.

3.4   Tool Implementation

In order to support the above approach, we extended the Objectiver GORE tool [22] mainly with the ability to tag goals and obstacles with their safety or security nature. The nature is modelled as an extra meta-model attribute. This nature is also graphically shown as decorator on the goal diagram. It can be used to filter them in reports and diagrams. In addition the notion of attacker which was not yet supported in the tooling was also added. Our extension takes the form of a tool plug-in that is easy to install and is illustrated in Fig. 2. Similar extensions can also be developed for other tools such as [29].

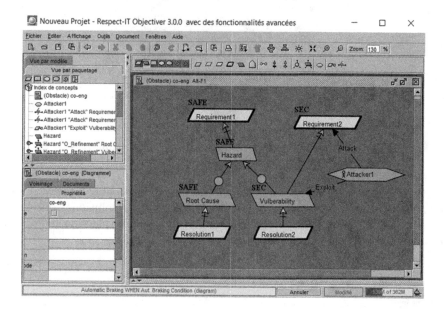

Fig. 2. Objectiver tool extension for safety and security co-engineering.

4   Automotive Case Study

Our case study is a connected car. Figure 3 shows the variety of subsystems and communication channels that can be found in a connected car. Our analysis is mainly inspired by the case study by Lotfi Ben Othmane [1] which considers a broader application framework initially before focusing on a safety case for the automatic braking subsystem. We also relied on a deeper threat model classifying communication channels that can be compromised [4].

For our case study, we start from that safety case and in particular the attack tree that we put in perspective through a co-engineering approach of safety and security with the KAOS method. Through this method of co-engineering, we make explicit the links between security and safety, links between attacks/hazards and the security/safety objectives and links with the counter-measures. By linking thus all the elements in this approach, we open pathways to semi-formal or formal validations and verifications.

We used our developed extension to experiment with some variants of co-engineering. Different scenarios involving different roles working together on the same model where experimented: the system engineer for the global system behaviour and architecture, the safety engineer to identify failure modes

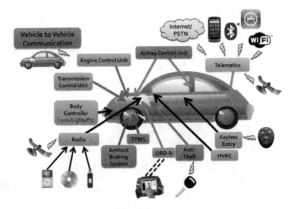

Fig. 3. Connected car subsystems and connection channels [4]

and their propagation, and security engineers to analyse possible attacks. A second step was then envisioned for reviewing the proposed resolutions addressing security and safety concerns. Regular reviews can also take place to perform a global validation gathering all analysts.

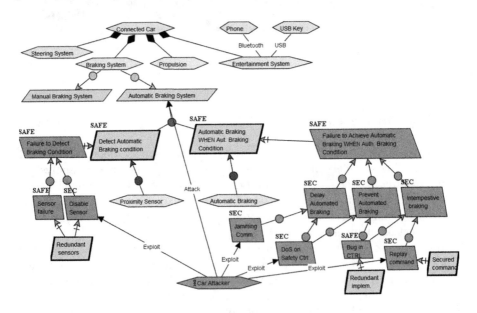

Fig. 4. Attack tree on a safety function.

Figure 4 shows an excerpt from the security/safety co-engineering of a connected car featuring automated braking based on SAE recommended practices [23]. The top level shows the general system structure and identifies the main sub-systems. The automated braking sub-system is then detailed based on two key milestones: condition detection and then braking. Next to each requirement, a mixed view of the result of the hazard/threat analysis is shown (those are usually presented in separate diagrams). Specific obstacles are tagged as SAFE or SEC depending on the process that identified them. Specific attacker profiles can also be captured (unique here). Some resolution techniques proposed in [12,13] can then be applied, e.g. to make the attack unfeasible or to reduce its impact. Some resolutions can also address mixed threats and reduce the global cost to make the whole system dependable.

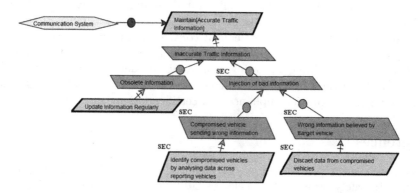

Fig. 5. Analysis of a distributed security problem

Figure 5 shows a security oriented analysis related to compromised cars reporting wrong traffic information. Safety could be impacted if the driver was to trust an immediate danger information like "Obstacle on the road at 20 m" and engaging in some braking (or even if the car was to engage the braking itself). This threat can be analysed using both ends of the chain: identifying the compromised car, e.g. by using data analytic techniques on the traffic information server. Such an information can be filtered out to avoid that it will reach the targeted car. Of course the compromised car should be quickly contacted for analysis and upgrade.

5 Conclusion and Perspectives

In this paper, we motivated the interest to develop a co-engineering approach for addressing safety and security requirements in systems like in the transport domain (automotive or railway) or smart cities/manufacturing where there is a growing trend to connect the related cyber-physical systems to the Internet. This possibly exposes safety critical cyber-physical systems to a new range of threats which are constantly evolving.

We presented on-going work on an approach to jointly address safety and security properties as well as compliance obligations during the requirements engineering phase. It was argued that a goal-oriented requirements engineering approach could be followed for initial specification of security and safety properties. It was also argued that the conditions and assumptions under which run-time adaptation of security functions and data may be made must also be specified thanks to the decomposition support offered by GORE-based co-engineering while assuring global safety properties. The approach was illustrated with an automotive case study showing how to model security threats on safety goals. From our limited current experiment, we already gained interesting knowledge about how different roles can interact. The approach is applicable to cyber-physical systems in general and was illustrated on an automotive case study.

Future work will conduct a deeper assessment of the feasibility of the approach in an industrial context, particularly considering the runtime case. We plan to carry out industrial case studies more specifically in the railway domain where cyber-security is becoming a growing concern while safety is a core requirement. The main aim of the work will be to co-engineer security and safety properties while taking into account compliance and certification obligations.

References

1. Ben Othmane, L., Al-Fuqaha, A., Ben Hamida, E., Van Den Brand, M.: Towards extended safety in connected vehicles. In: 2013 16th International IEEE Conference on Intelligent Transportation Systems-(ITSC), pp. 652–657. IEEE (2013)
2. Cartwright, R., Cheng, A., Hudak, P., OMalley, M., Taha, W.: Cyber-physical challenges in transportation system design. In: National Workshop for Research on High Confidence Transportation Cyber-Physical Systems (2008)
3. CENELEC: EN 50128:2001, Railway applications - Communications, signalling and processing systems - Software for railway control and protection systems. Technical report (2001)
4. Checkoway, S., McCoy, D., Kantor, B., Anderson, D., Shacham, H., Savage, S., Koscher, K., Czeskis, A., Roesner, F., Kohno, T.: Comprehensive experimental analyses of automotive attack surfaces. In: Proceedings of the 20th USENIX Conference on Security, SEC 2011, p. 6. USENIX Association, Berkeley (2011)
5. Du, S., Zhu, H.: Security assessment via attack tree model. In: Du, S., Zhu, H. (eds.) Security Assessment in Vehicular Networks. SpringerBriefs in Computer Science, pp. 9–16. Springer, New York (2013)
6. Fabian, B., Gürses, S., Heisel, M., Santen, T., Schmidt, H.: A comparison of security requirements engineering methods. Requirements Eng. 15(1), 7–40 (2010)
7. International Standardization Organization: ISO 26262: Road vehicles - functional safety. ISO (2011)
8. ITEA: MERGE Project. http://www.merge-project.eu
9. Kotenko, I., Chechulin, A.: A cyber attack modeling and impact assessment framework. In: 2013 5th International Conference on Cyber Conflict (CyCon), pp. 1–24. IEEE (2013)
10. van Lamsweerde, A.: Goal-oriented requirements engineering: a guided tour. In: Fifth IEEE International Symposium on Requirements Engineering, pp. 249–262 (2001)
11. van Lamsweerde, A.: Requirements Engineering - From System Goals to UML Models to Software Specifications. Wiley, Chichester (2009)

12. van Lamsweerde, A., Letier, E.: Handling obstacles in goal-oriented requirements engineering. IEEE Trans. Softw. Eng. **26**(10), 978–1005 (2000)
13. Lamsweerde, A.V., Brohez, S., Landtsheer, R.D., Janssens, D.: From system goals to intruder anti-goals: attack generation and resolution for security requirements engineering. In: Proceedings of the RHAS 2003, pp. 49–56 (2003)
14. Massacci, F., Mylopoulos, J., Zannone, N.: Computer-aided support for secure tropos. Autom. Softw. Eng. **14**(3), 341–364 (2007)
15. MERGE Project: Recommandations for Security and Safety Co-engineering. Delivrable (2016)
16. Moore, A.P., Ellison, R.J., Linger, R.C.: Attack modeling for information security and survivability. Technical report, DTIC Document (2001)
17. OECD: Digital Security Risk Management for Economic and Social Prosperity - OECD Recommendation and Companion Document (2015). http://www.oecd.org/sti/ieconomy/digital-security-risk-management.htm
18. Paul, S.: On the meaning of security for safety (s4s). In: Safety and Security Engineering VI, vol. 151, p. 379 (2015)
19. Paul, S., Rioux, L.: Over 20 years of research in cybersecurity and safety engineering: a short bibliography. In: Conference: 6th International Conference on Safety and Security Engineering (SAFE), May 2015
20. Rajkumar, R., Lee, I., Sha, L., Stankovic, J.: Cyber-physical systems: the next computing revolution. In: 2010 47th ACM/IEEE Design Automation Conference (DAC), pp. 731–736, June 2010
21. Rashid, A., Naqvi, S.A.A., Ramdhany, R., Edwards, M., Chitchyan, R., Babar, M.A.: Discovering unknown known security requirements. In: Proceedings of the 38th International Conference on Software Engineering, pp. 866–876. ACM (2016)
22. Respect-IT: Objectiver. http://www.objectiver.com
23. SAE: Recommended Practice J3061: Cybersecurity Guidebook for Cyber-Physical Vehicle Systems. http://articles.sae.org/14503
24. Schmittner, C., Ma, Z.: Towards a framework for alignment between automotive safety and security standards. In: Koornneef, F., van Gulijk, C. (eds.) SAFECOMP 2015. LNCS, vol. 9337, pp. 133–143. Springer, Heidelberg (2015)
25. Schmittner, C., Ma, Z., Schoitsch, E., Gruber, T.: A case study of fmvea and chassis as safety and security co-analysis method for automotive cyber-physical systems. In: Proceedings of the 1st ACM Workshop on Cyber-Physical System Security, pp. 69–80. ACM (2015)
26. Schneider, D., Armengaud, E., Schoitsch, E.: Towards trust assurance and certification in cyber-physical systems. In: Bondavalli, A., Ceccarelli, A., Ortmeier, F. (eds.) SAFECOMP 2014. LNCS, vol. 8696, pp. 180–191. Springer, Heidelberg (2014)
27. Schoitsch, E., Schmittner, C., Ma, Z., Gruber, T.: The need for safety and cybersecurity co-engineering and standardization for highly automated automotive vehicles. In: Schulze, T., Müller, B., Meyer, G. (eds.) Advanced Microsystems for Automotive Applications. Lecture Notes in Mobility, pp. 251–261. Springer, Switzerland (2016)
28. Sha, L., Gopalakrishnan, S., Liu, X., Wang, Q.: Cyber-physical systems: a new frontier. In: Machine Learning in Cyber Trust, pp. 3–13. Springer (2009)
29. Ottawa, U.: jUCMNav: Juice up your modelling (2001). https://www.openhub.net/p/jucmnav
30. Van Lamsweerde, A., et al.: Engineering requirements for system reliability and security. In: NATO Security Through Science Series D-Information and Communication Security, vol. 9, p. 196 (2007)

Practitioners' Perspectives on Change Impact Analysis for Safety-Critical Software – A Preliminary Analysis

Markus Borg[1]([✉]), Jose Luis de la Vara[2], and Krzysztof Wnuk[3]

[1] SICS Swedish ICT AB, Lund, Sweden
markus.borg@sics.se
[2] Carlos III University of Madrid, Madrid, Spain
jvara@inf.uc3m.es
[3] Blekinge Institute of Technology, Karlskrona, Sweden
krzysztof.wnuk@bth.se

Abstract. Safety standards prescribe change impact analysis (CIA) during evolution of safety-critical software systems. Although CIA is a fundamental activity, there is a lack of empirical studies about how it is performed in practice. We present a case study on CIA in the context of an evolving automation system, based on 14 interviews in Sweden and India. Our analysis suggests that engineers on average spend 50–100 h on CIA per year, but the effort varies considerably with the phases of projects. Also, the respondents presented different connotations to CIA and perceived the importance of CIA differently. We report the most pressing CIA challenges, and several ideas on how to support future CIA. However, we show that measuring the effect of such improvement solutions is non-trivial, as CIA is intertwined with other development activities. While this paper only reports preliminary results, our work contributes empirical insights into practical CIA.

Keywords: Change impact analysis · Safety-critical systems · Case study research

1 Introduction

Safety-critical software systems evolve during their lifecycle. As changes are made to the systems, change impact analysis (CIA) is needed, defined as "identifying the potential consequences of a change in a system, or estimating what needs to be modified to accomplish a change" [2]. CIA is essential for safety assurance, and it is indeed prescribed by safety standards, e.g. IEC 61508 states that "if at any phase of the software safety lifecycle, a modification is required pertaining to an earlier lifecycle phase, then an impact analysis shall determine (1) which software modules are impacted, and (2) which earlier safety lifecycle activities shall be repeated."

CIA is often a difficult task in practice due to the size and complexity of safety-critical systems [2, 7]. Inadequate CIA has further been among the causes of accidents and near-accidents in the past [10]. Industry can clearly benefit from new CIA technology and knowledge to more cost-effectively perform this safety assurance activity,

© Springer International Publishing Switzerland 2016
A. Skavhaug et al. (Eds.): SAFECOMP 2016 Workshops, LNCS 9923, pp. 346–358, 2016.
DOI: 10.1007/978-3-319-45480-1_28

enabling better risk avoidance and mitigation. Such technology and knowledge must be linked to current practices and targeted at meeting industry needs and expectations.

Despite the importance of CIA for safety-critical systems, the current knowledge about the state of the practice is limited. Our literature review identified no publications that studied the CIA activity in depth. The available knowledge is based on studies that (1) dealt with non-safety-critical systems, (2) analyzed data from past projects, (3) did not focus on CIA, or (4) surveyed practices for safety-critical systems from a general perspective. For example, Rovegård *et al.* [14] interviewed software practitioners to analyze CIA issue importance, whereas Borg *et al.* [3] studied past issue reports of an industrial control system. Some insights have been provided in studies on e.g. the alignment of requirements with verification and validation [1] and on traceability [13]. Regarding the surveys, Nair *et al.* [12] studied safety evidence management practices, including certain aspects related to change management, and de la Vara *et al.* [7] conducted a survey on safety evidence CIA to explore the circumstances under which it is performed, the tool support used, and the challenges faced.

We have conducted an industrial case study on CIA for safety-critical systems in practice, particularly exploring engineers' views on the work involved. The context is a distributed development organization offering industrial control systems to a global market. We interviewed 14 engineers in two units of analyses, constituted of two teams located in Sweden and India, respectively. This paper reports a preliminary analysis covering a subset of the interview guide.

Our long term goal is to support architectural decision making when evolving cyber-physical systems, an endeavor in which the CIA is fundamental. As a step in this direction, we explore three research questions: (RQ1) How extensive is the CIA work task?, (RQ2) What are the engineers' attitudes toward CIA?, and (RQ3) How could CIA be supported? By better understanding CIA in a particular case, we can take steps toward understanding how previous knowledge could be stored to support decision making in software evolution, in line with our previous work on traceability reuse [3] and knowledge repositories [6].

The rest of the paper is structured as follows: Sect. 2 presents the case, and Sect. 3 describes the research methodology. We report our results and discuss their implications in Sect. 4 and Sect. 5 concludes the paper and outlines future work.

2 Case Description

The case company develops safety-critical industrial control systems. The system under study has evolved since the 1980s and needs to fulfill the IEC 61511 standard via Safety Integrity Level 2 certification, according to the IEC 61508 standard. The developed software must be of high quality and therefore all changes to source code need to be analyzed prior to implementation. Moreover, detailed system documentation is created and mapped to the vertical abstraction layers in the V-model. The projects follow a rigid development process with hundreds of collaborating engineers distributed globally. The code base is over one million lines, dominated by C/C++ and some newer extensions in C# or VB.

Prioritized features originating from various customers (and sometimes pre-ordered feature requests) are incrementally added and extensively tested. When developing new features and also when fixing issues to previously delivered features, several changes are made to the source code. When the development is over, the development organization needs to present a safety case for an external assessor, illustrating that the system is acceptably safe for a given application in a given operating environment. The set of CIA analyses is a crucial component of the safety case. Therefore, the safety engineers at the case company have developed a semi-structured CIA report template, cf. Table 1, to support the safety case in relation to the IEC 61508 safety certification. The developers use this template to document their CIA before committing source code changes.

Table 1. CIA template used in the case company, adapted from Klevin [8].

(Q1) Is the reported problem safety critical?
(Q2) In which versions/revisions does this problem exist?
(Q3) How are general system functions and properties affected by the change?
(Q4) List modified code files/modules and their SIL classifications.
(Q5) Which library items are affected by the change? (e.g., library types, firmware)
(Q6) Which documents need to be modified? (e.g., reqts. specs, architecture)
(Q7) Which test cases need to be executed? (e.g., design/functional/sequence tests)
(Q8) Which user documents, including online help, need to be modified?
(Q9) How long will it take to correct the problem, and verify the correction?
(Q10) What is the root cause of this problem?
(Q11) How could this problem have been avoided?
(Q12) Which requirements and functions need to be retested by test organization?

Currently there is limited tool support available for CIA in the organization. The CIA process is tightly connected with the issue management process, as all changes to formal development artifacts require an issue report in the issue repository. All completed CIA reports are stored in the issue repository as attachments to issue reports. Developers typically access the issue repository using a simple web interface.

3   Research Methodology

We conducted a multiple unit industrial case study since the studied phenomenon could not be separated from its context [15]. The case under study is the CIA activity in the development organization described in Sect. 2. Two development teams constitute the units of analysis, referred to as Unit Sweden and Unit India, respectively. Figure 1 shows an overview of the study.

Four researchers iteratively (1) *designed* the case study and documented it in a case study protocol. All the steps in the design were reviewed by senior researchers other than the researchers. We constructed an interview guide (available online[1]) for semi-structured interviews to be able to ask both close and open-ended questions. We asked open questions in the beginning and end of the interviews, in line with the time glass

---

[1] http://serg.cs.lth.se/fileadmin/serg/ImpRec_EvalStudy/ImpRec_InterviewGuides.pdf.

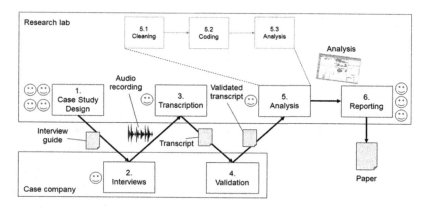

Fig. 1. Overview of the research process. Smileys depict the number of researchers involved in the various steps.

interview model [15]. This paper reports only on an analysis of a subset of the questions asked. Table 2 maps the RQs to specific parts of the interview guide.

Table 2. Breakdown from RQs to specific parts of the interview guide.

RQ	ID	Part of the interview guide1
RQ1. How extensive effort do engineers spend on CIA?	Pre2-b	Do you conduct CIAs daily/weekly/monthly?
	Pre2-c	How much time do you spend on a CIA?
	Pre2-d	What are the greatest CIA challenges?
RQ2. What are the engineers' attitudes toward CIA?	Pre2-a	What is your general opinion about the CIA work task?
RQ3. How could CIA be supported?	Pre4	What kind of support would you like to have access to when conducting CIAs?
	Pre3	We have collected data from your CIA history. Could you please comment on the metrics? - Pre3-b: Do the numbers reflect how long it takes to conduct a CIA? [TIME] - Pre3-c: Some CIAs have been modified. Does this mean they were harder? [MODS]

The data collection consisted of (2) *interviews* in Swedish or English. For confidentiality reasons, a single researcher conducted all interviews. The same researcher (3) *transcribed* all interviews word by word and sent them back to the interviewees for (4) *validation*. We interviewed 14 engineers of whom 10 are developers that write source code and its documentation. More specifically, we interviewed one R&D manager, one safety engineer, three senior developers (incl. the team leader), and one junior developer in Unit Sweden, and one product manager, one technical manager, four senior developers (incl. the team leader), and two junior developers in Unit India.

As a preliminary (5) *analysis* step, the transcripts were copied into a spreadsheet divided according to the interview guide. Longer answers were divided into smaller chunks. The spreadsheet was then (5.1) *cleaned* to remove obsolete and unimportant pieces of spoken language.

The iterative (5.2) *coding* process started by highlighting key statements, to establish a quick overview of the data and support subsequent data navigation. We then applied the following coding schemes: Pre2-a followed a two dimensional axial coding [16] with "connotation to CIA" vs. "importance of CIA" coded into the interval [−2, 2] to express positive/negative connotation and importance, respectively; Pre2-b used predefined closed codes: daily, weekly, bi-weekly, monthly, and rarely; Pre2-c was coded onto a timeline, expressing either point estimates or (min.-avg.-max.) intervals; Pre2-d employed open coding that evolved into 12 codes: test cases, documents, information overload, prolonged time, motivation, confidence, requirements, time estimation, avoidance, root cause, system version, and conformance; Pre3 used the interval [−2, 2] to signal whether the proposed metrics were indicative of time needed, and difficulty to conduct, a CIA; Pre4 used open coding that developed into: tool, training, template, search, traceability, and reviews. The coded interviews were then (5.3) *analyzed* to detect patterns and draw conclusions based on the qualitative data.

Finally, we (6) *report* our results in this publication. To preserve the confidentiality of the interviewees, we do not provide full traceability from the answers. We use the labels engineer/developer and junior/senior when needing to be more specific.

4   Results and Discussion

4.1   RQ1: Extensiveness of the Change Impact Analysis Task

To understand how extensive the engineers consider the CIA work task to be, we investigate: (1) how frequently engineers perform CIA, (2) how much time is needed to complete a CIA, and (3) what engineers consider as the major CIA challenges.

Change Impact Analysis Frequency. All the interviewees experienced with CIA stressed that the frequency of conducting CIA varies much, from daily to monthly CIAs, depending on the development phases. Four developers reported that they sometimes conduct CIA on a daily basis, and four other developers estimated that they do it weekly during the most intensive periods. Four other interviewees explained that their CIA intensity goes down to monthly during certain periods, while three interviewees answered bi-weekly CIAs at slow times. Five interviewees shared only estimates of their average CIA intensities: four reported weekly and one stated daily. A senior engineer in Unit Sweden estimated that a typical developer conducts 20 CIAs related to bug corrections per year. A senior engineer in Unit India stated a higher estimate: "in the thick of a project, a developer will do [a CIA] almost every day". We conclude that the engineers estimate the average intensity to be one CIA per week, considering variations due to cyclic development phases and parallel projects.

The main reason for the variation is the stage-gate development process employed by the company; at the initial stages of a project, when the bulk of the new development is conducted, there is considerable source code churn, and changes are not managed on the level of individual issues. A senior engineer explained "we package new development as generic items in our issue tracking system, and then we conduct one comprehensive CIA". Once a project reaches the "code complete" milestone and the formal verification phase is initiated, the goal is to stabilize the quality of the system, and all changes after this stage are considered bug corrections. The change management process then increases its granularity to individual bug resolutions.

Change Impact Analysis Effort. We asked the interviewees how much time they invested in a CIA, by providing the minimum, average, and maximum time needed. For the four non-developer interviewees, we instead asked them to approximate the time developers spend on CIAs. Four interviewees reported only an average CIA effort, i.e., a point estimate. Figure 2 presents an overview of the collected data. Similarly to the frequency results, the time required to conduct an individual CIA varies substantially. A senior developer stressed that the effort needed depends on the complexity of the involved component, and another senior developer expressed that it also depends on the structure of the corresponding documentation.

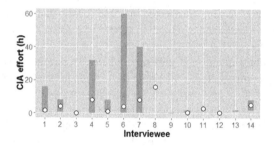

Fig. 2. Interviewees' estimates of CIA effort. Bars depict minimum and maximum effort, circles show the average. Interviewees 5–14 are developers.

Three interviewees estimated that the average CIA requires 1–2 h, four interviewees answered 4–6 h, and three interviewees reported 1–2 days. On the contrary, two interviewees answered that they complete the average CIA in less than an hour, more specifically 30–40 min and 5 min, respectively. A senior engineer shared his rule of thumb regarding issue management and CIA: "a normal issue, or slightly more challenging than normal, takes in total roughly a man week to resolve. I estimate the CIA to require 10 % of that time, 4 h. /.../ Then there are much faster issues that are resolved in a man day. 10 % of that means about 1 h for the CIA".

Eight of the interviewees claimed that the minimum time required to complete a CIA is 30 min or less, of which two answered 5 min or less. Two senior developers in India reported that quick CIAs still require an hour or two, motivated by "there are 13 questions to correctly answer" and "if you fill it in honestly, without copy-paste". Regarding the maximum time, four interviewees claimed 1–2 days, two answered a week, and a junior developer instead expressed "several months of calendar time". Two senior developers in India shared contrasting views, claiming that the most time-consuming CIAs still could be finished in 15–20 min.

We noted three main explanations for the reported variation. First, it is *hard to detach the CIA from the general issue resolution, thus the interviewees interpreted the questions differently*. The exploratory work involved in reproducing and understanding an issue is often intertwined with the CIA. To understand an issue well enough, developers must sometimes set up a specific test environment, stepping through source code, etc. As a senior developer put it: "there is considerable exploratory work, and it would require almost as much time without the formal CIA". Second, the *complexity among the parts of the system is not constant*. The same interviewee considers issues related to the embedded environment to be the most complex, and maintenance issues on isolated components to be simple. Quick CIAs occur when an issue needs to be corrected in several system versions, and parts of the CIAs can be reused. Third, *experienced developers conduct CIAs faster than novices*. Three junior developers reported relatively high estimates, and two senior engineers stressed the importance of experience and system understanding for successful CIAs.

Major CIA Challenges. We received 25 challenges from 14 interviewees that cover both general and specific aspects, presented in Table 1. Note that Table 1 comprises also questions that deal with issue management in general, e.g. Q9–Q11, as reflected by some interviewees' answers.

The most frequently mentioned general challenge was related to *motivation*, i.e., understanding why comprehensive CIAs are part of the process and recognizing their value. The difficulty to appreciate the CIA activity was primarily expressed in the Swedish unit of analysis, by both seniors and juniors alike; seniors struggling more with motivating others, whereas juniors talked about motivating themselves. A senior engineer explained: "my main challenge is to explain and motivate why we do CIA, because if you know why you have to do it, you accept it. But we must continuously remind ourselves why we do it." and "if we get the developer to see that the CIA is very good, it helps me in my work /.../ That's what we´re aiming for".

The second most commonly mentioned general CIA challenge is related to *information overload*. The three most senior engineers in the study, explained that obtaining a system understanding is hard due to the complexity. Apart from the source code, there are numerous documents describing the system. The sheer number of software artifacts contests the system overview, and makes traceability information highly complex. A senior engineer stated: "finding the right information has historically been the major challenge /.../ In principle you had to hunt down key people and ask for documents and dependencies, and you didn't necessarily get the answer".

Three additional general CIA challenges were mentioned. First, sometimes developers need to *update previous CIAs that were conducted a long time ago* (half a year before according to a junior developer). Returning to old issues is difficult and requires considerable time and effort. Second, one interviewee said that his major challenge was to *trust his own CIAs*, i.e., establishing confidence in the answers to the questions in Table 1. As he explained it: "I'm not sure whether my answers are true or not, I cannot evaluate it. I am the judge." Finally, one senior interviewee expressed that the major challenge was that the *developers do not follow the CIA guidelines*.

Interviewees reported three CIA challenges specific to the questions in Table 1, all of them reported by two or three interviewees: (1) *selecting which test cases should be executed* to verify the changes (Q7), (2) *understanding which requirements are affected* by a change (related to Q6 and Q12), and (3) *reporting which documents need to be updated* to reflect the change (Q6). A senior developer explained that "the question about test cases is supposed to cover both directly and indirectly affected test cases, and the indirect ones are quite difficult." Regarding the requirements, another senior developer said: "Requirements traceability is difficult. We do not have requirements that cover all aspects, and it is hard for developers to stay on top of all requirements. [As developers] we don't work continuously with the requirements."

Concerning the challenges that deal with issue management in general, the interviewees in Unit India reported four major challenges. Three interviewees explained that *finding the root cause of an issue* (Q10) is a major challenge. Two interviewees pointed out suggesting *how the issue could have been avoided* (Q11) as particularly difficult, and two others highlighted determining *which system versions are affected by the issue* (Q2). Finally, a senior developer in Unit India considered *estimating the resolution time* (Q9) as the major challenge. Our interviews suggest that developers answer the three questions Q9–Q11 with different levels of ambition, and two interviewees from Unit India indicated that they invest considerable effort answering these questions. Concerning determining affected system versions, a senior developer clarified: "sometimes you study the source code, sometimes you have to run tests in our lab [on multiple versions] /.../ This is not hard, but time-consuming."

Based on our interviews, it appears that determining how a change impacts the product source code is less of a challenge than determining impact on non-code artifacts, e.g., requirements, specifications, and test cases. Considerable research effort has been directed at CIA on the source code level [11], but neither junior nor senior engineers discussed source code in relation to the major challenges involved in CIA. Our results instead support conclusions from Lehnert [9] and de la Vara *et al.* [7], i.e., there is a need for CIA research that considers different artifact types.

4.2   RQ2: Connotations of Change Impact Analysis

We explored the engineers' connotation to "change impact analysis", i.e., the emotional association carried by CIA, in addition to the explicit or literal meaning (the denotation). Furthermore, we map the connotation to the impression of how important CIA is to the individual interviewee, as presented in Fig. 3.

The interviewees' attitudes toward CIA represent all quadrants in Fig. 3. No interviewees expressed very strong positive or negative connotations to "change impact analysis". Most answers are balanced and we note that a majority of the engineers consider their CIAs important. Several interviewees shared positive associations, e.g., "a healthy sign" and "shows that we do complex software engineering". Also, several interviewees had a neutral connotation: "no values on a personal level" and "just part of the job". On the other hand, two interviewees expressed negative connotations: "a

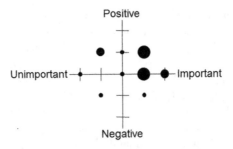

Fig. 3. Interviewees' attitudes toward CIA. The y-axis shows the general connotation of CIA, whereas the x-axis depicts how important interviewees consider the CIA.

too heavy construct in our organization", "unfortunately very rigid activity", and "could be done in a better way".

Considering the interviewees' perceived importance of the CIA activity to their work, all levels are covered. Responses range from "for some issues it is just worthless stuff, done for the process" to "professionally, it is very fundamental" and "side effects are extremely important in our complex product". We identified no indications of attitude differences between the two units of analyses. Regarding the level of seniority, there is a slight tendency of senior engineers considering CIA to be more important than juniors. This is no surprise, as the seniors have seen more cases of source code changes causing side effects, especially from earlier development work when the CIA was less formal, as explained by one senior engineer "we have seen many cases when fixes introduced bugs". On the other hand, lack of experience can also induce a positive attitude, as expressed by one junior developer in Unit India: "This is my first company. Whatever I see, I feel is good".

4.3   RQ3: Supporting Change Impact Analysis

Envisioned Change Impact Analysis Support. As one might expect when asking software engineers for solutions to support CIA, *the most frequent answer was tool support*. Three interviewees suggested increasing the level of automation in CIA by introducing some kind of tool. Interestingly, all these interviewees are seniors, and all discuss approaches to identify impact beyond the source code level. A possible explanation is that senior engineers are well-aware of the large efforts on establishing traceability in the organization, and that they consider the investment to be underutilized. One interviewee explained how a tool could iteratively follow traces through the system, from an input source code file or module, to a design description and its corresponding design tests, then continue up the abstraction layers to functional specifications and all the way up to the requirements. This could allow test identification directly from requirements, as a tool-oriented solution that would close the often challenging gap between requirements and test cases [1]. Another suggestion given by a recently employed senior developer was that "it is strange to attach a CIA report as a free-text string in a third party tool. In my previous company, this would have been done in an internally developed tool to better control the input [...] It would have been much easier to manage and interpret the data if the collection was more controlled." Indeed other companies use internal tools for CIA of safety-critical systems [7].

Two senior interviewees proposed *changes to the CIA template* in Table 1. A senior engineer considered security to be of critical importance to the future of the organization, and requested *adding explicit security questions* to the template. The other interviewee would like to see the question about *root cause analysis to be more elaborate* (Q10). The same interviewee also advocated *using more than one version of the CIA template, adapting the questions to the issue at hand*, to address the impression of having a too rigid CIA process. Another suggestion mentioned by two interviewees, a junior and a senior engineer, is to *increase the training of new employees on the specifics of CIA in the case company*, motivated by: "a new guy needs to be thoroughly trained on these questions /.../ I see newcomers just filling in things for the sake of moving the issue through the process".

Individual interviewees proposed additional improvement suggestions. First, *the search functionality in the issue tracking system should be improved*. Although no interviewee reported the current issue tracking system to be a major challenge to CIA, several mentioned that the tool was old and not user friendly. Another considerable limitation is a lack of full-test searchers in the issue tracker. Our previous work explored the potential of introducing state-of-the-art search technology to index full-text descriptions of issue reports [5]. Second, one senior engineer considered the source code and the documents to be two discrete information spaces with few connections. Despite all efforts to maintain traceability at the company, the interviewee wanted to *improve bidirectional connections between documents and source code*. Third, one junior developer thought that the CIAs "are not taken in a serious way", and proposed *introducing CIA reviews* before submitting them, as before committing code.

Measuring Change Impact Analysis Support. Prior to the interviews, we explored the CIA history stored in the issue tracking system, and constructed two measurements: TIME and MODS. We calculated these measurements for the relevant interviewees and presented the results during the interviews.

The first proposed measure, TIME, is the *time between a developer is assigned an issue and the first CIA report is submitted*. TIME thus targets CIA effort, but no interviewee considered the measure to be correlated with the time it takes to actually conduct the CIA. Six interviewees directly rebutted the measure, and two did not know how to interpret it. The most skeptical views explained: "it's definitely a question of priorities", "I work on several parallel products, and that measure can be anything", and "you have to measure when I start making related changes". We conclude that *TIME is a too confounded measure* to be used for evaluating solutions that aim at decreasing the time needed for CIAs.

The second proposed measure, MODS, is the *number of modifications on a CIA report after its first submission*. We suggested using this measure as a proxy for the difficulty of completing a particular CIA, thus related to CIA accuracy. The opinion about the validity of MODS differed. Three interviewees were positive or slightly positive to the measure, one of them claimed: "more modification clearly means it was a hard CIA. It means you couldn't immediately capture everything". On the other hand, two interviewees invalidated the measure entirely by showing that numerous modifications only deal with typos and copy-paste errors. One of them said: "I use Notepad without any spelling correction. /.../ When I paste it in the issue tracking system and submit, I get to see everything on a big screen and note the mistakes". Another interviewee instead writes the CIA directly in the issue trackers input field, but explained: "one of the problems with the tool is that it doesn't even stay open in five minutes, and it doesn't even save your data [before closing]. This is such a worst tool." When developers rush submitting CIA reports before the tool closes due to inactivity, the chances of introducing typos increases. We conclude that *MODS is not a reliable measure* for evaluating whether a solution leads to more accurate CIAs.

In conclusion, TIME appears to not at all be correlated with the time needed to conduct CIA. On the other hand, MODS received some supporters, but others show it is confounded by trivial changes to such an extent that it cannot be trusted. While both measures are easy to collect from most systems logging time stamps and revision history, they both need improvements. TIME should originate from actual changes related to an issue rather than when the issue is assigned, and MODS could possibly be filtered to remove insignificant changes such as spelling corrections.

5 Conclusion and Future Work

We report on an industrial case study on engineers' perspectives on Change Impact Analysis (CIA). We interviewed 14 engineers in two units of analysis in a global safety-critical software engineering context. Both the frequency of CIAs and the effort required to complete a CIA vary considerably, depending on the current phase of the development project as well as the complexity of the specific change. As a yearly average, our results suggest that developers in the case company spend roughly 50–100 h on CIA, corresponding to one CIA per week with 1–2 h effort each. A senior engineer also shared his rule of thumb: "CIA takes roughly 10 % of the time to resolve a normal issue". We reported several major CIA challenges including communicating to developers that CIAs are necessary and beneficial, and to navigate the large document space accompanying the source code, especially the requirements. We present empirical evidence confirming that CIA is an important but costly activity in safety-critical software development, worthwhile to address in future work.

We explored engineers' attitudes by mapping their connotation of CIA versus the perceived importance of their CIAs. All combinations were identified in our study, as well as a trend that CIAs are considered increasingly important with increasing seniority. Our interviewees shared eight CIA improvement suggestions, including additional tool support, improved traceability, newcomer training, and CIA reviews. Quantitatively measuring the value of CIA support appears difficult however, as CIA is rarely conducted as an isolated activity, but rather is deeply intertwined with issue management and development in general. We found that simple analysis of CIA revisions is too confounded to evaluate improvement suggestions, thus future work is needed to develop reliable quantitative measures.

Our preliminary study is subject to a number of limitations. Due to a non-disclosure agreement, both the interviews and the analysis were done by only the first author (cf. Fig. 1). In the next step of this study, we will address the single-perspective bias by adding another researcher in a validation step, e.g., to evaluate the coding schemes. Moreover, we plan to further increase the validity of our conclusions by data triangulation, i.e., by studying real CIAs stored in the issue tracker.

When making architectural decisions on how to evolve a software system, understanding the impact of competing alternatives is important, i.e., the CIAs are valuable input to the decision maker. In prior work, we have stored trace links from previous CIAs in semantic networks to help future developers by recommending potential impact [3, 4]. Now we aim to raise the level of abstraction to study impact of architectural decisions, i.e., to provide less granular recommendations for evolving software systems. As part of our ongoing work, we have proposed storing experiences from previous decisions in a knowledge repository [6]. As our current case study indicates that engineers put numerous hours into CIAs, and typically value their content, we argue that CIAs should also be incorporated in the knowledge repository.

Acknowledgement. The work is partially supported by a research grant for the ORION project (ref. number 20140218) from The Knowledge Foundation in Sweden.

References

1. Bjarnason, E., et al.: Challenges and practices in aligning requirements with verification and validation: a case study of six companies. Empir. Softw. Eng. **19**(6), 1809–1855 (2014)
2. Bohner, S., Arnold, R.: Software Change Impact Analysis. IEEE Press, Washington (1996)
3. Borg, M., Gotel, O., Wnuk, K.: Enabling traceability reuse for impact analyses: a feasibility study in a safety context. In: Proceedings of 7th International Workshop on Traceability in Emerging Forms of Software Engineering, pp. 72–79 (2013)
4. Borg, M., Runeson, P.: Changes, evolution, and bugs - recommendation systems for issue management. In: Robillard, M.P., et al. (eds.) Recommendation Systems in Software Engineering, pp. 477–509. Springer, Berlin (2014)
5. Borg, M., et al.: A replicated study on duplicate detection: using apache lucene to search among android defects. In: Proceedings of 8th International Symposium on Empirical Software Engineering and Measurement (2014)
6. Cicchetti, A., et al.: Towards software assets origin selection supported by a knowledge repository. In: Proceedings of 1st International Workshop on Decision Making in Software Architecture (2016)
7. de la Vara, JL., et al.: An industrial survey of safety evidence change impact analysis practice. Trans. Softw. Eng. (2016, to appear)
8. Klevin, A.: People, process and tools: a study of impact analysis in a change process. Master thesis, Lund University (2012). http://sam.cs.lth.se/ExjobGetFile?id=434
9. Lehnert, S.: A review of software change impact analysis. Technical report, Ilmenau University of Technology (2011)
10. Leveson, N.: Engineering a Safer World. The MIT Press, Cambridge (2011)
11. Li, B., et al.: A survey of code-based change impact analysis techniques. Softw. Test. Verif. Reliab. **23**(8), 613–646 (2013)

12. Nair, S., et al.: Evidence management for compliance of critical systems with safety standards: a survey on the state of practice. Inf. Softw. Technol. **60**, 1–15 (2015)
13. Regan, G., et al.: Investigation of traceability within a medical device organization. In: Proceedings of 13th International Conference on Process Improvement and Capability Determination, pp. 211–222 (2013)
14. Rovegård, P., Angelis, L., Wohlin, C.: An empirical study on views of importance of change impact analysis issues. IEEE Trans. Softw. Eng. **34**(4), 516–530 (2008)
15. Runeson, P., et al.: Case Study Research in Software Engineering. Wiley, New York (2012)
16. Strauss, A., Corbin, J.: Basics of Qualitative Research Techniques and Procedures for Developing Grounded Theory, 2nd edn. Sage Publications, Thousand Oaks (1998)

Seamless Integrated Simulation in Design and Verification Flow for Safety-Critical Systems

Ralph Weissnegger[1,2]($\boxtimes$), Markus Schuß[1], Christian Kreiner[1],
Markus Pistauer[2], Kay Römer[1], and Christian Steger[1]

[1] Institute for Technical Informatics, Graz University of Technology (TU Graz),
Graz, Austria
{ralph.weissnegger,markus.schuss,christian.kreiner,
roemer,steger}@tugraz.at
[2] CISC Semiconductor GmbH, Klagenfurt, Austria
markus.pistauer@cisc.at

Abstract. In the automotive domain, safety plays an ever increasing role in the development of future vehicles. Since the automotive market is heading towards fully automated driving cars, the amount of new assistance features for ensuring safe and reliable operations is rising. Today, requirements, design and verification must follow the stringent specifications from standards such as ISO26262 for functional safety. Thus, simulation in early design phases is key to develop safe and reliable systems and to reduce costs and time-to-market. UML as a model-based approach, helps to overcome the complexity issues of safety-critical systems and improves the communication between different stakeholders (e.g. hardware, software, safety, security). In this paper, we present a novel methodology to automatically generate testbenches for simulation based verification starting from a first safety analysis and derived safety requirements. Through early simulation of UML/MARTE models with constraint random stimuli and parameters we are able to derive further requirements for safety-critical system development. Furthermore, our approach is compliant with the requirements, design and verification flow of ISO26262. We will show the benefits by applying our methodology to an industrial use case of a battery management system.

Keywords: ISO26262 · Safety · Automotive · Process · UML · MARTE · Verification · Simulation · Model-based

1 Introduction

In the world of today, the increasing number of new assistance features for ensuring safe and reliable operation in modern vehicles, also have the implication of increasingly complex systems. The development and verification effort of these highly complex systems in an ever increasing and more elaborate task, since the amount of electric/electronic (e/e) components is steadily growing. In safety terms, these systems must fulfill standards such as ISO26262 [4] (functional safety standard for

© Springer International Publishing Switzerland 2016
A. Skavhaug et al. (Eds.): SAFECOMP 2016 Workshops, LNCS 9923, pp. 359–370, 2016.
DOI: 10.1007/978-3-319-45480-1_29

road vehicles). Therefore, OEMs and their suppliers are required to develop and test their systems according to certain levels, alias ASIL levels.

In the effort to cope with the high complexity in the design of safety-critical systems, a model-based approach helps to unite stakeholders from different domains. Furthermore it supports non-safety specialists in understanding the problems of the design of safety-critical systems. In addition to this, provides great help in coping with the vast range of requirements that must currently be met. MARTE was introduced as an extension of UML2 to overcome the high complexity in the design of real-time and embedded systems. MARTE provides capabilities to model hardware and software, as also timing, resource and performance behavior. It is used by many semiconductor vendors and suppliers and is the driving system-design language in the European Catrene project entitled OpenES [3].

Simulation plays an ever increasing and important role in the verification of the modern car because of its advantages in easily varying the virtual environment and also representing the car in different variations, and this not least from an economic perspective. These tests can be monitored and reproduced every time. Another advantage of simulation is not only can it be run day and night, but also massively in parallel.

In this work, we present a novel methodology to simulate and verify MARTE designs supported through our Eclipse framework called SHARC [1] (Simulation and verification of HierARChical embedded microelectronic systems). With the help of our library, we link fast executable digital, analog mixed signal and mechanical simulation-models with MARTE design models. These simulation-models are implemented in open-source languages such as SystemC (-TLM) and SystemC-AMS. Through these reusable components we achieve an early behavior simulation of the whole system. The advantage of our approach is that design models are tightly and seamlessly integrated into the design flow of ISO26262. From this early system level simulation we are able to obtain further requirements for the design of hardware and software for real-time applications (timing, power, thermal). With our proposed solution there is no need to switch between several design or verification tools. Both state-of-the-art analytical methods and simulation-based verification can be handled by using MARTE, SysML and our approach. Tests derived from safety requirements can be reused throughout the entire development cycle until final system integration and validation. We use constraint random verification, as defined in the UVM standard, to cover all possible parameters and various variants of a vehicle. Any shortcomings in the design can thus be detected much earlier in the development process to reduce costs and time-to-market.

2   Related Work

Popular approaches [5,8,10] have shown that analysis and verification of UML models with methods methods such as failure mode and effect analysis (FMEA), fault tree analysis (FTA), design space exploration (DSE), design walk through, hardware architectural metrics evaluation or even code-generation are very efficient for testing safety-critical systems. The drawback of UML, in terms of code-generation and simulation to verify the system-behavior is that this is done at a very late stage or even at the end of the design process when all details are well known. Later changes in design are costly, they result in inconsistent models and furthermore reverse engineering is an error prone and cumbersome task. The majority of components in new projects are reused and simply extended by the addition of new features to reduce costs and time-to market. The reuse of complete safety concepts, well-trusted designs and mechanisms is thus growing more important as a means to reduce the effort in developing complex systems. This situation prompts the urgent demand for new techniques to simulate the behavior in early development phases by reusing verified system components.

In [9] the authors presented three different analysis techniques for architectural models described in EAST-ADL, to guarantee the quality in the context of ISO26262. One of the proposed techniques is the simulation of EAST-ADL functions in Simulink. The behavior of each function was linked to FMU or Simulink models to facilitate the simulation. The authors also described mapping rules for the EAST-ADL to Simulink transformation (one-to-one mapping). The results of the simulation have been traced back to the requirements. This approach was applied to an industrial use case of a brake-by-wire system on design level. In contrast to our approach, however, they use proprietary simulation engines with high license costs and external tools which are not integrated into the design and development flow.

The authors of [11] demonstrated how to use MARTE for hardware design and simulation. They introduced a step-by-step methodology for hardware modeling with Hardware Resource Models (HRM) stereotypes. The platform models are refined until the final platform class is reached. In a later step, these models are used to generate code with the help of a Java plugin. A tool under the name Simics was used to facilitate the simulation. Instead of using the whole MARTE spectrum for simulation, this approach only uses HRM models for code generation of very detailed platforms instead of system level design.

In [6] the authors presented a simulation-based methodology for requirements verification of SoC designs. This automatically generated a white-box and black-box verification platform from requirements specified in textual specification format. During a simulation-based verification these very fication platforms are simulated together with the SoC design to verify whether or not they fulfill the given requirements. Lexical, syntax and semantic analysis were used to parse textural requirements into a semi-formal format. This approach would benefit from a standardized format such as SysML to define the requirements in tight interaction with the system design. Furthermore, this approach cannot be adapted to an industrial use case.

3   Methodology

Since the design and development of safety-critical systems is a cumbersome and costly task, it needs novel methods to test evaluate the design both in the early phases and also during and throughout the entire development process. The reusability of well-tested designs, mechanisms or even complete safety concepts is an issue that is currently becoming ever more prominent. Against this background we thus propose simulation-based verification of UML/MARTE design models on the preliminary architectural assumption (preAA) level, depicted in Fig. 1. For this simulation we are using our reusable components from our System Component Library (SCL). This library includes all major components for a high level simulation of systems from different domains e.g. automotive, mobile computing, health care or multimedia. It also includes components in different versions and on different abstraction levels. These models serve on the one hand as the starting-point for future developments and furthermore as the verified and golden reference for integration aspects. The properties of the models are all taken from the standard definition for UML/MARTE system, hardware and software models. In order to bring the components of the SCL to life, they are linked to executable models in SystemC(-TLM) or SystemC-AMS. More information on this methodology is given in [12,13]. Based on the functional SRs from the functional safety concept, defined as SysML models, and the information from the preAA we are able to obtain further requirements for the technical safety concept, described in Sect. 3.1. By also taking non-functional properties (timing, power, thermal) into account, we are able to refine the functional SR and to define the technical SR. Furthermore we are able to obtain inputs for our final system design before the step of costly implementation of faulty design is taken.

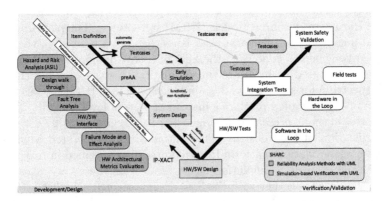

Fig. 1. Seamless integration of simulation-based verification in the ISO26262 design flow

Testbenches in the Universal Verification Methodology (UVM), to test the design on preAA level through simulation are automatically generated from the information and constraints of the functional SR defined in SysML. Furthermore constraint random verification helps to cover all possible parameters and variants of the system, but also to vary environmental conditions, to find corner cases.

These testbenches can be used throughout the whole development cycle through to the final system integration and validation.

3.1   UVM Testbench Generation from SysML Requirements

We use a simple semi-formal language to define our requirements as approaches such as [6] have shown that informal languages can be too ambiguous for our application. The ISO26262 also promotes the view that informal languages should only be used for applications with low ASIL levels such as A and B and highly recommends the use of semi-formal requirements specifications for higher safety goals such as C and D. We thus we decided to use the benefits of the UML profile SysML for the definition of the requirements. As SysML for requirements lacks in proper definition for safety, we defined an extension as depicted in Fig. 2. Besides standard attributes id and text, following attributes such as type (functional SR, technical SR, hardware SR, software SR), status (proposed, assumed, accepted, reviewed), ASIL level, and pass/fail have been added to the definition. Attributes such as id, text, status and ASIL level are also recommended by the ISO26262 standard. Each safety goal in our approach is therefore clearly defined by our extension for safety requirements. As mentioned in the previous chapter, the top level safety requirements (Safety Goals) are derived from the hazard and risk analysis. These safety goals lead to the definition of the functional safety concept. Here the functional SR are derived from the safety goals in conjunction with the preAA. At least one functional SR shall be specified for each safety goal, but also one functional SR can also be valid for several safety goals. Each functional SR is described by the defined attributes in our extension for safety requirements. Furthermore each functional SR in our approach has several defined constraints for functional and non-functional properties. These constraints are defined in the MARTE value specification language (VSL) and specify the boundaries for a fail-safe operation of the system. These constraint precisely captures the original requirement and opening up, through computer readable formalism, the possibility of subsequent computer-aided analysis of the characteristics of this design. The MARTE *nfpConstraint* are defined by arithmetic; logical or time expressions formed by combining oper-

Fig. 2. An extension to the SysML profile to cope with safety requirements and to achieve traceability

ators such as ('$<$','$\leq$','$=$','$\neq$','$\geq$','$>$') but also 'and', 'or' and 'xor'. The syntax used for our constraints follows the following patterns:

`Requirement = Signal/Pin/Port <,≤,=,≠,≥,> Value/Signal`

Multiple constraints can be connected via simple Boolean statements such as:

`NOT ( temp > 100°C AND current < 10A )`

"The current shall not exceed 10A if the battery temperature is above 100°C"

The technical SR can be derived after the systematic specification of the functional SR and design of the preAA with the help of our SCL. The ISO26262 specifies the technical safety requirements as following [4]:

"The technical SR shall be specified in accordance with the functional safety concept, the preliminary architectural assumptions of the item and the following system properties: the external interfaces, such as communication and user interface; the constraints, e.g. environmental conditions or functional constraints; and the system configuration requirements. The ability to reconfigure a system for alternative applications is a strategy to reuse existing systems."

"Safety Mechanisms: The technical safety requirements shall specify the response of the system or elements to stimuli that affect the achievement of safety goals. This includes failures and relevant combinations of stimuli in combination with each relevant operating mode and defined system state."

"The system design shall be verified for compliance and completeness with regard to the technical safety concept using the verification methods e.g. Simulation for ASIL level higher than B."

In order to support the specification of the technical SR and furthermore enable the verification in compliance with the technical safety concept, we defined a novel methodology to derive further requirements and inputs from the functional SR in coherence with the early system design (preAA). Using the syntax for safety requirements we are able to generate UVM verification components and whole testbenches from the definition of the functional SR and their constraints. For each constraint of the functional SR, a new UVM validator is added on the ports or one end of the signal. A validator consists of a configurable comparator with the pin/port/signal attached to one input and a reference signal or constant value attached to the second input. The outputs of the comparator can be either 1 (true) or 0 (zero) and are connected via arithmetic or algebraic function blocks to create the boolean operations. In addition we use non safety requirements in the SysML specification to provide stimuli blocks for relevant operating modes and driving maneuvers. Depending on the non safety requirements and constraints and if the pin/port/signal is an unused input of a block the testbench generator creates a stimuli block and attaches it. This block generates either values that are within the specifications in order to validate proper operation or to generate invalid stimuli to verify safety mechanisms within the model. To vary the parameters and stimuli of our system and to cover up corner cases we use the benefits of Coverage-Driven Verification (CDV), with its aim to detach from direct - user depended - testing [2]. This methodology provides the definition of so called verification goals, which can be verified by smart test scenarios. The intelligence is mainly achieved by creating simulation configurations (stimuli), with respect to some predefined constraints. This concept is widely known as Constraint Random Verification (CRV) [7]. CRV mainly consists of two core concepts, which is on one hand the usage of Markov-chain Monte Carlo to guarantee coverage through probability and on the other hand the processing of constraints with SAT solvers. As described above, it is important to vary parameters such that many different input combinations can be covered. The defined internal values of the DUT vary according to a predefined probability distribution. In this case we use Gaussian distribution with the definition of a value of 3 sigma.

4   Usecase: Battery Management System

We have applied our methodology to an industrial use case, an electric vehicle (eVehicle) system provided by CISC Semiconductor, to more fully illustrate its innovative capabilities and benefits. As more and more vehicles are now powered by Li-ion batteries, the challenge for engineers to ensure reliability and fault tolerance is also greatly increasing. It is crucial for ensuring safe operating conditions that the battery management systems (BMS) measure voltage, temperature and current of the battery very precisely. This information must be forwarded to a vehicle wide controller network to ensure a reliable and fully utilized system. Problems with overheating or even explosions have been frequent in the past. The main cause of these problems was an excessively high energy intake from regenerative braking or harsh environmental conditions. Management systems and mechanisms are thus essential to assure that persons are not put at risk and that no damage is caused. The overall system model of the eVehicle is depicted in Fig. 3. This model gives an early view of the system on preAA design level with little to no assumption about the actual hardware. It is composed of the *battery, controller, inverter, dc-motor* and the *battery management unit (BMU)*. The *BMU* is included in the *battery* model. The *driver* provides the desired speed for the eVehicle. This can be set according to standardized maneuvers such as the New European Drive Cycle (NEDC). The *controller* is a model for a PI state-space controller and maintains a constant speed based on the information about the state variables, motor armature current and motor-speed. The *inverter* model implements an inverter function for a PM-DC motor driving stage. It compares the actual battery voltage and the requested controller voltage to maintain the PM-DC motor terminal voltage. The *battery* model simulates the behavior of a Li-ion battery pack composed of a defined set of single cell Li-ion batteries. The appropriate number of single cells is connected in parallel and series to obtain the necessary capacity, maximum current and terminal voltage. The battery pack's terminal voltage is calculated based on the defined parameter and the battery current. A BMU is connected to the battery to measure voltage,

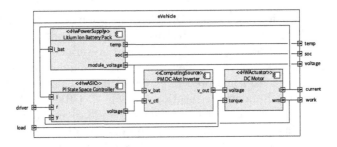

Fig. 3. Design under test (DUT): ports on the outside of the eVehicle class enables the connection to verification components

current and temperature of the cells/modules. The BMU computes the SOC, State-Of-Health (SOH) and is responsible for cell balancing, cell protection and demand management of the battery. These computed values can then processed via a CAN controller as digital values to the power train controller. In addition, the external load environmental conditions such as temperature can be changed during the simulation.

In a next step the functional SR are derived from the definition of the safety goals. An example for this would be to reuse the battery pack from a prior design which has known operating conditions and test if it is powerful enough to power the motor chosen for the new design (using a preliminary specifications provided by the manufacturer).

- The maximum operation temperature allowed for the battery cells is 100° C, therefore this temperature shall never be reached.
- Due to the choice of battery the maximum current drawn from the cells shall not exceed 10A.
- The cell/module voltage shall remain between 2.5 V (empty) and 4.25 V (maximum charging voltage)
- The state of charge for the individual cells shall not be lower than 10 % nor higher than 110 % of design capacity.

While textual or informal definition is easy to read, according to ISO26262 a semi-formal notation for requirements specifications is best qualified for ASIL levels higher than B, shown in our requirements diagram in Fig. 4.

These requirements and constraints can be used to test only the battery to be included as DUT. As i_bat is modeled as an input (e.g., a current sense ADC in the BMU) and temp as output, it would merely sweep the current from 0–10A (0 as no lower boundary was defined) and evaluate if the temperature, voltage and SoC remain within their respective bounds.

We use non-safety requirements to define driving maneuvers with an assumed load and different environmental conditions. By this means we can automatically create a testbench for the entire design as shown in Fig. 5, including stimuli, validators and scoreboards. The validator verifies that an input signal does not exceed a given threshold or remains bounded between two limits. This can

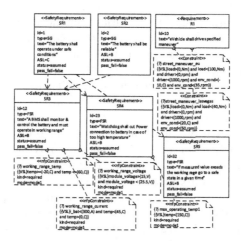

Fig. 4. Definition of safety and non-safety requirements to derive automatically testbenches for verification

basically be represented as a comparator with a user configurable operation ('<','≤','=','≠','≥','>') and one or two constants. Nevertheless, these descried thresholds are not stringed constants. The constraints can also describe temporal parameters as a certain peak current may be drawn from the battery but not for a prolonged period of time. The validator components are provided by our SCL and exists in many common configurations. Each validator has a boolean output that indicates if the constraints have been violated by the monitored signal. The scoreboard can be configured to terminate the simulation upon violation or continue and flag the simulation accordingly. Using our tool these problematic simulations can be filtered and re-run using more output or a smaller timestep to gain more insight into the problem. Testbenches from each design step can be reused for the further steps in order to improve test coverage. This means that while the preAA will not contain exact timing information for every specific subsystem, its testbenches can still be reused in later design phases to verify that

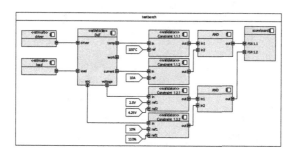

Fig. 5. Automatically generated testbench for the eVehicle model using UVM components derived from specification

the overall system is still behaving as initially intended. This design approach incorporates elements from the test-driven, continuous integration design flows commonly used in agile software development in the sense that for each step the constraints from parent and current level serve as unit-tests. The scoreboard is used to check every commit/change for errors. This is also useful in case of refactoring e.g., if for reasons of supply problems a part/component has to be replaced rather late in the design.

As mentioned previously stimuli are required in order to correctly evaluate the overall design (integration testing) and not only individual components (unit testing). While it would be possible to automatically generate the stimuli for the overall systems from the constraints (e.g., linear search of the entire value space for an input in correlation with each other input trying to find corner cases that best test the design) most of them would not represent any realistic environment. For this reason we decided to use non-safety requirements and derive stimuli from these. Using the eVehicle as an example this could be a standardized driving maneuver using a number of predefined locations for environment parameters (e.g., ambient temperature and humidity). It is also important to test if the designed safety mechanisms and safe states operate as designed. For this reason we could either define stimuli that provoke the triggering of a mechanism (e.g., driving at full speed for a prolonged period of time under high ambient temperature to test if the system can prevent overheating) or due fault injection. To the terms of software development this would represent a form of mutant testing where a deliberate fault is simulated in order to verify that a safe state can be reached. This is especially useful if existing designs are reused or a fault tree is given by the vendor to define the stimuli. The traces of our simulation-based verification within UML/MARTE are depicted in Fig. 6.

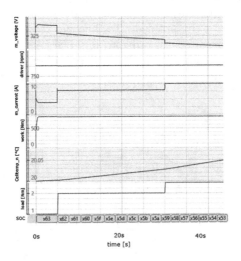

Fig. 6. This figure presents traces from one run of our seamless simulation-based verification methodology, e.g. temperature, voltage, current and SOC of the battery

This shows the analog signals such as module_voltage, driver, module_current, load, celltemperature and work, which are monitored by our UVM components. The DUT was stimulated by a driver with the *street_maneuver_eu* driving scenarios. Only one run, with a specific configuration, is shown in this figure. As the number of the simulation tasks for different parameter configurations can be relatively high and are independent of each other, we use a cloud-based solution for UVM [14] in order to parallelize our simulations to a very significant extent and gain a virtually linear acceleration. This provides a flexible way to allocate several worker instances to speed-up the time needed to simulate thousands of tasks.

5   Conclusions

In this paper we presented a simulation-based verification methodology tightly and seamlessly integrated in the safety-lifecycle (v-model) of the functional safety standard ISO26262. Our tool-aided methodology can be used from early system design, throughout the entire safety-lifecycle through to system integration and validation. Since millions of testkilometers now need to be managed, our simulation-based and constraint random approach helps to cover up a high percentage of possibilities. From an early safety analysis in conjunction with the early system design, testbenches have been automatically generated to test the preliminary architectural design. From this early analysis further technical but also hardware and software requirements have been derived. Furthermore, our approach provided important inputs for the more detailed system design. These testbenches have been generated from the requirements and constraints defined in the semi-formal SysML/MARTE format with our extension for safety requirements and can be used throughout the entire safety-lifecycle. We used standardized UVM components and the benefits of constraint random verification to provide different stimuli and configurations to find corner cases in our system. To randomly stimulate our UML/MARTE design models, these models have been linked to fast-executable analog, digital but also mechanical implementation models in SystemC (-AMS). This framework was tested by a complex example from the automotive industry in order to demonstrate its efficiency. The use cases showed how to define constraints in the MARTE constraint language and to generate verification components to automatically test the current preliminary design. In addition our approach was developed as a plugin in Eclipse, with the result that every Papyrus UML editor is now capable of simulation simply by installing our plugin. This tool will be published for download and is also to be used for educational purposes. Further work will include the definition of safe-states and timing behavior and the generating of testbenches from it. Furthermore, sequence diagrams will be used for the generation of the test stimuli.

References

1. CISC Semiconductor GmbH. https://www.cisc.at/
2. Accellera: Universal Verification Methodology (UVM) 1.2 User's Guide. Technical report, Accellera, May 2015
3. Catrene: OpenES CATRENE Project: CA703 (2016). http://www.ecsi.org/openes
4. ISO: Functional Safety ISO26262 - Part 4: Product development at the system level 2011, pp. 1–35 (2011)
5. Kim, H., Wong, W.E., Debroy, V., Bae, D.: Bridging the gap between fault trees and UML state machine diagrams for safety analysis. In: 2010 Asia Pacific Software Engineering Conference, pp. 196–205 (2010)
6. Kirchsteiger, C.M., Grinschgl, J., Trummer, C., Steger, C., Weiß, R., Pistauer, M.: Automatic test generation from semi-formal specifications for functional verification of system-on-chip designs. In: 2008 IEEE International Systems Conference Proceedings, SysCon 2008, pp. 421–428 (2008)
7. Kitchen, N., Kuehlmann, A.: Stimulus generation for constrained random simulation. In: Proceedings of the 2007 IEEE/ACM International Conference on Computer-Aided Design, Piscataway, NJ, USA, pp. 258–265, November 2007
8. Mader, R., Armengaud, E., Leitner, A., Kreiner, C., Bourrouilh, Q., Grießnig, G., Steger, C., Weiß, R.: Computer Safety, Reliability, and Security. In: 30th International Conference, SAFECOMP 2011, Naples, Italy, September 19–22, 2011, pp. 113–127. Springer, Heidelberg (2011). Chap. Computer-A
9. Marinescu, R., Kaijser, H., Mikučionis, M., Seceleanu, C., Lönn, H., David, A.: Analyzing industrial architectural models by simulation and model-checking. In: Artho, C., Ölveczky, P.C. (eds.) FTSCS 2014. CCIS, vol. 476, pp. 189–205. Springer, Heidelberg (2015)
10. Mhenni, F., Nguyen, N.: Automatic fault tree generation from SysML system models. In: 2014 IEEE/ASME International Conference on Advanced Intelligent Mechatronics (AIM), Besancon, France (2014)
11. Taha, S., Radermacher, A., Gérard, S.: An entirely model-based framework for hardware design and simulation. In: Hinchey, M., Kleinjohann, B., Kleinjohann, L., Lindsay, P.A., Rammig, F.J., Timmis, J., Wolf, M. (eds.) DIPES 2010. IFIP AICT, vol. 329, pp. 31–42. Springer, Heidelberg (2010)
12. Weissnegger, R., Kreiner, C., Pistauer, M., Römer, K., Steger, C.: A novel design method for automotive safety-critical systems based on UML/MARTE. In: Proceedings of the 2015 Forum on Specification & Design Languages, Barcelona, Spain, pp. 177–184 (2015)
13. Weissnegger, R., Schuss, M., Kreiner, C., Pistauer, M., Römer, K., Steger, C.: Simulation-based verification of automotive safety-critical systems based on EAST-ADL. Procedia Comput. Sci. **83**, 245–252 (2016)
14. Weissnegger, R., Schuß, M., Schachner, M., Pistauer, M., Römer, K., Steger, C.: A novel simulation-based verification pattern for parallel executions in the cloud. In: 21st European Conference on Pattern Languages of Programs Proceedings (2016)

1st International Workshop on Timing Performance in Safety Engineering (TIPS)

Note: **In the online version, the abstracts of the keynotes can be found in the back matter of the proceedings.**

TIPS 2016: The 1st International Workshop on Timing Performance in Safety Engineering

Chokri Mraidha[1], Laurent Rioux[2], Julio L. Medina Pasaje[3], and Marc Geilen[4]

[1] CEA, LIST, Point Courrier 174, 91191 Gif-sur-Yvette, France
chokri.mraidha@cea.fr
[2] Thales R&T, 1 Avenue Augustin Fresnel, 91767 Palaiseau Cedex, France
laurent.rioux@thalesgroup.com
[3] Department of Computer Science and Electronics, University of Cantabria, Spain
julio.medina@unican.es
[4] Eindhoven University of Technology, Eindhoven, The Netherlands
m.c.w.geilen@tue.nl

1 Introduction

Welcome to the first edition of the workshop on Timing Performance in Safety Engineering (TIPS'16), which has been held in conjunction with the International Conference on Computer Safety, Reliability and Security (SafeComp 2016).

Safety and certification are key issues in various domains such as automotive, medical, avionics and space. Today, designing safety critical real-time systems becomes more and more complex not only because the safety standards are more strict and rigorous, but also because the number of functions to realize is increasing while timing performance must continue to be guaranteed within an acceptable overall cost. For such systems, an increasing portion of design effort is therefore spent on timing performance verification and the corresponding safety and certification argumentations.

Currently, in the industrial design practices, performance engineering and safety engineering are rarely interconnected or integrated, thus requiring additional efforts from the timing performance verification community to fill the gap between the design model and its temporal semantics with techniques to produce proofs and argumentations required by the safety and certification standards. The challenge addressed by this workshop is therefore to link both engineering activities to increase the design efficiency of safety critical real-time systems.

2 Program

We are pleased to announce an excellent program that covers some of the latest research and development activities on timing, safety and security analysis and their integration challenges in various application domains. This year's program consists of eight presentations and a panel to have fruitful discussions and foster collaborations between workshop attendees.

3 Acknowledgments

We thank the SafeComp Workshop Chairs and the SafeComp Organizing Committee for providing the opportunity to organize this workshop. Finally, we are deeply grateful to all the members of our Technical Program Committee, as well as the authors, presenters, and attendees of the TIPS'16 workshop, the community with and for whom all these efforts are done.

TIPS 2016 Program Committee
Liliana Cucu-Grosjean, INRIA, France
Zain A.H. Hammadeh, TU Braunschweig, Germany
Huascar Espinoza, Tecnalia, Spain
Loic Frejoz, Realtime@work, France
Bran Selic, Malina Software Corp., Canada
José Merseguer, Univ. de Zaragoza, Spain
Rafik Henia, THALES, France
Bernhard Schatz, Fortiss, Germany
De-Jiu Chen, KTH, Sweden
Dorina C. Petriu, Carleton University, Canada
Yiannis Papadopoulos, University of Hull, UK
Emmanuel Grolleau, ENSMA, France

Model-Based Real-Time Evaluation of Security Patterns: A SCADA System Case Study

Anas Motii[1(✉)], Agnès Lanusse[1], Brahim Hamid[2], and Jean-Michel Bruel[2]

[1] CEA, LIST, Laboratory of Model Driven Engineering for Embedded Systems,
P.C. 174, 91191 Gif-sur-Yvette, France
{anas.motii,agnes.lanusse}@cea.fr

[2] IRIT, University of Toulouse, 118 Route de Narbonne, 31062 Toulouse Cedex 9, France
{brahim.hamid,bruel}@irit.fr

Abstract. Securing critical systems such as cyber physical systems (CPS) is an important feature especially when it comes to critical transmitted data. At the same time, the implementation of security counter-measures in such systems may impact other functional or non-functional concerns. In this context, we propose a model-based approach for securing critical systems at early design stage. This approach combines security analysis and mitigation solution proposals with multi-concern architectural evaluation. It exploits two views of security counter-measures patterns: abstract and concrete. The abstract view is used to select relevant solutions to security requirements on a logical point of view. Then, the concrete view helps the architect evaluating different possible implementation alternatives against other design constraints. The modeling is based on accepted OMG standards such as UML and MARTE. In this paper, the approach is illustrated on a SCADA (Supervisory Control and Data Acquisition) system case study and a tool chain based on Papyrus UML supports the approach.

Keywords: Architecture evaluation · MBE for cyber-physical systems · Model-based system analysis · Security patterns

1 Introduction

Cyber-physical systems (CPS) consist of computational units controlling physical entities. The complexity of such systems during their design comes from the involvement of transdisciplinary concerns. Indeed, such systems must satisfy a number of requirements (real-time, physical, energy efficiency and others). In addition, critical cyber-physical systems have to satisfy assurance requirements (IEC 61508 and ISO 27005 [1], for dependability and security concerns). This brings the complexity of such systems to a higher level. In particular, security concerns have an impact on other concerns such as real-time performance. For example, encryption adds a delay to the transmission time of data from one point to the other and affects real-time constraints. Therefore, architects must apply trade-offs to satisfy functional requirements (real-time), and security requirements as two categories of constraints.

© Springer International Publishing Switzerland 2016
A. Skavhaug et al. (Eds.): SAFECOMP 2016 Workshops, LNCS 9923, pp. 375–389, 2016.
DOI: 10.1007/978-3-319-45480-1_30

Model-Based System Engineering (MBSE) provides a useful contribution for the design and evaluation of secure systems. It makes easier the enactment of the separation of concern paradigm (security, real-time, performance, etc.). It helps the architect specify in a separate view non-functional requirements such as security at a high level of abstraction. Moreover, expertise and knowledge in system architecture and security can be captured within patterns that provide generic solutions for recurring problems. In particular for security, where protecting data and services is an important issue, security pattern catalogues [2] provide guidelines to build secure architectures.

Previous work have focused on security and real-time requirements separately: dependability and security modeling and analysis [3, 4]; and real time requirements [5]. A survey of dependability modeling and analysis frameworks with UML can be found in [3]. It focuses on software systems Reliability, Availability, Maintenance and Safety (RAMS). In [4], the authors have extended MARTE with a Dependability Analysis and Modeling (DAM) UML profile and applied it to an intrusion-tolerant message service case study. In [5], the authors presented a staged approach to optimize the deployment in the context of real-time distributed systems.

Other works focused on large scale architecture optimization, decision and trade-off analysis [6, 7]. In the automotive domain, a multi-objective automatic optimization approach based on EAST-ADL modeling is proposed [6]. It supports the evaluation of alternative architectures according to dependability, timing performance, cost etc. More specifically in security and performance interplay, the study in [7] focused on the analysis of the performance effects of security solutions modeled as UML non-functional aspects. It used SPT UML profile for annotating a UML design with schedulability, time and performance data. The resulting model and the security aspects were transformed separately and composed into one model which was then analyzed.

In this paper we present an approach to select and evaluate possible candidate improvements in order to find the best set of security patterns respecting timing constraints. To this end, we propose a model-based approach for the development of secure critical systems based on architectural evaluation driven by security concerns. This work is part of a more general process devoted to incremental pattern-based modeling and safety and security analysis for correct by construction systems design. In previous works, we have proposed a model-based approach for guiding the selection of security patterns based on risk analysis and pattern classification [8]. In a recent paper in [9], we proposed an approach to support Security, Dependability and Resource Tradeoffs using Pattern-based Development and Model-driven Engineering. In this paper, we go one step further, we study the impact of implementation alternatives of these security solutions onto the system architecture. A special emphasis is paid to timing performance concerns using model-based real-time evaluations. In this context, the system architect starts from a functional architecture and an abstract platform. The artifacts are abstract at this stage of development but contain temporal information (e.g., computation cost, deadlines and period of event for each function). Once security requirements are specified (resulting from a security risk analysis), several security pattern solutions are proposed from a repository of patterns. The real-time evaluation helps the architect to select the best candidates that respect timing concerns (e.g., maximum utilization capacity in the platform).

The remaining sections are organized as follows: Sect. 2 describes the SCADA system case study and its security issues. Section 3 illustrates the real-time evaluation approach of security solutions on the case study and gives its steps and modeling principles. Section 4 discusses the obtained experimental results. Section 5 concludes the paper and discusses future work.

2 Case Study: SCADA System

2.1 Description

SCADA systems are meant to control processes through local controllers, acquiring field data and returning it to a SCADA master computer system. Figure 1 shows a typical SCADA system architecture. It consists of a SCADA master, an operator workstation and a number of field devices connected by a communication infrastructure. Field devices can be Programmable Logic Controllers (PLC), Remote Terminal units (RTU), sensors and actuators.

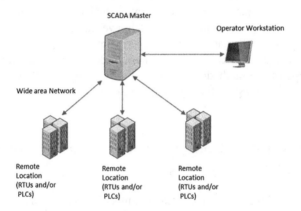

Fig. 1. A typical SCADA system architecture [10]

The SCADA master provides the operator with a Human-Machine Interface (HMI) through a work station to issue commands to PLCs and gather field data from them. PLCs are digital computers programmed to continuously monitor sensors and control actuators (e.g., valves, pumps, etc.). RTUs are used for converting sensor data into digital data. As SCADA systems cover large areas, they use Wide Area Networks (WAN). SCADA systems provide the following functionalities: data acquisition and handling (e.g., polling data from controllers, alarm handling, calculations, logging and archiving) on a set of parameters, typically those they are connected to.

2.2 SCADA Security

It is very important for SCADA systems to be safe and reliable. They have a good reputation in this field. However, the key issue nowadays is SCADA security.

Governments all over the world are worried about the security of SCADA systems that run over critical infrastructures. First generation of SCADA systems were introduced in the 1970's and second generation in 1980's. Many of these are still in operation especially second generations. They relied on two approaches for security: (1) Security by isolation: based on the principle that if the system is not connected to the Ethernet then it cannot be attacked by external attackers. However it is still vulnerable to insider attacks. (2) Security through obscurity: based on the fact that SCADA systems used unusual programming languages and communication protocols. However this is also vulnerable to insider attackers who know about these technologies. In addition the documentation can be found on internet or can be stolen.

Third generation SCADA systems use standard IT technologies and protocols (e.g., organizational wireless networking, Microsoft windows, TCP/IP and web browsers as interfaces). The third generation systems which are web connected are integrated with an interface to second generation systems. Opening SCADA systems rises a major issue for guarantying security since the "security by isolation" principle is violated.

Proposing security solutions for critical systems, and in particular SCADA systems, requires an early architecture evaluation analyzing the impact of these solutions on quality attributes. In this paper, we treat one quality attribute which is real-time performance. The aim is to help the architect, at a high level design, selecting the best set of security solution implementations that respect timing requirements (if any). As mentioned earlier, the selection of security patterns is driven by a risk analysis performed in previous steps of the methodology [8]. This risk analysis follows a model-based implementation of EBIOS[1] methodology described in [11]. However this step is not described in this paper. The foundations of the approach are described in the next section.

3   Model-Based Real-Time Evaluation of Security Pattern Configurations

In this section we present the foundations of a model-based seamless approach for an incremental architecture securing process involving both: solutions identification, integration, evaluation and comparison. We present here the corresponding workflow, and illustrate each step of this process over the SCADA system case study.

3.1   Approach Workflow Overview

The process workflow proposed for architectural solutions evaluation follows 3 main steps (1 to 3) as illustrated in Fig. 2. Actually, the workflow itself is part of a more global process not described here that encompasses security analysis of design architecture proposal, and issues security requirements. Step0 here refers to a preliminary stage aimed at selecting appropriate pattern solutions satisfying these requirements. The main

---

[1] EBIOS: Expression of Needs and Identification of Security Objectives from ANSSI, the french agency for security of information systems (Agence nationale de la sécurité des systèmes d'information).

objective of the workflow presented below is to support the real-time evaluation of various possible security pattern configurations to assess their soundness regarding temporal (and possibly resource) constraints.

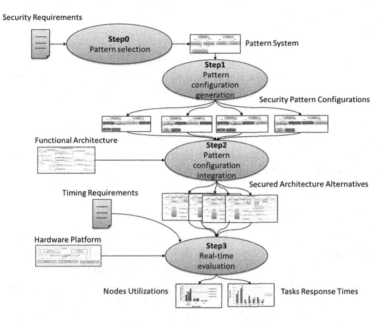

Fig. 2. Process of real-time evaluation of security pattern configurations

This seamless process relies on three main kinds of artifacts: (1) *functional architectures* to describe system and software functions, (2) *security patterns* to describe system security solutions and (3) *platform models* to describe hardware resources. The approach is centered on the concepts of security patterns. In this context, we consider the following definitions.

3.2   Definitions

Definition 1 (Security Pattern):   A security pattern provides a generic solution of recurring security problem. Security patterns follow templates such as the ones proposed by GoF [12] and include several attributes e.g., "Name", "Context", "Problem", "Solution", "Consequences" and "See Also". "Structure" contains information about the functional structure of the pattern and uses generally semi-formal languages e.g., UML.to describe it. "Consequence" contains information about the impact of using this pattern on the target architecture quality attributes e.g., availability and performance.

The level of abstraction of the pattern depends on the detail of its solution. We distinguish: (1) abstract pattern providing an abstract solution without clear details of the used techniques (2) concrete pattern refining the solution provided by an abstract pattern possibly using other patterns. There are thus two types of relationships: refinement and usage relationships.

Definition 2 (System of Security Patterns): A System of security patterns is a collection of security patterns with their relationships. In our context, patterns have different refinement alternatives.

Definition 3 (System of Security Patterns Configuration): A configuration is a subset of a System of security patterns. It will be used to specify the possible refinement alternatives (concrete patterns). It will be also referred to as "security solution alternative".

Definition 4 (Pattern Integration): Pattern integration means refining the functional architecture by adding security pattern functions. Each security solution alternative is integrated producing secured architecture alternatives. In the context of MDE, pattern integration is a "model refinement".

3.3   Process Description

As stated earlier, the evaluation process is composed of three main steps (see Fig. 2), and a preliminary one for patterns selection. This process considers as inputs security requirements resulting from prior risk analysis and the design model.

In the case of SCADA systems, such security requirements can be: (1) There should be a mechanism for secure communication that guarantees data integrity, confidentiality and authenticity, (2) There should be a mechanism that protects against denial of service attacks at the level of the SCADA master.

Step 0 (Pattern Selection). Selecting appropriate security solutions, here presented as security patterns, from security requirements is an important step during the development of secure software and systems. In this context, we use the selection method described in [4] which is based on the use of risk analysis to derive security properties and constraints; along with pattern selection principles using pattern classifications [13, 14] to select concrete security patterns. The method is based on a library of patterns stored in the SEMCO repository [15]. The System and software Engineering Pattern Metamodel (SEPM) [15] is used to model Security and Dependability (S&D) patterns which are then stored in a repository. Patterns provide their functionalities through interfaces. Their characteristics are described by properties.

After analyzing security requirements, the architect identifies a set of security patterns along with their refinement alternatives, i.e. concrete patterns. It is important to note that the selection of security patterns takes into account conflicts due to inconsistencies between patterns. For example, Limited view and Full view pattern are conflictual by nature so that implementing both of them in a system will surely bring inconsistencies.

The search in the repository leads to the identification of two abstract patterns:

- *SecureComm* pattern [2]: ensures that data passing across a secure network is secure. It can be refined by two patterns: *SecureCommSSL* (P1) and *SecureCommIPsec* (P2).

SecureCommSSL uses *X.509 certificates* for authentication and *secure channel* for creating a cryptographic tunnel.

- *Firewall* pattern [2]: restricts access to internal networks which can be refined by *PacketFilter* (P3) and *StatefulFiltering* (P4).

The result of this step is the System of security patterns represented in Fig. 3.

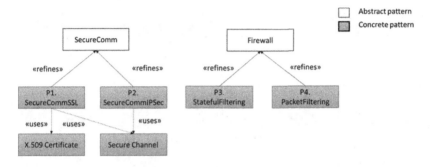

Fig. 3. System of security patterns

Step 1 (System of Patterns Configuration Generation). The goal of this step is to create the possible security solution alternatives from a system of patterns using system of patterns configuration management based on variability models.

Security variability consists of documenting all alternative security solutions for a given problem. Security variability is important in the context of architecture design because it helps the architect understanding (1) which security solution varies and how it varies, (2) if there are security solutions satisfying several security objectives, (3) possible conflicts between security solutions, (4) security solutions that supports others.

Several works have treated this concern [9, 16]. In [16], the authors present a modeling approach based on aspect engineering. In [9], the author have presented an algorithm for pattern system configuration management. It takes as input a pattern system with its relationships, a base configuration and a reference kind (i.e. relationship type); and outputs a security solution alternative.

In the context of the paper [9] is used. For the case study, Fig. 3 can be considered as a possible security variability model. Then, Fig. 4 shows the corresponding possible security solution alternatives. Each system of security solution alternative consists of a set of concrete patterns in dark grey.

Step 2 (Pattern Configuration Integration). The goal of this step is to integrate each security solution alternative into the functional architecture thus obtaining refined design architecture candidates.

The difficulty of this step is not only the verification of the correct integration of the pattern but also the management of possible conflicts between the functional architecture and a security pattern or between security patterns themselves.

The integration of concerns; and security in particular has been treated in [17–19]. Pattern integration consists of composing security patterns with a functional

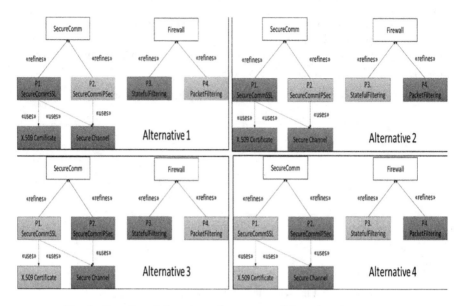

Fig. 4. Security solution alternatives generated from the pattern system

architecture. It requires techniques such as: role bindings merge techniques, checking techniques prior and after the integration to detect possible conflicts.

In the context of this work, [19] is used. Each security solution alternative is applied into the SCADA system functional architecture. Figure 5 depicts the initial SCADA

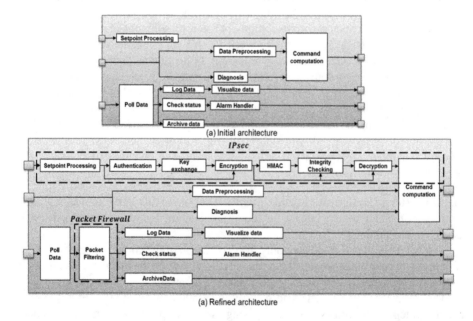

Fig. 5. SCADA functional architecture before (a) and after the integration of Alternative 4 (b)

functional architecture (a) and the result of the integration (b) of *security solution alternative 4*.

Step 3 (Real-Time Evaluation). Real-time evaluation principles are based on works by [20] with the Optimum methodology[2]. This methodology was previously applied in other modeling contexts such as EAST-ADL in the MAENAD project. In this approach design models are evaluated at early stages to help make architectural decisions. Here we use it on UML design models and patterns stored in SEMCO Library.

Modeling Principles. The Optimum methodology is used to build a task model from the design in order to evaluate, compare architectural solutions and/or optimize deployment. We describe here the modeling principles and main steps of the methodology. Note that in our context, it is applied to high level functional design to get preliminary decisions on the overall architecture security improvement solutions. The input is thus a functional view of the application and patterns annotated using MARTE profile[3].

A task model is obtained following four steps: (1) identification of event-chains in the functional model, (2) specification of timing constraints (on event-chains and on behaviors corresponding to functions), (3) computation of a MARTE task model (end-to-end flows), and (4) tasks Allocation Specification (tasks on nodes).

To support the approach several diagrams are used: composite diagrams for (1) and (2); activity diagrams for (3); and composite diagrams showing task model and platform model together with allocation links for (4). This Optimum workflow and MARTE notations used are summarized in Fig. 6.

Event Chains Identification. The functional organization of the application is described in a Composite diagram showing functions and their connections. From this global view several timing views corresponding to end-to-end flows are selected.

Timing Constraints Setup. Selected event chains are then tagged to setup timing constraints. MARTE annotations are added to these diagrams to set: (1) event chains timing constraints (between 2 ports), (2) execution time constraints on functions (actually expected for the behavior implementing the function).

Task Model Setup. The task model structure is described using activity diagrams and can be directly obtained from the event chains specifications above. Each of them is translated into a MARTE end-to-end event flow. Each flow is activated by the reception of an event and described by the consequent behaviors implementing the various functions traversal connected through connectors.

MARTE annotations are used to: (1) characterize a timing configuration, (2) specify a data arrival pattern for the activating event (workflowEvent) and (3) specify constraints on the different steps (behaviors involved in the event flow).

---

[2] Optimum methodology is developed at LIST CEATech and is integrated within Papyrus open-source modeling tool.

[3] MARTE profile is a standard from the OMG (UML Profile for MARTE™: Modeling and Analysis of Real-time Embedded Systems™). http://www.omgmarte.org/.

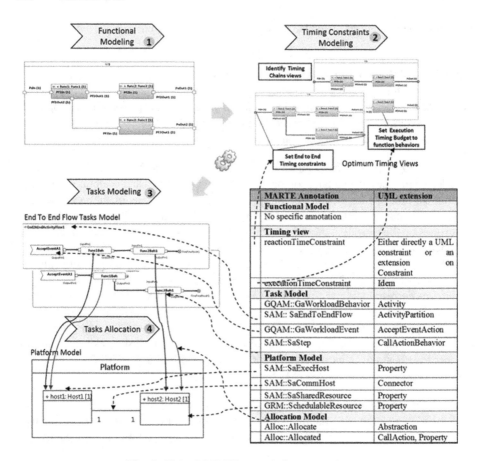

Fig. 6. Using MARTE to set timing constraints

Allocation Model Setup. Finally an allocation model is described in a composite diagram that shows the allocation between functions (actually the tasks corresponding to their behaviors) onto a platform model.

MARTE annotations are used to: (1) set allocation relations and (2) set hardware architecture characteristics on execution hosts and communication channels.

Real-Time Evaluation Steps. The modeling principles described earlier allow the specification of task and allocation models exploitable by scheduling algorithms such as Rate Monotonic scheduling (RMS) and offset-based scheduling [21, 22]. Let P be a platform consisting of connected nodes $\{N_1, N_2, \ldots, N_a\}$ and F be a set of functions $\{f_1, f_2, \ldots, f_b\}$. Each function has a computation cost c_{f_i}. The execution nodes are connected through buses. Both nodes and buses have a maximal capacity that must not be exceeded. In the context of multiple processors, each node runs an independent real-time operating system. Each platform node N_i executes a set of tasks $T_i = \{t_{i,1}, t_{i,2}, \ldots, t_{i,ni}\}$. Each task consists of a subset of functions from F. Each task $t_{i,j}$

has an activation period $P_{i,j}$, an execution time $c_{i,j}$ (computed as the sum of computation costs of all allocated function) and a deadline $D_{i,j}$. Real-time evaluation consists of two steps:

1. **Preliminary evaluation.** A preliminary real-time evaluation is used to compute nodes utilizations. If one of the refined architectures exceeds the node maximum capacity, it is rejected. The node utilization is computed as: $U_{Ni} = \sum_{t_{i,j} \in Ti} \frac{c_{i,j}}{P_{i,j}}$.

   In case of RMS, the utilization U_{Ni} for each node must at least be: $U_{Ni} \leq n(2^{\frac{1}{n}} - 1)$ with n being the number of tasks assigned to Ni. If not, the node is overloaded and *response time analysis* is not performed.

2. **Response time analysis.** The response time analysis is performed for architectures succeeding the preliminary evaluation. At this step, response time analysis is performed following the principles proposed in [22] for distributed systems. It concerns the computation of the worst case response time $R_{t_{i,j}}$ of every task. All response times must verify: $R_{t_{i,j}} \leq D_{i,j}$. If not, the tasks are not schedulable and the corresponding architecture is rejected.

   In the context of this work, we use RMS for preliminary evaluation and offset-based scheduling for response time analysis using QOMPASS tool that supports Optimum methodology.

4   Preliminary Experimental Results

As a preliminary experiment, we apply the approach to a SCADA system case study. Figure 7 shows the input functional architecture together with hardware platform. The functional model contains ten functions in three transactions with their deadlines and trigger periods. The hardware topology in the platform contains a SCADA master and a PLC connected with Modbus. The partitioning of functions into tasks and assignment of tasks onto hosts is also shown. In addition, the signal between "Set point processing" and "Command computation" is mapped onto a message. The execution budgets of the

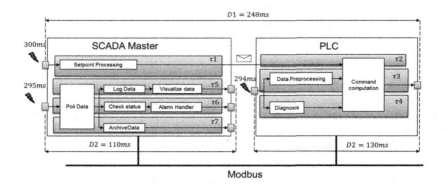

Fig. 7. Input functional architecture, hardware platform and deployment

functions, the assigned tasks and hosts are showed in Table 1. The values of the SCADA function timing parameters are based on IEEE 1646 standard [28] specifying communication deadlines and IEC 61850 [29] specifying communication network delays in different information categories.

Table 1. Timing parameters and deployment of SCADA functions

Functions	Execution time	Task	Host
Setpoint processing	8.7	$\tau1$	*SCADA master*
Poll data	9.6	$\tau5, \tau6, \tau7$	*SCADA master*
Log data	8.5	$\tau5$	*SCADA master*
Check status	9.6	$\tau6$	*SCADA master*
Visualize data	10.5	$\tau5$	*SCADA master*
Alarm handler	10.3	$\tau6$	*SCADA master*
Archive data	9.5	$\tau7$	*SCADA master*
Command computation	10	$\tau2, \tau3, \tau4$	*PLC*
Data preprocessing	9.5	$\tau3$	*PLC*
Diagnosis	8.9	$\tau4$	*PLC*

Similarly, the timing and placement parameters of the used security patterns are showed in Table 2. The concrete patterns have the same functions but have different execution times (two execution time columns). The timing parameters are based on a review of technical reports of SSL/IPsec [23], and stateful/packet firewall [24].

Table 2. Timing parameters and deployment of security pattern functions

Patterns	Functions	Execution times		Task
		(1)	(2)	
SecureCommSSL (1)	Authentication	9.7	38.7	$\tau1$
SecureCommIPsec (2)	Key exchange	10.1	39.6	$\tau1$
	Encryption	9.9	9.9	$\tau1$
	HMAC	9.2	9.2	$\tau1$
	Decryption	10.3	10.3	$\tau2$
	Integrity checking	10.2	10.2	$\tau2$
PacketFiltering (1)	Filtering	10	40	$\tau7$
StatefulFiltering (2)				

One important point is that the experiment has required some effort in quantifying real-time parameters of security pattern functions. Some functions execution times were estimations and averages. For example, in *SecureComm* pattern function "HMAC" does not have the same execution time as it depends on the used algorithm (e.g., HMAC-SHA-1-96, HMAC-MD5). However, we believe that estimations and averaging is enough as the approach is meant for high level evaluation and architecture decision making. For example, if none of the security solution alternatives respected the timing requirements because of overload; the architecture of SCADA can be rethought leading to adding an execution node.

4.1   Results

The preliminary analysis consists in evaluating the placement of SCADA and pattern functions on hosts described in Table 1 for each security solution alternative (1, 2, 3 and 4) in Fig. 4. The left side of Fig. 8 shows the node utilization results of each alternative. The utilization bound of the SCADA master and PLC are up to 75.68 % (four tasks) and 77.97 % (three tasks) respectively. Security solution alternatives 2 and 4 are rejected because the SCADA master utilization in the two cases (83.33 % and 103.33 %) exceeds the threshold. Response time analysis given in [22] is performed for security solution alternatives 1 and 3 since they pass the preliminary evaluation. Task $\tau2$ response time is up to 280 ms in alternative 3 and violates its deadline of 248 ms. This is due to the offset added by task $\tau2$ and the message transmission time. All tasks of configuration 1 respect their deadline: $\tau1$ (150 ms), $\tau2$ (240 ms), $\tau3$ (60 ms), $\tau4$ (120 ms), $\tau5$ (70 ms), $\tau6$ (100 ms) and $\tau7$ (30 ms). From the evaluations, alternative 1 is the best security solution alternative that fulfils security requirements and respects real-time constraints.

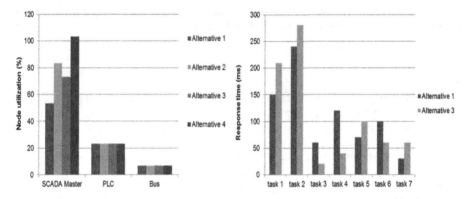

Fig. 8. Node utilization for security solution alternatives 1, 2, 3 and 4, and tasks response times for alternatives 1 and 3

4.2   Discussion

From this first experimentation, we conclude that the approach fulfils the objective of finding the best set of security patterns respecting timing constraints.

The work has two main contributions: (1) the proposal of abstract security pattern solutions fulfilling security requirements and (2) the evaluation of the possible implementations fulfilling real-time requirements by the integration of possible security solution alternatives. In this context, this work can be beneficial to resource constrained embedded systems e.g., automotive, avionics. For instance in EAST-ADL, trade-off analysis is performed for one design model with different parameters whose values determine whether the design satisfies the model or not. Our work adds a step forward which is the evaluation of different design alternative models against non-functional concerns (security in this paper). This work can benefit from EAST-ADL concepts for configurations management using features diagrams.

5   Conclusion and Future Work

The paper presents a model-based approach for evaluating security solutions based on patterns applied to a SCADA system case study. It shows the applicability of the approach. The main benefits are to provide a tooling support for early evaluation of different implementation of security measures using: pattern composition and integration, automatic configuration generation and evaluation. The evaluation focuses on temporal performance concerns. This work is part of a process devoted to incremental pattern-based modeling and safety and security analysis for correct by construction systems design. The results obtained help the designer select appropriate design solution to reinforce security. The methodology relies on UML/MARTE for modeling and makes extensive use of MARTE to perform architectural evaluation for timing concerns. This work will be extended to address other concerns (e.g., cost, reliability, memory consumption, power supply).

Acknowledgements. This work is conducted in the context of a Ph.D. thesis funded by CEA LIST and co-leaded by CEA (LISE) and IRIT (MACAO).

References

1. ISO/IEC 27005: Information Technology — Security Techniques — Information Security Risk Management (2011)
2. Fernandez, E.B.: Security Patterns in Practice: Designing Secure Architectures Using Software Patterns. Wiley, New York (2013)
3. Bernardi, S., Merseguer, J., Petriu, D.C.: Dependability modeling and analysis of software systems specified with UML. ACM Comput. Surv. **45**, 2 (2012)
4. Bernardi, S., Merseguer, J., Petriu, D.C.: A dependability profile within MARTE. Softw. Syst. Model. **10**, 313–336 (2011)
5. Mehiaoui, A., Wozniak, E., Piergiovanni, S.T., Mraidha, C., Natale, M.D., Zeng, H., Babau, J.-P., Lemarchand, L., Gérard, S.: A two-step optimization technique for functions placement, partitioning, and priority assignment in distributed systems. In: SIGPLAN/SIGBED Conference on Languages, Compilers and Tools for Embedded Systems 2013, LCTES 2013, Seattle, WA, USA, June 20–21, 2013, pp. 121–132 (2013)
6. Walker, M., Reiser, M.-O., Tucci-Piergiovanni, S., Papadopoulos, Y., Lönn, H., Mraidha, C., Parker, D., Chen, D., Servat, D.: Automatic optimisation of system architectures using EAST-ADL. J. Syst. Softw. **86**, 2467–2487 (2013)
7. Petriu, D.C., Woodside, C.M., Petriu, D.B., Xu, J., Israr, T., Georg, G., France, R., Bieman, J.M., Houmb, S.H., Jürjens, J.: Performance analysis of security aspects in UML models. In: Proceedings of the 6th International Workshop Software Performance, pp. 91–102 (2007)
8. Motii, A., Hamid, B., Lanusse, A., Bruel, J.-M.: Guiding the selection of security patterns based on security requirements and pattern classification. In: Proceedings of the 20th European Conference on Pattern Languages of Programs, pp. 10:1–10:17. ACM, New York (2015)
9. Hamid, B.: Interplay of security and dependability and resource using model-driven and pattern-based development. In: 2015 IEEE Trustcom/BigDataSE/ISPA, pp. 254–262 (2015)
10. Technical Information Bulletin 04-1: Supervisory Control and Data Acquisition (SCADA) System (2004)

11. Abdallah, R., Motii, A., Yakymets, N., Lanusse, A.: Using model driven engineering to support multi-paradigms security analysis. In: Desfray, P., et al. (eds.) MODELSWARD 2015. CCIS, vol. 580, pp. 278–292. Springer, Heidelberg (2015). doi:10.1007/978-3-319-27869-8_16

12. Gamma, E., Helm, R., Johnson, R., Vlissides, J.: Design Patterns: Elements of Reusable Object-Oriented Software. Addison-Wesley Longman Publishing Co., Inc., Boston (1995)

13. Fernandez, E.B.: Using security patterns to develop secure systems. In: Software Engineering for Secure Systems: Industrial and Research Perspectives, pp. 16–31 (2011)

14. Bunke, M., Koschke, R., Sohr, K.: Organizing security patterns related to security and pattern recognition requirements. Int. J. Adv. Secur. 5, 46–67 (2012)

15. Hamid, B., Percebois, C.: A modeling and formal approach for the precise specification of security patterns. In: Jürjens, J., Piessens, F., Bielova, N. (eds.) ESSoS. LNCS, vol. 8364, pp. 95–112. Springer, Heidelberg (2014)

16. Dai, L.: Security variability design and analysis in an aspect oriented software architecture. In: Third IEEE International Conference on Secure Software Integration and Reliability Improvement, SSIRI 2009, pp. 275–280 (2009)

17. Alam, O., Kienzle, J., Mussbacher, G.: Concern-oriented software design. In: Moreira, A., Schätz, B., Gray, J., Vallecillo, A., Clarke, P. (eds.) MODELS 2013. LNCS, vol. 8107, pp. 604–621. Springer, Heidelberg (2013)

18. Nguyen, P.H., Yskout, K., Heyman, T., Klein, J., Scandariato, R., Le Traon, Y.: Model-driven security based on a unified system of security design patterns (2015)

19. Hamid, B., Percebois, C., Gouteux, D.: A methodology for integration of patterns with validation purpose. In: Proceedings of the 17th European Conference on Pattern Languages of Programs, pp. 8:1–8:14. ACM, New York (2012)

20. Mraidha, C., Tucci-Piergiovanni, S., Gerard, S.: Optimum: a MARTE-based methodology for schedulability analysis at early design stages. SIGSOFT Softw. Eng. Notes 36, 1–8 (2011)

21. Harbour, M.G., Gutiérrez, J.J., Drake, J.M., Martínez, P.L., Palencia, J.C.: Modeling distributed real-time systems with MAST 2. J. Syst. Archit. 59, 331–340 (2013)

22. Tindell, K., Clark, J.: Holistic schedulability analysis for distributed hard real-time systems. Microprocess. Microprogram. 40, 117–134 (1994)

23. Alshamsi, A., Saito, T.: A technical comparison of IPSec and SSL. In: 19th International Conference on Advanced Information Networking and Applications (AINA 2005), Volume 1 (AINA papers), vol. 2, pp. 395–398 (2005)

24. Design and Performance of the OpenBSD Stateful Packet Filter (pf). http://www.benzedrine.ch/pf-paper.html

Invited Papers

ASIL-Conformant Deployment
and Schedule Synthesis Using Multi-objective
Design Space Exploration

Sebastian Voss$^{(\boxtimes)}$ and Bernhard Schätz

Fortiss GmbH, Guerickestrasse 55, 80805 Munich, Germany
voss@fortiss.org

The growing complexity of functionalities in automotive vehicles and their safety-criticality, including timing requirements, demands sound and scalable approaches to deal with the increasing design space. Most often, such complex automotive systems are composed of a set of functions that are characterized by a set of contradicting requirements when it comes to a valid system architecture and configuration.

These functionalities perform more and more safety-critical tasks, thus increasing the challenge on assuring the safety of such systems. Furthermore, as safety-critical systems must perform the desired behavior within guaranteed time bounds, a valid system configuration is needed including a time-correct schedule that fulfills all timing requirements. This contribution proposes a systematic and correct deployment and scheduling synthesis of complex automotive software systems that ensures multi objective design constraints (e.g. ASIL-conformant deployments) of software components.

© Springer International Publishing Switzerland 2016
A. Skavhaug et al. (Eds.): SAFECOMP 2016 Workshops, LNCS 9923, p. 393, 2016.
DOI: 10.1007/978-3-319-45480-1

Model-Based Contract and Service for Self-managed Components in Cyber-Physical Systems

DeJiu Chen$^{(\boxtimes)}$

Mechatronics, Department of Machine Design,
KTH Royal Institute of Technology, Stockholm, Sweden
chen@md.kth.se

Abstract. Modern automotive vehicles represent one category of cyber-physical systems that are inherently safety&time-critical. Future automotive technology will to an increasingly large extent be based on an integration of general purpose components for shortening the innovation loops and enabling efficient product evolution. Nevertheless, the adoption of general purpose solutions in automotive vehicles will not be a trivial task. Currently, while domain-specific frameworks like AUTOSAR and ISO26262 facilitate component-based system development based on well-formulated assumptions and interfaces, challenges remain in the areas of contract synthesis, conformity assessment, and diagnostics when issues like mode behaviors, timing, and failures are of concern. This talk presents the EAST-ADL modeling framework and discusses an EAST-ADL based approach to system modularity and risk analysis in order to integrate separately developed electronic components into safety-critical automotive systems. Special attention is paid to the synthesis of both component contracts and the associated runtime services for lifecycle and quality management, anomaly treatment according to ISO26262.

Keywords: Cyber-Physical Systems (CPS) · Model-Based Development (MBD) · Domain-Specific Modeling (DSM) · Component-Based Engineering (CBE) · Real-Time System (RTS) · Functional safety · EAST-ADL · ISO2626

© Springer International Publishing Switzerland 2016
A. Skavhaug et al. (Eds.): SAFECOMP 2016 Workshops, LNCS 9923, p. 394, 2016.
DOI: 10.1007/978-3-319-45480-1

Automotive Ethernet:
Towards TSN and Beyond

Zhonghai Lu[(⊠)]

Department of Electronics and Embedded Systems, School of ICT,
KTH Royal Institute of Technology, Stockholm, Sweden
zhonghai@kth.se

Abstract. As a new generation of E/E architecture, Ethernet is rapidly pene-
trating into the automotive domain. To accommodate the stringent quality-
of-service (QoS) requirements of automotive applications, Ethernet is evolving
towards mixed criticality aware time-sensitive networking (TSN). This talk will
first present a landscape brought by TSN for complex automotive distributed
real-time applications such as advanced driver assistance systems (ADAS). Then
we will exemplify how TSN can better cope with application requirements than
conventional Ethernet, in particular, in adaptively delivering QoS assurances
under vehicle internal conditions and external situations. Finally we shall discuss
challenges and opportunities on deploying TSN as a new E/E infrastructure for
advanced automotive applications under safety concerns.

Keywords: Automotive E/E architecture · Automotive ethernet · Time
sensitive networking (TSN) · Mixed criticality systems · Quality of service
(QoS) · Functional safety

© Springer International Publishing Switzerland 2016
A. Skavhaug et al. (Eds.): SAFECOMP 2016 Workshops, LNCS 9923, p. 395, 2016.
DOI: 10.1007/978-3-319-45480-1

Dataflow-Based Verification
of Temporal Properties
for Virtualized Multiprocessor Systems

Mladen Skelin[✉] and Marc Geilen

Eindhoven University of Technology, Eindhoven, The Netherlands
{m.skelin,m.c.w.geilen}@tue.nl

Over the last decade we have witnessed ever increasing use of virtualized multi-processor platforms in the design of advanced digital systems. This is due to the fact that virtual platforms, by means of virtual machines, facilitate the design of complex systems involving large numbers of applications by providing both spatial and temporal isolation between them. In particular, each application is assigned with a fraction of the platform's (spatial and temporal) capacity and can be treated as if it were executing on a platform of its one. This means that in cases where applications have stringent temporal constraints we can analyze their temporal behavior in isolation because the behavior of one is not affected by the other. In this talk we reflect on the model-based design flow developed at Eindhoven University of Technology that by the use of aforementioned virtualization principles guarantees composability and predictability. In particular, we discuss how timed dataflow-based design flow implemented in the SDF^3 tool enables real-time dataflow applications to be automatically mapped, verified and executed on the CompSOC temporally composable platform providing strongly temporally isolated virtual multiprocessor platforms.

© Springer International Publishing Switzerland 2016
A. Skavhaug et al. (Eds.): SAFECOMP 2016 Workshops, LNCS 9923, p. 396, 2016.
DOI: 10.1007/978-3-319-45480-1

WARUNA: Modeling and Timing Verification Framework

Rafik Henia[✉]

Thales Research & Technology, Palaiseau, France
rafik.henia@thalesgroup.com

WARUNA is a French research project aiming at developing a framework to model and verify timing properties in real-time embedded systems. The framework covers all design phases and allows evaluating the impact of the design decisions on the response times. It also allows merging the timing results obtained at different design levels from the different analysis tools. The WARUNA framework is integrated in the modeling environment.

In the talk, the WARUNA framework will be presented, as well as the project objectives and the partners' role. More details about the WARUNA project can be found on the project website: http://www.waruna-projet.fr/.

© Springer International Publishing Switzerland 2016
A. Skavhaug et al. (Eds.): SAFECOMP 2016 Workshops, LNCS 9923, p. 397, 2016.
DOI: 10.1007/978-3-319-45480-1

Author Index

Agirre, Irune 273
Azkarate-askasua, Mikel 273

Bando, Koichi 55
Bate, Iain 17
Borg, Markus 346
Bruel, Jean-Michel 375

Cârlan, Carmen 30
Carlson, Jan 43
Cazorla, Francisco J. 273
Chaari, Moomen 144
Chen, DeJiu 394
Cohen, Myra B. 75
Couce-Vieira, Aitor 246

Dallons, Gautier 334
de la Vara, Jose Luis 270, 311, 346
Denney, Ewen 2
Dillinger, Oliver 157
Druml, Norbert 183

Ecker, Wolfgang 144
Espinoza, Huáscar 311

Firestone, Justin 75
Fockel, Markus 298
Fröhlich, Joachim 105
Frtunikj, Jelena 105

Gallina, Barbara 43, 311
Gassilewski, Martin 286
Geilen, Marc 372, 396

Habli, Ibrahim 2
Hamid, Brahim 375
Hansson, Hans 43
Hegedűs, Csaba 234
Henia, Rafik 397
Höfig, Kai 322
Holweg, Gerald 183
Houmb, Siv Hilde 246

Ishigaki, Yang 55
Izosimov, Viacheslav 286

Jaradat, Omar 17
Jarzębowicz, Aleksander 87
Johansson, Rolf 286

Kelly, Tim 270
Kido, Hiroyuki 55
Kinoshita, Shuji 63
Kinoshita, Yoshiki 63
Koller, Thomas 210
Kreiner, Christian 359
Kruse, Thomas 144

Lanusse, Agnès 375
Larrucea, Asier 273
Liggesmeyer, Peter 171
Lu, Zhonghai 395
Lukkien, Johan J. 130

Ma, Zhendong 157, 195
Mak, Rudolf H. 130
Massonet, Philippe 334
Matsuno, Yutaka 55
Mazzini, Silvia 311
Medina Pasaje, Julio L. 372
Meitner, Matthias 118, 222
Motii, Anas 375
Mraidha, Chokri 372
Müller, Sebastian 171
Myklebust, Thor 5

Netland, Øyvind 256
Novello, Cristiano 144

Pai, Ganesh 2
Perez, Jon 273
Pierobon, Massimiliano 75
Pistauer, Markus 359
Plank, Hannes 183
Plósz, Sándor 234
Ponsard, Christophe 334
Puschner, Peter 157, 195

Ratiu, Daniel 30, 322
Reyes, Carolina 157

Richthammer, Valentina   222
Rioux, Laurent   372
Römer, Kay   359
Rothbauer, Stefan   105
Ruiz, Alejandra   270, 311

Saglietti, Francesca   118, 222
Schätz, Bernhard   30, 393
Schmittner, Christoph   157, 195
Schoitsch, Erwin   100
Schuß, Markus   359
Skavhaug, Amund   100, 256
Skelin, Mladen   396
Sljivo, Irfan   43
Soltani Nezhad, Amir   130
Spengler, Ralf   118
Stålhane, Tor   5
Steger, Christian   183, 359
Stückjürgen, Christoph   105

Tabacaru, Bogdan-Andrei   144
Tanaka, Kenji   55
Tryggvesson, Jörgen   286

van den Heuvel, Martijn M.H.P.   130
Vardanega, Tullio   273
Varga, Pál   234
Verhoeven, Richard   130
von Wardenburg, Lars   222
Voss, Sebastian   393

Wardziński, Andrzej   87
Warg, Fredrik   286
Weber, Donatus   210
Weissnegger, Ralph   359
Werneman, Anders   286
Wnuk, Krzysztof   346

Zeller, Marc   322

Printed in the United States
By Bookmasters